REVISED SECOND EDITION

THE
Scriptural
TEMPLE

UNDERSTANDING THE TEMPLE
THROUGH THE SCRIPTURES

MARK H. GREENE III

Horizon Publishers
An Imprint of Cedar Fort, Inc.
Springville, Utah

ISBN 13: 978-1-4621-1760-4

Published by Horizon Publishers, an imprint of Cedar Fort, Inc.
2373 W. 700 S., Springville, UT 84663
Distributed by Cedar Fort, Inc., www.cedarfort.com

LIBRARY OF CONGRESS CATALOGING-IN-PUBLICATION DATA

Names: Greene, Mark H., III, author.
Title: The scriptural temple : understanding the temple through the
  scriptures / Mark H. Green III.
Description: Springville, Utah : Horizon Publishers, an imprint of Cedar
  Fort, Inc., [2016] | "2016 | Includes bibliographical references and index.
Identifiers: LCCN 2015039079 | ISBN 9781462117604 (perfect bound : alk. paper)
Subjects: LCSH: Temple endowments (Mormon Church) | Mormon temples. |
  Spiritual life--Mormon Church. | Church of Jesus Christ of Latter-day
  Saints--Doctrines. | Mormon Church--Doctrines.
Classification: LCC BX8643.T4 G74 2016 | DDC 246/.9589332--dc23
LC record available at http://lccn.loc.gov/2015039079

Cover design by Shawnda T. Craig
Cover design © 2016 Cedar Fort, Inc.

Printed in the United States of America

10 9 8 7 6 5 4 3 2 1

Printed on acid-free paper

To Brian, the son I met again in the scriptural temple

Contents

Contents

Introduction

When I finished the first edition, I had a strong impression to read the scriptures again. This I have done, adding much to the writing of the first addition. This new material has confirmed my impression in the first addition that *The Scriptural Temple* keeps expanding. I hope new expansions will develop in the minds and lives of those who understand that the power of love generated as a temple endowment will always be the great message of Mount Zion. This is what the tree of life found in Lehi's dream and the temple is all about. Understanding the power of love is what goes on forever.

At the end of the introduction to the first addition, I expressed a hope for a bond of joy with the reader. However, for the most part the reaction to this book has been silence. I can only speculate what this means. Perhaps the book is not known or widely read. Perhaps the whole subject of temple worship is not of interest to most people. Perhaps the first edition was difficult to read and understand. I do admit in the second addition that reading and understanding this book is like climbing a mountain, step by step, requiring effort. However, the view at the top and the understanding gained from the climb is worth the effort. Looking up to the mountain from the valley will not give the glorious perspective from the peak. This book is not a casual weekend read. It is like the scriptures in requiring searching. There is some repetition of scripture and ideas in this book but usually with a new perspective and with the hope that repetition will reinforce meaning. This is a method used by the Lord in revealing scripture.

I have discovered that the scriptures can stimulate thought that can reveal great knowledge if the reader will search the scriptures. To me the means connecting repeated words and phrases in the scriptural text and then searching with study and prayer until the meanings God intends to convey are found. For example the words *seed*, *god*, and *receive* and the phrases *one flesh*, *great and last promise*, *cast off*, or *cut off* are repeated enough to draw attention to layered or deeper meanings. Because *The Scriptural Temple* is a book drawn from the scriptures whose burden it is to revel the temple, I have tried to associate these repeated words and phrases to draw messages and meaning about temple worship. Once we understand the importance of Christ's Atonement in our lives we see that He leads us to the temple to fully partake of His atoning power.

While I have made the effort to write this book and take responsibility for its content, I testify that it came by the power of prophecy and revelation in my own life. Some of the ideas of this book may be purely mine and even incorrect. However, every time I read this book, I feel an overwhelming assurance of its truthfulness. I feel inspired, wanting to know more. I feel the power of the Lord's love in its pages. It is my desire to share this assurance and feeling with the reader.

The Temple Paradigm

The intent of this book is to bear witness of a great view from a mountain top. The view is an understanding in my mind and heart of scriptural messages about the temple mountain. This view has changed my life. I hope it will change your life too. As you understand the mysteries and feel the love of God while climbing the scriptural temple mountain, you will learn to worship in the house of the Lord.

Those That Forget My Holy Mountain

My expanding view of the temple began a few years ago with a calling to the stake high council that included the assignment to teach a temple preparation class. I was obliged to learn about a subject that had been of occasional interest to me, but largely ignored. I was surprised when I reviewed our stake's statistics of those holding a current temple recommend with those having received their own endowment. I found that only ⅓ to ½ of our stake's members who had received their own endowment had current temple recommends, and that number may even have been better than Churchwide figures.

How many new members actually receive their own endowment? What happens between the first endowment and subsequent temple recommend interviews? Why are there so many temple dropouts? While I was not a part of this "dropout" group, I was part of a larger, nonreported group in the Church that I will call temple inactives. Isaiah described temple dropouts and inactives as those "that forget my holy mountain" (Isaiah 65:11).

At a temple recommend interview, the stake president asked me when I last attended the temple. I told him it had been the prior month, but I didn't respond with conviction. In fact, I felt so guilty that I had to return and confess to him that it had been a whole year since I had really attended the temple. I knew that he was not asking me about temple attendance for a family wedding, but rather temple service for my own salvation and for that of the departed. I was so occupied with my profession and other secular matters that temple endowment attendance had been excluded from my calendar for a whole year. However, the real reason for being a temple inactive was not the typical excuses of a busy life, but rather I did not fully understand that Moroni atop the temple was blowing his trumpet for me. I did not hear his call (see Isaiah 65:12).

Few Comprehend the Full Meaning of the Temple Endowment

My first temple experience was in Los Angeles. I was eight years old, and the Los Angeles California Temple had just been completed. My parents invited me to go to the dedication. I remember walking into a magnificent room and sitting on an aisle seat. Soon, a procession of men dressed in white entered. One was tall, with white waved hair. He was such an impressively divine figure that I could have imagined it was God Himself. My mother whispered to me that the prophet David O. McKay had just passed by.

Years later I read an interesting statement concerning President McKay's visit to the Los Angeles California Temple dedication. While addressing member leaders before the dedication, he told about his niece who regarded her initiation into a sorority superior in effect and meaning to her endowment in the temple. Then he said:

Brothers and Sisters, she was disappointed in the temple. Brothers and sisters, I was disappointed in the temple, and so were you. There are few, even temple workers, who comprehend the full meaning and power of the temple endowment. *Seen for what it is, it is the step-by-step ascent into the Eternal presence. If our young people could but glimpse it, it would be the most powerful spiritual motivation of their lives!*[1]

When I read this statement by President McKay, I became uncomfortably aware that the temple had not been the most powerful spiritual motivation in my life. I did not comprehend the temple endowment as the step-by-step ascent into the presence of God. Why not? My parents attended the temple. I was taught to be worthy to go to the temple and certainly to be married in the temple. But little was said about temple worship, either at home or at Church. I had a notion that it was mysterious and secret. Even after first going to the temple, I didn't fully comprehend its significance, and I considered it more as a church annex for specialized work. My state of temple inactivity may have come in part from President Benson's observation that "because of [the temple's] sacredness we are sometimes reluctant to say anything about the temple to our children and grandchildren. As a consequence, many do not develop a real desire to go to the temple, or when they go there, they do so without much background to prepare them for the obligations and covenants they enter into."[2]

I am grateful that the Lord has blessed me over the past few years with a new paradigm. This paradigm is a great change in my frame of reference toward understanding the temple. In this paradigm I have increased insight and find greater personal meaning for the temple. I hope to explain this new frame of reference by revealing the temple paradigm found throughout the scriptures.

The Term *Scriptural Temple* as Used in This Book

The term *scriptural temple* in this book refers to scriptural verses that directly or indirectly reveal true temple worship, "expounding the mysteries thereof out of the scriptures" (D&C 71:1). This term may intrigue many and cause them to ask where temple worship is found in the scriptures. Perhaps too many are looking for references to the sacred ritual while missing the profound temple teachings of the scriptural temple.

The Scriptural Temple

The temple is a marvelous template for scripture study because if we enhance what we learn inside temple walls with the rich temple teachings of the scriptures, temple worship will have great and glorious meaning in our lives. The scriptural temple will help us understand important concepts of true temple worship, such as growing up in the Lord, the bond of perfectness, and many other important temple concepts and principles.

This book is a broad synthesis of scriptural relationships and messages designed to create a temple paradigm in the image of a mountain and our ascent of this mountain. However, it is not a comprehensive scriptural temple. I have discovered that the scriptural temple keeps expanding as we are taught by the Holy Spirit. Many verses of the scriptural temple are quoted in this book. In addition, references are made to many more. Reading and understanding this book will require personal effort as needed in climbing a mountain. The view at the summit from "eyes of our understanding" (D&C 110:1) will be worth the effort. It is recommended that this book be read with a pondering and prayerful heart and with the scriptures in hand.

By constructing a temple paradigm from the perspective of the scriptures, I bear testimony that the temple will become central in our lives and our most powerful spiritual motivation.

A Whale of a Tale and Its Message

If understanding the temple is so important, why isn't it revealed more fully in the scriptures? Previously, I rarely saw the temple reflected in the scriptures. Now the scriptures and the temple come to life in the scriptural temple. A major burden of the scriptures is to reveal the temple[3] and to "show us concerning the buildings of the temple" (Joseph Smith—Matthew 24:2).

For example, I have been told and read the story of Jonah many times. It was at first a curiosity, a whale of a tale, like the story of Pinocchio. But then it took on believable significance as a sign of the Crucifixion and Resurrection of Christ. When the Savior was challenged by the scribes and Pharisees to produce a sign from heaven, He made reference to "the sign of prophet Jonas" (see Matthew 12:39–40; 16:4; Luke 11:29–30), as a sign of His own Crucifixion and Resurrection.

4

Probably fearing for his life, Jonah thought he deserved better after receiving his mission call to the hostile Assyrian city of Nineveh. He foolishly thought he could flee from the Lord by sailing to Tarshish. En route, a tempest threatened the lives of those aboard. Jonah identified himself as the possible cause of the peril and then volunteered to be thrown overboard to save the others.

> Wherefore they cried unto the Lord, and said, We beseech thee, O Lord, we beseech thee, let us not perish for this man's life, and lay not upon us innocent blood: for thou, O Lord, hast done as it pleased thee.
> So they took up Jonah, and cast him forth into the sea: and the sea ceased from her raging. (Jonah 1:14–15)

These verses imply the Atonement with reference to mercy, innocent blood, and the voluntary sacrifice of Jonah to save others from the raging demands of justice.

Jonah was swallowed by a "great fish" (a whale) and taken to the depths of the sea where he "prayed unto the Lord his God out of the fish's belly . . . the belly of hell" (Jonah 2:1–2). Can the Lord hear our cries from the belly of hell? From the depths of the sea? Yes! Oh, yes, He can, "for these things are not hid from the Lord" (Moses 5:39). Thus, we should all pray to the Lord in the depths of our despair, in our most miserable conditions.

Can we run or hide from the Lord? Like Jonah, Adam and Eve learned that Satan will try to convince us that we can, but the Lord will find us wherever we go, even in the belly of hell (see Amos 9:3; Deuteronomy 30:4).

In the story of Jonah and the whale, we see a reflection of Adam and Eve being cast out of the Garden of Eden. To be swallowed by a whale and cast out of the sight of the Lord is a description of the depth of the Fall. After his fall into the belly of the whale, it was the thought of the Lord's temple that sustained Jonah. "I am cast out of thy sight; *yet I will look again toward thy holy temple*" (Jonah 2:4; emphasis added).

It's this key verse that first alerted me to the temple significance of the book of Jonah. Adam and Eve did the same thing, looking back to the garden, which represented the temple, for direction from the Lord.

> And Adam and Eve, his wife, called upon the name of the Lord, and they heard the voice of the Lord from the way toward the Garden of Eden, speaking unto them, and they saw him not; for they were shut out from his presence.
>
> And he gave unto them commandments, that they should worship the Lord their God, and should offer the firstlings of their flocks, for an offering unto the Lord. And Adam was obedient unto the commandments of the Lord. (Moses 5:4–5)

What happened to Adam and Eve happens to us. Because of the Fall, we are cast out of the presence of the Lord. We must look towards the garden, the Lord's temple, and hear His voice to receive His commandments, that we may find the way to return to His presence.

For Jonah, the memory of the Lord was in His holy temple. He hallowed the memory of being in the presence of the Lord or being in His holy temple. What a contrast to Jonah's current surroundings!

Through his memory, Jonah was teaching us that Christ didn't die just to save sinners from physical death, but to draw all sinners to Him to elevate them from the belly of hell to His level. Justification before God is not just a matter of acquittal from guilt and sin. To dwell in God's presence also requires sanctification or a mighty change in our fallen nature where we have no more weakness or desire for sin. This change is required to pass a future divine judgment.[4] The repentant sinner needs to be set free from sin to stand righteously in the presence of the Lord. "And my Father sent me that I might be lifted up upon the cross; and after that I had been lifted up upon the cross, *that I might draw all men unto me*" (3 Nephi 27:14; emphasis added; see also John 12:32).

Being able to dwell in the presence of the Lord is true deliverance from the Fall. I see in the account of Jonah a broad, glorious metaphor, a whole series of comparisons between Jonah's experience and various facets of the plan of salvation. As in the case of Adam and Eve, transgression facilitated yielding again to Satan and the compulsion to "hide themselves from the presence of the Lord" (Moses 4:14). As Jonah discovered, even in the belly of hell you cannot hide yourself from the Lord.

There are many other metaphors and parallels between the story of Jonah and Christ's sacrifice. As Christ was pressed under the weight of the Atonement (as Jonah was pressed under the weight of the sea) and the Father withdrew, He cried unto the Father that he not drink the bitter cup and that He not be forsaken (just as Jonah cried to the Lord). Yet Christ's sacrifice was out of love for his Father and for us. Thus, He obediently kept His vow to complete the Atonement as Jonah kept his vow to go to Nineveh.

Because of this obedience (because of Jonah's desired obedience to his temple vows), the Father delivered His beloved Son to His celestial presence on His right hand (Jonah was delivered to dry ground, a celestial place compared to the belly of hell).

The Lord can take each of us from the belly of hell to His celestial realm if we are obedient to Him.

> The waters compassed me about, even to the soul: the depth closed me round about, the weeds were wrapped about my head.
>
> I went down to the bottoms of the mountains; the earth with her bars was about me for ever: *yet hast thou brought up my life from corruption, O Lord my God*. (Jonah 2:5–6; emphasis added)

This description of the increasing depth (bottoms), the pressure (bars), the darkness (weeds) is vivid. Jonah was on the verge of drowning. These verses are symbolic of our great fall, the depth of corruption in this life. Jonah knew that only one person could save him and bring him up from corruption. That person was his Savior.

Do we sense our impending drowning in this world of carnal security? If we find ourselves in the belly of hell do we deserve better? Do we forsake our own mercy because of "lying vanities" (see Jonah 2:8)? Do we realize there is only one person who can save us? Jonah would have rejoiced at the words of Jacob: "My soul delighteth in proving unto my people that save Christ should come all men must perish" (2 Nephi 11:6).

When all hope was apparently gone, Jonah remembered the Lord in the temple: "When my soul fainted within me, I remembered the Lord: and my prayer came in unto thee, into thine holy temple (Jonah 2:7; emphasis added).

This verse is similar to a verse in King David's song of thanksgiving:

> In my distress I called upon the Lord, and cried to my God: and *he did hear my voice out of his temple*, and my cry did enter into his ears. (2 Samuel 22:7; Psalm 18:6; emphasis added)

I wonder if I would have thought of the temple if I were in David's or Jonah's condition. Yet, am I not also in the belly of hell like David and Jonah? (See Acts 2:27, 31)

To be delivered from the belly of hell, we must have faith unto life and salvation. This requires sacrifice with real intent (thanksgiving) in covenants (vows) (see Jonah 2:9), sacrificing all things to the Lord as Joseph Smith taught: "Let us here observe, that a religion that does not require the sacrifice of all things never has power sufficient to produce the *faith necessary unto life and salvation*."[5]

We must keep our covenants (vows) through strict obedience to the Lord. We must be willing to sacrifice anything for this obedience. Strict obedience to God is our work (see D&C 11:20). We must have hope that the Lord's grace is sufficient for our rescue (salvation is of the Lord; see Jonah 2:9). No wonder Jonah thought of the temple and his vows. The way of salvation is paved with repentance, sacrifice, obedience, hope in Christ, and covenants with Him. All of these are important temple teachings.

> And the Lord spake unto the fish, and it vomited out Jonah upon the dry land. (Jonah 2:10; see also Exodus 15:19)

As miraculous as this seems, we should have confidence and expectation that the Lord can do something just as miraculous, if not more so, for us:

> But the Lord knoweth all things from the beginning; wherefore, he prepareth a way to accomplish all his works among the children of men; for behold, *he hath all power* unto the fulfilling of all his words. And thus it is. Amen. (1 Nephi 9:6; emphasis added)

Jonah's rescue was symbolic of the power of the Resurrection and of exaltation. Do we see ourselves resurrected and perfected because of the power, work, and glory of the Lord (see Alma 5:15)? I can imagine that Jonah used words and feelings similar to Nephi's psalm (see 2 Nephi 4:16–35) after being "encompassed about" but "preserved upon the water of the great deep" and then becoming a successful missionary to the Assyrians.

For years, I had not noticed the reference to the temple in this whale story. Now, with my new temple paradigm, this story has become not only an important witness for the Savior but one of the most glorious accounts of temple deliverance in all of scripture.

I realized, as I studied and read, that *the temple was central to Jonah* in his peril, even in his sin. Why wasn't the temple central in my life? Why wasn't it the most powerful spiritual motivation in my life? Why had I not seen the temple in the scriptures?

The Fall, the Plan of Redemption, the Atonement, the Resurrection, the celestial potential of man, the power and grace of Christ all taught in this whale of a tale are central temple doctrines. The story of Jonah teaches us that the temple should be the center of our lives, even in the moment of our greatest tribulations, because it represents the presence of the Lord and teaches us the process of true deliverance from the Fall, including our personal falls.

The Mighty Change: The Great Paradigm Shift of the Gospel

Prior to recognizing the temple message in the scriptures, I had become intrigued with the Book of Mormon doctrine of "the mighty change," as taught by King Benjamin and the prophet Alma:

> And they all cried with one voice, saying: Yea, we believe all the words which thou has spoken unto us; and also, we know of their surety and truth, because of the Spirit of the Lord Omnipotent, which has wrought a mighty change in us, or in our hearts, that we have no more disposition to do evil, but to do good continually. (Mosiah 5:2)

> And now behold, I ask of you my brethren of the church, have ye spiritually been born of God? Have ye received his image in your countenances? Have ye experienced this mighty change in your hearts? (Alma 5:14)

I wondered seriously if any of us really do change except by the modifications of time and experience. Does our basic nature change, our hearts, our countenance? What does it mean to be spiritually born of God? How does one change from a state of "evil continually" to "good continually" (see Moroni 7:12–13)? "Good" is a definite term in the scriptural temple. Its source (see Genesis 1:3–4; James 1:17; Moses 2:4, 12, 18, 25, 31; Mosiah 4:12; Alma 32:35; Moroni 7:24; 10:25; D&C 11:12;) and actions (see Moroni 10:6; D&C 11:12; 21:7; 35:12) are clearly defined. Good comes from those that are good (see Abraham 3:23) and the plan that is good (see Abraham 4:21). In this plan we are "agents unto [ourselves]. And inasmuch as [we] do good, [we] shall in nowise lose [our] reward" (D&C 58:28). "Fear not to do good . . . [for] if ye sow good ye shall also reap good for your reward" (D&C 6:33). What does God see as "very good" (Genesis 1:31; Moses 2:31; compare Abraham 4:31) in our lives today?

The mighty change seems to be something quite separate from the changes imposed by the natural process of mortality. It is, according to King Benjamin and Alma, a change of heart. King Benjamin further said that this change of heart requires putting off the natural man, acquiring the qualities of a child, and becoming a Saint through the Atonement (see Mosiah 3:19). I call this mighty change of heart *the great paradigm shift of the gospel*. Alma, the converted son of Alma, testified of this great shift in his own life and witnessed it in the lives of those he taught, calling it a "great check" (Alma 15:17). He said further that all mankind must make this shift to be born of God:

> For, said he, I have repented of my sins, and have been redeemed of the Lord; behold I am born of the Spirit.
>
> And the Lord said unto me: Marvel not that all mankind, yea, men and women, all nations, kindreds, tongues and people, must be born again; yea, born of God, changed from their carnal and fallen state, to a state of righteousness, being redeemed of God, becoming his sons and daughters. (Mosiah 27:24–25; see also Moses 6:59)

The major events of life (birth, family, schooling, marriage, children, profession, aging) reflect the seven acts on the stage of life as described in Shakespeare's *As You Like It*.[6] If "all the world's a stage and all the men and women merely players," then as Hugh Nibley asked: "if all this is so, which is the real you?"[7] Discovering "the real you" is centered in our agency or our ability to choose. Regardless of any external forces upon us, our unique identity is linked to responsibility for our own choices. The fundamental nature of each living soul is a "light of truth" that "can act for itself" (see D&C 93:29–30). Therefore, we have the potential to act out our true selves.

We have the power to be true to the truth within us. This truth is illuminated and enhanced by obedience to God because "no man receiveth a fulness [of truth] unless he keepeth his commandments" (see D&C 93:26–28). C. S. Lewis embraced the ultimate choice of obedience so clearly when he said:

> There are only two kinds of people in the end: Those who say to God, "Thy will be done," and those to whom God says, in the end, "Thy will be done."[8]

For "it shall be unto thee according to [thy] desire" (Moses 5:23). One who said to the Lord "Thy will be done" through his beliefs and actions was Deitrich Bonhoffer, a Lutheran minister imprisoned and executed by the Third Reich of Germany. A few days before his execution and impending liberation by the allied forces, he wrote the following verses:

> Who am I? They often tell me
> I stepped from my cell's confinement
> calmly, cheerfully, firmly,
> like a Squire from his country house.
> Who am I? They often tell me
> I used to speak to my warders
> freely and friendly and clearly,
> as though it were mine to command.
> Who am I? They also tell me
> I bore the days of misfortune
> equably, smilingly, proudly,
> like one accustomed to win.
> Am I then really that which other men tell of?
> Or am I only what I myself know of myself?
> Restless and longing and sick, like a bird in a cage, struggling for
> breath, as though hands were compressing my throat,
> yearning for colours, for flowers, for the voices of birds,
> thirsting for words of kindness, for neighbourliness,
> tossing in expectation of great events,

powerlessly trembling for friends at an infinite distance,
weary and empty at praying, at thinking, at making,
faint, and ready to say farewell to it all.
Who am I? This or the Other?
Am I one person today and tomorrow another?
Am I both at once? A hypocrite before others
and before myself a contemptible woebegone weakling?
Or is something within me still like a beaten army
fleeing in disorder from victory already achieved?
Who am I? They mock me, these lonely questions of mine.
Whoever I am, Thou knowest, O God, I am thine![9]

In spite of successfully acting out the major scenes of our lives, with their attendant rewards, trials, and teachings, there remains a nagging variation of Deitrich Bonhoffer's question: "Am I true to my real self or am I just acting?" In the end, will we feel that we were just acting and God knows it? Perhaps this is the feeling that we have when we contemplate the declaration of Amulek: "this life is the time for men to prepare to meet God" (Alma 34:32). What does it take to prepare to meet God? What labors are to be done for this preparation? Have I not prepared by acting out the major scenes of my life in acquiring knowledge, developing talents and character, and even striving to keep the commandments of God?

Yes, all of these are part of the labors and preparation to meet God because learning to choose correctly between good and evil and act accordingly in these major events of our lives is preparation in discovering who we are and what we can become. However, Amulek had a more profound preparation and discovery in mind. It is the discovery of "the real you" by preparing for a mighty change "that your hearts might be prepared" (D&C 58:6). He even implied the nature of this mighty change when he referred to a witness in the heart (see Alma 34:30–31). The mighty change is the core, the crux, of the gospel of Jesus Christ because it requires Christ and His Atonement to happen for us individually. It is the great paradigm shift of the gospel, the mighty change of heart. The Apostle Paul and Alma the Younger taught that it is a literal change in our nature:

For all things are for your sakes, that the abundant grace might through the thanksgiving of many redound to the glory of God.

For which cause we faint not; but though our outward man perish, yet the inward man is renewed day by day. (2 Corinthians 4:15–16)

Therefore if any man be in Christ, he is a new creature: old things are passed away; behold, all things are become new. (2 Corinthians 5:17)

And thus they become new creatures; and unless they do this, they can in nowise inherit the kingdom of God. (Mosiah 27:26)

I found myself wondering like Enos, "Lord, how is it done?" The answer Enos received is so simple yet profound: "Because of thy faith in Christ" (Enos 1:7–8). The answer is that we must choose Christ.

Faith in Christ leads to repentance, which is obedience to the words of Christ. This obedience leads to the gifts of the Spirit which bring the mighty change of heart (see Helaman 15:7). Therefore, in this life we have the choice of either a mortal suffering relieved through repentance and faith in Christ now, or else procrastinating repentance until we die and must suffer spiritually in spirit prison with weeping, wailing, and gnashing of teeth (see D&C 19:45; Moses 1:22). This is why Amulek said, "I beseech of you that ye do not procrastinate the day of your repentance until the end" (Alma 34:33).

As a missionary, I saw a mighty change in some of my investigators, and certainly in myself. Most missionaries experience the same, and they testify that faith and obedience in Christ is the power behind this mighty change. Stephen, my missionary son in Korea, discovered this truth as expressed in one of his letters: "I often wondered why missionaries had that special spirit about them. I always just thought it came with the calling but I don't know if that's the case anymore. Sure it comes with the calling somewhat but it's due to the strict rules that the missionary abides by." *The only reason that this mighty change does not continue in our lives is that we do not continue to seek and follow the Lord with the same missionary conviction and obedience,* having faith that He can change us mightily and permanently.

When I find myself crossing the straight and narrow path I get a glimpse of what I really want and hope to be. But alas, "O wretched man that I am!" (Romans 7:24; 2 Nephi 4:17). We have only one hope to acquire this divine nature, this mighty change of heart in becoming a new creature. This hope comes through faith in Christ who promises to make weak things strong unto us according to our faith and His grace (see Ether 12:27). For the power of Christ to work in my life, I must be meek enough to seek Him, and draw near to Him as He draws near to me (see D&C 88:63). I "return" or draw near to Christ when I keep His commandments. Then He will "return" or draw near to me (see 3 Nephi 24:78). In this returning the stage is set for the great and last promise of the temple.

While I believe the mighty change to be a true doctrine of the gospel, I had difficulty seeing it consistently taking place within me in this life until I connected the great paradigm shift of the gospel with my changing paradigm of temple worship through the scriptural temple. I truly believe, as I will explain in detail, the mighty change of heart—the change from an unbelieving hard heart to a pure heart—is the pinnacle of the temple paradigm. It is the highest peak of Mount Zion, the Temple Mount, that we can climb in this life. It is the pure heart that is needed in preparation to meet God. This preparation, the mighty change of heart, is possible in this life by the power of the Atonement manifest through the ordinances and covenants of the fulness of the gospel starting with the ordinance and covenant of baptism. As Joseph Smith stated, "being born again comes by the Spirit of God through ordinances."[10]

Truman Madsen placed our most important spiritual rebirth or change in the ordinances and covenants of the temple when he said, "The birth [mighty change] that climaxes all rebirths is in the House of the Lord. The perfecting of His work (D&C 76:106) is the perfecting of His people. Are any perfected? Only those who are 'made perfect through Jesus the mediator of the new covenant, who wrought out this perfect atonement through the shedding of his own blood.' "[11]

The *scriptural temple* teaches that to "be in Christ" (2 Corinthians 5:17) requires the full priesthood of God through the ordinances and covenants of the temple. By the power of His full priesthood and love, "all things shall become new" (D&C 101:25) even the "renewing of our bodies" that makes a "new creature" both physically and spiritually (see D&C 84:32–33). He can even take a hard heart, soften it, and make it pure.

Moroni's Heralding Call to Commune with God

In a memorable lecture on temple worship, the apostle John A. Widstoe said the following:

> There is at present an unusual increased interest in temple activity. Our temples are crowded. The last time I attended the Salt Lake Temple I was a member of the third company. One started early in the morning, one late in the forenoon, and my company started about 2 o'clock in the afternoon. It was about 6 p.m. before we had completed the day's work. The number of temples is also increasing. The Hawaiian temple has only recently been dedicated; the Cardston temple is being rushed to completion, the Arizona temple is being planned and numerous communities in the Church are anxiously waiting and praying for the time that they may have temples. There is a renewed spirit in behalf of temple work, not because people are wealthier than they were before, nor because temples are more accessible, but because the time has come for more temple work to be done. The spirit is abroad among the people, and those who are honest in heart and understand the Gospel of Jesus Christ, are willing to give their time and means more liberally in behalf of temple work.[12]

This is an interesting statement, especially in context of what is happening to temple activity in the Church today. If Elder Widstoe were alive now, I believe he would declare another era of "unusual increased interest in temple activity."

Elder Widstoe mentioned a few new temples. He would be overwhelmed with the ambitious temple construction today. Yet this construction is an expression of renewed temple desire and understanding of the Saints. President Hinckley's announcement of the smaller "stake" temples during the October 1997 general conference[13] as well as the plans to build many more of these temples announced in subsequent general conferences, is fulfillment of prophecy:

> For it is ordained that in Zion, and in her stakes, and in Jerusalem, those places which I have appointed for refuge, shall be the places for your baptisms for your dead. (D&C 124:36)

Perhaps with prescience, Samuel Francis Smith wrote the phrase: "I love thy rocks and rills, Thy woods and templed hills" in his famous anthem "My Country, 'Tis of Thee."[14] While the description of his country was the eastern United States, we are literally seeing hills templed not only in the entire United States but throughout the world.

The expansion of temple construction and worship throughout the world is also a significant part of the fulfillment of the supplication of Joseph Smith in his Kirtland temple dedicatory prayer: "That the kingdom, which thou hast set up without hands, may become a great mountain and fill the whole earth" (D&C 109:72).

Last January, I decided to attend the Bountiful Utah Temple one Friday evening. I traveled the few miles from Salt Lake and climbed the gently winding streets of the foothills of Bountiful. My eyes and thoughts were naturally lifted above to the elegant white house of the Lord.

As I entered the parking lot, it was evident that either there was a very large wedding or many other members had decided to visit the Bountiful Utah Temple this particular Friday. I could not find a parking place either in the parking lot above or under cover. I had to park on the street. I intended to go on the six o'clock session, but I became concerned about this start time when I couldn't find a vacant locker. Before entering the chapel, I was directed to an overflow area already full of waiting people. It was obvious that I was in for a long evening.

The six o'clock session did not start until eight o'clock. The temple workers had never seen such attendance at the temple. Explanations could have been the cleaning closure of the Salt Lake temple or simply the fulfillment of New Year's resolutions. Regardless of the reason, it was an impressive experience to be in the temple so full of worshippers that it could scarcely accommodate them. How wonderful if every weekend could draw such crowds to the temple as we all look with great anticipation for the work-week to end.

Truly, the time has come "for more temple work to be done," not only in construction, but in understanding, worship, and practice in our daily lives. It is time for the temple to become the center of our lives to teach us the way of salvation.

Moroni's trumpet call from atop the temple should not be "an uncertain sound" (1 Corinthians 14:8) in our ears. It is time we hear Moroni as a "voice like a trumpet" (Isaiah 58:1), even "a trumpet talking with [us]" saying, "come up hither, and I will shew thee things which must be hereafter" (Revelation 4:1).

Similar to the two silver trumpets used to call the camps of Israel to assemble at the door of the tabernacle (see Numbers 10:2–3), Moroni's trumpet calls us to come to the mountain of the Lord. Surely, one golden trumpet is worth two silver trumpets. Therefore,

> Blow ye the trumpet in Zion, and sound an alarm in my holy mountain: . . . for the day of the Lord cometh, for it is nigh at hand. (Joel 2:1)

> And it shall come to pass in that day, that the great trumpet shall be blown, and they shall come which were ready to perish . . . and shall worship the Lord in the holy mount. (Isaiah 27:13)

President Thomas S. Monson once said that

> The Moroni statue which appears on the top of several of our temples is a reminder to us all that God is concerned for all His people throughout the world, and communicates with them wherever they may be.[15]

In response to Moroni's heralding call to commune with God, and to increased desire to understand temple worship, I would like to take a journey through the scriptural temple. Throughout the scriptures the Lord weaves a clear temple message. The word of God teaches us how and why we should center our lives in the temple. It beckons us to climb Mount Zion, the spiritual mountain of the Lord's house, to see the great view of God's kingdom. The ensign from which "bloweth a trumpet" (see Isaiah 18:3) is the temple that the Lord lifted up upon the mountains to all inhabitants of the earth. "For, verily, the sound must go forth from this place into all the world" (see D&C 58:57, 64). For "he shall send his angels before him with the great sound of a trumpet, and they shall gather together the remainder of his elect" (Joseph Smith—Matthew 1:37).

Moroni's calling trump reaches the dwellers on the earth not in musical notes, but with the "sound of rejoicing, as with the voice of a trump" (D&C 29:4) in "the sound of the gospel" (D&C 84:114). This sound is in the words of the everlasting gospel revealing the scriptural temple:

And I saw another angel fly in the midst of heaven, having the ever-lasting gospel to preach unto them that dwell on the earth, and to every nation, and kindred, and tongue, and people,

Saying with a loud voice, Fear God, and give glory to him; for the hour of his judgment is come: and worship him that made heaven, and earth, and the sea, and the fountains of waters. (Revelation 14:6–7; see D&C 133:36–39)

Seeking the Source of Temple Worship in the Holy Land

One event that greatly changed my understanding of the importance of the temple was a visit to the Holy Land. In preparation for this trip, I read history and religious books about the Near East. One of these was *Jerusalem, the Eternal City* by David Galbraith, Kelly Ogden, and Andrew Skinner. A statement in this book impressed me not only as particularly significant for my developing temple paradigm, but also as a testimony for the religion to which I belong:

> Though the land certainly was holy, this transfer of sanctity to sites and buildings within Jerusalem reveals, in the words of Hugh Nibley "Christian envy of the Temple." In every ancient culture, temples represented the meeting place of heaven and earth. The destruction of the Temple in Jerusalem left a gaping hole in the life of the Christian movement after the first century, especially in theology. Thus, "many Christian writers have expressed the conviction that the church possesses no adequate substitute for the Temple." After the first century, Christianity seems always to have been looking for a surrogate to replace the rituals as well as the physical structure of the Temple.[1]

After reading these words, I again realized that the temple was not as central in my life as it had been in the lives and cultures of those in Jerusalem. I began to see a "gaping hole" in my own religious life. I then appreciated the great blessing in the restoration of true temple worship through the restored gospel. We as Latter-day Saints have something extraordinarily marvelous that distinguishes us from all other religions: a true understanding of temples and the practice of true temple worship.

This understanding and practice is great evidence of the principle of revelation from God on which our beliefs are based. We could not build a temple structure and perform covenants and ordinances acceptable to God, unless they were revealed from God (see Psalm 127:1) with His authority. Loss of this authority and revelation makes it impossible to fill the "gaping hole" from loss of true temple worship because the priesthood keys that validate all temple ordinances are lost. The surrogates try to fill the hole by "[administering] that which was sacred unto him to whom it had been forbidden because of unworthiness" (4 Nephi 1:27). Without the keys of the kingdom of heaven that "bind" (see Matthew 16:19; D&C 110:16;132:46), these surrogates defile sacredness and thwart the Plan of Salvation. They become harlots on a hilltop (see Isaiah 57:7). The only church that has the keys to open the blessings of binding or sealing individual relationships beyond death is the church that has true temple worship. The authority of all other churches ends at "death do [we] part" (compare D&C 132:15, 19).

True temple worship is as great an evidence of the truthfulness of our religion as the Book of Mormon. Both could only have come by the power of God through revelation "according to the pattern which I will show unto them" (D&C 115:14; see Exodus 25:8–9). Therefore, the temple should be as important in our lives as the Book of Mormon. It should be, as President Howard W. Hunter said, "the great symbol of [our] membership."[2] and what it makes of our lives should be the real "symbol of our worship."[3]

Granite and Gossamer Veils

The day I visited the Western Wall and contemplated the scene of men divided from women as they worshipped, I immediately thought that this is the veil of the Jewish temple today. Its Herodian stone is as thick as the disbelief of those who worship before it. Their rejection of the One who saves brought ruin to their temple, with only a stony veil as its remnant memorial. Even the veils that separated the Holy of Holies from the Holy Place in the Aaronic Priesthood temples on Mount Moriah were heavy and thick compared to the veil in Melchizedek Priesthood temples today. This thick veil was consequent to the rejection of the fulness of the priesthood and the "rest" of the Lord offered to the children of Israel in the Sinai (see 2 Corinthians 3:13–16).

In the Doctrine and Covenants, we learn that the Lord's temple is covered with a veil, hiding the whole earth from the presence or celestial temple of the Lord (see D&C 101:23). This is a result of our fall from His realm. This scripture also teaches us that the veil will be removed at the Second Coming, but only those who are purified enough to see through the "veil of darkness" will endure the event (see D&C 38:8).

In preparation for this event, if we keep ourselves as a temple (see 1 Corinthians 6:19), a veil of darkness which Moroni called the "veil of unbelief" (Ether 4:15) can be lifted from our mortal eyes so that we see with "eyes of our understanding" (see D&C 110:1; 138:11). However, before we see with "eyes of our understanding," we must first see with "an eye of faith" (Ether 12:19). If this faith is strong enough, the "veil of unbelief" and even the veil separating us from the presence of the Lord will be rent.

The Prophet Isaiah implied that "the veil that is spread over all nations" will be destroyed in the temple mountain (see Isaiah 25:7). By learning in the temple how to part the veil, we become purified to endure the presence of the Lord. The Lord expects us to seek after Him and part the veil even in this life. This is what Paul taught the Athenians on Mars Hill:

> That they should *seek the Lord* , if haply they might *feel after him,* and *find him,* though He be not far from every one of us:
>> For in Him we live, and move, and have our being; as certain also of your own poets have said, for we are also His offspring. (Acts 17:27–28; emphasis added)

This scripture stirs in me the impression of an orphan striving to find a true parent. Would we not earnestly and persistently seek our natural parents? Yet are we not all spiritual orphans?

Some mistakenly feel they can part the veil and find the Lord simply by communing with nature, but avoiding worship in His temple. While appreciating nature brings us closer to the Lord, the scriptural temple teaches that there is more to finding Him:

> And this *greater priesthood* administereth the gospel and holdeth the key of the mysteries of the kingdom, *even the key of the knowledge of god.*
> Therefore, *in the ordinances thereof, the power of godliness is manifest.*
> (D&C 84:19–20; emphasis added)

The "greater priesthood" is the fulness of the Melchizedek Priesthood found in the ordinances and covenants of the temple. Therefore, the Lord said to the Prophet Joseph Smith:

> For I have conferred upon you the keys and power of the priesthood, *wherein* I restore all things, and *make known unto you all things in due time.* (D&C 132:4; emphasis added)

It is with ordinances and truths revealed in the temple that the veil of darkness that is spread over all nations will be removed to make known all things in due time. *Revelare*, the Latin root for the word *reveal*, means "to part the veil."

Abraham is a prime example of one who diligently sought after the Lord and found Him through the ordinances of the "greater priesthood." Through this priesthood, he possessed "great knowledge" and held "the right belonging to the fathers" (Abraham 1:2). With this right, Abraham could declare, "Thy servant has sought thee earnestly; now I have found thee" (Abraham 2:12).

The most important message of the story of Abraham to all of us is that he went from relative obscurity and family instability to become a god-like figure as the father of nations *because he sought God and found Him through the fulness of the priesthood* in the temple. He learned and practiced the doctrine of the priesthood as he lived its laws of pure love in his world of turmoil. It is important to remember that "Abraham received all things, whatsoever he received, by revelation and commandment" (D&C 132:29).

Linking the priesthood with the temple, President Ezra Taft

Benson said: "To enter in the Order of the Son of God is the equivalent today of entering into the fulness of the Melchizedek Priesthood, which is only received in the house of the Lord."[4]

This is exactly what Abraham did, receiving the great and last promise of the temple. This promise is that the "right belonging to the fathers," the Second (Other) Comforter or presence of the Lord, can be obtained in this life as Joseph Smith explained:

> Now what is the other comforter? It is no more nor less than the lord Jesus Christ himself . . . this is the state and place the ancient Saints arrived at when they had such glorious visions. Isaiah, Ezekiel, John upon the Isle of Patmos, St. Paul in the three heavens, and *all the Saints* who held communion with the general assembly and "Church of the Firstborn" the Lord taught them face to face and gave them a perfect knowledge of the mysteries of the Kingdom of God.[5]

Moroni told of the power of faith referring to this great and last promise of the temple as a heavenly gift:

> For it was *by faith* that *Christ showed himself unto our fathers ,* . . . and he showed not himself unto them until after they had faith in him. . . . But because of the faith of men he has shown himself unto the world . . . and prepared a way that thereby others might be *partakers of the heavenly gift.* . . .
>
> Wherefore, ye may also have hope, and be *partakers of the gift,* if ye will but have faith. Behold it was by faith that they of old were called after the *holy order of God.* (Ether 12:7–10; emphasis added)

There is an impressive list of Book of Mormon "fathers" who where partakers of the gift of the great and last promise of the temple: Lehi (1 Nephi 1:9), Nephi (2 Nephi 11:2), Jacob (2 Nephi 11:3), Lamoni (Alma 19:13), Bountiful Saints (3 Nephi 11:8), twelve disciples (3 Nephi 27:2), Brother of Jared (Ether 3:14), Emer (Ether 9:22), Mormon (Mormon 1:15), and Moroni (Ether 12:39). Like David (see Psalm 63:2) and Isaiah (see 2 Nephi 11:2) of the Old Testament, others of the Book of Mormon probably received this gift such as Alma and the sons of Mosiah and Nephi the son of Helaman. "There were many . . . who were made pure and entered into the rest of the Lord their God" (Alma 13:12). They, like the brother of Jared, were "sanctified" (see Ether 4:7; compare D&C 88:68) and did not "contend against the word of the Lord" (Ether 4:8). The more we develop faith in Christ, His life and salvation, the more we become obedient to the ordinances and covenants of His Holy Order, the fulness of the Melchizedek Priesthood. With this faith and obedience under the Melchizedek Priesthood, the more gossamer the veil becomes, and the easier it is to be partakers of the gift and find the presence of the Lord. This is why the Apostle Paul, speaking of the Aaronic Priesthood temple under the law of Moses said, "the Holy Ghost this signifying, that the way into the holiest of all was not yet made manifest" (Hebrews 9:8). Today, we learn this obedience and we experience the thinning of the veil by the Holy Ghost through the ordinances and covenants of a Melchizedek Priesthood temple.

Topographical Temples in Israel

Topographical settings of the land Israel provide a marvelous symbol of the importance of the temple. In every region of Israel are natural temples reminding the people of the land that no matter their place in life, be it in the cities, fertile valleys, or the desert, they have need of a temple.

Located in the Sinai Desert is Mount Horeb, where Moses and Elijah had great temple experiences.

In the Judean hills rising from the Dead Sea we find the Mount of Temptations where the Savior dwelt 40 days like Moses, facing Satan's temptations and preparing for His ministry.

From the fertile Jezreel Valley rises Mount Tabor, called "the holy mount" by Peter (2 Peter 1:18). Many feel that on this holy mount the marvelous temple experience of the Transfiguration occurred.

On the Mediterranean coast near Haifa is Mount Carmel which means the garden place, as though it were a symbol of Gethsemane and a reminder of the Garden of Eden. Mount Carmel's dews are likened unto the knowledge of God distilling upon us, as in the temple (see D&C 128:19; 121:45).

At the northern end of Israel, in the Golan Heights, Mount Hermon, the highest mountain of Israel, becomes a major source of Israel's water supply as it captures snow and stores the melted crystal in its aquifers. At the southern end of Mount Hermon is a massive rock wall from which flows the river Jor, emptying the subterranean aquifers. It is here that the Savior taught his apostles the importance of revelation and of living waters flowing from the presence of God when He asked them "Whom do men say that I the Son of Man am?" (see Matthew 16:13–19). Mount Hermon is symbolic of the spiritual Mount Zion (see Deuteronomy 4:48), the celestial temple source of spiritual water that quenches our spiritual thirst.

In the center of these natural temple mounts of the land Israel is Mount Zion, including Mount Moriah, "the mountain of [the Lord's] holiness" (Psalm 48:1).

Just east of Mount Zion, across the Kidron valley, is the Mount of Olives. On both of these mounts (Mt. Zion and the Mt. of Olives or Golgatha and Gethsemane), the great atoning sacrifice of the Savior occurred. Here the Savior rent the thick veil of the Jewish temple and opened the way as the "forerunner" to "that within the veil" meaning the celestial presence of God (see Hebrews 6:19–20). *Through His Holy Order, Christ is the forerunner and High Priest for all those willing to follow Him up the holy mountain of the Lord.*

The manmade temple became an architectural expression of the natural or mountain temple.[6] Its construction of natural materials; its separation from the world as sacred space representing holiness and the presence of the Lord; its beauty, peace, and order as representation of the creation of cosmos out of chaos; its orientation as a climb to a higher order and celestial state; all these represented an extension of the natural mountain temple.

As a mountain is a vertical elevation on the horizon, so also is the manmade temple, elevating one's thoughts and actions toward God. Even within the temple, the altar is a vertical elevation on the horizon, where our covenants of sacrifice are made with God.

The mountain of the house of the Lord, Mount Moriah, is like a natural altar, where sacrifices and offerings to the Lord have been made for centuries. True to the Mosaic law (see Leviticus 1:11), on the northern side of this natural altar, the greatest sacrifice of all and for all, the crucifixion of our Lord and Savior, occurred in the meridian of time, thus lifting our thoughts and devotion to Christ.

The Concept of a Holy Nation: Then and Now

The temple was the center of many ancient Near Eastern civilizations where kings were coronated, laws codified, civil and religious authority established, and God revealed to man. John Lundquist has shown that a temple was the central organizing, unifying institution of ancient Near Eastern nations.[7]

A distinguishing characteristic of Joseph Smith's work from 1830 and continuing beyond his death was gathering a people to a city whose center or high point was a temple. This work was in distinct contrast to other religious leaders and organizations of Joseph's time who diffused God into the hearts of believers with church buildings scattered across the land. Richard Bushman observed, "as if the temple was a vital part of the work and chapels and Sunday meeting were incidental . . . Joseph's temples, like temples throughout history, focused sacred power at a single spot."[8]

The reality that a nation could come out of a temple experience was given to Moses and the children of Israel in the Sinai: "Now therefore, if ye will obey my voice indeed, and keep my covenant, then ye shall be a peculiar treasure unto me above all people. . . . And ye shall be unto me a *kingdom of priests*, and an *holy nation*" (Exodus 19:5–6; emphasis added). The king of this holy nation was to be Jehovah. This holy nation could only function as a kingdom of righteous priests and priestesses because only they would have access to the presence of their holy king, in His holy temple. However, the formation of a holy nation did not occur in the Sinai because of the "provocation" (see D&C 84:23–25). A Mosaic holy nation, a level below the intended holy nation of the Lord, yet above secular government, was the result.

The nation-state of Israel did not really solidify until a mortal king was chosen and a central temple constructed. This occurred when Saul became king and Solomon's temple was constructed. Until these events, the "state" of Israel did not exist: "In those days there was no king in Israel: every man did that which was right in his own eyes" (Judges 21:25).

This last verse in *The Book of Judges* summarizes a dark period for the house of Israel. The contrast between the perfidious king Abimelech (see Judges 9:6) and Gideon, who refused to be king, attests the constant difficulty the Israelites had in following Gideon's proclamation: "the Lord shall rule over you" (Judges 8:23).

However, the Israelites desired a mortal king in order to become like other nations instead of a holy nation: "Nevertheless the people refused to obey the voice of Samuel; and they said, Nay; but we will have a king over us; That we also may be like all the nations; and that our king may judge us, and go out before us, and fight our battles" (1 Samuel 8:19–20).

The choice of a mortal king over Jehovah was a sign of rejection to the Lord, similar to the rejection of the fulness of the Lord in the Sinai:

> And the Lord said unto Samuel, Hearken unto the voice of the people in all that they say unto thee: for they have not rejected thee, but they have rejected me, that I should not reign over them. (1 Samuel 8:7)

It is interesting that God established himself as king over the promised American land of Gentile and Israelite inheritance with a warning that "he that raiseth up a king against me shall perish" (see 2 Nephi 10:14). "For I will be your king . . . for I am your lawgiver" (see D&C 38:21–22).

The dedicatory prayer of Solomon's temple emphasized the central role of the temple in establishing a nation-state (see 1 Kings 8:22–54). The Lord's acceptance of this temple established Him as the real king of Israel with His name, eyes, and heart there perpetually (see 1 Kings 9:3). If the temple in ancient Near Eastern society was the very venue of universal order establishing conditions under which civil law was possible, our concept of separation of church and state would have been quite foreign to these civilizations. Yet we need to remember that the founding fathers of the United States stood on higher laws than the laws of men when they declared, "We hold these truths to be self evident" (see D&C 134:2). "Governments [and religion, see D&C 134:4] were instituted of God for the benefit of man; and . . . he holds men accountable for their acts in relation to them" (D&C 134:1).

In our zeal to protect religious freedom, have we cut the umbilical cord to the greatest lawgiver of all (see D&C 38:22)? The best we can say about the nations of the world today is that they represent the precepts of men mingled with the laws of heaven to a greater or lesser degree. The idea of the higher laws of the cosmos revealed through the temple to guide our societies in both religious and civil needs is appealing if, in fact, "in God we trust."

Is a "holy nation" possible? The scriptures answer this question with an emphatic yes, illustrating with examples of holy nations in past dispensations and prophecies of Zion, the New Jerusalem, the holy nation of the dispensation of the fulness of times, and the millennial dispensation. The King of this holy nation will be Jehovah (see D&C 38:21) and the place from which He will reign will be the temple. As in past dispensations (see Exodus 33:7), this is where those who seek Him will find Him for the Lord whom we seek will "suddenly come to His temple" (see Malachi 3:12; D&C 36:8).

God: The Primordial Source of Temple Worship in All Civilizations

True temple worship in its purity was revealed to Adam and Eve. Joseph Smith taught that this truth was perverted and adapted to the worldly desires and cultures of man in every dispensation until true messengers from God returned some believing listeners to true temple worship:

> It is reasonable to suppose that man departed from the first teachings, or instructions which he received from heaven in the first age, and refused by his disobedience to be governed by them. But that man was not able himself to erect a system or plan with power sufficient to free him from a destruction which awaited him is evident from the fact that God . . . prepared a sacrifice in the gift of His own Son who should be sent in due time, to prepare the way, or open the door through which man might enter into the Lord's presence, whence he had been cast out for disobedience. From time to time these glad tidings were sounded in the ears of men in different ages of the world.[9]

In spite of the cultural and religious differences in ancient societies, the similarities in temple worship speak for a primordial source. This source is revealed in the establishment of temple worship in ancient Egypt, which was established after "the government of Ham, which was patriarchal" but without the right of the Priesthood (see Abraham 1:25–27). The source of the true Holy Order and Priesthood received by the patriarchs was God Himself (see Moses 5:58–59). This was the source of Noah's ordination to this Holy Order (see Moses 8:19).

Even after the Babylonian destruction of Solomon's temple, it was the Lord who "stirred up" (2 Chronicles 36:22) the Persian ruler Cyrus to proclaim a new temple in Jerusalem:

> All the kingdoms of the earth hath the Lord God of heaven given me; and he hath charged me to build him an house in Jerusalem, which is in Judah. (2 Chronicles 36:23)

As Joseph Smith learned, *the form of godliness without the power (the priesthood) is desecration in the eyes of God* (see Joseph Smith—History 1:19; emphasis added). This is why the Lord had to "proceed to do a marvellous work . . . and a wonder" (Isaiah 29:14) in restoring the gospel and its holy order in our dispensation.

The Holy Order of God, with its holy ordinances practiced in righteousness under the direction of the King of Righteousness and those appointed by Him, is what makes a nation a holy nation and a temple a holy temple (see Daniel 9:17; Helaman 10:7–9; D&C 84:19–21). Just as the gates of Jerusalem were shut on the sabbath because it was defiled (see Nehemiah 13:17–19), so are the doors of the temple shut when the Lord and His true messengers are rejected (see Acts 21:30).

The remnants of past civilizations reveal a connection to God and the cosmos that is little understood in modern times. The loss of the temple truly left a gaping hole for the lands of the Near East and its cultures today. For me, the inescapable comparison after this revealing travel through the Near East was between the central role the temple played in this land and the esoteric annex the temple was in my personal religious life. Once again I faced the same question: Why wasn't the temple of central importance to me?

After my trip to Israel and the Near East, I marveled at the pervading influence of the temple on this land and its cultures. My overwhelming impression was that the temple and temple worship is a fundamental and primordial necessity for the salvation of man. The temple is God's gift to man, to remind us of the higher order from which we fell and to teach us how to return to that order.

I will be forever grateful for the assignment to teach a temple preparation class on the stake level. I now know that this assignment was given to me as the consolidation of my developing temple paradigm. When I was given the assignment, I certainly wasn't an expert on the temple. I had never taught a class about the temple. I still considered it something associated with marriage and genealogy and a place to be visited when one had the time. However, my Holy Land experience had given me a strong desire to make the temple central in my life. Now I had to know all about it because I had to convince others to make it central in their life.

The Mountain of Holiness

A dominant theme of the scriptural temple is the representation of God's temple as a holy mountain. Mount Sinai was called "the mountain of God" (Exodus 3:1) and the portable Tabernacle was a horizontal representation of this vertical mountain. In Isaiah we learn that those who are adopted into the house of Israel by keeping covenants with the Lord will be brought to the holy mountain of God through the holy temple of God (see Isaiah 56:67; 49:11). The image of a holy mountain is important in symbolizing our fall and the need to climb back to the elevated level of God. It is in climbing this mountain that our nature changes in preparation to meet God. As we climb, we get glimpses of the great view to be seen at the summit.

After Adam and Eve fell from the holy mountain of God, they learned how to climb back to the garden presence of God and even beyond to a greater presence called "eternal life." This climb back was through their Guide and Savior, Jesus Christ. Sacrifice of all worldly distractions and possessions, in strict obedience to the commandments, covenants, and ordinances of the Holy Order of the Son of God, was the technique or "pattern" taught to them:

> And Adam and Eve, his wife, called upon the name of the Lord, and
> they heard the voice of the Lord from the way toward the Garden of
> Eden, speaking unto them, and they saw him not; *for they were shut
> out from his presence.*
>
> And he gave unto them *commandments*, that they should worship
> the Lord their God, and should offer the firstlings of their flocks, for
> an offering unto the Lord. And *Adam was obedient* unto the com-
> mandments of the Lord. (Moses 5:4–5; emphasis added)

Once Adam demonstrated obedience to the Lord, he received a
heavenly gift in the form of a heavenly messenger with more instructions about the climb back to the presence of God. From this messenger, Adam learned that the only way "all mankind" could return
to God's presence would be through the grace of the sacrifice of the
Son of God, "even as many as will" repent and remain obedient to
the truths of His holy order.

> And after many days an angel of the Lord appeared unto Adam,
> saying: Why dost thou offer *sacrifices* unto the Lord? And Adam said
> unto him: I Know not, save the Lord commanded me.
>
> And then the angel spake, saying: This thing is a *similitude of the
> sacrifice of the Only Begotten of the Father*, which is full of grace and truth.
>
> Wherefore, thou shalt do all that thou doest in the name of the
> Son, and thou shalt *repent and call upon God* in the name of the Son
> forevermore. . . .
>
> I am the Only Begotten of the Father from the beginning, hence-
> forth and forever, that *as thou hast fallen thou mayest be redeemed*, and
> all mankind, even as many as will.
>
> And Eve, his wife, heard all these things and was glad, saying:
> Were it not for our transgression we never should have had seed, and
> never should have known good and evil, and the *joy of our redemption*,
> and the *eternal life* which God giveth unto all the obedient. (Moses
> 5:6–9, 11; emphasis added)

The reason that Adam then "blessed God" (Moses 5:10) was
because of his joy in receiving the gospel from the beginning of his
mortal existence. This gospel provided the way back to the presence
of God. Adam began to return to God through "an holy ordinance":
the first four principles and ordinances of the gospel (see Moses 5:89;

6:50–52, 64–66), then the higher temple ordinances of the fulness of the Order of the Son of God. And thus may all become one in God, His sons and daughters (see Moses 6:68–69).

> And thus *the Gospel* began to be preached, from the beginning, being declared by holy angels sent forth from the presence of God, and by his own voice, and by the gift of the Holy Ghost.
>
> And thus all things were confirmed unto Adam, by an holy ordinance, and the Gospel preached, and a decree sent forth, that it should be in the world, until the end thereof; and thus it was. Amen. (Moses 5:58–59; emphasis added)

The Tower of Babel: An Apostate Temple

The story of an apostate temple, the Tower of Babel, opens to us one of the great temple events in the scriptural temple. In this amazing scriptural story, the true and false paths to the presence of God are closely contrasted. This contrast teaches us a fundamental gospel truth: that *anything built or done under the name of man or his precepts will never reach God.* Only those who follow the plan of redemption in the name of the Son will reach heaven (see Alma 12:34–35).

Nimrod, the great grandson of Noah, esteemed himself more powerful than God and influenced his followers to build a mountain tower to reach heaven. The tower Babel, which means "gate of God," was a manmade counterfeit of a true temple, built in rebellious mocking of God.[1] The comparison of this temple with the one seen by Jacob is also a striking contrast (see Genesis 28:17).

Jared and his family rejected the apostasy of those building the Tower of Babel and sought to maintain a oneness with the true God. This Jaredite community was led away to a promised land by God himself, much as He led Lehi's family and Moses with the children of Israel.

When the Jaredites came to Moriancumer near the sea that separated them from the land of promise, the Brother of Jared inquired of the Lord about the problem of air and light in crossing the sea. The answer to the question of light occurred on a temple mountain, a mountain of holiness, where the brother of Jared demonstrated a fulness of faith that became a perfect knowledge when he saw and knew with "eyes of understanding" beyond his "eyes of faith":

> And it came to pass that the brother of Jared, . . . went forth unto the mount, which they called the *mount Shelem*, because of its exceeding height, and did molten out of a rock sixteen small stones; and they were white and clear, even as transparent glass; and he did carry them in his hands upon the top of the mount. (Ether 3:1; emphasis added)

Now that the brother of Jared had entered a temple mount he rehearsed his fallen condition. Like Adam, he again expressed his desired relation with the Lord by obedience to His commandments because the Lord "has all power." These of course are prominent themes in the drama of temples today.

Like Jonah, the Brother of Jared "again cried unto the Lord, saying":

> O Lord, thou hast said that we must be encompassed about by *the floods* . . . for we know that thou art holy and dwellest in the heavens, and that we are unworthy before thee; because of *the fall* our natures have become evil continually; nevertheless, O Lord, thou hast given us a commandment that we must call upon thee, that from thee we may receive according to our desires.
>
> I know, O Lord, that thou hast all power, and can do whatsoever thou wilt for the benefit of man; therefore touch these stones, O Lord, with thy finger, and prepare them that they may shine forth in darkness. (Ether 3:2, 4; emphasis added)

Because of the faith of the brother of Jared he literally received the promised blessing of Adam (see Moses 5:10). To be brought back into the presence of the Lord is the great and last promise of the temple. Similar to Adam, the brother of Jared learned that becoming a spiritually begotten son or daughter of Christ is necessary in becoming an exalted son or daughter of God the Father:

> The Lord stretched forth his hand and touched the stones one by one with his finger. And *the veil was taken from off the eyes of the brother of Jared,* and he saw the finger of the Lord; and it was as the finger of

a man, like unto flesh and blood. . . . And the Lord said unto him: Because of thy *faith* thou hast seen that I shall take upon me flesh and blood; and never has man come before me with such exceeding faith as thou hast; for were it not so ye could not have seen my finger. Sawest thou more than this?

And He answered: Nay; Lord, show thyself unto me. . . . And when he had said these words, behold, the Lord showed himself unto him, and said: Because thou knowest these things *ye are redeemed from the fall; therefore ye are brought back into my presence;* therefore I show myself unto you. . . .

Behold, I am he who was prepared from the foundation of the world to redeem my people. Behold, I am Jesus Christ. I am the Father and the Son. *In me shall all mankind have life, and that eternally, even they who shall believe on my name;* and they shall become my sons and my daughters. (Ether 3:6, 9–10, 13–14; emphasis added)

Moroni recalled the account of the brother of Jared and then encouraged the Gentiles and the house of Israel to be like the brother of Jared in rending the veil of unbelief and calling upon the Father in the name of Christ with a broken heart and contrite spirit. Then God will remember His covenant and reveal "great things" which have been laid up for them from the foundation of the world (see Ether 4:4, 13–15).

With the teachings of the Fall and the covering veil of this life, and with the need for faith in the Lord Jesus Christ through a change of heart in covenants with Him, this marvelous mountain temple endowment of the brother of Jared again defined the way back to the presence of the Lord. Like Adam, the brother of Jared described the steps of this ascension: (1) rejecting apostasy and following true messengers of God, (2) having enough faith in Christ to sacrifice all worldliness in strict obedience to His covenants, and (3) rending the veil of disbelief by a change of heart from unbelief to exceeding faith in order to receive the Second Comforter.

The brother of Jared received the gift of the patriarchs or the Second Comforter, the great and last promise of the temple. This gift is the face to face ministry of the Savior, with one's calling and election made sure. With this gift, we are assured a full knowledge of the Lord and His realm of existence called eternal life.

Eden's Temple: The Holy Mountain of God

It is notable that the scriptural account of man on this earth began in a temple setting. The presence of the Lord in the Garden of Eden, a place of beauty, cleanliness, and innocence, defines a temple setting.

One might wonder how Satan could be present in such a place (see 2 Thessalonians 2:4). The agency of man was introduced in the Garden of Eden as it is in all temple settings. This agency specifically applies to choosing between Christ and Satan. Therefore, we must confront Satan's temptations and make choices using our own free will in order to learn how to abide the presence of the Lord. In other words, we must "work out [our] own salvation with fear and trembling before God" (Philippians 2:12; Alma 34:37; Mormon 9:27). Then, as taught in the temple and the casting out of the unclean spirit present in the synagogue (see Luke 4:31–37), if we hear God's voice and choose His salvation, He has the power to free us from Satan's captivity (see Moses 4:4) and to cast him out of our lives. Conversely, as Adam and Eve discovered, the choice to follow Satan's temptations removes us from the presence of the Lord.

Old Testament temples alluded to the Eden temple with such symbols as eastward orientation, cherubim on the curtain divisions protecting the holy places, the menorah representing the tree of life, and water flowing from the temple like the river that flowed out of Eden. As one would expect in the Eden temple, reference to "the upper chambers" (see 2 Chronicles 3:9) described by Josephus (see *Antiquities of the Jews* 8.3.2–3) and temple worship described in D&C 124:38–39 establish a Melchizedek Priesthood component to these Old Testament temples. This was the case in Book of Mormon temples (see 2 Nephi 5:16; Alma 4:20).

The pervading idea in Old Testament temples and celebrations, such as the seventh Sabbath year and the Jubilee year in return to the conditions of Eden on the sixth day of creation, was that *return to the garden of Eden is a return to the presence of the Lord*. Likewise, one could say that leaving the celestial room in today's temples, and exiting the temple, is like leaving the presence of the Lord and going to the lone and dreary world. Significantly, we learn in the endowment that the Savior led Adam and Eve and thus their posterity into the

Garden of Eden. The Savior leads us in the temple, and therefore to the presence of the Father.

The Eden temple was probably an elevated or mountain dwelling. The river of Eden flowed outward (downward) becoming four rivers that proceeded to the four corners of the earth.[2] The Fall of man can easily be visualized as falling from an elevated or mountain height. Ezekiel made reference to the Garden of Eden as "the holy mountain of God" in his warnings to the King of Tyre, who became a fallen Adam when iniquity was found in him (see Ezekiel 28:13–15).

The Temples of Adam-Ondi-Ahman

Three years before Adam died, he gathered his righteous posterity in the valley of Adam-ondi-Ahman which most likely means "Adam in the presence of God."[3]

Joseph Smith had a vision of this gathering. He said, "I saw Adam in the valley of Adam-ondi-Ahman. He called together his children and blessed them with a patriarchal blessing. The Lord appeared in their midst. . . . *This is why Adam blessed his posterity; he wanted to bring them into the Presence of God.*"[4] D&C 107 gives us additional detail about this family gathering when "the Lord appeared unto them" (see verses 53–56). This gathering, precursor to a future assembly at Adam-ondi-Ahman in fulfillment of the events told by the prophet Daniel (see Daniel 7:9–22; also D&C 116:1), is a temple gathering because of the presence of the Lord.

It is interesting that the altar built by Adam to call on God and to offer sacrifice, as implied in Moses 5:46, was probably built on a hill described as the "mountains of Adam-ondi-Ahman" overlooking Adam-ondi-Ahman, "the land of my people, even Zion" (see D&C 117:8–9). Joseph Smith identified the remains of this altar, which still existed in his day.[5] The altar of Adam and the temple site marked by the Saints in 1831, lie in the center of a future city near Adam-ondi-Ahman.[6] "Behold, the place which is now called Independence is the center place; and a spot for the temple" (D&C 57:3). This city is the land of the Lord's people "for an everlasting inheritance" (D&C 57:5), even Zion, the New Jerusalem, "the city of the heritage of God" (D&C 58:13). *Thus the temple site at the beginning of man on this earth (the Garden of Eden) will become the temple site at the beginning of the earth's millennial existence (the New Jerusalem)*. The city of the New Jerusalem will be the new Mount Zion (see D&C 84:2), and therefore the Holy Mountain of God that Adam knew as the Garden of Eden. Brigham Young declared this truth when he said, "Right where the Prophet Joseph laid the foundation of the Temple was where God commenced the Garden of Eden, and there he will end or consummate his work."[7]

Literally, worthy Saints from past and present will be "gathered in one" (see D&C 42:9) in the presence of the Lord in the Garden of Eden of the New Jerusalem (see D&C 133:56; see also Joel 2:3). This gathering will start at the temple (see D&C 84:4, 32), suggesting that *in preparation for this gathering in one we must climb, through the temple endowment, the spiritual Mount Zion.*

Men to Match His Mountains

One of my favorite books is Irving Stone's *Men to Match My Mountains*. I even have an autographed copy of this book dated May 8, 1961. It is a captivating book written in the grand Irving Stone style about the courageous men and women who explored and settled the mountains and plains of the West. It's about men such as John Fremont, Jim Bridger, and others who met the challenge of the mountains.

While reading their stories I could envision myself with them because I live in the land they explored. My orientation is with mountains and my horizon is defined as the next range of mountains. When I lived in Michigan, I missed the defined mountain horizons of the West. In this flat land of the Great Lakes, visual horizons fade to vanishing points at any degree of a circle. Orientation is not by mountain ranges but rather by shopping centers.

On the title page of this book is a quatrain from Samuel Foss's poem "The Coming American": "Bring me men to match my mountains, Bring me men to match my plains / Men with empires in their purpose, And new eras in their brains."[8]

In the temple paradigm, the men who match the mountains are the men and women worthy to stand in the Lord's presence on His mountain or in His temple. Men who match the plains are those obedient servants who are true messengers of the Lord acting as "savor" in the plains of humanity.

These men and women have great views ("empires") in their purpose and anticipation of a new celestial order ("new eras"), because they understand the magnificent promises in store for those who are obedient to the Lord (see 1 Corinthians 2:9). They, like the patriarchs and prophets of old, would sacrifice anything to follow the straight and narrow path to the presence of the Lord. With this sacrifice, they obediently seek the path and make the climb of Mount Zion to the summit of the mountain of the Lord, thus becoming men and women who match His mountain.

Men Who Matched His Exceedingly High Mountains

On the mountain top one is nearer to God and the veil between man and God, like the air, is thinner. It is God who calls man to the mountain, symbolic of the requirement that man elevate himself to the level of God as best he can before God descends to the level of man. Perhaps the scriptural term *exceedingly high mountain* does not mean elevation from sea level as much as it does spiritual height of the realm of God or the place of encounter as a holy place. Yet, it is a place we can attain in mortality as Nephi described: "And upon the wings of his Spirit hath my body been carried away upon exceedingly high mountains" (2 Nephi 4:25).

It is our faith in Christ and our righteousness through His Holy Order that qualifies and empowers us to summit an "exceedingly high mountain." *The presence of God makes a mountain an "exceedingly high mountain."*

Joseph Smith once said, "The rich can only get [blessings] in the temple—the poor may get them on the mountain top as did Moses."[9] Before Solomon's temple was built, "the people sacrificed in high places" (1 Kings 3:2). The connection between a mountain top and a temple is seen in scriptural temple parallels (compare Ezekiel 37:22, 28).

The rich are those blessed by the Lord with the means and money to construct a temple mountain wherever they gather and are instructed by the Lord to build a temple. Often they were not rich in material possession but by collective sacrifice produced a richness in sacrifice acceptable to the Lord. "In the days of your poverty, wherein ye are not able to build a house unto me" (D&C 124:30), the Lord will accept his sacred ordinances outside a constructed temple. "The poor," who certainly were rich in spirit, have left us inspiring accounts of "exceedingly high mountains" or sacred place encounters with the Lord.

After **Adam** and **Eve** fell from the holy mountain of God, they learned how to climb back to the garden presence of God, and even beyond, to a greater presence called "eternal life." Following Adam's example, other great patriarchs and prophets like the brother of Jared had temple experiences and endowments on mountaintops or secluded sacred places as they returned to the presence of the Lord.

Enoch, who had known Father Adam (see D&C 107:53), testified about Adam and the Plan of Salvation and then opened a window to his temple experience on Mount Simeon:

> As I was journeying, and stood upon the place Mahujah, and cried unto the Lord, there came a voice out of heaven, saying—Turn ye, and get ye upon the mount of Simeon.
>
> And it came to pass that I turned and went up on the mount; and as I stood upon the mount, I beheld the heavens open, and I was clothed upon with glory;
>
> And *I saw the Lord*; and he stood before my face, and he talked with me, even as a man talketh one with another, face to face; and he said unto me: Look, and I will show unto thee the world for the space of many generations. (Moses 7:2–4; emphasis added)

Abraham arose from the plains of Moreh "and removed from thence unto a mountain on the east of Bethel . . . and there [he] built another altar unto the Lord" (Abraham 2:20).

Moses on Mount Sinai is the dramatic and classic example of the ascension of the mountain of the Lord:

> Now Moses kept the flock of Jethro his father in law, the priest of Midian: and he led the flock to the backside of the desert, and came to the mountain of God, even to Horeb,
>
> And he said, Certainly I will be with thee; and this shall be a token unto thee, that I have sent thee: When thou hast brought forth the people out of Egypt, *ye shall serve God upon this mountain*. (Exodus 3:1, 12; emphasis added)

Here are the words of God, which he spake unto Moses at a time when Moses was caught up into an *exceedingly high mountain*: "And *he saw God face to face*, and he talked with him, and the glory of God was upon Moses; therefore Moses could endure his presence" (Moses 1:12; emphasis added).

King David, challenged by his son Absalom, fled Jerusalem. As a forerunner of the real King of Israel, he ascended to the top of Mount Olivet weeping, with his head covered, and his feet bare "where he worshipped God" (2 Samuel 15:32).

Isaiah, who had seen the Lord (Isaiah 6:1–10), was vivid in temple mountain imagery:

> And it shall come to pass in the last days, that the *mountain of the Lord's house shall* be established in the top of the mountains, and shall be exalted above the hills; and all nations shall flow unto it.
>
> And many people shall go and say, Come ye, and let us go up to the *mountain of the Lord*, the *house of the God* of Jacob; and he will teach us of his ways, and we will walk in his paths: for out of Zion shall go forth the law, and the word of the Lord from Jerusalem. (Isaiah 2:2–3; emphasis added)

> Even them will I bring *to my holy mountain*, and make them joyful in my *house of prayer*: their burnt offerings and their sacrifices shall be accepted upon *mine altar*; for mine house shall be called an house of prayer for all people. (Isaiah 56:7; emphasis added)

> But he that putteth his trust in me shall possess the land, and shall *inherit my holy mountain*. (Isaiah 57:13; emphasis added)

The **Prophet Nephi** was carried away to a high mountain where he had a great vision:

> For it came to pass after I had desired to know the things that my father had seen, and *believing* that the Lord was able to make them known unto me, as I sat pondering in mine heart I was caught away in the Spirit of the Lord, yea, into an *exceedingly high mountain*, which I never had before seen, and upon which I never had before set my foot. (1 Nephi 11:1; emphasis added)

The Scriptural Temple

Ezekiel's vision of a future temple to be built on the mountain of the house of the Lord in Jerusalem occurred on a high mountain: "In the visions of God brought he me into the land of Israel, and set me upon a *very high mountain,* by which was as the frame of a city on the south" (Ezekiel 40:2; emphasis added).

John the Revelator also had a high mountain experience: "And he carried me away in the spirit to *a great and high mountain,* and shewed me that great city, the holy Jerusalem, descending out of heaven from God" (Revelation 21:10; emphasis added).

During his mortal ministry, the **Savior** returned to mountains for solitude, prayer, and holy mountain temple events:

> And when he had sent the multitudes away, *he went up into a mountain apart to pray:* and when the evening was come, he was there alone. (Matthew 14:23; emphasis added)

> And after six days Jesus taketh **Peter, James,** and **John** his brother, and bringeth them up into an *high mountain apart,* And he was transfigured before them. (Matthew 17:1–2; emphasis added)

Even after His resurrection, the Savior in similitude of the great and last promise of the temple returned to a mountain where His disciples saw and worshipped Him (see Matthew 28:16–17).

Does the Lord call us to match His mountain today? If so, how can we have these sacred mountaintop experiences? Consider these callings of old and liken them to us, for truly the modern-day temple of the Lord is the holy mountain of the Lord.

While warning Lot who lived in Sodom, angels urged him: "Escape for thy life; look not behind thee, neither stay thou in all the plain; *escape to the mountain,* lest thou be consumed" (Genesis 19:17).

Having arrived in the Arabian Bountiful, Nephi received instruction on a mountain to build a ship to carry his people to the promised land: "And it came to pass that after I, Nephi, had been in the land of Bountiful for the space of many days, the voice of the Lord came unto me, saying: Arise, and *get thee into the mountain.* And it came to pass that I arose and went up into the mountain, and cried unto the Lord" (1 Nephi 17:7; emphasis added). A few verses later, Nephi notes that he "did *go into the mount oft,* and I did pray oft unto the Lord; *wherefore the Lord showed unto me great things*" (1 Nephi 18:3; emphasis added).

The Savior foretelling the abomination of desolation upon Jerusalem said, "stand in the holy place" (Joseph Smith—Matthew 1:12). Then He said, "flee into the mountains" (Joseph Smith—Matthew 1:13). *The admonitions to "escape to the mountain," "Arise, and get thee into the mountain" and even "flee into the mountains" are equivalent to "escape to the temple," "arise and get thee into the temple" and "flee into the temple."* This was the commandment of the Lord to our patriarch fathers and Saints of old. They were men and women of faith who could match His "exceedingly high" mountains.

The Lord is making the same call to us, both through His living prophets and through His prophets of old, whose admonition centuries ago is still valid today: "O Zion, that bringest good tidings, *get thee up into the high mountain*" (Isaiah 40:9; emphasis added). Are we of such faith to hear and obey the command "arise, and get thee into the temple"? This is what Moroni's trumpet is sounding: "Come unto Christ, Arise and get thee into the temple." Do we hear Moroni's call? Do we have enough faith in Christ to leave the precepts of men and follow a more excellent way through the Holy Order of God in the temple? If so, we may be partakers of the gift which is a knowledge of God even in the glory of His "rest" (see Ether 12:9–11). Joseph Smith taught this more excellent way:

> How do men obtain a knowledge of the glory of God, his perfections and attributes? By devoting themselves *to his service,* through prayer and supplication *incessantly strengthening their faith in him,* until like Enoch, the brother of Jared and Moses, they obtain a manifestation of God to themselves.[10]

Are we so desirous to know "great things" that we will cry and pray unto the Lord in His temple and go often as did Nephi? Are we men and women who can learn to worship the Lord in His temple (see Psalm 5:7; 100:4–5) to match His holy, exceedingly high mountain?

> *Who shall ascend into the hill of the Lord?* or who shall stand in his holy place? He that hath clean hands, and a *pure heart*; who hath not lifted up his soul unto vanity, nor sworn deceitfully.

He shall receive the blessing from the Lord, and righteousness
from the God of his salvation.
This is the generation of them that seek him, that seek thy face, O
Jacob. (Psalm 24:3–6; emphasis added)

Mount Zion: The Cosmic Mountain

A central idea in most Near Eastern philosophies is the primordial mound or hillock as the first solid ground to emerge from
the chaotic waters of creation. This can vividly be imagined in the
Hebrew designation of Mount Moriah as the primordial hillock, the
most holy ground in all the earth. It is the center of the earth to
which is attached the umbilical (*omphalos*) from heaven which sustains the earth.[11] The concept of a cosmic Mount Zion, a holy mount
from which the Lord reigns (see Isaiah 24:23) and from which His
knowledge and laws of the cosmos are revealed to man, centered on
the concept of a "primordial hillock"[12] and "omphalos."

The Old Testament temples were architectural representations of
the cosmic mountain experience in the Sinai. Moses on Mount Sinai
in the presence of the Lord is the classic cosmic experience. It was the
pivotal event of the Exodus of the children of Israel, one of the most
often-referenced episodes in all of scripture.

Climbing the Spiritual Mountain
Embodied in Physical Temples

The cosmic mountain before us today—as at the time of Paul—
is not a physical mountain like Mount Sinai, which our fathers in
the desert refused to ascend. It is not the physical Mount Zion of
Jerusalem which our fathers ascended to worship in the house of the
Lord. Rather, it is "Mount Zion in the Lord's house" (D&C 84:32).
It is a spiritual mountain embodied in our physical temples. It is what
Paul called the heavenly Mount Zion and the glory at its summit is
worth the climb.

Ye are come unto *Mount Sion*, and unto the city of the living God,
the heavenly Jerusalem, and to an innumerable company of angels,
To the general assembly and church of the firstborn, . . . and to God

the judge of all, and to the spirits of just men made perfect, And to Jesus the mediator of the new covenant. (Hebrews 12:22–24; emphasis added)

Joseph Smith, explaining the process of climbing the heavenly Mount Zion, observed that: "Men have to suffer that they may come upon Mount Zion and be exalted above the heavens."[13]

Suffering is synonymous with sacrifice in the context of obedience. The sacrifices acceptable to the Lord are those made in obedience to His commandments and covenants (see D&C 132:50). Suffering on our part is the internal struggle to change our nature to one of pure righteousness through obedience, until we learn to emulate the Savior, who "suffered the will of the Father in all things" (3 Nephi 11:11; see also Hebrews 5:8; Philippians 1:29). After we have "[suffered] all manner of affliction for Christ's sake" (see Alma 4:13; 2 Timothy 3:12), He will "make [us] perfect" (see 1 Peter 5:10). The climb of Mount Zion is done with obedient faith and sacrifice that may require both external and internal suffering in our metamorphosis to exaltation. As Christ's and His Father's condescension or suffering and sacrifice were for the benefit of others, so should ours become.

The spiritual Mount Zion is the holy mountain of the Lord before us today. It is the mountain whose summit is Zion, the heavenly kingdom of God (see D&C 105:32). We learn how to climb to the summit of this Mount Zion through the temple endowment at the temple altar of sacrifice. We must climb the spiritual Mount Zion of the temple to see and be part of the great view of eternal life.

Ascending the
Mountain of Holiness

A memorable event in my tour of Old Jerusalem was the visit to the Temple Mount. Much of the recent excavation has occurred along the Western Wall and the southwestern corner of the Mount. The remainder of Robinson's arch and the stairs to the southern gates of Herod's temple have been excavated. These gates were probably a principle entrance to the temple, requiring the worshippers to ascend as they approached the courts of the temple.

In this ascent, they climbed what are known as the Ophel steps which in Hebrew means "ascend." The Ophel steps are unusual in that they do not accommodate quick ascent. This is because the steps have alternating deep and shallow cuts. One cannot simply run up these steps. This type of stair may have been for crowd control, but I favor the explanation of our tour guide, Wayne Brickey. As I sat on these stairs in the late afternoon, with long and short shadows cast obliquely across them, this is what I recorded in my diary based on his comments: "*These stairs symbolize the need for steady slow pace in our spiritual progress. Spiritual things are cut out of rock.*"

In Psalm 122 we read one of the psalms of ascent, recited as worshippers climbed the stairs, symbolizing the progressive climb in their journey to become like God:

> I was glad when they said unto me, Let us go into the house of the Lord.
>> Our feet shall stand within thy gates, O Jerusalem
>> Whither the tribes go up, the tribes of the Lord, unto the testimony of Israel, to give thanks unto the name of the Lord.
>> Pray for the peace of Jerusalem: they shall prosper that love thee.
>> Because of the house of the Lord our God I will seek thy good.
> (Psalm 122:1, 2, 4, 6, 9)

"A prevalent theme of the writings of Isaiah," my diary continues, "is that our life should be great and small steps of repentance as we ever refine ourselves to become like God. *It is not good intentions that make us Godlike, but rather climbing the steps of repentance to the house of the Lord where the powers of righteousness are released by the ordinances and covenants of the temple.* The foundation of these ordinances and covenants is unselfishness and service to others, with a true love of God and man. In other words, righteousness and holiness are closely connected to unselfishness in one's love to God and man. This is especially true in marriage."

The Admission Requirement: A Defined Level of Spiritual Maturity and Obedience

As I climbed the ramp and entered the temple courtyard, I remember being overcome with a feeling of reverence and peace even though I saw no temple and was surrounded by Moslem shrines with somber Arab guards. The aged, noble trees, with sacred memory etched in their bark, were the reverent sentinels. I was standing on the ancient court of the Gentiles where Jesus had taught and healed and cast out the irreverent.

Looking to where Herod's temple probably stood, I had to look up. It was on an elevated plane above the court of the Gentiles. I pictured the Balustrade or Soreg with its strict warning in Greek and Latin: "No Gentile shall enter inward of the partition and barrier surrounding the Temple, and whosoever is caught shall be responsible to himself for his subsequent death."

This five-foot stone wall was a physical barrier between the court of the Gentiles and the courts of the inner temple. It was symbolic of the barrier the Lord created around the holy mount in the Sinai (see Exodus 19:12) and the warning of the Lord in the Mosaic law (see Leviticus 15:31). I thought of the many gentile visitors wondering why they were kept out of the inner temple and then recalled the barriers confronted by the many visitors to Salt Lake City's Temple Square who ask, "Why can't I go inside the temple?"

A defined level of spiritual maturity and obedience is the price of admission to the higher realms of the mountain of the House of the Lord. We must ascend to God's defined level of worthiness and readiness, willing to "separate from [our] uncleanness," before He will descend to our level. The temple recommend is the defined level today.

It is interesting that at the foot of the Ophel steps are excavated houses of ablutions (washings). Baptism, the Lord's sign of our humility (see Alma 32:16), is the gate through which we must pass before we climb the steps to the defined level of the temple. There we can pray, "O Lord, wilt thou not shut the gates of thy righteousness before me, that I may walk in the path of the low valley, that I may be strict in the plain road" (2 Nephi 4:32). "Open to me the gates of righteousness. . . . This gate of the Lord, into which the righteous shall enter" (Psalm 118:19–20). Of course, in the Melchizedek Priesthood temples of today, "Jew and Gentile alike," are welcome if they will meet the standard required for admission: "Thus we see that *the gate of heaven* [baptism through the temple] *is open unto all,* even to those who will *believe on the name of Jesus Christ*" (Helaman 3:28; emphasis added). "For he is our peace, who hath made both one, and hath broken down the middle wall of partition between us" (Ephesians 2:14).

It is the intent of the Lord to bring all His children to His holy mountain as "an house of prayer for all people" (Isaiah 56:7; see also Isaiah 57:13). If we could look at an aerial drawing of the temple mount at the time of the Savior's earthly ministry, the image of ascending levels is evident from street level, up the Ophel steps, into the court of the Gentiles, to the Holy of Holies. A description of these ascending levels is found in the book *Jerusalem, the Eternal City*:

Overall, the Temple area consisted of a series of rising platforms. From the Court of the Gentiles one ascended stairs to the Court of the Women; from there, one ascended fifteen curved stairs (possibly singing fifteen Psalms of Ascent; see Psalm 120; 134) to the Court of the Men of Israel and the Court of the Priests; and a final ascent was required to enter the Holy Place itself. Thus the phrase "Jesus went up into the temple" (John 7:14) is literal. The three courtyards surrounding the holiest place where the Divine Presence could be manifest may appropriately be compared to three degrees of glory and three settings for instruction in modern temples: telestial, terrestrial, and celestial. It is not enough to progress into the third courtyard or heaven; it is incumbent upon each worshiper, now that the Great High Priest has made it possible for all, to actually enter into the highest degree of that realm, to symbolically enter into the Presence of God and be exalted.[1]

The ascension from baptism to the temple and climbing the temple to the exalted presence of God is a process of passing through gates of righteousness until we can say "Lift up your heads, O ye gates; and be ye lift up, ye everlasting doors; and the King of glory shall come in" (Psalm 24:7). This is the great and last promise for ascending through the gates of the mountain of holiness.

Pressing Forward with a Steadfastness in Christ

When we enter the temple, we must press forward with a steadfastness in Christ having, as Paul said, "the full assurance of hope" (Hebrews 6:11) or "a perfect brightness of hope" as Nephi said. Then we pass the final gate and enter the Holy of Holies, standing in the presence of the Father:

And then are ye in this strait and narrow path which leads to eternal life; yea, ye have entered in by the gate [baptism]. . . .

And now, my beloved brethren, after ye have gotten into this strait and narrow path, I would ask if all is done? Behold, I say unto you, Nay; for ye have not come thus far save it were by the word of Christ with unshaken faith in him, relying wholly upon the merits of him who is mighty to save.

Wherefore, *ye must press forward with a steadfastness in Christ*, having a *perfect brightness of hope*, and *a love of God and of all men*. Wherefore, if ye shall press forward, *feasting upon the word of Christ*, and *endure to the end*, behold, thus saith the Father: ye shall have eternal life. (2 Nephi 31:18–20; emphasis added)

This scriptural verse of Nephi beautifully describes the climb to the highest level of the temple, which is eternal life. To reach this summit we must press forward in the word of Christ found in the temple until we have a perfect love of God and all men. In our climb we will be pressed into what the climb will make of us because "every man who seeketh truth presseth into it" (Joseph Smith Translation, Luke 16:18).

The Temple Falls, but Ascending to It Lives On

Many writings, which draw a variety of conclusions, try to explain the destruction of the house of the Lord in Jerusalem and expulsion of the Jews in AD 70 and again in AD 135. The fall of this people and their temple as in all of the "falls" of man from the presence of God, can be due only to the rejection of the Savior through disobedience to His laws. Except for unrighteousness, "the master will not suffer his house to be broken up" (D&C 104:86; see D&C 105:2).

What did the Jewish faithful do when they no longer had the temple? This loss definitely left a hole in their manner of religious worship. The practice of the law of Moses was centered in the temple as the way to ascend to the Lord.

The Pharisaic leaders, such as Rabbi Zakkai and Gamaliel II, established a Jewish religious and governmental center at Jamnia and Jabneh.[2] They developed a modified Mosaic law through the techniques of the Mishnah and Midrash, which excluded temple worship but anticipated the return of the temple and a religious Jerusalem.

These exiled rabbis and Jewish sages created a New Jerusalem in their minds with remembrance of the destroyed Jerusalem temple. The rituals of this remembrance have been passed on from generation to generation. An example of such a ritual is the well known breaking of a glass under foot at a Jewish wedding.[3]

For the Orthodox Christians, the temple destruction was the fulfillment of Christ's prophecy (see Matthew 24:12). They reason that Christ and His Atonement eliminated the need for the Mosaic temple.

The Ascent from an Aaronic Priesthood Temple to a Melchizedek Priesthood Temple in Jerusalem

Evangelist creeds today speak of a spiritual temple, a temple without walls, defined as a collective body of true believers. "It is this community of true believers from various denominations who are a 'spiritual temple' that replaced the temple building of the Old Testament" wrote Luke P. Wilson.[4]

These creeds show no understanding or need of physical temple worship. They misinterpret Paul's writings about the individual human body, a unified group of believing Saints, and a physical place with covenants and ordinances as all being necessary temple concepts, but not being mutually exclusive. They fail to recognize that Paul and the other apostles continued to worship at the Jerusalem temple long after the Savior's ascension. These apostles gave us scriptural hints that they made the transformation from an Aaronic Priesthood temple to a Melchizedek Priesthood temple that truly led them to the presence of the Lord. For instance, the Epistle to the Hebrews says,

> If therefore perfection were by the Levitical priesthood, (for under it the people received the law,) what further need was there that another priest should rise after the order of Melchisedec, and not be called after the order of Aaron?
>
> For the priesthood being changed, there is made of necessity a change also of the law.
>
> And it is yet far more evident: for that after the similitude of Melchisedec there ariseth another priest,
>
> Who is made, not after the law of a carnal commandment, but after the power of an endless life. (Hebrews 7:11–12, 15–16)

Before His ascension, Jesus had promised his disciples, "And, behold, I send the promise of my Father upon you: but tarry ye in the city of Jerusalem, until ye be *endued with power* from on high" (Luke 24:49).

The events in the upper room at Pentecost and the forty-day ministry of the Savior after his resurrection give us further insight of this ascent to the covenants, ordinances, and endowments of an "endless life" through "a greater and more perfect tabernacle" (Hebrews 9:11).

The Ancient Concept of the Celestial Ascent

Some Jewish scholars reasoned that if they could not worship God on the mountain of the house of the Lord in Jerusalem, then they would ascend to him in their minds. This concept evolved into an even more physical transformation to the celestial temple of God. The personal ascension to God in his celestial temple certainly had scriptural foundation as seen in the verses concerning the ascensions of Enoch, Moses, Isaiah, Ezekiel, John the Revelator, and even the Savior.

The idea of personal ascension to the presence of God is known in Jewish theological literature as Merkavah (chariot), Hekhalot (temple palace), and Bereshit (creation) mysticism.[5] These Jewish ascension themes became more mystical in the Jewish creed called *Kabalism.* This creed developed mainly in medieval Spain.[6] Safed, the geographically highest city in Israel, located at the northwestern end of the Sea of Galilee, became the center of this Jewish mysticism.[7]

Along with the social importance of the temple, *the concept of celestial ascent is one of the most persisting and prevalent religious concepts in history.*[8] Writing about ascension texts, William Hamblin said:

> The parallels between Jewish, early Christian, Hellenistic Gnostic, and Egyptian ascension texts and rituals are too numerous and exact to be explained by random chance. . . .
>
> It is remarkable that nearly all of these visionary ascents to the celestial temple—whether from Jewish, pagan, or Christian sources—exhibit many parallels, indicating that all of these ideas and documents were somehow conceptually and historically linked together.[9]

One of the more remarkable ascension texts in the Bible is Jacob's staircase vision. Jacob had been given the birthright by his father, Isaac. He was warned by his mother, Rebekah, to flee from Esau and choose a wife from the daughters of her brother Laban, who lived in Haran. While traveling northward from Beershebe to Haran, Jacob had a descriptive temple vision (see Genesis 28:11–22).

It is interesting to compare this staircase erected by God with the Tower of Babel which means "gate of God."[10] The staircase experienced by Jacob was "set up on the earth" by God, unlike the Tower of

Babel, because "the top of it reached heaven." Truly, the staircase seen by Jacob was the "gate of heaven" because "the Lord stood above it" (Genesis 28:13). The building of an altar, the ordinance of anointing, and making covenants with the Lord who stood above it established the place Bethel as "the house of God."

The free descending of angels established that Jacob's staircase was connected to the celestial realm of God, as true heavenly messengers descend from God (see John 1:51). *The ascending of angels implies the possibility of ascent to the presence of God if one becomes angelic, then God-like, by making and keeping covenants represented by each step of the ladder.*

Jacob learned that by making a covenant with the Lord ("Jacob vowed a vow") and through the blessings ("I am with thee, and will keep thee in all places whither thou goest") of the God of Abraham (Christ), he could become angelic and come again to his father's house in peace (which ultimately meant the house of his Father in heaven). In this covenant, Jacob promised to be obedient to God ("then shall the Lord be my God") and offer sacrifice acceptable to the Lord in this obedience ("I will surely give the tenth unto thee"). Jacob received the same covenant and blessings that his grandfather, Abraham received. Indeed, Jacob received the Abrahamic Covenant, which comprises the greatest blessings of the temple.

The teachings of Jacob's vision are the Fall, the path of return to our Father's house through the gate of God which ultimately is the temple, and the ascent up its staircase by the power and blessings of Christ. We receive these blessings by ascending through the ordinances, covenants and endowments of the temple. The technique of the ascent is faith in Christ and obedience through sacrifice to His commandments. The sacrifice we offer is our time and means in edifying others.

The greatest book of scripture that describes in vivid detail the ladder of ascent and descent from the presence of God is the Book of Isaiah. Avraham Gileadi has "decoded" Isaiah by describing the levels of ascent and descent on this ladder.[11] The different rungs of the ladder represent spiritual levels of maturity. The entry level into mortality for most is what Isaiah calls "Jacob / Israel." This level will eventually disappear because all in mortality will have to choose to either ascend or descend the ladder. There is no neutral point on this ladder.

The temple teachings for ascending the mountain of the Lord have been passed down from Adam who received them from God. Therefore, God is the source and conceptual link of all the celestial ascension themes. The glory of true temple ascension is that we not only climb it ourselves, being helped and led by Christ, but we lead and help our friends and ancestors in their ascent as well. This help did not occur on the Tower of Babel where the attitude was "let us make us a name" (Genesis 11:4) instead of working for other names and receiving a new name from the Lord.

Ascending to the Great View

While in high school, I was introduced to the techniques of mountain climbing through my experiences at *Outward Bound* in Colorado and the *National Outdoor Leadership School* in Wyoming. I have had the chance to climb some of the grand mountains of Colorado and Wyoming. Out of concern, many have asked, "why did you do something so dangerous?"

I didn't answer with George Mallory's famous statement "Because it is there." Rather, my answer was "Because of the view," *not only the glorious, panoramic view that rewarded me for reaching the summit, but the new view of me within.* I found a totally different perspective of myself on the summit.

In his great temple sermon, King Benjamin apparently spoke about this concept of views, for his listeners responded to him by saying, "And we . . . through the infinite goodness of God, and the manifestations of his spirit, have *great views* of that which is to come" (Mosiah 5:3).

King Benjamin defined this great view as an understanding of "the mysteries of God" (Mosiah 2:9), and he even contrasted the "great view" with an "awful view" (Mosiah 3:25). God said, "Except [a man] humble himself . . . acknowledge unto me the things he has done wrong . . . covenant with me to keep my commandments, and exercise faith in me . . . he shall have no such views (D&C 5:28). When we exercise humility, repentance, obedience, and faith in Christ, His gifts of revelation "throw greater views upon [His] gospel" (D&C 10:45; Helaman 11:23). The great view that King Benjamin taught and his people saw was not a point of view. Rather, it was a compound in one of all points of view in a panoramic view of the glory of God.

Since being on the stake high council and having the occasion to sit on the stand in sacrament meeting, I have seen a different perspective, a point of view, that unfolded a great view of those coming to hear the word of God. It reminds me of my boyhood fascination with a magnet and iron filings, as though there were some kind of polarity with the pulpit affecting the response of the congregation. For example, the concentration of the congregation is often directly proportional to the distance from the pulpit. I know that the distribution of the congregation is similar in most wards and has nothing to do with faith and intent. It has more to do with the location of entry, the tendency to be a spectator in the chapel, or the fear of being on the other side of the pulpit giving a talk.

From his great view on the tower, King Benjamin saw, as I did on the stand, the effect of the power of the word of God in the hearts of those who heard it. The soul overcome by the Spirit, shedding tears; the wayward soul finding the miracle of forgiveness; a child radiating the love of God; a servant of God speaking with the power of the Spirit: all these uncover the private corners of the chapel, lifting eyes and hearts in unison to the pulpit as though its polarity were irresistibly drawing all to it. This is a great and glorious view, and it comes by the power of the Spirit when the word of God penetrates the heart.

This image of the polarity of the pulpit is symbolic of our understanding of the temple and our relation to it. Like the Children of Israel in the Sinai who feared the Holy Mount, some of us distance ourselves from the temple, not understanding its power to change lives. Similarly, we distance ourselves from the pulpit, not understanding how bearing testimony of the gospel from behind it can give us a great view of ourselves. Both the pulpit and the altars of temple symbolize a commitment to change in our lives. Why do we fear change for the better? Yet we are drawn to the pulpit as listeners, and thus to God when the power of His word penetrates our hearts. Likewise, God beckons us to draw near and climb His holy mountain. Therefore, "fear not to do good" (D&C 6:33).

The temple is a powerful, positive magnet that penetrates and cleanses the negatives in our hearts, propelling us into the presence of God. If our hearts are charged with false-positive pride of the world, we are repelled from the true-positive power of the temple. As a chapel pulpit and the sacrament table are the focal points of resolve to remove the negatives and false-positives in our lives, so should the temple, where "we worship God before the altar" (Alma 15:17; 17:4), be the focal point of positive spiritual rebirth. There we will begin to see the great view of that which is to come as the word of God penetrates our hearts.

The Lead Climber and His Rope

When I lived in Durham, North Carolina, I resided in a region called the Piedmont, which translated from French means "foothill." It was pleasant to live there, but nothing like going up to the Smoky Mountains of North Carolina and Tennessee.

In his epistle to the Hebrews, Paul admonished the Jewish Saints to no longer tarry in the foothills of spiritual experience. In essence he said to get to the mountain of perfection. Paul's words even give the impression of climbing a mountain with a rope:

> Therefore not leaving the principles of the doctrine of Christ, let us go on unto perfection:
> That ye be not slothful, but followers of them who through faith and patience inherit the *promises* . . . lay hold upon the *hope* set before us.
> Which hope we have as *an anchor of the soul*, both sure and steadfast, and which entereth into *that within the veil*. (Joseph Smith Translation, Hebrews 6:1, 12, 18–19; emphasis added)

Picture this hope as a rope that we grasp. This rope, anchored to Christ, is an anchor of the soul. The rope is the Atonement in which we have hope. Where do Christ and His rope lead? They lead "by a new and living way" (Hebrews 10:20) to the summit of Mount Zion ("to that within the veil"). The summit is the presence of God.

Paul's descriptive phrases imply the promises: obtaining a good report, entering into the Lord's rest, going on to perfection, entering into the holiest, being made a high priest forever, knowing the Lord, pleasing God, obtaining a witness of being righteous and having the law written in the heart.[12] Paul is talking about the promises obtained during and after the climb to the summit of the temple. The view and realization of these promises is worth the climb.

In climbing, it is important that the rope is securely fixed to the mountain by a nail or piton. I love the image of this piton in Isaiah:

> And I will fasten him as *a nail in a sure place*; and he shall be for a glorious throne to his father's house.
> And *they shall hang upon him* all the glory of his father's house, the offspring and the issue, all vessels of small quantity, from the vessels of cups, even to all the vessels of flagons. (Isaiah 22:23–24; emphasis added)

This Messianic prophecy refers to the Savior as the nail (see Zechariah 10:3–4) in a sure place, which is the temple. We all hang on Him, holding fast to His hope, whether we are a small cup or a flagon.

Ezra identified the sure place of escape, confession and recommitment as the temple because there we have "a nail in His holy place" (Ezra 9:8). The image of the nail in this verse refers to the surety of escape from iniquity because of the grace of the Savior.

In mountain climbing, both literally and figuratively, the lead climber is most important because the followers hang their lives on his abilities. Who is the lead, the guide in our ascension of the mountain of the Lord? The Lord tells us with certainty that "I am Messiah, the King of Zion, the Rock of Heaven. . . . Whoso cometh in at the gate and *climbeth up by me shall never fall*" (Moses 7:53).

The Psalms beautifully describe the Savior guiding us ever upward to higher levels, line upon line, precept upon precept, rock upon rock, until we reach the summit: "From the end of the earth will I cry unto thee, When my heart is overwhelmed: *Lead me to the rock that is higher than I*" (Psalm 61:2).

It is His words, in laws and covenants, that refresh us and lead us like a light on the ascending path of holiness (see Psalm 119:103, 105). As we climb to higher levels of spirituality and are secured by our guide upon His rock we can feel safe against the blast of storms: "That when the devil shall send forth his mighty winds, yea, his shafts in the whirlwind, yea, when all his hail and his mighty storm shall beat upon you, it shall have no power over you to drag you down to the gulf of misery and endless wo, because of the rock upon which ye are built, which is a sure foundation, a foundation whereon if men build they cannot fall" (Helaman 5:12; see also Matthew 7:25; D&C 6:34).

The Scriptural Temple

The Lord warns us that if we do not hold his rope (oracle) and the rope of his true servants (oracles) firmly with conviction, we will stumble and fall relinquishing the rope: "And all they who receive the *oracles* of God, Let them beware how they *hold* them lest they are accounted as a light thing, and are brought under condemnation thereby, and *stumble and fall* when the storms descend, and the winds blow, and the rains descend, and beat upon their house" (D&C 90:5; see also 1 Nephi 8:24–28).

When we climb to a higher rock and discover our true spiritual nature and the spirit within us resonates with the words of Christ, we become a light to those climbing below. "The spirit of man is the candle of the Lord" (Proverbs 20:27).

As the Savior is drink to our thirsting soul, so we become drink to those thirsting below because "out of [our] belly shall flow rivers of living water" (John 7:37–38) when we speak the spiritual words of truth. Those thirsting below are also those who are waiting in the world of spirits for us to give them the chance to fully grasp the rope. As we climb the temple with an ancestor, one by one, the thirst in both of our souls is quenched with the love of the Savior.

What a wonderful image of this mountain ascent the scriptural temple gives us. We are all roped together with hope in our lead climber, Jesus Christ. We all hang on Him, and He is secure in a sure place, the celestial temple of His Father. As He holds the rope for us until we reach a higher and more secure level then we in turn must belay for those below us until they reach the same secure level. The sure place in which we learn how to belay and elevate others, both living and dead, and continue our own climb is in the temples of the Lord. This is where we should drive our pitons through covenants with Christ, and hang our hope on Him for He is "able to keep [us] from falling" (Jude 1:24).

The Great View of Ourselves

What if we do wander and fall? Does our guide let us fall to our death? Ammon, one of the sons of Mosiah, while recalling the fall of himself, his brothers, and Alma the younger, said they were "snatched" by the Lord while falling into an everlasting gulf of death and misery:

Who could have supposed that our God would have been so merciful as to have *snatched* us from our awful, sinful, and polluted state?

Oh, my soul, almost as it were, fleeth at the thought. Behold, he did not exercise his justice upon us, but in his great mercy hath brought us over that *everlasting gulf* of death and misery, even to the salvation of our souls. (Alma 26:17, 20; emphasis added; see Psalm 37:23–24)

When I was a young boy about six years old, my family went to a favorite vacation site, a quiet bay near Balboa Beach. I was limited to the shore line under the watch of my parents since I didn't know how to swim. In the middle of the bay was a bridge supported by wooden columns. Fastened to the wood were a variety of sea creatures such as starfish and shellfish.

I was fascinated by these columns and was determined to touch them. Early one morning, without telling my parents, I got up before anyone else and went to the beach. There was no one to watch me paddle out to the bridge but I felt confident that I could make it. I paddled an inflated raft slowly toward the wooden columns. As I approached them a speed boat made a sharp turn on the opposite side of the bridge. Its wake quickly capsized me. I saw my raft floating away as I began to sink to the bottom.

I have a vivid memory of pushing from the bottom three times and frantically trying to find surface air. As I started to descend the fourth time, I remember thinking I wouldn't have the strength to surface again. Then suddenly, I was snatched by the anxious hands of four girls who had come to the beach just in time. I was not only snatched but severely scratched in their excitement. As I sat shivering with foolishness and fear on the beach, I'm not sure I had the gratitude of being snatched and even scratched that I have now.

Recalling this fortuitous event in my life, I remember the prophet Jonah who was snatched from the depths of the sea by the Lord. The Lord will go to any depth, even the belly of hell, to deliver us if we will believe on His name. When the Lord snatches and delivers us, we, with faith, grab hold of his rope (the hope of His Atonement) secured in a sure place (the rock of His holy mountain or temple). We then go from the awful view spoken of by King Benjamin to the great view of the mysteries of God he also described.

The 76th section of the Doctrine and Covenants fills me with the grandeur of this view and explains how to see it:

Great and marvelous are the works of the Lord, and the mysteries of his kingdom which he showed unto us, which surpass all understanding. . . .

Neither is man capable to make them known, for they are only to be seen and understood by the power of the Holy Spirit, which God bestows on those who love him, and purify themselves before him

To whom he grants this privilege of seeing and knowing for themselves;

That through the power and manifestation of the Spirit, while in the flesh, they may be able to bear his presence in the world of glory. (D&C 76:114, 116–118; see also verses 5–10)

We must learn to obey and be taught by the Spirit to see the "great view." When we do, we will be purified and see the great view of ourselves as holy like the Savior. He said: "For I am the Lord that bringeth you up out of the land of Egypt, to be your God: ye shall therefore *be holy, for I am holy*" (Leviticus 11:45; emphasis added).

Can we see that it is in ascending the staircase of the gospel (which climbs the mountain of holiness, the temple) with our Guide and Savior, Jesus Christ, that we become holy? For He is able to make us holy (see D&C 60:7).

Therefore, to see this great view we must center our lives in worshipping the Lord in "the beauty of holiness" (Psalm 29:2), in His beautiful and holy temple, for here we are taught by the Spirit and led by our Savior. By worshipping in the temple we can have a "godly walk and conversation . . . walking in holiness before the Lord" (D&C 20:69). Then we will exclaim as Jeremiah: "The Lord bless thee, O habitation of Justice, and mountain of holiness" (Jeremiah 31:32).

The mountain of holiness that we climb in the temple is the spiritual Mount Zion. Before we ascend this mountain we must come to base camp and prepare for the climb.

The Camp of Israel: Base Camp of Mount Zion

*A*t *Winter Quarters* on the banks of the Missouri River, Brigham Young, the latter-day Moses, received the "Word and Will of the Lord" in January 1847. This word, revealed on the threshold of the great trek through the unknown West to a promised land, is recorded in the 136th section of the Doctrine and Covenants.

This revelation was given during the "Exodus to Greatness"[1] which started in Nauvoo. There are many striking similarities between this exodus and the exodus from Egypt including the fact that both journeys began with expulsion then refuge in a base camp at the foot of a mountain ascent. The approach to the promised land of the mountain was in both cases from East to West.

In January 1847, Winter Quarters was a base camp, a "Camp of Israel" preparing the pioneer Saints "in their journeyings to the West" (D&C 136:1) to became men and women who would match His Mountains. In base camp, these Saints were organized into groups of multiples of tens with "captains" and presiding men. They were led by a man like unto Moses (see D&C 103:16), and by the Lord, "the Lord your God, even the God of your fathers" whose "arm is stretched out in the last days, to save my people Israel" (D&C 136:21–22). The camp of Israel was prepared and would be saved with "a covenant and promise" to "walk in all the ordinances of the Lord" (D&C 136:2–4). But the revelation said that the Lord's people "must be tried in all things" and must "be prepared . . . [for] the glory of Zion" (D&C 136:31).

This base camp at Winter Quarters was similar to the camps of Israel in the Sinai. The base camp at the foot of the Holy Mountain in the Sinai was a place of preparation for the children of Israel to match God's mountain. It is where "Israel camped before the mount" (Exodus 19:2) and received the ordinances and laws to teach them "the way wherein they must walk" and "the work that they must do" (Exodus 18:20). The camp of Israel was organized into groups of multiples of ten and led by "men of truth" (Exodus 18:21).

Moses said to the camp of Israel: "The Lord God of your fathers" (Exodus 3:15) has delivered you "with a mighty hand, and with an outstretched arm" (Deuteronomy 26:8) so "fear not: for God is come to prove you . . . that you sin not" (Exodus 20:20). With those willing to be proved, the Lord made a covenant witnessed by the "blood of the covenant" (Exodus 24:78). By this covenant and ordinance the camp of Israel would know that "I am the Lord that doth sanctify you" (Exodus 31:13), therefore, "ye shall be holy men unto me" (Exodus 22:31).

Israel Lost the Melchizedek Priesthood Ordinance and the Lord's Rest

Unfortunately, the people of the camp of Israel in the Sinai were not sanctified enough to bear the presence of the Lord. Therefore, the Lord said to them: "I will send an angel before thee; . . . for I will not go up in the midst of thee; for thou art a stiffnecked people: lest I consume thee in the way" (Exodus 33:23).

Joseph Smith clarified why the presence of the Lord would not "go up in the midst of thee" and what the consequences were when he recorded the Lord saying: "For I will take away the priesthood out of their midst; therefore my Holy Order, and the ordinances thereof, shall not go before them; for my presence shall not go up in their midst" (Joseph Smith Translation, Exodus 34:1).

Now this [the ordinances of the higher priesthood, meaning temple ordinances] Moses plainly taught to the children of Israel in the wilderness, and sought diligently to sanctify his people that they might behold the face of God;

But they hardened their hearts and could not endure his presence; therefore, the Lord in his wrath, for his anger was kindled against them, swore that they should not enter into his rest while in the wilderness, which rest is the fulness of his glory.

Therefore, he took Moses out of their midst, and the Holy Priesthood also;

And the lesser priesthood continued, which priesthood holdeth the key of the ministering of angels and the preparatory gospel. (D&C 84:23–26; see also Joseph Smith Translation, Exodus 34:2)

In spite of losing the blessing of the Lord's rest, the camp of Israel was organized into family groups around their "own standard, with the ensign of their father's house: far off about the tabernacle" (Numbers 2:2; see also D&C 30:4). By this organization surrounding the tabernacle, the Lord was teaching the children of Israel that the tabernacle was to remain the center of their lives as their true "father's house."

The chastisement of the Israelites in the Sinai continued 40 years in a prolonged base camp, until Joshua and Caleb and a new generation of Israelites, who had not breached the Lord's promise, were finally led into the promised land (see Numbers 14:27–34). Nephi reminded his brothers Laman and Lemuel of the recalcitrant Israelites, declaring, "He did straiten them in the wilderness with his rod; for they hardened their hearts, even as ye have" (see 1 Nephi 17:41–42).

The Sinai chastisement and wandering of the children of Israel became the archetype for "in the wilderness" themes of the scriptural temple. The basic principle is that "the Lord God will lead away the righteous out from among you" (Jacob 3:4) because "the tares choke the wheat and drive the church into the wilderness" (see D&C 86:3). He will lead them into the wilderness (see 1 Nephi 2:4; 2 Nephi 5:7; Omni 1:12, 16; Mosiah 9:2, 4; 18:34; 8:7; 7:4; 22:2, 8; 24:20; 25:2; Ether 2:5) or the world where God is unseen (see D&C 88:66) to hear "the voice of one crying in the wilderness" (D&C 88:66; Isaiah 40:3). This voice is the voice of the Spirit (see D&C 88:66) which can only be heard by our spirits. To hear the voice of the Spirit, it often requires a wilderness where the rest of the world is silent. We must hear this voice in order to be "led by [God] through the wilderness" (Alma 9:9) before the great and last promise of the temple and the promised land are obtained.

The Lord will lead His people into the wilderness to flee for protection, "to pass under the rod" (Ezekiel 20:37) of chastisement to "straiten them" (1 Nephi 17:41), and to "receive great strength" (see Ether 14:7–8). There, God will humble them "to pour out [their] souls . . . in [their] wilderness" (Alma 34:26) until "thou has heard [their] prayer . . . in the wilderness" (Alma 33:4). He will "plead with [them]" (Ezekiel 20:35) and polishes them in the sands of trial and tribulation until "many of them [are] converted in the wilderness" (Alma 25:6). If they don't learn God's "power in delivering" (Mosiah 25:10) by showing them "the course [they] should travel in the wilderness" (Alma 37:39), they will wander and tarry in "bondage" (see Alma 5:5) and "[die] in the wilderness of their wounds" (Alma 2:38). It is revealing to reflect on how the Lord has led each of us into the wilderness of our lives and how He has shown us there the power of His deliverance.

After the provocation, it was nearly 1,500 years before the camp of Israel would again be offered the fulness of the priesthood and the Lord's rest. Then, only a small number of faithful Saints understood the Savior's earthly ministry as the ultimate preparation to receive the fulness of His priesthood and the promise of His rest. This is because they let the words of the Savior penetrate their hearts to an understanding of His Atonement and how this final great sacrifice would open the way to that within the veil. Then they sought greater blessings beyond the preparatory gospel of baptism, repentance, the remission of sins, and the law of carnal commandments (see D&C 84:26–27) through the fulness of the Holy Ghost in a great endowment.

The Apostle Paul understood these greater blessings. He taught the Hebrew Saints that they needed to be taught again "the first principles of the oracles of God" (see Hebrews 5:12–13; compare Isaiah 28:9–13) then "go on unto perfection" (Hebrews 6:1) a sanctification far greater than they or their ancestors had known for centuries under the Levitical law. He taught them about "the Order of the

Son of God" at the time of Melchizedek emphasizing that all those ordained to this order are "made like unto the Son of God" (Joseph Smith Translation, Hebrews 7:3; see also 3 Nephi 28:10). He reasoned that if another high priest (Jesus Christ), "after the order of Melchisedec" was necessary, then "perfection" could not come by the Levitical order but could only come after the order that has "the power of an endless life" (see Hebrews 7:11, 15–16).

Too often we fail to appreciate the incredible offer, this same offer of a perfected knowledge of God and His power of an endless life the Lord made to the camp of Israel in the Sinai. The God of the Old Testament was going to "come down in the sight of all the people" (Exodus 19:11). Jehovah, the God of the Old Testament and the Messiah of the New Testament, was going to reveal himself in His glory to an estimated one and a half million people. After all this great camp of Israel had witnessed as the power of the Lord, delivering them from Egypt, it is incredible that most of these people rejected the "rest" of the Lord (see D&C 84:24).

Receiving the Lord's Rest: A Preparation of the Heart

It is interesting to compare this potential event with the humble, mortal advent of the Savior in the meridian of time. Thousands of Jews saw Him but only a few recognized Him. While "all men mused in their hearts of John, whether he were the Christ, or not" (Luke 3:15), those who should have recognized Christ as a true prophet could not (see Luke 7:39). The Jews at that time were looking for their God to come in might and glory as He would have appeared to their fathers in the Sinai. In both "Sinai Israel" and "Meridian Israel," the Savior of mankind came and went, with only a few recognizing their God and receiving a witness of His rest. In both cases it required an unerring heart to really recognize Him and behold His glory.

When the Lord appears to a future camp of Israel, again in might and glory, to deliver them from their enemies, the Jews will finally recognize Him for what He is. However, this appearance will be less than a sublime encounter. It will be a time of profound sorrow when the Jews see again the wounds in the hands and feet of their Savior and He says to them: "These wounds are the wounds with which I was wounded in the house of my friends. . . . I am Jesus that was crucified. I am the Son of God" (see D&C 45:51–52; Zechariah 13:6).

The Savior's crucifixion wounds, witnessing His declaration as the crucified Son of God is recorded in a glorious temple event that occurred in the Book of Mormon. At the temple of Bountiful, 2,500 faithful Nephites, heard the heart-piercing voice of God the Father and saw His crucified and resurrected Son. They even had the unforgettable privilege of feeling His crucifixion wounds:

> And it came to pass, as they understood they cast their eyes up again towards heaven; and behold, they saw a Man descending out of heaven; and he was clothed in a white robe; and he came down and stood in the midst of them. . . . And it came to pass that he stretched forth his hand and spake unto the people, saying:
>
> Behold, I am Jesus Christ, whom the prophets testified shall come into the world.
>
> And it came to pass that when Jesus had spoken these words the whole multitude fell to the earth. . . .
>
> And it came to pass that the Lord spake unto them saying:
>
> Arise and come forth unto me, that ye may thrust your hands into my side, and also that ye may feel the prints of the nails in my hands and in my feet, that ye may know that I am the God of Israel, and the God of the whole earth, and have been slain for the sins of the world.
>
> And when they had all gone forth and had witnessed for themselves, they did cry out with one accord, saying:
>
> Hosanna! Blessed be the name of the Most High God! And they did fall down at the feet of Jesus, and did worship him. (3 Nephi 11:8–10, 12–14, 16–17)

The personal privilege to feel the Savior's wounds by these Nephites was not just a tangible witness but also a spiritual witness of His divinity. They knew by feeling, both in their mind and in their heart, that the Savior had been slain for the sins of the world. This is why they cried out "Hosanna! Blessed be the name of the Most High God!" and fell at the feet of Jesus.

One of the most tender, sublime moments in all of scripture occurs in chapter 17 of this great temple event with the Savior:

For I perceive that ye desire that I should show unto you what I have done unto your brethren at Jerusalem. . . .

And it came to pass that when he had thus spoken, all the multitude, with one accord, did go forth with their sick and their afflicted, . . . and He did heal them every one as they were brought forth unto him.

And they did all, both they who had been healed and they who were whole, bow down at his feet, and did worship him; and as many as could come for the multitude did kiss his feet, insomuch that they did bathe his feet with their tears. . . .

And it came to pass that when they had knelt upon the ground, Jesus groaned within himself, and said: Father, I am troubled because of the wickedness of the people of the house of Israel.

And when he had said these words, he himself also knelt upon the earth; and behold he prayed unto the Father, and the things which he prayed cannot be written. (3 Nephi 17:8–10, 14–15)

So great and marvelous were the words that Jesus spoke to the Father that the multitude was overcome with joy (see 3 Nephi 17:18–19). Because of the faith of this multitude the Savior's joy was so full that he wept.

And it came to pass that Jesus spake unto them, and bade them arise.

And they arose from the earth, and he said unto them: Blessed are ye because of your faith. And now behold, my joy is full.

And when he had said these words, he wept, and the multitude bare record of it, and he took their little children, one by one, and blessed them, and prayed unto the Father for them.

And when he had done this he wept again. (3 Nephi 17:19–22)

Another tender temple encounter with the Savior occurred the week before His crucifixion in Jerusalem:

And in the day time he was teaching in the temple; and at night he went out, and abode in the mount that is called the Mount of Olives.

And all the people came early in the morning to him in the temple, for to hear him. (Luke 21:37–38)

These brief verses evoke a multitude of meaningful questions: Was the night time "abode in the mount" a harbinger of the dark hours of the Atonement? Who were "all the people"? Why did they go "early in the morning"? What words did they "hear" from the Savior? I can imagine an intimate, sacred gathering during these early hours on the threshold of the great Atonement. I can imagine the Savior also wept with those He taught at the temple in Jerusalem.

Can you imagine over a million people seeing the fulness of the glory of the Lord who brought them out of Egypt, worshipping Him at His feet? What might the wonderful words of scripture have been, had the camp of Israel in the Sinai not rejected such a glorious moment with their God? This pivotal event and the initial rejection of the Lord to lead His people into the promised land (see Numbers 14:11–12), is known throughout scripture as *the Provocation*. The Apostle Paul, recalling the warning to their ancestors, again admonished the Hebrew Saints to harden not their hearts as in the Provocation:

> *Harden not your hearts*, as in the *provocation*, in the day of temptation in the wilderness:
>> When your fathers tempted me, proved me, and saw my works forty years.
>> Wherefore I was grieved with that generation, and said, They do alway err in their heart; and they have not known my ways.
>> So I sware in my wrath, they shall not enter into *my rest*. (Hebrews 3:8–11; emphasis added; compare Psalm 95:8–11)

Jacob, the brother of Nephi, recalled the *provocation* when he wrote,

> Wherefore we labored diligently among our people, that we might persuade them to come unto Christ, and partake of the goodness of God, that they might enter into *His rest,* lest by any means he should swear in His wrath they should not enter in, as in the *provocation* in the days of temptation while the children of Israel were in the wilderness. (Jacob 1:7; emphasis added)

The "rest" of the Lord is the great and last promise of the temple (see Enos 1:27). It comprises the exaltation of eternal life when we "rest with them" (see D&C 15:6) and "rest with him in heaven" (Moroni 7:3). In this life, "rest" with the Lord is possible in the great blessing of the second comforter, the personal ministry of the Savior Himself, in His glory. This rest requires that we "are chosen in this thing, even as one, that you may enter into my rest" (D&C 19:9). This mortal "rest" occurred at the temple in the Book of Mormon when the Savior appeared. It occurred to the "peaceful followers of Christ" who heard the words of Mormon in the synagogue (see Moroni 7:13). Some early Christian Saints who believed and entered into "rest" (see Hebrews 4:13) unlike their fathers in the Sinai received this great and last promise. It is a promise that comes by faith, hope, and repentance to a change of heart that we may become chosen as one with the Savior.

> Therefore, whosoever repenteth, and hardeneth not his heart, he shall have claim on mercy through mine only begotten son, unto a remission of his sins; and these shall enter into my rest. (Alma 12:34)

Alma taught that hardness of heart is the primary condition keeping us from the Lord's rest (see Alma 12:10, 33–37; 13:4–6; 16:16–17), but the promised rest is possible only through the cleansing power and mercy of the Atonement: "Therefore nothing entereth into *his rest* save it be those who have washed their garments in my blood" (3 Nephi 27:19; emphasis added).

Since the scriptural definition of the "rest" of the Lord is the fulness of His glory (see D&C 84:24) as a great and last promise of the temple (see Isaiah 66:1) as well as God's planned destination for His children (compare Hebrews 4:3–4, D&C 121:32), perhaps there is a deeper meaning in what we know as "the day of rest." While the Sabbath was a day set aside to rest from our mortal labors, it is even more a day to spiritually labor to enjoy the "rest" of the Lord (see Matthew 11:28). "Thou shalt go to the house of prayer and offer up thy sacraments upon my holy day" (D&C 59:9). This concept gives a defined meaning to keeping the Sabbath day holy. We should not "profane the sabbath" (Matthew 12:5) which from its Latin root, *profanum*, literally means "outside of the temple." We should observe and keep the entire Sabbath day as though we were in the temple. Like the Jews who looked to the Sabbath as the coming of the Bridegroom and "his rest shall be glorious" (Isaiah 11:10), the rest of the Lord that we should find on the Sabbath is preparation for the greater rest of the Lord that we will experience in the temple, the house of our Bridegroom (see Ruth 1:9). It is not surprising, therefore, that one of the blessings listed by the Lord for keeping the Sabbath day holy is "to ride upon the high places of the earth" (see Isaiah 58:13–14) by having His "tabernacle among [us]" that He "will walk among [us]" (see Leviticus 26:11–12).

The Preparatory Redemption

In these last days, the Missouri Saints' failure to establish a Zion community is compared to the failure of the Camp of Israel in the Sinai to establish a holy nation. The Saints in Missouri did not climb Mount Zion, like the Israelites in the Sinai, because they did not obey the Lord's commandment to be unified and build a temple to receive its protection. Therefore they were chastened by the Lord "for a little season with a sore and grievous chastisement" (D&C 103:4).

The sore and grievous chastisement came through tribulation with a promise of redemption:

> For after much tribulation . . . cometh the blessing.
>
> Behold, this is the blessing which I have promised after your tribulations, and the tribulations of your brethren—your redemption, and the redemption of your brethren, even their restoration to the land of Zion. . . .
>
> Behold, I say unto you, the redemption of Zion must needs come by power. (D&C 103:12–13, 15)

Before the redemption of Zion, the Saints must be prepared by wandering through the Sinai wilderness of chastisement and tribulation then receive a "preparatory redemption" (Alma 13:3) by power.

> Therefore, in consequence of the transgressions of my people, it is expedient in me that mine elders should wait for a little season for the redemption of Zion—
>
> That they themselves may be prepared, and that my people may be taught more perfectly, and have experience, and know more perfectly concerning their duty, and the things which I require at their hands.

And this cannot be brought to pass until mine elders are endowed with power from on high. For behold, I have prepared a great endowment and blessing to be poured out upon them, inasmuch as they are faithful and continue in humility before me. (D&C 105:9–12)

The preparation and perfection spoken of in this revelation will come to pass when the Saints are chastened to obedience, then endowed with power through the temple endowment.

The idea of power (see D&C 103:15) was introduced in Kirtland at the conception of Zion's Camp. Its meaning may have been interpreted by many in the camp as armed force. Near the end of the 1834 Zion's Camp march, in the Fishing River Revelation, the word *power* (see D&C 105:11) was again mentioned by the Lord. In this revelation it is clear that power to the Lord means the power of love (see D&C 105:23–27), as a temple endowment. This endowment of power (see D&C 105:33, 37) will prepare the called "strength of mine house" (see D&C 101:55; 103:22, 30, 34; 105:16–17, 27) to become the chosen "strength of mine house" (see D&C 105:35–36) when they receive the fulness of the power of the priesthood in the temple. The full power of God's love in our lives is necessary and sufficient for the redemption of Zion.

The preparation of chastisement, tribulation, and power, concentrated in Zion's Camp continued into Nauvoo and to the banks of the Missouri River with the Camp of Israel. It continues today as we camp in the tops of the mountains near the House of the Lord or wherever there is a House of the Lord, preparing us for the day of redemption. Therefore, Zion's Camp marches on until Zion is redeemed!

Base camp, or the camp of Israel, is a place of preparation to climb Mount Zion, the mountain of the Lord's house. It is a camp within the mountains (above the world) preparing to climb the mountain of the Lord's house (see Micah 4:1–2). It is a camp at the base of an exceedingly high and glorious mountain that humbles the pride of the world. "Thou shalt no more be haughty because of my holy mountain" (Zephaniah 3:11). The climb of Mount Zion will prepare us for the redemption of Zion and "the great day of the Lord" (see D&C 133:10, 12–13).

Base camp is where we begin to learn to be separate from the world and "touch not the unclean thing," turning completely to our

Father in Heaven that "[He] will receive [us]" (see 2 Corinthians 6:17–18). It is where we practice what we learn and acclimatize ourselves for the higher levels of Mount Zion. By so doing, we begin to develop an unerring, broken heart in preparation to climb His holy mountain. There we will receive a pure heart for His rest. Base camp is where we submit ourselves to the chastisement of our real Father "until [we] learn obedience" to Him even by "the things which [we] suffer" (D&C 105:6). It is where we are straitened by His rod but comforted by His outstretched arms.

Separating Covenant People from the World to Become the Lord's Jewels

The Lord calls us to be separate, and separates us from the world to His base camps in order to prepare us to become His jewels. This He did with the children of Israel living in bondage along the Nile. He separated them from the world of the Nile to make of them His jewels because of the covenants He made with Moses and their fathers: "Now therefore, if ye will obey my voice indeed, and keep my covenant, then ye shall be a peculiar treasure unto me above all people. . . . And ye shall be unto me a kingdom of priests, and an holy nation" (Exodus 19:5–6). The term *peculiar treasure* comes from the Hebrew word *segullah* which means a precious possession like a jewel.[2]

In spite of transgression, the Lord still numbered His Saints in Missouri as His potential jewels because of His love and mercy for them. However, like the children of Israel, they had to be chastened (polished) by the power of God to become His jewels: "Yet I will own them, and they shall be mine in that day when I shall come to make up my jewels. Therefore, they must needs be chastened and tried, even as Abraham, who was commanded to offer up his only son" (D&C 101:3–4; see also Malachi 3:17; 3 Nephi 24:17). "In the day when I shall make up my *jewels*, all men shall know what it is that bespeaketh the power of God" (D&C 60:4). These scriptures remind me of the jewels worn in the temple vestments of Aaron and his successors (see Exodus 28:9, 12, 15, 17). These jewels represented the house of Israel. They were worn both on the shoulders and near the heart of the high priest who represented the Lord. Therefore the

Lord carries His Saints, those who covenant with Him, on His shoulders and in His heart,[3] even through tribulation.

Why are those who leave the world and covenant with the Lord, His jewels? Moses' farewell speech to the Children of Israel provides perspective:

> For thou art an holy people unto the Lord thy god: The Lord thy God hath chosen thee to be a special people unto himself. . . .
>
> The Lord did not set his love upon you, nor choose you, because ye were more in number than any people; for ye were the fewest of all people;
>
> But because the Lord loved you, and because he would keep the oath which he had sworn unto your fathers. . . .
>
> Know therefore that the Lord thy God, he is God, the faithful God, which keepeth covenant and mercy with them that love him and keep his commandments to a thousand generations. (Deuteronomy 7:6–9; see also 3 Nephi 20:25–27)

Nephi summarized Moses's speech when he said: "Behold, the Lord esteemeth all flesh in one; He that is righteous is favored of God" (1 Nephi 17:35; see also Mosiah 10:13; Ether 1:34; 1 Timothy 4:10). To be "chosen" by the Lord does not automatically mean one is "choice." It means anointed or set apart to become, through righteousness, His jewels.

The righteous are favored of God because they keep the covenant He made with the fathers. The righteous are His jewels because they "are bought with a price" (1 Corinthians 6:20). The price is the "precious blood" of His only begotten Son (see 1 Peter 1:1819). This price the Father and the Son paid because of their love for their children, expecting they would become righteous jewels reflecting the price paid.

When the Lord gathers us from the banks of the Nile (the world), He leads us to His base camps in preparation to climb His temple. In climbing the temple, He will make us His righteous jewels as we become a "compound in one" (2 Nephi 2:11) with Him. Then we will be "as the stones of a crown, lifted up as an ensign upon his land" (Zechariah 9:16). The chosen of the Lord cannot be polished to become His jewels by the pagan world. Holiness cannot be contaminated with unholiness. This truth was dramatically demon-strated when the Philistines tried to mix the holiness of the Arc of the Covenant with Dagon, their unholy god (see 1 Samuel 5, 6). For this reason, Joseph Smith declared:

> The main object of gathering the people of God in any age of the world is to build unto the Lord a house whereby He could reveal unto His people the ordinances of His house and the glories of His kingdom, and teach people the way of salvation.[4]

Therefore, the Lord commanded the Latter-day Saints to "gather together" and build a temple in Far West "that they may worship me" (D&C 115:8; see also D&C 101:64–65). In keeping the cov-enants He made with the fathers, the Lord makes righteous jewels by first gathering uncut, unpolished gems from the plains of the world. He does this through true messengers, such as missionaries, parents, and prophets who bear testimony to the souls of these gems. Then He gathers these gems as potential jewels, for "the worth of souls is great" (D&C 18:10), to His base camps, His stakes of Zion, where He prepares them to match His mountain and climb His holy temple. It is in climbing His temple (Mount Zion) while passing through mor-tality, the "furnace of affliction" (see Isaiah 48:10), that He polishes and purifies these gems to make them His "gems for the sanctified" (D&C 135:6) so they can enter within the veil and abide His rest. In His temple, God will "purify unto himself a peculiar people, zealous of good works" (Titus 2:14).

Put Away Strange Gods, Be Clean, and Change Your Garments

There is an important lesson to be learned from an incident in the life of Jacob, the grandson of Abraham. When Jacob returned from Haran, he lived among the Canaanites. A conflict arose when Shechem the Hivite violated Dinah, the daughter of Jacob. Sensing his peril with the Canaanites, Jacob obeyed a directive from the Lord to go to Bethel where he had seen his great temple staircase vision, "and make there an altar unto God" (see Genesis 35:1). The Lord was tell-ing Jacob to get out of the world, go to the temple, and worship there.

In response, "Jacob said unto his household, and to all that were with him, Put away the strange gods that are among you, and be clean, and change your garments" (Genesis 35:2). Jacob was teaching his household to prepare to be worthy to enter the temple.

Christ dramatically taught the importance of worthiness to enter the temple when He cleansed His house of prayer (see Matthew 21:12–14). In casting out thieves before He exercised the power of His priesthood to heal the blind and the lame, the Savior taught that *we as individual temples must cast out the thieves in our own lives that rob us of holiness before we can experience the power of God.* To cast out the thieves of our lives, we should follow Jacob's advice. We need to put away strange gods by giving up our worldly idols and showing obedience to the one true God, keeping a defined set of His commandments. This is the requirement for admission to His holy house so we are not cast out. We give written proof of this obedience by obtaining a temple recommend, our pass to the inner courts of the temple.

However, final proof of obedience to the Lord requires a spiritual stamp on our pass. It is the stamp or certifying "seal" of justification and sanctification by the Holy Spirit of Promise (see Ephesians 1:13; D&C 76:53; D&C 20:31). This seal is given when we obey all the laws of the gospel and demonstrate strict obedience to the covenants of the Lord, "doing the will of God from the heart" (Ephesians 6:6). It is "by the voice of the Spirit" that the called shall be chosen, justified, and sanctified (see D&C 105:36; Moses 6:60; Alma 13:12; 3 Nephi 27:20; D&C 84:33). Until then we are only called and anointed to be sealed.

Our obedience to the Lord cleanses us as temples so we can invite the Spirit to enter our lives and teach us the way of salvation. To be polished and purified in the temple, we not only need the ordinances but we need to be taught by the Spirit. The Spirit will teach us personally about the power and grace of Christ that is needed in our individual lives to make the mighty change in our hearts. The Spirit will show us our weaknesses and inspire us with the confident hope that we can do better, so that our weaknesses will become strengths. Christ and the Holy Spirit are "[our advocates] who knoweth the weakness of man and how to succor them who are tempted" (D&C 62:1). When we follow the personal teachings of the Spirit, we become "new creatures," desiring above all else to be sealed to our Father in Heaven.

The Spirit prompts us to be clean enough to go to the temple. There we symbolically leave the world behind by changing our worldly garments. We change into clothing of white, symbolic of the Atonement cleansing, as if we were washed white in the blood of the Lamb.

Before we climb Mount Zion and receive the polishing purification of the temple, we must pay a price, demonstrating a preparatory worthiness in obtaining and maintaining a temple recommend. We must keep ourselves as a temple so we can be worthy to be guided in our climb by the Holy Spirit. This preparation for the climb of Mount Zion is how we "get root" that we may "grow up" in climbing Mount Zion to "bring forth fruit" (see Alma 32:37). Preparing to climb Mount Zion is the ultimate goal of base camp.

Equipped for the First Ascent: Initiation to Mount Zion

*P*art *of the* explicit instructions Moses received for the tabernacle included the preparation of those acting as its priests:

> And this is the thing that thou shalt do unto them to *hallow* them, to minister unto me in the priest's office. . . .
>
> And Aaron and his sons thou shalt bring unto the door of the tabernacle of the congregation, and shalt *wash* them with water.
>
> And thou shalt take the *garments,* and put upon Aaron. . . .
>
> Then shalt thou take the anointing oil, and pour it upon his head, and *anoint* him. (Exodus 29:1, 4–5, 7; emphasis added)

Modern Temple Preparations Follow Ancient Scriptural Patterns

Ezekiel poetically described the same preparation and blessings given to Moses for temple service and endowment. Ezekiel compared Jerusalem (the Israelites) to an abandoned child at birth, orphaned with the Canaanites but loved and redeemed by the Lord. He found them, then He washed away their blood, anointed them with oil, covered their nakedness with His skirt, and clothed them with broidered work of fine linen and silk. He entered into a covenant with them, which caused the Lord to declare to them that "thou becamest mine" (see Ezekiel 16:8–10; see also Isaiah 43:1).

To be washed, anointed, and clothed in a garment are likewise preparatory or initiatory ordinances of temples in this dispensation: "Therefore, verily I say unto you, that your anointings, and your washings, . . . are ordained by the ordinance of my holy house" (D&C 124:39).

The school of the prophets (D&C 95:10), organized just prior to the construction of the Kirtland temple, was a preparatory function for those intending to "magnify [their] calling" (D&C 88:80) for temple worship. The preparatory functions of this school were washings, anointings, and instructions to purify feet, hands, and hearts (see D&C 88:74). It was a "solemn assembly" (D&C 88:70), where the principles of love (see D&C 88:133) "in love greeting" (D&C 90:32) were practiced and the "law of the gospel" (D&C 88:78) taught.

In temple initiation today, we are symbolically washed, then covered with the "garment of salvation." Both of these ordinances represent the cleansing and covering power of the Atonement. We are also anointed with oil, symbolizing a setting apart to holiness by reception of the Holy Spirit, whose power directs us and sanctifies us in a new covenant relationship with Christ. The final ordinance of the initiation is to receive a new name as a token of this covenant relationship in which we more fully take upon us the name of Christ.

In the initiatory of the temple we are equipped for the first ascent of Mount Zion. *During this ascent we will be clothed with the robes of righteousness, which represent the acquisition of a divine or holy nature.* In order to reach the summit of Mount Zion, it is important that we are equipped properly by understanding the meaning of these initiatory ordinances and blessings in our personal lives.

Covering Our Nakedness with the Power of the Atonement

The cleansing power of the Atonement is symbolically taught in the scriptural temple by a comparison between the Savior's blood

(His atoning sacrifice) and our blood (our sins). Truly, the blood of Christ is "precious blood" (see 1 Peter 1:18–19), of great price because it does not stain our garments nor our robes. In contrast, it is our blood that stains our garments and His garments (see Alma 5:22 and Isaiah 63:23).

Christ's blood is precious because it can "cleanse [our] blood" (Joel 3:21) and wash our bloodstained garments and robes, making them "white in the blood of the Lamb" (Revelation 7:14). The whitening of Christ's blood is so complete that it "cleanseth us from all sin" (1 John 1:7), making us "clean every whit" (John 13:10) that our "garments be always white!" (Ecclesiastes 9:8). If we "repent sufficiently before God that He would take away our stain" (Alma 24:11), then we will be "washed bright through the blood of the Son of our great God" (Alma 24:13) because He will "cleanse [our] hearts and [our] garments" (D&C 112:33).

In the temple, we are taught even deeper truths about the cleansing and covering power of the Atonement as we learn about the clothing of the Holy Order: the "garments of salvation" and the "robe of righteousness" foretold by the prophet Isaiah: "My soul shall be joyful in my God; for He hath clothed me with the *garments of salvation*, He hath covered me with the *robe of righteousness*" (Isaiah 61:10; emphasis added; see also Psalm 132:9, 16).

In the first temple setting, a beautiful moment of hope occurred when God the Father explained the plan of salvation to Adam and Eve. Then their "nakedness" from the Fall was covered with coats of skin as they made a covenant of obedience to the Father and the Son. It is significant that this benevolent act of covering Adam and Eve occurred when the first animal sacrifice was performed by the Lamb of God (see Genesis 3:21). Perhaps in symbolic reverence, this is why the covering of animal skins was removed and not consumed in a burnt offering under the law of Moses (see Bible Dictionary "Sacrifices"). In a similar manner today, the nakedness of our fall is completely covered with this Atonement clothing as we make covenants with the Lord.

The garment of salvation symbolizes complete covering of salvation from physical death and the first spiritual death (see Helaman 14:16; Alma 40:11; Mormon 9:13; D&C 29:32, 41). This salvation garment is given as a gift "to every needy, naked soul" (Mosiah 18:28) by the power of the Atonement (1 Corinthians 15:22; Helaman 14:17). For those who enter the temple and keep temple covenants, clothing to cover spiritual nakedness is "[imparted] more abundantly" (Mosiah 18:27), even "cloth of every kind, that we might clothe our nakedness" (Mosiah 10:5; see also Ether 10:24).

In the temple the garment of salvation becomes the first covering leading to exaltation, reminding us that *eternal life, the greatest gift of God, comes also by the cleansing and covering power of the Atonement.* "Eternity [is] our covering and our rock and our salvation" (Abraham 2:16). Because of Christ's saving and exalting power, "He that overcometh shall not be hurt of the second death" (Revelation 2:11, see Revelation 2:26; 12:11).

During my trip to Israel, I was taught an interesting lesson about the covering of the Atonement while visiting Galilee. In my diary, I recorded the instructions of our guide, Wayne Brickey, who explained the significance of Capernaum, the Lord's resident city:

> When Moses talked about the day of atonement he used the word *Kippur* or *kfar*. It was a word that had no direct translation in English. In Near Eastern languages it means to protect, to cover, or to pay. The Hebrew *kfar* means a covering that heals rather than one that hides. The English word *atonement* is the traditional substitute. The Jordanians use the word *kfar* to mean a robe that is used in ceremony to cover a candidate who is embraced or accepted into a family clan. The embracing image of the arms and hands of God in the Book of Mormon (see 2 Nephi 1:15; Alma 34:16; Mormon 5:11; 6:17) is consistent with the meaning of *kfar*. Therefore the word *Capernaum* is very significant. *Caper* is equivalent to *Kippur* or *kfar* and means a covering. *Naum* is translated to mean repentance. Thus, Capernaum means a covering for repentance. It refers directly to the Atonement of the Savior. No wonder Capernaum was the center of His Galilean ministry.

John the Baptist understood the concept of the atonement covering when he said to the unbelieving Pharisees and Sadducees: "For your sins ye have no cloak" (Joseph Smith Translation, Matthew 3:34; see also John 15:22). Hasidic Jews, today, practice a ritual called Kapparot during Yom Kippur, the Day of Atonement. In this ritual, a man swings a cock and a woman a hen above their heads while saying: "This is my substitute, my vicarious offering, my atonement. This cock shall meet death, but I shall find a long and pleasant life of peace." The animal is then sacrificed and donated to the poor.

Perhaps there is no better example in the scriptural temple than the story of the prodigal son to teach us of God's desire to cover us with His robe of acceptance. The "best robe" is a covering of acceptance for seeking our Father in Heaven and desiring His mercy:

> The son said unto him, Father, I have sinned against heaven, and in thy sight, and am no more worthy to be called thy son.
> But the father said to his servants, Bring forth *the best robe*, and put it on him. (Luke 15:21–22; emphasis added)

It is significant that the prodigal son was received into this father's house while the older brother only "drew nigh to the house" and "would not go in" (Luke 15:25, 28). We will not go into the Lord's house with a broken heart and contrite spirit until we recognize the sin within us and the need for the Lord's help to overcome that sin. Our Father in Heaven will forever cover us with the best robe if we repent and come unto Him in His house as a little child.

It is natural for a mother to hold and cover her naked, little child. Therefore, the maternal image is a type of Christ who described His relationship with us, "As one whom His mother comforteth, so will I comfort you" (Isaiah 66:13).

Christ spiritually begets us then stands "with open arms to receive [us]" (Mormon 6:17), desiring to encircle us with the best robe. He will hold us in His outstretched arms and feed us with "the sincere milk of the word, that [we] may grow thereby" (1 Peter 2:2). He will be to us "a nursing father" (Numbers 11:12). This He will do with the love and tenderness of a mother if we become as a little child before Him. Yet, Christ's love for us is even greater than our mother's love, "For can a woman forget her sucking child, that she should not have compassion on the son of her womb? Yea, they may forget, yet will I not forget thee, O house of Israel" (1 Nephi 21:15; see Psalm 27:10) because, "I have graven thee upon the palms of my hands" (1 Nephi 21:16). *Christ has engraved all of mankind on the palms of His hands with the wounds of His Atonement.*

The Scriptural Temple

The words of Nephi give the image of *kippur*, pleading to be covered with the best robe, which is the robe of righteousness: "O Lord, wilt thou encircle me around in the robe of thy righteousness!" (2 Nephi 4:33).

After we are anointed in the temple initiatory to become kings and queens unto God, we are symbolically clothed during the endowment with the robes of righteousness. These regal robes, as well as the garment of salvation, are the covering of the fulness of the priesthood. These priesthood robes (see Revelation 1:13) symbolize the purity (see 2 Nephi 9:14) and righteousness (see Revelation 19:8; Isaiah 11:5) of the divine nature of a Saint who "[follows] the Lamb whithersoever he goeth" (Revelation 14:4). They also must be washed white by the cleansing power of the Atonement (see Revelation 1:5–6; 7:14).

Discovering Our Spiritual Nakedness

At the time of judgment, "the righteous shall have a perfect knowledge of their enjoyment, and their righteousness, being clothed with purity, yea, even with the robe of righteousness" (2 Nephi 9:14). Discovering our spiritual nakedness with a perfect knowledge, then covering it to withstand the Judgment, is the challenge of this life because, "all things are naked and opened unto the eyes of him with whom we have to do" (Hebrews 4:13).

"For in this we groan, earnestly desiring to be clothed upon with our house which is from heaven. If so be that being clothed we shall not be found naked. For we that are in this tabernacle do groan, being burdened: not for that we would be unclothed, but clothed upon, that mortality might be swallowed up of life" (2 Corinthians 5:2–4). Therefore, "Why do ye adorn yourselves with that which hath no life?" (Mormon 8:39). Satan will try to convince us that we should conceal our physical and spiritual nakedness by hiding from God in a covering of worldliness (see Revelation 3:17). When we discover our spiritual nakedness or our spiritual fall (see D&C 29:41, 44) and are "brought to see [our] nakedness before God" (Mormon 9:5), we want to be clothed with His righteousness because He loves us in spite of our nakedness. Then our shame will turn from the despondency of worldly sorrow to the hope of godly sorrow.

God's covering includes modesty, the art of deflecting attention from ourselves, "for the good of men unto [the glory of God]" (D&C 63:12; see Exodus 18:19; Mosiah 2:19; D&C 84:19). Therefore, "let your light so shine before men, that they may see your good works, and *glorify your Father which is in heaven*" (Matthew 5:16; emphasis added). The association of righteousness and modesty is conveyed by the temple garment. This temple covering, both physical and spiritual, is in direct contrast to the uncovering of the world which is still discovering and exposing its nakedness in the literal, immodest sense (see Exodus 32:25). This uncovering is in defiance of God's love which covers our shame. Therefore, "Blessed is he that watcheth, and keepeth his garments, lest he walk naked, and they see his shame." (Revelation 16:15).

It is interesting that Adam and Eve, while in the garden temple, "were both naked, . . . and were not ashamed" (Genesis 2:25). The male and female body reveal a divine dignity in sharing the gifts of pure love to become "one flesh." In the context of holiness, shame disappears because the dignified goodness of male and female intimacy, created to comprehend the love of God, is protected. Where there is pure love there is no shame.

Mortal dangers require that our mortal nakedness is covered (see Alma 43:37–38; 49:6) but the spiritual nakedness of our fall requires that we be clothed by the "garments of salvation" (the Atonement), and the "robes of righteousness" (the divine nature). Otherwise, we will remain spiritually naked, unprepared for the Kingdom of God and His rest (see 3 Nephi 27:19).

Contrast the "beautiful garments" with which the Savior covers us (see 3 Nephi 13:28–30) to the immodest covering offered by Satan to Adam and Eve. His is the only temple clothing for which we do not initially "arise" and "put on," standing in the presence of God (ponder Ephesians 6:14). "For Zion must increase in beauty, and in holiness; her borders must be enlarged; her stakes must be strengthened; yea, verily I say unto you, Zion must *arise* and *put on* her *beautiful garments*" (D&C 82:14; emphasis added). "Awake, awake; *put on thy strength*, O Zion; put on thy *beautiful garments*, O Jerusalem, the holy city: for henceforth there shall no more come into thee the uncircumcised and the unclean" (Isaiah 52:1; emphasis added).

The Scriptural Temple

The term *put on thy strength* means to put on the authority and power of the priesthood (see D&C 113:78) with the clothing of the fulness of the Savior's Atonement in His Holy Order. To "put on the whole armour of God" (Ephesians 6:11; D&C 27:15) is to put on the fulness of the priesthood of God in the temple "that [we] may be able to withstand the evil day, having done all, that [we] may be able to stand" (D&C 27:15) in the presence of God. "The strength of mine house" (see D&C 101:55) are those endowed with the priesthood power of pure love as an "armour of light" (Romans 13:12).

These scriptures emphatically call us to the temple that we might be covered with the fulness of the Atonement being clothed with righteousness. There we "put on" the power of the Holy Order of God. By this power we "put off . . . the old man" (Ephesians 4:22) and "put on the new man, which after God is created in righteousness and true holiness" (Ephesians 4:24). This beautiful covering will prepare us and empower us for the Lord's rest and the redemption of Zion if "above all these things [we] put on charity" (see Colossians 3:14).

In the dedicatory prayer of the Kirtland temple, the Prophet Joseph Smith called us to the temple "that our garments may be pure":

> And let these, thine anointed ones, be clothed with salvation. . . . That our garments may be pure, that we may be clothed upon with robes of righteousness. (D&C 109:76, 80)

If we keep our garments undefiled, then we will be "clothed in white raiment," the robes of righteousness (see Revelation 3:45).

When Jesus made His triumphal entry into Jerusalem, He went to the temple. There He confounded the Pharisees and chief priests and taught several parables. It is significant that He taught the parable of the marriage of the King's son in the temple. This parable tells of a king who invited close neighbors and friends (those who were bidden) to the wedding feast of his son, "yea, a supper of the house of the Lord" (D&C 58:9). It is in the temple that this feast will occur since "in this mountain shall the Lord of hosts make unto all people a feast of fat things" (Isaiah 25:6; see D&C 58:8; Ezekiel 39:17–20). But those who were bidden made light of this invitation and killed the king's servants who invited them. The king was angered by this rejection and sent his army to destroy the murderers. The king then sent his servants into the highways, to both the bad and good and invited them to the wedding (see D&C 58:9–11). "Blessed are they which are called unto the marriage supper of the Lamb" (Revelation 19:9). When the king came to greet his guests at the wedding, he saw one man who was not dressed in a wedding garment:

> And he saith unto him, Friend, how camest thou in hither not having a wedding garment? and he was speechless.
>
> Then said the king to the servants, Bind him hand and foot, and take him away. . . .
>
> For many are called, but few *chosen* ; wherefore all do not have on *the wedding garment.* (Joseph Smith Translation, Matthew 22:12–14; emphasis added)

In this symbolic context, the wedding garment is the garment of salvation and the robes of righteousness. It is the garment that we will wear as "chosen" for the marriage of the King's Son at the redemption of Zion. There we will be "clothed upon, even as I am, to be with me, that we may be one" (see D&C 29:12–13; D&C 38:24–27).

It is perhaps a significant custom that a bride usually wears a white wedding gown. It is symbolic of the marriage covenant relationship that we have with the Bridegroom so that in being one with Him, He will wash our garments white and cover us "as with a mantle" in His pure love (see D&C 88:125). The acceptable wedding garment is our divine nature, washed white in His blood, covered with His mantle of charity, and filled with the Holy Spirit (see 2 Nephi 9:14; D&C 85:7).

It is in the temple that we learn how temple clothing symbolically prepares the temple "anointed" to one day be "chosen" (see D&C 95:36). To be chosen by God is to be the elect of God. The elect "are the elect according to the covenant" (Joseph Smith–Matthew 1:22). By this covenant the "elect of God" "put on" the nature of God (see Colossians 3:12–13). Joseph Smith implied that we will be called up and chosen if we remain faithful to the wedding garment by abiding the covenant of the celestial laws it symbolizes:

> How many will be able to abide a celestial law, and go through and
> receive their exaltation, I am unable to say, as many are called, but
> few are chosen.[1]

All of these passages combine to present a clear scriptural temple
message: *To be chosen we must first discover our spiritual nakedness; then
we must cover it with salvation and exalting righteousness by receiving the
cleansing and covering power of the Atonement of Christ.* His complete
power flows to us when we keep temple covenants.

Anointing with the Spirit: A Preparation to Be Taught in the Temple

The anointing of the temple sets us apart to become a kingdom
of priests, a royal priesthood, a holy nation, a chosen generation, a
peculiar people (see 1 Peter 2:9). Therefore, the anointing symbolically introduces candidates for the endowment into the Holy Order
of God, anointing them to become kings and queens, priests and
priestesses (see 1 Corinthians 4:8; Revelation 1:56).[2] The anointing
not only sets us apart for this royalty, but also like King David's
anointing (see 1 Samuel 16:13), *it is symbolic of receiving the Holy
Spirit with His powers to teach, reveal, and seal.* This anointing will be
"sealed upon [us] with power from on high" (see D&C 109:35) when
we receive the fulness of the temple endowment.

The oil in the lamps of the ten virgins was symbolic of the light
provided by the Holy Spirit as a guide that they be not deceived
(see D&C 45:56–57). After baptism in water, we receive the gift of
the Holy Ghost which gift is ultimately to be baptized with the fire
of this symbolic oil. This baptism by fire will enlighten us with the
mysteries of God to sanctify and save us (see 1 Corinthians 3:15). It
is in the temple that we are anointed to receive a fulness of this gift
(see D&C 109:15).

Our text for learning in the temple is the scriptures. A symbolic witness for this truth is the temple altar upon which the scriptures rest.
Our most important teacher in the temple is the Holy Spirit, because to
understand and partake of the great view in the text of the scriptural
temple we need His teaching and revealing powers. The Comforter
has "the peaceable things of immortal glory; the truth of all things;

that which quickeneth all things, which maketh alive all things; that which knoweth all things, and hath all power according to wisdom, mercy, truth, justice, and judgment" (Moses 6:61).

The Apostle John said the "anointing teacheth":

> But the anointing which ye have received . . . *ye need not that any man teach you*: but as the same *anointing teacheth* you of all things, and is truth, and is no lie. (1 John 2:27; emphasis added)

Jacob described the teaching and revealing power of the Holy Spirit in similar terms: "For the spirit speaketh the truth and lieth not . . . *it speaketh of things as they really are,* and of things as they really will be" (Jacob 4:13; emphasis added). In this world of deceit and half truths, it is refreshing to have someone teach us the truth and speak of things as they really are, even things not seen by the natural eye! We need not that any man teach us because we can be "taught from on high" (Ether 6:17). Mormon, who inquired of the Lord concerning a disputation over infant baptism, testified of the source of his instruction when he said, "The word of the Lord came to me by the power of the Holy Ghost" (Moroni 8:7).

To Be Taught by the Holy Spirit We Must Become as Temples

Christ declared that His body is a temple (see John 2:19–21). The *scriptural temple* teaches that our bodies also are temples (see D&C 93:35; 1 Corinthians 6:19). Our body as a temple and Christ's body as a temple come together in His holy house. There, as "a sanctuary, a tabernacle of the Holy Spirit to [our] edification" (D&C 88:137), we are taught Christ's words by the power of the Holy Spirit. The Holy Spirit can teach us in the temple if we become temples in which He can teach (see Ephesians 2:19–22; Mosiah 2:37; Alma 7:21; Helaman 4:24).

In the *scriptural temple*, there is a beautiful expression of the potential for each of us to become a temple in which the Holy Spirit can teach: "And if your eye be single to my glory, your whole bodies shall be filled with light, and there shall be no darkness in you; and that body which is filled with light comprehendeth all things" (D&C 88:67). With this light and by the power of the Holy Ghost, "The day shall come when you shall comprehend even God. . . . Then shall ye know that ye have seen me, that I am, and that I am the true light that is in you" (D&C 88:49–59). These verses give the image of constructed temples with their great and last promise to know, comprehend, and see God because they concentrate the light of God. Temples are filled with light as glowing beacons in the dark night "that they may shine forth in darkness" (Ether 3:4) "and the darkness comprehendeth it not" (D&C 88:49).

The new Nauvoo Illinois Temple has a particularly beautiful lambent light coming from the inside out at night. While visiting the vacant temple lot in Independence, Missouri which was surrounded on a smaller scale like the temple lot in Jerusalem by multiple religions of the same source, claiming it as sacred ground, I noticed flashes of light as miniature beacons from the dark, grassy covering. I couldn't miss the symbolism as these fascinating fireflies seemed only active on the temple lot, revealing light within.

Other scriptures speak of the light of the body as the eye, stating that "when thine eye is single, thy whole body also is full of light" (see Luke 11:33–34, 36; 3 Nephi 13:22). Like a magnifying glass, our own personal seer stones which "magnify to the eyes of men" (Ether 3:24), eyes single to God's glory (see Mormon 8:15) concentrate all the rays of truth from the Son into a single powerful beam. This beam, the powerful light of God, can penetrate our blind eyes and hard hearts with understanding of spiritual knowledge (see Psalm 36:9; John 12:35–40). Then we see spiritually with "singleness of heart" (D&C 36:7) to "let the affections of [our] heart be placed (focused) upon the Lord forever" (Alma 37:36). Our whole body, spirit and element connected, is filled with light and joy (see D&C 93:32–33) because "the Lord shall be unto [us] an everlasting light" (see Isaiah 60:19–20). Truly, the eye is the light of the body because it not only receives light from heaven but reveals the light within us.

While most mortals receive and understand light or other physical signals through physical senses such as eyes, to every mortal is given a gift of some spiritual light through the light of Christ (see D&C 84:46; 93:9). The light of Christ which gives light to everything and everyone both physically and spiritually is "the light which shineth, which giveth you light [and] is through him who enlighteneth your eyes, which is the same light that quickeneth your understandings" (D&C 88:11). This "Spirit of Jesus Christ" (see D&C 84:45; Moroni 7:16) or "the light of truth" (see D&C 88:6–7) is also "the word of the Lord" spoken to us in our conscience by the Holy Spirit. When we receive the gift of Holy Ghost, the voice of God within us is spiritually enlightened such that we can understand the mysteries of God, even though His voice usually remains a still small voice or a feeling.

Analogous to the plant process of photomorphogenesis, it is imperative that we convert physical light or understanding into spiritual light or understanding within us for our spiritual survival and growth. This is how "things of the Spirit" are discerned (see 1 Corinthians 2:14). Paul called this process the "treasure in earthen vessels" (see 2 Corinthians 3:6–7; Proverbs 20:27). The catalyst or seer stone of this conversion is the Holy Spirit (see D&C 88:11). By the power of the Holy Spirit (see Ether 4:11) the Lord confirms all His words (see Mormon 9:25) to us. This is why receipt of the gift of the Holy Ghost is called the confirmation (see D&C 84:47–48).

The process of this spiritual conversion of light is seen in young Nephi who had "great desires to know of the mysteries of God, wherefore, I did cry unto the Lord; and behold he did visit me, and did soften my heart that I did believe all the words which had been spoken by my father" (1 Nephi 2:16). Then Nephi "spake unto Sam, making known unto him the things which the Lord had manifested unto [him] *by his Holy Spirit*" (1 Nephi 2:17). Conversion of light occurred in Nephi because he desired to know and believe the mysteries of God (see Alma 32:27) and gave place that the word of God was planted in his heart so that he might have "root in [himself]" (see Mark 4:17). He did not "resist" (see Alma 32:28), "quench" (see 1 Thessalonians 5:19), or "choke" (Mark 4:19) the word of the Lord until his understanding (see Matthew 13:23) was "enlightened" (see Alma 32:27–28) by the Holy Spirit.

As taste is a discernible sense (see Alma 32:35; compare Mormon 1:15), "whatsoever is light, is good," because it discerns truth (see Ether 4:11–12). Heavenly light or spiritual light is good because it is not found in evil (see Moroni 7:17; Moses 1:13–15). With this light we can discern good from evil (see Moroni 7:18).

The Scriptural Temple

A symbolic reason that we have two eyes is that we need two "I"s to discern truth. One eye represents *Information.* The other eye represents *Inspiration* which "quickens" our understanding of information. The Prophet Joseph Smith explained this truth when he said, "We consider that God has created man with a mind capable of instruction, and a faculty which may be enlarged in proportion to the heed and diligence given to the light communicated from heaven to the intellect."[3] This light is communicated both physically and spiritually through information and inspiration.

The inspirational process of spiritual photomorphogenesis in which light is converted into spiritual roots, prepared Nephi to bring forth spiritual fruit in that the word, or the truth of light, was converted to "take root in [him]" (see Alma 32:42). The Lord confirmed and continued the spiritual conversion process of light in Nephi when He said, "Blessed art thou, Nephi, because of thy faith, for thou hast sought me diligently, with lowliness of heart. And inasmuch as ye shall keep my commandments, ye shall prosper" (1 Nephi 2:19–20). Because Nephi was "faithful in keeping the commandments of the Lord" (see 1 Nephi 3:16, 21; 4:1), he always found a way prepared (see 1 Nephi 3:7; 10:18; 14:17) so that he prospered (see 1 Nephi 17:3). Nephi then became a ruler over his brethren and a teacher of spiritual truth because of his obedience to God and his love for his fellow men.

Failure in this spiritual conversion of light is seen in the case of the Nephites and Lamanites who "forgot those signs and wonders" of physical light just three years after they occurred at the birth of the Savior. These people forgot because they were not remembering the spiritual disciplines in obeying all God's commandments. Therefore, they "began to be less and less astonished at a sign or a wonder from heaven." Without this spiritual conversion of light, they became "hard in their hearts, and blind in their minds, and began to disbelieve" (see 3 Nephi 2:1–2). "Forgot" is in stark contrast to the repeated warning by Book of Mormon prophets to "remember, remember" (see Mosiah 2:41; Alma 37:13; Helaman 14:30) in the "ways of remembrance" (1 Nephi 2:24). King Benjamin explained the difference between forgotten and retained remembrance. To "remember to retain the name [of Christ] always written in [our] hearts" (see Mosiah 5:12) requires keeping God's commandments and spiritual photomorphogenesis. While keeping God's commandments facilitates spiritual photomorphogenesis, without doing so in the love of God (see Mosiah 13:14) with "meekness and lowliness of heart" (see Moroni 8:26) there will be no visitation of the Holy Spirit and no remembrance nor understanding of spiritual truth in the laws of God (see Mosiah 11:27–28;12:31–37;13:27–32). Then the commandments of God "are not written in [our] hearts" (see Mosiah 13:11) in "the ways of remembrance" (1 Nephi 2:24).

It is interesting that Satan's mimic of light as flashes of "fiery darts" overpowers "unto blindness" (see 1 Nephi 15:24). Those blinded by Satan are still "the guilty [but they] taketh the truth to be hard" (see 1 Nephi 16:2). This is because of their hard hearts through which the light of truth painfully "cutteth them to the very center." Yet, "they *receive* not the light" (D&C 93:31) in not receiving spiritual photomorphogenesis. Elder John A. Widtsoe taught that spiritually receiving with the light of God is what happens to us in the temple.

> Spiritual power is generated within temple walls, and sent out to bless the world. Light from the house of the Lord illumines every home within the Church fitted for its reception by participation in temple privileges.[4]

As informational light is focused by inspirational light, our eyes become single to the light of God. We become the "children of light" (John 12:36; Ephesians 5:8; 1 Thessalonians 5:5; D&C 106:5), with the "light of life" (John 8:12). As such, we learn a great truth: the light of Christ is more powerful than the darkness of Satan (see D&C 6:21; 14:9; 21:6; 50:25; John 12:35) because darkness is the absence of light. Christ's light is "a light that is endless, that can never be darkened" (Mosiah 16:9). Those who abide in the light of Christ through spiritual photomorphogenesis receive more spiritual light and "that light groweth brighter and brighter until the perfect day" (D&C 50:24) of "perfect knowledge" (see 2 Nephi 9:13–14).

The *scriptural temple* message is clear: To become temples in which the Holy Spirit can teach and thus become the "children of light," we must have faith, hope and charity as a beam of light through an eye single to the glory of God (see D&C 4:5). Our eyes become single when we "embrace [the gospel] with singleness of heart" (D&C 36:7). That is, we must seek God only for His glory and not divide our devotion in serving "two masters" (3 Nephi 13:24). We seek God in total devotion when we believe in Him and receive Him. Then God will be our only master because He can provide the power to free us as subjects to the master of our own wills (see Alma 42:7). When God is our only master, His light will be the light in our eyes filling our whole body with light and joy (see D&C 88:50).

We want the Holy Spirit to teach us in the temple, not only because the Spirit "speaketh the truth and lieth not" (Jacob 4:13) to "guide [us] into all truth" (John 16:13) and show us "the way whither [we] should go" (see D&C 79:2), even "shew [us] things to come" (John 16:13), but because He "searcheth all things, yea, the deep things of God" (1 Corinthians 2:10) and "knoweth all things" (D&C 35:19). "God shall give unto you knowledge by his Holy Spirit, yea, by the unspeakable gift of the Holy Ghost, that has not been revealed since the world was until now" (D&C 121:26).

Joseph Smith declared that "no man can receive the Holy Ghost without receiving revelations. The Holy Ghost is a revelator."[5] To know all things, to have this great view of all things, can be our gift if we seek the Lord and become holy like a temple. As we continue to obey the commandments of the Lord and follow His true messengers, we become more like a temple, filled with "truth and light" until we "knoweth all things" (see D&C 93:28) and "[receive] a fulness of truth" (see D&C 93:26–27).

On the first ascent of Mount Zion, we are anointed and set apart to be holy like a temple. To help us in the quest to one day reach the summit, being called up and chosen as part of the great view, we are anointed to receive the fulness of our Guide and Teacher, the Holy Spirit. *It is paramount that we learn of the power of the Holy Spirit and how He teaches us in our minds and hearts if we are to reach the summit of Mount Zion.* Therefore, the Prophet Joseph Smith challenged us in our temple worship:

> The things of God are of deep import; and time, and experience, and careful and ponderous and solemn thought can only find them out. Thy mind, O man . . . must stretch as high as the utmost heavens, and search into and contemplate the darkest abyss, and the broad expanse of eternity—*thou must commune with God.*[6]

In order to commune with God in the temple we must understand how God and the Holy Spirit commune with us. We must learn how to "incline [our] heart unto the Lord God of Israel" (Joshua 24:23) so the Lord will "pour out his Spirit . . . to prepare [our] hearts" (Alma 16:16) in order to have "an heart to perceive" (Deuteronomy 29:4).

Understanding the Scriptural Concept of the Heart

> But the Lord said unto Samuel, Look not on his countenance, or on the height of his stature; because I have refused him: for the Lord seeth not as man seeth; for man looketh on the outward appearance, but the Lord looketh on the heart. (1 Samuel 16:7)

The Lord can "tell [me] that which no man knoweth save [Him and me] alone" (D&C 15:3) because "there is none else save God that knowest thy thoughts and the intents of thy heart" (D&C 6:16). What is this heart that the Lord looketh upon and knowest (see Deuteronomy 8:2)? Can we call it the center of our deepest feelings, the interpreter of our thoughts, our intuitive, therefore "feeling" nature?

Is not the heart the individual spiritual self? There are scriptures that imply close association between the heart and the spirit such as Ezekiel 18:31 and 3 Nephi 9:20. Poetic Isaiah made this association in a parallel couplet: "to revive the spirit of the humble, and to revive the heart of the contrite ones" (Isaiah 57:15; see also Isaiah 65:14). This is why God looks on and understands our heart. Our spirit is what God engendered as His offspring. It is what He desires to develop in His likeness.

Many scriptures talk about a hardened heart, but the verse that connects such a heart with such a spirit is Deuteronomy 2:30. To be "spiritually begotten" is to "say that your hearts are changed" (Mosiah 5:7). Deductive reasoning for the equivalence of heart and spirit could come from associating Romans 10:8–10 with Romans 8:16 and 1 Corinthians 2:14 concerning where we should place the word of God and how we come to know of its truthfulness (see also Alma 32:28). This reasoning could be applied in combining the words of Abinadi to the priests of Noah when he said, "Ye have not applied your hearts to understanding" (Mosiah 12:27), with the words of Elihu when he said, "But there is a spirit in man: and the inspiration of the Almighty giveth them understanding" (Job 32:8). The Nephites who heard a voice out of heaven (see 3 Nephi 11:3) and the Savior's prayer to His Father expressing words that cannot be spoken or written (see 3 Nephi 19:33) had a spiritual understanding because "it did pierce them to the very soul, and did cause their hearts to burn" and because they "did understand in their hearts the words which he prayed."

God the Father looks deeply and fondly upon our hearts or our spirits because we are His spiritual offspring. Therefore, He remembers well our spiritual existence with Him and desires to know how we are doing spiritually. The important question is how well we recall this spiritual relationship with our Father in Heaven. How well do we recognize "a familiar spirit" (2 Nephi 26:16)? For if we "pour out [our] hearts to him; . . . he [will] know the thoughts of [our] hearts" (Mosiah 24:12) and we will know that He does.

If a gift or power of the Holy Spirit is to quicken our spirits and "bring all things to [your] remembrance" (John 14:26), is not the heart, the spiritual body, laden with spiritual memory especially of our true nature and potential? The feelings of our hearts are spiritual memories from matter more refined (see D&C 131:7) that is native to spiritual truth and understanding. In fact, the uncreated core (see D&C 93:29) or "the very center" (1 Nephi 16:2) of "the very soul" (see 3 Nephi 11:3), both our spiritual soul (see Abraham 3:21–23) and mortal soul (see Abraham 5:7), is an "intelligence, or the light of truth" that can "act for itself" (see D&C 93:29–30). Such is the core of God's soul (see D&C 93:36).

A volcano is a window to the creation process of the soul for through it we see light captured in the core of a surrounding earth. Galaxies photographed by the Hubble telescope often show images like the pupil and iris of the eye. Planets and other matter are patterned around a brilliant light just as light is at the center of the eye. Is light the center of all God's creations (see D&C 88:13) including our spiritual rebirth because the light is good (see Genesis 1:1–4, 31; Moses 2:1–4, 12; Abraham 4:1–4, 21; Alma 32:35)? As the sun in our solar system witnesses, the measure of our creation is to let our light so shine that it warms and brightens others while maintaining our own identity. Such is the description of a celestial person. Because "the great God . . . loveth our souls" (see Alma 24:14; D&C 18:10), His great plan is to bring "life and immortality to light [our intelligence] through the gospel" (2 Timothy 1:10). Our eternal nature is to be lit up by truth and to radiate truth. The Prophet Joseph F. Smith taught that, "All those salient truths which come home so forcibly to the head and heart seem but the awakening of the memories of the spirit. . . . But in order to tap into that knowledge we must struggle to get past 'the prisonhouse of mortality.'"[7]

The difficulty we have in the prisonhouse of mortality is getting through the surroundings of our physical and mental impressions to the enlightenment of our spiritual impressions (see D&C 30:2). This is the challenge of converting physical light to spiritual light. It is disobedience and the traditions of our fathers (see D&C 93:39) that keep us in the prisonhouse of mortality without the enlightenment of spiritual truth from the Spirit of truth. This was the case of Laman and Lemuel contrasted with Nephi (see 1 Nephi 17:8, 13, 15, 17–18). The challenge is casting off "the dark veil of unbelief" (Alma 19:6; see also Ether 4:15) and finding "the hidden man of the heart" (1 Peter 3:4). The Holy Spirit helps us get past the prisonhouse or veil of mortality that blinds our minds and hardens our hearts. This is God's gift for obedience to His commandments with diligence and lowliness of heart.

Concerning the Israelites from Moses through his time, Paul described their prisonhouse of mortality as the "veil upon their heart" (see 2 Corinthians 3:13–15). Therefore, they did not have "an heart to perceive" or as Paul said, they had "the spirit of slumber" (Romans 11:8). This "slumber of death" (Jacob 3:11) eliminated "eyes to see" and "ears to hear" (see Deuteronomy 29:4). Paul said that when their hearts "shall turn to the Lord, the veil shall be taken away" because "where the Spirit of the Lord is, there is liberty" (see 2 Corinthians 3:16–17; Alma 61:15) from the prisonhouse of mortality. Therefore, "abide ye in the liberty wherewith ye are made free" (D&C 88:86).

While our spirit body does not usually speak to us in audible tones, it feels to us "with groanings which cannot be uttered" (Romans 8:26). The Prophet Joseph Smith testified of this feeling when he said of the biblical verse of James 1:5: "Never did any passage of scripture come with more power to the heart of man. . . . It seemed to enter with great force into every *feeling* of my heart" (Joseph Smith—History 1:12; emphasis added). We can come to recognize these feelings of *peace, assurance*, and even *burning in our hearts* from righteousness (see 3 Nephi 11:3; Luke 24:34) or sin.

Women have been telling men for a long time that there is a level of understanding beyond logic because there is "a peace of God, which passeth all understanding, [that] shall keep your hearts and minds through Christ Jesus" (Philippians 4:7). Most women know that the art of listening is not just hearing the words but also understanding the feelings. Women are motivated as much by understood feelings as by logical thinking but they have a gift for this sense of feeling, to know when something feels right.

The endowment drama implies that Eve had this feeling of assurance, that partaking of the forbidden fruit was the better choice for her and Adam. Abraham was advised by the Lord to listen to Sarah's feelings (see Genesis 21:12). It was not only their husband's and father's visions but the great faith and persistent feelings of assurance that kept the Queen of Ishmael and Abish her servant, like many women in adverse situations, "converted unto the Lord for many years" (see Alma 19:10, 16). Therefore, Rahab of Jericho, concealed the two spies of Israel, bore testimony of the true God, and saved the lives of her family with a passover sign (see Joshua 2:1–24). Even the wife of Pontius Pilate warned him about Christ with her feelings from a dream (see Matthew 27:19).

Appropriately, wisdom is given a feminine gender (see Mosiah 8:20). If we apply our hearts to understanding (see Mosiah 12:27), we are "wise hearted," filled with "the spirit of wisdom" (Exodus 28:3). The feminine nature of this wisdom characterized Ammon who was "wise, yet harmless" (Alma 18:22).

We can be cunning and a wise, as to the wisdom of the world (see Mosiah 27:7; Alma 2:1), but there is a difference between the carnal "wise and the learned" and godly "wisdom and prudence" (Abraham 3:21; compare 2 Nephi 9:42, 43; see also Mosiah 12:27; Isaiah 5:21; 29:14). There may even be something lacking in the "wise and prudent" compared to "babes and sucklings" when receiving truth from God (see D&C 128:18). It is the desire of God that we "learn wisdom and . . . find truth" (D&C 97:1) for "it is impossible for a man to be saved in ignorance" (D&C 131:6). If the sense of feeling in our hearts is by the power of the Holy Spirit, it will be the logical truth and the wisdom of God to help us become "wise and prudent" babes.

Arriving at wise and logical truth by the power of the Holy Spirit is demonstrated in the reasoning and feeling process that Nephi experienced when he was constrained by the Spirit to kill Laban. He said in his heart, "never at any time have I shed the blood of man. And I shrunk and would that I might not slay him" (1 Nephi 4:10). After reasoning with the Spirit, Nephi "did obey the voice of the Spirit" (1 Nephi 4:18).

To deny feelings and reason from the witness and teaching of the Holy Ghost, whether they confirm our thoughts and actions as right or wrong, can bring great condemnation "because that which may be known of God is manifest in them" (Romans 1:19). "Behold, here is the agency of man, and here is the condemnation of man; because that which was from the beginning is plainly manifest unto them, and they receive not the light. And every man whose spirit receiveth not the light is under condemnation" (D&C 93:3–132; see John 3:18–19). "Let that therefore abide in you, which ye have heard from the beginning" (1 John 2:24).

To receive the light is to be "enlightened" by the light of God in the "Spirit of truth" (see Alma 32:28; D&C 6:15; 93:26). It is to make the conversion of God's light into spiritual light that the light of our hearts receives. Our intelligences receive and even cleave (see D&C 88:40) to the light of truth because they *are* the light of truth (see D&C 93:26). We are condemned if we don't receive this light because we are not true to our basic natures. The light of God as "the light of truth" (see D&C 88:6) is "the Spirit of Jesus Christ" (see D&C 84:45). Since this light is a gift "that lighteth every man that cometh into the world" (D&C 93:2) and is the light by which truth and good are determined (see Moroni 7:16), we are condemned if we don't *receive it* (see D&C 88:33; D&C 45:57). "He who sins against the greater light shall receive the greater condemnation" (D&C 82:3).

As good loves light and evil shuns light (see 2 Nephi 26:10; 27:27; Alma 32:35), there is a *test of light* to expose whether or not thoughts and deeds are good meaning "wrought of God" (see John

3:19–21; Matthew 10:26–27; Ephesians 5:13–14; 1 John 1:5–7). This test occurs when we "search diligently in the light of Christ that [we] may know [light from dark, or] good from evil" (Moroni 7:19) because "intelligence cleaveth unto intelligence . . . light cleaveth unto light" (D&C 88:40). The light of Christ will penetrate our hearts, exposing both good and evil to our intelligence. To be "brought into the light" we must first learn what it means to ask, knock (see 2 Nephi 32:4), and seek diligently (see 1 Nephi 2:19) in the light of Christ.

The light of Christ is "the law of Christ" (D&C 88:21) "by which all things are governed" (see D&C 88:13), "preserved . . . perfected and sanctified" (D&C 88:34). "All things which are good cometh of Christ" (Moroni 7:24; see also Moroni 10:6–7, 25). "That light [is] good" (Moses 2:4) because "it [is] bright" (Abraham 4:4) with truth. The light of Christ is "a light which cannot be hid in darkness" (D&C 14:9). Therefore, the test of the light of Christ is the ultimate test to determine good from evil. Stepping into the darkness of the unknown is a test of our faith in the light of Christ because "there is no work of darkness save it shall be made manifest in the light" (2 Nephi 30:17). Therefore, we may "chase darkness" (D&C 50:25) by the light of Christ such that "prejudices may give way before the truth" (D&C 109:56). The test of light continues to "enlighteneth" only those who "hearkeneth to the voice of the Spirit" (see D&C 84:46; Alma 5:7) for they receive more light in order to comprehend all things (see D&C 50:24; 88:67), "even the Father" (see D&C 84:47; 88:47).

Those who fail to apply this test, fail to "ask of me," the "Father of lights" (D&C 67:9; James 1:17) because "they love darkness rather than light" (see D&C 10:21) and "their works [are] in the dark" (Moses 5:51). "By this you may know they are under the bondage of sin, because they come not unto me" (D&C 84:50). They "[seek] their own counsels in the dark" (Moses 6:28). It is not surprising that the "unpardonable sin" starts by denying the witness of the Holy Spirit when "[we] know that [we] deny it" (see Alma 39:6) and eventually "altogether turneth therefrom" (see D&C 84:41). When we "withdraw [ourselves] from the Spirit of the Lord, that it may have no place in [us] to guide [us] in wisdom's paths, . . . the same cometh out in open rebellion against God" (Mosiah 2:36–37). Then we risk being "led away captive by [Satan] even as was the son of perdition, . . . [selling Christ] for silver and gold" (3 Nephi 27:32; 29:7; see D&C 132:27). As spiritual captives, we cannot choose to repent.

Because the spiritual body has already been programmed with spiritual truth that is at the heart of feeling spiritual truth, *we will be judged by the Lord according to how we receive this feeling of truth in our minds and hearts*, and how well we respond to it: "For I, the Lord, will judge all men according to *their works*, according to the desire of *their hearts*. (D&C 137:9; see also Alma 41:3)

The Lord will "make manifest the counsels of the hearts" (1 Corinthians 4:5) for "there is none else save God that knowest [the] thoughts and the intents of [the] heart" (D&C 6:16). "[He] will give unto everyone of [us] according to [our] works" (Revelation 2:23; see also D&C 1:10; 128:6) that come from the desires and feelings of our hearts even if works can't be accomplished in this life (see D&C 137:8). Seeking the Lord with a "sincere heart" (Moroni 10:4) by responding to His will with "real intent of heart" (Moroni 7:9) is the real intent of obedience out of love. Real intent of heart is what matters to the Lord, otherwise our outward actions "profiteth [us] nothing" (Moroni 7:6, 9). We are to "walk uprightly before [the Lord] with all [our] hearts" (D&C 109:1). True conviction comes from the heart. Notice that "there is nothing that the Lord thy God shall take *in his heart* to do but what he will do it" (Abraham 3:17). The concept of heart quality was a dominant theme in afterlife theology of ancient Egypt. The deceased pharaoh's final judgment was to have his heart weighed against the Feather of Truth. The Apostle John taught that the heart is the best source of the truth of God within us:

> My little children, let us not love in word, neither in tongue; but in deed and in truth.
>
> And hereby we know that we are of the truth, and shall assure our hearts before him.
>
> For if our heart condemn us, God is greater than our heart, and knoweth all things.
>
> Beloved, if our heart condemn us not, then have we confidence toward God. (1 John 3:18–21)

When we "obey not the truth, but have pleasure in unrighteousness," and "seek to counsel in [our] own ways," then *[our] hearts are not satisfied"* (see D&C 56:14–15; emphasis added). The Apostle Paul perceptively described such persons as "those that oppose themselves" (2 Timothy 2:25). This opposition occurs because of the two kinds of hypocrisy—those who willfully pretend to be something they are not and those who willfully refuse to be something they are. In both cases, the true self is opposed because it is not exposed in the light of truth.

The Holy Spirit intimately knows our hearts because He has been dwelling and striving with our personal spirits during their mortal probation. This dwelling is not figurative since Christ "cast out devils, or the evil spirits which dwell in the hearts of the children of men" (Mosiah 3:6). For the Lord, "the hearts of the righteous" become holy temples in which He can dwell (see Alma 34:36). Dwell means an intimate association. As the word of God, the Holy Spirit is a "discerner of the thoughts and intents of the heart" (D&C 33:1; Hebrews 4:12; see also Alma 18:16, 32). The Lord and the Holy Spirit not only looketh upon and knoweth the heart but also the thoughts and intents of the mind (see Ezekiel 11:5). No man or woman can deceive the Holy Spirit. Perhaps, this is why all acts, covenants, and ordinances that have eternal consequences are only valid if sealed (certified) by the Holy Spirit of promise (see D&C 132:7).

Before his conversion, Amulek experienced a mind unreceptive to spiritual knowledge because he did not respond to the feelings of his heart: "Nevertheless, I did *harden my heart*, for I was called many times and I would not hear; therefore *I knew* concerning these things, *yet I would not know"* (Alma 10:6; emphasis added). To harden one's heart like Amulek is to stifle the feelings of spiritual truth within. This occurs from unbelief and slothfulness in looking up to God (see Alma 33:21). Such was the case of Laman and Lemuel who were "desirous that they might not labor, for they did not believe" (1 Nephi 17:18) in "the simpleness of the way." For "the labor which they had to perform was to look" (1 Nephi 17:41) by keeping God's commandments with real feeling of heart.

Unbelief with slothfulness was King Lamoni's problem most of his life but in an environment different than the one influencing Amulek. King

Lamoni believed in a "Great Spirit of whom our fathers have spoken" by tradition and "that whatsoever [he as king] did was right" (Alma 18:4–5). Both Amulek and King Lamoni eventually responded to the internal feelings of their hearts through the power of God from true messengers (see Alma 10:7–8; 18:5, 23; 19:13) because it takes the "Spirit to soften our hearts" (Alma 24:8). By this power in their hearts, "the dark veil of unbelief was being cast away from [their] mind" (Alma 19:6).

When we deny or stifle the feelings of our spirits, hardening our hearts with an encasement of unrighteousness, worldliness, and traditions of men like Amulek and King Lamoni, the Holy Ghost will have difficulty in teaching us and activating our spiritual recall to bring all things to our remembrance. If we harden our hearts too much, the Holy Spirit will withdraw and refuse to enlighten us. Then our hearts will become more and more subordinate to the traditions of men and the lies of Satan. This is why we are instructed in the scriptures to "trust in the Lord with all thine heart; and lean not unto thine own understanding" (Proverbs 3:5). When we trust too much in the arm of flesh and lean unto our own understanding, we learn only in our natural minds. We become like the preconverted Amulek, whose type Paul described as "ever learning, and never able to come to the knowledge of the truth" (2 Timothy 3:7).

We may receive the words of spiritual knowledge in our minds through our eyes and ears unless we have "the spirit of slumber" (Romans 11:8). This slumber is "gross darkness [that covers] the minds of the people" (D&C 112:23) such that they have "eyes that they should not see, and ears that they should not hear" (Romans 11:8). However, until we feel the words of spiritual truth in our hearts by the power of the Holy Spirit, and keep "that good thing which was committed unto [us] by the Holy Ghost which dwelleth in us" (2 Timothy 1:14), we cannot elevate ourselves from the physical world and hear or "see afar off" (see Moses 6:27) the great view of the spiritual world. In other words, we cannot climb the spiritual mountain of the Lord's House without the light and power of spiritual photomorphogenesis. Therefore, "he that hath an ear, let him hear what the Spirit saith" (Revelation 2:11).

It is only in feeling with our hearts that a true relationship to the Father of our spirits is remembered (see Romans 8:16; 2 Chronicles

16:9). Without this feeling of the heart, we cannot "prophesy unto the people whatsoever things should come into [our hearts]" (Helaman 13:3). "Our conversation is [not] in heaven" (Philippians 3:20) and we "do not know the heavens" (Alma 18:29) because we don't fully comprehend the things of God. For "the things of God knoweth no man, but the Spirit of God" (1 Corinthians 2:11).

By living in and experiencing mortality, we see the view of the world and understand the "spirit of man" (1 Corinthians 2:11), but the Lord declared, "I give not unto you that ye shall live after the manner of the world" (D&C 95:13). Within each of us there is a spirit that feels for a "better world" (see Ether 12:4). It looks "beyond this vale of sorrow into a far better land of promise" (Alma 37:45).

The *scriptural temple* teaches us that, "We have received, not the spirit of the world, but *the spirit which is of God*; that we might know the things that are freely given to us of God. Which things also we speak, not in the words which man's wisdom teacheth, but which *the Holy Ghost teacheth*" (1 Corinthians 2:12–13; emphasis added).

The condition of the "natural man," with only "the spirit of man" and not the influence of the Holy Spirit, is similar to someone who has never experienced the power of electricity. The "electric" power of the Spirit of God was vividly contrasted to his natural power when Nephi said, "Behold, I am full of the Spirit of God, insomuch that my frame has no strength" (1 Nephi 17:47; see also Alma 19:6). Those who have felt the power of the Spirit of God, suddenly experience their dependence on it when the power goes out. They suffer "in the least degree . . . at the time I [withdraw] my Spirit" (D&C 19:20). The Lord will "turn off the power" if we reject Him and His true messengers (see Helaman 13:8).

Once we have felt and seen the power of spiritual electricity in our lives as a personal witness of the Spirit, we risk condemnation unless we are honest with ourselves in declaring the truth as did the Prophet Joseph Smith: "For I had seen a vision [or felt the Spirit]; I knew it, and I knew that God knew it, and I could not deny it, neither dared I do it; at least I knew that by so doing I would offend God, and come under condemnation." (Joseph Smith—History 1:25)

In order to fully understand the imperative necessity for each of us to be influenced and taught by the Holy Spirit, it is necessary to understand our natural condition and potential state if the Holy Spirit does not influence and teach us.

The State of the Natural Mind and Potential State of the Hardened Heart

If the word of God is not illuminated by the power of the Holy Spirit in our hearts, it deteriorates to misunderstanding, unimportance, or disbelief in our natural minds: "But the natural man receiveth not the things of the Spirit of God: for they are foolishness unto him: neither can he know them, because they are spiritually discerned" (1 Corinthians 2:14).

The natural man is an enemy to God because of natural reactions like fear, doubt, and greed. It is difficult for such a man to become meek and seek God (see Mosiah 3:19). Instead, with a "carnal nature" (Mosiah 16:5; see Moses 5:13), he moves in ways contrary to the Plan of Salvation and happiness (see Alma 41:11). He may intensely guard his right to choose and proclaim freedom, but his choices increasingly lead to captivity by Satan, resulting in a loss of his freedom to choose (see 2 Peter 2:19). Even unwittingly, the natural man is captive of Satan (see 2 Nephi 9:8–9). He is enrolled in Satan's army as "the [servant] of Satan" (D&C 10:5), "being an enemy to God" (Mosiah 16:5) to "continually" fight against God (see Moroni 7:12) until he "listeth to obey the evil spirit" (Mosiah 2:37) and "wilfully rebel[s] against the gospel of Christ" (4 Nephi 1:38). The natural man who does not recognize that he is also a spiritual man, for "man is spirit" (D&C 93:33), will not receive the things of the Spirit. If the natural man does not learn how to "cheer up [his] heart and remember that [he is] free [or responsible] to act for [himself]" (2 Nephi 10:23), he will not learn how to become "free forever, knowing good from evil; to act . . . and not to be acted upon" in the redeeming love of God (see 2 Nephi 2:26). Such a natural man without a cheerful or activated heart to receive the things of the Spirit will be "without Christ and God in the world" (Mormon 5:16; Alma 41:11) and ultimately in the world to come. *Therefore, the natural man can never receive "eternal life" which is the great and last promise of the temple* (see D&C 67:11–12).

Only the man who becomes meek in his mind and heart, then seeks God with his mind and heart, "[yielding] to the enticings of

The Scriptural Temple

the Holy Spirit" (Mosiah 3:19), can know these things (see Alma 26:21–22) of the absolute nature of good and evil. Such a man learns in the humility and sweetness of "butter and honey . . . to refuse the evil, and choose the good" (Isaiah 7:15). This condition of obedience brings true freedom because freedom forever comes not by defining good and evil for ourselves, but by choosing to be obedient to the spiritual light that defines absolute good and evil.

It is interesting that the Constitution of the United States "supporting that principle of freedom in maintaining rights and privileges" was "justifiable before [God]" (see D&C 98:5; 109:54). It was established by the Lord "according to just and holy principles; that every man may act in doctrine and principle pertaining to futurity [or eternal principles], according to the moral agency which I have given unto him" (see D&C 101:77–80). "I, the Lord God, make you free, therefore ye are free indeed; and the law also maketh you free" (D&C 98:8). "That which is governed by law [if the law is justified by God] is also preserved by law and perfected and sanctified by the same" (D&C 88:34). The Lord compared the Constitution, this "law of man" (D&C 98:7), with His laws of freedom under His gospel by the expression "whatsoever is more or less than this, cometh of evil" (compare D&C 98:7 with 3 Nephi 11:39–40; D&C 10:67–68; 93:25; 124:119–120).

In America, a promised land just like the lands of Enos and the residue of the people of God (see Moses 6:17), the brother of Jared and his followers (see Ether 2:7), and of Abraham's and Lehi's families (see Hebrews 11:9; 1 Nephi 2:20), we must remember that our freedom depends on our alignment with the laws of God (see Ether 2:10, 12). "Unto every kingdom [including the promised land] is given a law [by God] and unto every law [of God] there are certain bounds also and conditions" (D&C 88:38). "None shall be exempted from the justice and the laws of God" (D&C 107:84; see also 107:81).

Maintaining rights and privileges of the individual without the principle of sacrifice of these rights and privileges for the common good and higher principles of love, as defined by God, is a principle of freedom "more or less than this" law of God. Such a principle, "without Christ and God in the world," today threatens the Constitution of the United States when individual rights seem more important than the collective good. Let us "abide . . . in the liberty wherewith [we] are made free" (D&C 88:86).

For the Apostle Paul, agency is truly free when it is obedient to Christ, for His liberty is inextricably linked to love (see Galatians 5:13–16). There is no love without liberty to choose. "Under this head ye are made free, and there is no other head whereby ye can be made free" (Mosiah 5:8). In remembering this connection of our freedoms with God's laws of love, let us choose "honest . . . wise . . . and good men" (D&C 98:10) who make this connection because they understand the scriptural definition of one who is wise (see Ephesians 5:17).

Disbelief of the natural mind or lack of faith, permits Satan to blind it to the light of the gospel (see 2 Corinthians 4:4). Those hearing the "great and marvelous" prophecies of Ether "did not believe, because they saw them not" (Ether 12:5). Their hearts were hardened by disbelief. Lack of faith can also be expressed as rationalization when the thoughts of the natural mind overpower the feelings of the heart (see D&C 10:25, 28). With rationalization, we risk "[calling] evil good, and good evil" (Isaiah 5:20).

We can rationalize and develop a heart murmur (see D&C 75:7), "[thinking] in [our] hearts . . . to anger" (D&C 10:16, 24) or "evil continually" (see Moses 8:21–22). We can become "slow of heart" (Luke 24:25) making "the heart . . . fat" (see Isaiah 6:9–10) or lazy with indifference. These are cardiac conditions of "unsteadiness of [heart]" (Helaman 12:1) which lead to a "doubtful heart" (D&C 58:29), then hardness of heart. With such cardiac conditions we cannot climb Mount Zion.

This unsteady then hardened condition of the heart opens the door for Satan to "get hold upon our hearts" with "the chains of hell." Alma defined the chains of hell in relation to hardness of heart. Those who continue to harden their hearts to the word of God will be "given the lesser portion of the word until they know nothing concerning his mysteries. . . . Now this is what is meant by the chains of hell" (see Alma 12:11).

The contrast of knowing the mysteries of God "in full" (Alma 12:10) and knowing "nothing concerning his mysteries" (Alma

12:11) is deeply revealing. Those who reject the word of God until they know nothing of His mysteries lose the ability to distinguish between good and evil because *they lose the light* (see D&C 1:33) *by which good is determined.* They are "kept in chains of darkness" (see D&C 38:5–6) in which they "die a spiritual death: yea, [they] shall die as to things pertaining unto righteousness" (Alma 12:16; see Alma 5:42). Even those who have been enlightened by God and then reject or don't use this light, will have "taken away, even that which they have" (see D&C 60:2–3) and "become more hardened" (see Alma 24:30, 47:36) because "unto that soul who [continues to sin] shall the former sins return" (D&C 82:7).

Without distinction between good and evil there is an effective loss of ability to choose wisely. This loss of agency is the main problem with intoxicating substances and addicting habits. Without clear distinction between good and evil the mind and heart succumb to the pride of rationalization. Then the "snare of the adversary, [is] laid to catch this people that he might bring [them] into subjection unto him, that he might encircle [them] about with his chains, that he might chain [them] down to everlasting destruction" (Alma 12:6; see also D&C 90:17). In spite of the resurrection and immortality of the spirit, when loss of agency is finalized, the freedom of "both body and soul" become "extinct" (see Alma 36:15) because then the body and soul become completely subject to the will of Satan being led "captive at his will" (Moses 4:4; see 1 Nephi 14:3–4). If an intelligence cannot be an "[agent] unto [itself]" (Moses 6:56) and "act for itself, . . . there is no [meaningful] existence" (see D&C 93:30).

Ironically, the loss of knowledge of good and evil because of "hardened hearts against the word" (Alma 12:13) will be reversed at the judgment of God (see D&C 38:5). Those without the word of God in them will stand before His glory "condemned" (Alma 12:13) to "acknowledge to [their] everlasting shame that all his judgments are just . . . and that he is merciful" (Alma 12:15). They will condemn themselves (see Alma 41:7) because, with "remorse of conscience," they will admit their agency to choose good or evil (see Alma 29:5). They will acknowledge with "a perfect knowledge" (see 2 Nephi 9:14, 46) and a "perfect remembrance" (see Alma 5:18) that their words, works, and thoughts condemn them (see Alma 12:14) and that "justice [can] not be destroyed" (Alma 12:32). "The demands of divine justice [will] awaken [their] immortal soul to a lively sense of [their] own guilt . . . and fill [their] breast with guilt, and pain, and anguish, which is like an unquenchable fire" (Mosiah 2:38). "Their torments shall be as a lake of fire and brimstone, whose flame ascendeth up forever and ever" (Alma 12:17; compare Satan's mocking mimic in Alma 14:14). This is the "sting of death" (see 1 Corinthians 15:56) and the torment of the second death (see D&C 63:17). Those with such an inflamed conscience before God will realize that their "first provocation" of God, or hardening their hearts (see Alma 12:37), has continued as their "last provocation" (see Alma 12:36) because they have "cast out the righteous" and therefore righteousness, becoming "ripe for destruction" (Helaman 13:14) even "ripening for an everlasting destruction" (Helaman 6:40). This destruction is to be cast out of the presence and therefore mercy of God forever and ever (see D&C 63:18).

Zeezrom, "the foremost to accuse Amulek and Alma, he being one of the most expert . . . lawyers . . . in the devices of the devil" (Alma 10:31–32; 11:21), witnessed the dreadfulness of these chains as potentially unquenchable fire of guilt, pain, and anguish. After hearing the words of Amulek, "he began to tremble under a consciousness of his guilt" (Alma 12:1). When Alma spoke to the great multitude of people, explaining "things beyond, or to unfold the scriptures beyond that which Amulek had done" (Alma 12:1), "Zeezrom began to tremble more exceedingly, for he was convinced more and more of the power of God" (Alma 12:7). "He began to be encircled about by the pains of hell" (Alma 14:6) until he was "scorched with a burning heat" (Alma 15:3). Alma could certainly empathize with Zeezrom for Alma also had been "racked with eternal torment . . . with all his sins" . . . [at] the very thought of coming into the presence of [his] God" (Alma 36:12, 14).

To "fill up the measure of their iniquities" (D&C 103:3) instead of the measure of their creation is to be "fully ripe" (see Ether 2:15) with "the cup of their iniquity full" (D&C 101:11). It is to be "strong in . . . perversion, . . . [delighting] in everything save that which is good," "without principle, and past feeling" (Moroni 9:20–21). It is to "love to have others suffer" (D&C 121:13). This state of complete hardness of heart is the inability to repent because agency is lost. The Spirit will no longer strive with someone unable to repent whose "[heart is] set to do evil" (Abraham 1:6). Until then, "have mercy, O Lord, upon the wicked . . . if repentance is to be found" (D&C 109:50). Those in such a state will be cut off from the presence of the Lord forever because "they cannot be redeemed from their spiritual fall" (D&C 29:44). They die "a second death . . . an everlasting death as to things pertaining unto righteousness" (Alma 12:32) because they have "sinned unto death" (see D&C 64:7). "They cannot be redeemed" because they "cannot die" (Alma 12:18) the "first death" (Alma 11:45) again, "having no preparatory state" (Alma 12:26) seeing they are immortal. Then "they shall be chained down to an everlasting destruction, according to the power and captivity of Satan" (Alma 12:17). Mercifully, "the only ones on whom the second death shall have any power" are the sons of perdition (see D&C 76:32–37). Christ "shall redeem all things, except that which he hath not put into his power" (D&C 77:12). Even those "who receive not of his fulness in the eternal world" (D&C 76:86), "who shall not be redeemed from the devil until the last resurrection" (D&C 76:85), shall have "glory of the telestial, which surpasses all understanding" (D&C 76:89). Christ "saves all the works of his hands, except those sons of perdition" (D&C 76:43).

Ironically, "It [would have] been better for them [the sons of perdition] never to have been born" (D&C 76:32). Was it better for Satan and a third of the spiritual hosts of heaven to be cast out forever without obtaining a body? Since a unified immortal body and spirit produces a fulness of joy as a chosen vessel, does an unrepentant spirit in an immortal body produce a fulness of misery as a "vessel of wrath" (see D&C 76:33; Alma 12:26)? Without the plan of redemption, "as soon as [men are] dead, their souls [are] miserable, being cut off from the presence of the Lord" (Alma 42:11). Thus, the "chains of hell" is a very descriptive term because the chains of hell can everlastingly captivate in the "pains of hell" (Alma 14:6). To be "captive of the devil" (Alma 12:11) in the chains of hell is to lose our agency and thus our ability to repent in order to receive happiness in varying degrees. It is to be in a state of constant justice without mercy.

The resurrection will "[bring] forth" (see D&C 76:39) a celestial compound in one (see 2 Nephi 2:11) and "all the rest" in a degree of glory except for the sons of perdition. Without the protective power of the Atonement and the resurrection to redeem the soul (see D&C 88:16; Moses 3:7; 6:59), we would "[look] upon the long absence of [our] spirits from [their] bodies to be a bondage" (D&C 45:17). Our spirits, in an unresurrected state void of agency, would become "like unto him . . . devils, angels to a devil" (2 Nephi 9:9).

Physically, when the heart stops so does the physical mind. The heart stopping is the final cause of complete physical death. It is symbolic of the final cause of spiritual death when "men's hearts [fail] them" (Moses 7:66). Just as our spirit preserves the temple of our body as "a living soul" (see Moses 3:7; 6:59; Abraham 5:7), the Spirit of the Lord spiritually and physically preserves holy temples (see Helaman 4:24). This relationship is revealed in Jacob's query, "harden not your hearts; for why will ye die?" (Jacob 6:6). Both physical and spiritual deaths are seen in the case of Nabal and his heart attack (see 1 Samuel 25:10–11, 37–38).

Our hearts have great influence on how we perceive spiritual truth in our minds (see Daniel 5:20). Since the heart is a strong receptor of spiritual truth, it will continue "beating" to influence the spiritually weak mind. Perhaps Jacob best expressed the importance of the heart's influence on the mind when he said, "To be carnally-minded is death, and to be spiritually-minded is life eternal" (2 Nephi 9:39). Satan must stab us in the heart spiritually or "put into the heart" to "get hold upon the hearts of the children of men" (see Helaman 6:26, 30) in order to blind our minds and bind us in his chains of hell. Notice the connection between a pure heart and firmness of mind (see Jacob 3:1–2). When the heart is hardened, its beat is weakened, causing the mind to risk blindness to spiritual light (see 1 Nephi 17:30; Alma 13:4) that "shined in our hearts" (2 Corinthians 4:6). The mind is blind to spiritual light when it no longer maintains a reciprocal connection with the heart (see Jarom 1:3; Mosiah 11:29). Then both will suffer (see Isaiah 1:5) from "blindness of [the] heart" (Ephesians 4:18) and mind (see Alma 48:3). The heart then risks becoming even more hardened until it is bound with the chains of hell or spiritually dead to the influence of the Holy Spirit. Then "Satan [has] full power over the hearts of the people" (see Ether 15:19).

After abridging the account of the Jaredites, Mormon witnessed a similar tragic condition of the hearts of his own people bound in the "chains of hell." They hardened their hearts against the word of God to the point that the Spirit of the Lord ceased to strive with them (see Ether 15:19; 2 Nephi 26:11). When this happened, they "lost their love" for their fellow men and became as "wild beasts," without order and mercy, "[delighting] in everything save that which is good" (see Moroni 9:45, 10, 18–19; see also Hosea 4:1–2). When iniquity abounds, "the love of men shall wax cold" (D&C 45:27).

The wicked people at the time of Enoch were in a similar state: without affection, hating their own blood, with their hearts bound in the chains of hell (see Moses 7:33). Laman and Lemuel were also "without principle, and past feeling" (Moroni 9:20; 1 Nephi 17:45), hating their own blood. Their hearts were hardened "like unto a flint" (2 Nephi 5:21). Therefore, they sought the life of their brother Nephi and "remembered not the brotherly covenant" (Amos 1:9).

Other scriptural examples of binding of the heart with the chains of hell include the Pharisees and Zoramites. Their hearts were hardened and bound by pompous piety. Isaiah called such an hardened heart "stouthearted" (see Isaiah 46:12). The Zoramites' hearts were so hardened that Alma said they were totally encased with the chains of hell or "swallowed up in their pride" (see Alma 31:25, 27).

The principle of "natural affection" (see 2 Timothy 3:13), or the self evident truths of human kindness and liberty, are the final qualities of love that are lost when the heart is bound with the chains of hell. With our hearts bound in these chains, we cannot feel the self evident truths of natural affection because they are truths of the nature of godliness known and felt only if we "open [our] hearts" (D&C 63:1).

Without the power of the Holy Spirit to ignite spiritual feelings in our hearts, we can know but not know, like Amulek. Consequently, we will have little faith and little resolve *to look* or seek and act on a spiritual plane. Ultimately, if we continue to harden our hearts against the feelings of the Spirit, He will "not tarry with [us]" (D&C 130:23) permitting Satan to have full power over our hearts. This was the case of Korihor who not only deceived others but also himself. Alma recognized the source of Korihor's self-deception when he said, "Behold, I know that thou believest, but thou art possessed with a lying spirit, and ye have *put off the Spirit of God* that it may have no place in you; but the devil has power over you, and he doth carry you about, working devices that he may destroy the children of God" (Alma 30:42). Korihor finally recognized his self-deception of knowing but not knowing when he said, "And I always knew that there was a God. But behold, the devil hath deceived me . . . I taught them [the lies of Satan] because they were pleasing unto the *carnal mind*; and I taught them, even until I had much success, insomuch that *I verily believed* that they were true; and for this cause I withstood the truth, even until I have brought this great curse upon me" (Alma 30:52–53). When Satan has power over us, we risk being deceived about our true selves and becoming like "wild beasts" without natural affection, delighting in everything save that which is good (see Romans 1:24–31). Then "cometh speedy destruction" (2 Nephi 26:11; D&C 1:33). When the light of the Holy Spirit leaves our hearts, so does our ability to establish order and to show love and mercy. Our hearts are bound and locked with the chains of hell.

Since our hearts or spiritual selves are the centers of remembering and learning spiritual truths, it is not surprising that a primary emphasis of the work of Satan is to weave strands of doubt and disbelief upon our hearts, "that he might lead away the hearts of the people" (Jacob 7:3). We are led away and bound as the strands become the chains of hell, even those "everlasting chains" (2 Nephi 28:19) and "awful chains, from whence there is no deliverance" (2 Nephi 28:22). Enoch saw Satan with the chain of hell in his hand which "veiled the whole face of the earth with darkness" (see Moses 7:26). Satan's weaving the strands of darkness and disbelief may start with a "flaxen cord" of flattering and carnal security (see 2 Nephi 26:22; 28:21–22; 1 Nephi 17:21–22) which becomes "the cords of vanity [and then] a cart rope" (Isaiah 5:18) of pride "until he grasps them with his awful chains." Or, in another form of pride, Satan may "rage in the hearts of the children of men, and stir them up to anger against that which is good" (2 Nephi 28:20; Moses 6:15). From the spectrum of divers ways to commit sin (see Mosiah 4:29–30) the chains of hell are forged, for they are made from the "bands" and the "bonds of iniquity" (see Mosiah 23:12–13).

As Alma taught, the only thing that can loosen "the bands of death" and "the chains of hell" is "the light of the everlasting word," which illuminates the soul, meaning both mind and heart, to produce "a mighty change wrought in [the] heart" (see Alma 5:7, 10, 12). Such was the source of Captain Moroni's righteous power. "If all men had been, and were, and ever would be, like unto Moroni, behold, the very powers of hell would have been shaken forever; yea, the devil would never have power over the hearts of the children of men" (Alma 48:17). With hearts bound by Satan we should pray like Nephi: "O Lord, according to my faith which is in thee, . . . give me strength that I may *burst these bands* with which I am bound" (1 Nephi 7:17; emphasis added). We cannot climb Mount Zion bound in the chains of hell. It is only the Son of God who can deliver "from death and the chains of hell" (see D&C 138:23). It is only his straight and sure rope that will lead us to the summit.

The power of Satan to bind our hearts will be lifted during the Millennium when "Satan shall be bound, that he shall have no place *in the hearts* of the children of men" (D&C 45:55). Ironically, it is Satan who will then be bound with "a great chain" (see Revelation 20:1–2) "for he hath no power over the hearts of the people" (see 1 Nephi 22:26). Until this millennial binding of Satan, we should heed the warning of Lehi and "awake from a deep sleep, yea, even from the sleep of hell, and shake off the awful chains by which [we] are bound" (2 Nephi 1:13), before it is nothing, save the power of God threatening our destruction, that can soften our hearts (see 1 Nephi 18:20; D&C 19:7).

To Find God We Must Seek the Lord on His Terms

Seeking the Lord on His terms has been a major problem for mankind in every generation. The state of the world at the dawn of the dispensation of the fulness of times was similar to the Israelite nation in 1100 BC, the Nephites in 24 BC, and the world at the time of the Apostle Paul (see Judges 17:6; Helaman 6:31; Philippians 2:21). Therefore, the Lord again declared in our dispensation:

> They seek not the Lord to establish His righteousness, but every man walketh in his own way, and after the image of his own god. (D&C 1:15–16)

And the anger of God kindleth against the inhabitants of the earth; and none doeth good, for all have gone out of the way. (D&C 82:6)

But it must needs be done in mine own way. (D&C 104:16)

The importance of finding and following Jesus' way by seeking Him in His mortal and immortal life was implied when He asked "what seek ye" (John 1:38) and "whom seekest thou" (John 20:15).

It is a great paradox of life that we pass each other as ships in the night yet we are all in the same boat on the same sea. This same boat is a life boat that is launched at birth and docks at death. This life boat travels on both smooth and turbulent waters that we might learn by our own experience and agency how to keep the boat afloat in waters of both good and evil. Why is it so difficult to go beyond superficial or hostile relationships and seek in others and ourselves the meaning of this life boat? Why is it so hard to seek to know who we are and where we are going? Why are worldviews so private? Nephi wrote of this lack of seeking as not asking, knocking, and searching in the light of God for great knowledge of good and evil:

> Wherefore, now after I have spoken these words, if ye cannot understand them it will be because ye ask not, neither do ye knock; wherefore, ye are not brought into *the light*, but must perish in *the dark*. . . .
> And I am left to mourn because of the unbelief, and the wickedness, and the ignorance, and the stiffneckedness of men; for they will not *search knowledge, nor understand great knowledge*, when it is given unto them in plainness, even as plain as word can be. (2 Nephi 32:4, 7; emphasis added)

The state of ignoring the Lord occurs when we yield to the "enticing words of man's wisdom" (1 Corinthians 2:4) instead of the "enticings of the Holy Spirit" (Mosiah 3:19). Then, under Satan's influence, we begin to esteem the words of God as "things of naught" (see 2 Nephi 33:2; Moses 1:41). Therefore, we do not seek "great knowledge" (see D&C 6:67; 76:114) and even "greater knowledge" (see Abraham 1:2) in the mysteries of God. The Lord promises us that if we seek His knowledge, "things which are not, [will] bring to nought things that are" (1 Corinthians 1:28) in that "the wisdom of the wise shall perish, and the understanding of the prudent shall come to naught" (D&C 76:9). This is because the works, designs, and purposes of God "cannot be frustrated" or "come to naught" (see D&C 3:1). If we "set at naught his counsels" (Helaman 12:6; D&C 3:4) and do not seek the great knowledge of God in learning truth in our world of choice between good and evil, we risk "[setting] at naught the Atonement" (Moroni 8:20) and becoming a "thing of naught . . . [having] no purpose in the end of [our] creation" (2 Nephi 2:12).

Remember how the apostle Paul instructed us to seek the Lord? We must "feel" after Him (see Acts 17:27), even feeling His words (see 1 Nephi 17:45), as though we were deaf and blind men and women. We more readily recognize our helpless condition and the need to "feel after [God]" in "the day of [our] trouble" (see D&C 101:8). Yet, we must continually seek God with a "sincere heart," "real intent," and complete "faith in Christ" our guide (see Moroni 10:4). "For we walk by faith, not by sight" (2 Corinthians 5:7). Then, when our faith is tested true, the Lord will feel after us and heal our blindness (see D&C 112:13). We are invited to "feel [God's] power" in the temple (see D&C 109:13).

Amulek and Lamoni did not seek the Lord because they did not respond to the feelings of their hearts. Laman and Lemuel were condemned by Nephi, stating they were "past feeling" (1 Nephi 17:45; see also Ephesians 4:19). They were not only past the feeling of natural affection but they "knew not the dealings of that God who had created them" (1 Nephi 2:12) because they did not inquire of the Lord (see 1 Nephi 15:8–11; see also D&C 10:21) on His terms by feeling after Him with humility. *We begin to seek the Lord on His terms by responding to the feelings of our hearts with a broken heart and contrite spirit.* The Lord's ancient promise to the captive Jews in Babylon is applicable to all:

> Ye shall seek me, and find me, when ye shall search for me with all your heart. (Jeremiah 29:13)

He that finds God on His terms, "prepareth his heart to seek God" (2 Chronicles 30:19) and seeks Him early "with [the] spirit within" (see Isaiah 26:9). For "they who have sought me early shall find rest to their souls" (D&C 54:10). The object of seeking God is not just to find Him but to sup (see Revelation 3:20) and dwell with Him . This truth is taught in the inquiry of Jesus to the two disciples of John the Baptist who followed the newly baptized Lamb of God:

Then Jesus turned, and saw them following, and saith unto them, What seek ye? They said unto him, Rabbi, . . . where dwellest thou? They came and saw where he dwelt, and abode with him that day. (John 1:38–39)

Christ "received all power, both in heaven and on earth, and the glory of the Father was with him, for he dwelt in him" (D&C 93:17). To dwell with or in God, we must become like Him by following His "conditions of repentance" (Helaman 14:11) and terms for perfection. Then "the spirit of God [will descend] out of heaven, and [abide] upon [us]" (Moses 6:26). Good intentions and our own brand of righteousness will not bring us to abide with Him because "if a man also strive for masteries, yet is he not crowned, except he strive lawfully" (2 Timothy 2:5).

It is a matter of recognizing that we are "not right before [God]" (see D&C 49:2) that "inasmuch as [we] erred it might be made known" (D&C 1:25). Then our responsibility is getting "all things right" (see D&C 41:3), "that all things may be right before me, as it shall be proved by the Spirit" (D&C 57:13). It is a blessing from God, "a privilege of organizing [ourselves] according to [God's] laws" (D&C 51:15), "by conforming to the ordinance and preparation that the Lord ordained and prepared before the foundation of the world" (D&C 128:5). If we don't conform to this blessing we will be "cut off" (see D&C 51:2; 56:10) from the Lord.

It is not from a Rameumptom, a tower of pride like the Zoram-ites built (see Alma 31:21), that we will see the great view and find the Lord. C. S. Lewis captured this truth when he said, "As long as you are proud, you cannot know God . . . as long as you are looking down, you cannot see something that is above you."[8]

Isaiah advised us in acquiring a true perspective while climbing Mount Zion when he said: "Lift up your eyes to the heavens, and look upon the earth beneath" (Isaiah 51:6). Compare the pride of the Zoramites on the Rameumptom or King Noah on his tower (see Mosiah 11:6–15) with the humility and service of King Benjamin, who from his tower saw great views (see Mosiah 2:7, 12–17). It is only through the depths of humility with the feelings of a meek and lowly heart that this view and knowledge come (see D&C 5:23–24) because "he that humbleth himself shall be exalted" (Luke 18:14; see also 1 Peter 5:6).

We cannot feel God with faith and hope if our hearts are encased in worldly pride, being set upon the things of this world and the honors of men. *It is only the meek and lowly heart that is acceptable before God* (see Moroni 7:43–44) *for this is the heart that the Savior has* (see Matthew 11:29).

The Power of the Holy Ghost Is Learning Truth in the Mind and Heart

When we seek the Lord with a meek and lowly heart, we are given a gift (see Moroni 8:26) because "[God] is a rewarder of them that diligently seek him" (Hebrews 11:6). This gift is "the power of the Holy Ghost" (see 1 Nephi 10:17). Notice that even Jesus of Nazareth received this gift (see Acts 10:38).

For the fulness of the power of the Holy Ghost, we must not only seek God with a meek and lowly heart, but we must convince Him, just like His chosen Nephite disciples (see 3 Nephi 19:9), that this gift is "most desired" above anything else in our lives. We convince God by seeking Him with faith in hungering and thirsting for righteousness (see 3 Nephi 12:6), and then by keeping all of His covenants. *Obedience is the foundation of true faith.* Then we will be filled with the Holy Spirit. With the fulness of the Holy Spirit, "the mysteries of God" (1 Nephi 10:19) and "the truth of all things" (Moroni 10:5) are unfolded to us.

Within the word *seek* is the word *see,* which is the gift for seeking. By the power of the Holy Spirit, we see things with eyes of understanding as they really are. If we keep seeking on His terms, we will see the "King Immanuel" (D&C 128:22).

Oliver Cowdery learned about the power of the Holy Ghost in his request for the gift of translation:

> Yea, behold, I will tell you in your *mind* and in your *heart, by the Holy Ghost,* which shall come upon you and which shall dwell in your heart.

> Now, behold, this is *the spirit of revelation*; behold, this is the spirit by which Moses brought the children of Israel through the Red Sea on dry ground. (D&C 8:23; emphasis added; see also Moses 1:25)

Note in verse two that we can learn from the Holy Ghost in our minds and our hearts because He can dwell in our hearts. That is, *He can dwell with and influence our spiritual selves.* His presence in our hearts will influence not only the feeling of our hearts but the thinking of our minds, being "renewed in the spirit of [our] mind" (Ephesians 4:23; see also Romans 12:2). The voice of the Spirit may first come to our minds (see Enos 1:10), but unless we hear His voice pressing us (see D&C 128:1) with the feelings of our hearts, we will not act with conviction upon the "mind" or will of the Spirit. Therefore, the Apostle Paul wrote, "he that searcheth the hearts knoweth what is the mind of the Spirit" (Romans 8:27). The Holy Spirit has the power to penetrate the veil of unbelief, both in our minds and our hearts, if we will seek the Lord and cleanse ourselves as a temple (see Ether 4:15).

The *scriptural temple* teaches that we come to know of spiritual truth and the mysteries of God not just with logic nor just with feelings. Rather, *spiritual truth is learned in both our minds and our hearts.* That is, spiritual truth must be logical and feel right. For our faith we need reason and the feeling of hope (see 1 Peter 3:15). "Truth is reason," as stated in the hymn "O My Father." When we "lay it to heart" (D&C 58:5), reasoned truth will burn as a feeling in our hearts until we come to "perfect understanding" (Alma 48:11). Therefore, Oliver Cowdery was instructed by the Lord to "study it out in [his] own mind . . . ask me if it be right, and if it is right . . . you shall *feel* that it is right" (D&C 9:8).

Paul said there is a natural body, "our earthly house," and a spiritual body which is "a building of God, an house not made with hands, eternal in the heavens" (2 Corinthians 5:1; see 1 Corinthians 15:44). Man is composed of a spirit and flesh soul in likeness of God our Father who is a spirit and flesh soul (see D&C 93:33; John 4:24). The physical difference is that we are mortal "flesh and blood" (1 Corinthians 15:50) while God is immortal "flesh and bones" (Luke 24:39; D&C 129:1; 130:22; see also Genesis 2:23).

Much speculation and controversy has occurred from the statement that God created man "in our image, after our likeness"

(Genesis 1:26). A similar expression is used after Adam "begat a son [Seth] in his own likeness, after his image" (Genesis 5:3; see also D&C 107:43). This event certainly gave common sense meaning to the terms *image* and *likeness* unless one gets lost in academic speculation. Ezekiel's vision of the glory of the Lord described His likeness "as the appearance of a man" (Ezekiel 1:26). In the sense of glory, likeness is more than image because it infers what a man can become.

The plural term *our* in Genesis 1:26 can be understood from the following verse: "And I, God, created man in mine own image, *in the image of mine Only Begotten* created I him; male and female created I them" (Moses 2:27; see also D&C 20:18). The plural *our* means God the Father and the Son.

The fact that we were created after the image of the Son is profoundly significant in establishing the literal nature of "the image of man" as God's image (see Mosiah 7:27). When we see our image in a mirror we see the image of God (see D&C 130:1). This was the startling discovery of the brother of Jared who saw the pre-mortal Christ in the image of a man (see Ether 3:6, 8, 15).

The image of the spirit Christ is the same image as the mortal Christ and even the resurrected Christ (see Ether 3:9, 16). The body takes the image or form of the spirit. The Savior's response to Philip's request to see the Father was, "he that hath seen me hath seen the Father" (John 14:9). When the resurrected Savior appeared before His apostles He said, "behold my hands and my feet, that it is I myself: handle me, and see; for a spirit hath not flesh and bones, as ye see me have" (Luke 24:39).

Christ demonstrated to man in His pre-mortal, mortal, and post-mortal states, that man is literally in the image of God in all of these states. Image means "*in the image of his own body*, male and female, created he them" (Moses 6:9; emphasis added). We are literal offspring of God because "the seed in itself yieldeth its own likeness" (Abraham 4:11; see also Alma 32:31). If we are in the image and likeness of God, we are His seed! "And this is the genealogy of the sons of Adam, who was the son of God" (Moses 6:22). If we are God's seed or offspring, we should think of our Father in Heaven as what we are and what He promises we can become (see Acts 17:28–29).

The ultimate goal of our creation for a fulness of joy, even in this life, is to have the body and spirit or the mind and heart "inseparably connected" (D&C 93:33), thinking, feeling, and acting as one. This is not only an individual goal but also a collective goal of unity (see 2 Nephi 1:21; Moses 7:18). We demonstrate this oneness of body and spirit, understanding in both mind and heart, by "[glorifying] God in [our] body, and in [our] spirit" (1 Corinthians 6:20) and serving God with both mind and heart (see D&C 4:2). "The Lord requireth the heart and a willing mind" (D&C 64:34).

The mind and heart, body and spirit, coming to think and feel with one accord was demonstrated by the Jerusalem Council concerning the application of the law of Moses to the Gentile disciples. After "much disputing" (Acts 15:7), the apostles and elders declared their unity with "one accord" (Acts 15:25). This occurred through the spirit of revelation witnessed by their statement, "For it seemed good to the Holy Ghost, and to us" (Acts 15:28). If this council had relied only in reasoning on the written word of God as the final arbiter in the matter, circumcision would have been imposed. Since the apostles and elders knew the importance of continued revelation from God, they sought to know the will of God in both their minds and their hearts by reasoning with revelation from the Holy Ghost. This is how we obey God's commandment to "assemble [ourselves] together to agree upon [His] word" (D&C 41:2). By this process we counter Satan who "doth stir up the hearts of the people to contention concerning the points of my doctrine" (D&C 10:63). The doctrine of learning in heart and mind taught in the *scriptural temple* is what King Benjamin preached in his great sermon at the temple of Zarahemla:

> I have not commanded you to come up hither to trifle with the words which I shall speak, but that you should hearken unto me, and open your ears that ye may hear, and your hearts that ye may understand, and your minds that the mysteries of God may be unfolded to your view. (Mosiah 2:9)

It is interesting that a similar opening of ears, eyes, minds, and hearts occurred at the temple of the land Bountiful when the glory of the Savior and the mysteries of God were revealed to the Nephites (see 3 Nephi 11:3, 5). If we only learn in our minds and resist the feelings of our hearts, never getting mind and heart to think and feel as one, we will not acquire the righteousness of God because, "with the heart man believeth unto righteousness" (Romans 10:10).

The opening of ears, eyes, minds and hearts occurs when obedience to God ceases to be a burden and becomes a blessing. Then God will endow us with powers from on high such that the mysteries of God will be revealed by the power of the Holy Spirit. This is what Adam and Eve realized in the garden when their eyes were opened and they received the blessings of willful obedience to God. Now as fallen and no longer in the presence of God, it is extremely important that we connect, through willful obedience to God, with the Holy Spirit of prophecy and revelation because anything that comes "according to the spirit of prophecy" comes "according to the truth" (Alma 3:27). We need this connection in order to reach the summit of Mount Zion and not fall.

The Power of the Holy Ghost Is the Spirit of Prophecy and Revelation of Jesus Christ

The Apostle John defined the spirit of prophecy as the testimony of Jesus (see Revelation 19:10; see also Jacob 1:6). The Apostle Paul confirmed that this testimony is a gift of the Spirit when he wrote that, "No man can say that Jesus is the Lord, but by the Holy Ghost" (1 Corinthians 12:3; see also D&C 46:13). For "ye may know that he is, by the power of the Holy Ghost" (Moroni 10:7). A revealing and prophesying testimony of Jesus Christ is exactly what Adam received when the Holy Ghost fell upon him (see Moses 5:9). Concerning the blessings from the Holy Ghost, Joseph Smith said:

> The Spirit of Revelation is in connection with these blessings. A person may profit by noticing the first intimation of the spirit of revelation; for instance, when you feel pure intelligence flowing into you, it may give you sudden strokes of ideas. . . . Thus by learning the Spirit of God and understanding it, you may grow into the principle of revelation until you become perfect in Christ Jesus.[9]

The first intimation of the spirit of revelation is to hear the voice of God in our conscience. Then, with the gift of the Holy Ghost to hear the voice of God in both our hearts and minds, the principle of personal revelation expands to reveal the mysteries of God. This is how "the Lord God [calls] upon men by the Holy Ghost everywhere" (Moses 5:14). Joseph Smith instructed John Taylor in this principle:

> Elder Taylor, . . . you have had hands laid upon your head for the reception of the Holy Ghost. . . . Now, if you will continue to follow the leadings of that spirit, it will always lead you right. Sometimes it might be contrary to your judgment; never mind that, follow its dictates; and if you be true to its whisperings it will in time become in you a principle of revelation, so that you will know all things.[10]

To know all things is to have Jesus Christ revealed by the power of the Holy Spirit. By this power we can receive, like Oliver Cowdery, the "spirit of revelation" (D&C 8:3) of Jesus Christ in our minds and our hearts. The spirit of revelation of Christ from the Holy Ghost is powerful because:

- with this spirit we will emulate the Christlike qualities of a child and will never be tempted above that which we can bear. (See Alma 13:28.)
- with this spirit we can know "the thoughts and intents of [the] hearts" of others. (See Alma 12:7.)
- with this spirit we can recognize true messengers of the Lord because we can know in our hearts Christ's words of truth they speak. (See 2 Nephi 33:1; D&C 50:17–22.)
- with this spirit we can become true messengers of the Lord and "prophecy" (see D&C 34:10) speaking with "the tongue of angels" the words of Christ. (See 2 Nephi 32:2–3; D&C 18:33–35.)
- with this spirit we can "speak much" (Ether 12:23) with "the power of God unto the convincing of men" (D&C 11:21) to come unto Christ.
- with this spirit "which giveth utterance" we "stand as witness . . . and declare repentance unto this generation" (D&C 14:8).
- with this spirit we are "brought to the knowledge of the truth" (see Alma 23:6; Ether 4:11) even the truth of God's written words. (See D&C 18:2–3.)

- with this spirit "we [know] concerning the true points of [Christ's] doctrine. (See Helaman 11:23; 3 Nephi 21:6.)
- with this spirit we can "receive revelations to unfold the mysteries of the kingdom." (See D&C 90:14.)
- with this spirit we can know God's will for us because "the words of Christ will tell [us] all things what [we] should do" (2 Nephi 32:3).
- with this spirit the Holy Ghost will "manifest all things which are expedient unto the children of men" (D&C 18:18) and "show unto us all things [we] should do" (see 2 Nephi 32:5) to come unto Christ.
- with this spirit we will "know all things whatsoever you desire of me, which are pertaining unto things of righteousness, in faith believing in me that ye shall receive" (D&C 11:14).
- with this spirit we will know when to preach, exhort, pray, supplicate or sing in conducting the church. (See Moroni 6:9.)
- Therefore, with this spirit the words of Christ are confirmed unto us. (See Mormon 9:25.)

As Nephi explained (see 2 Nephi 32:2–3), "feasting upon the word of Christ" (2 Nephi 31:20) requires dining with the Holy Ghost because He serves the feast. When we "enter in by the way, and receive the Holy Ghost" (2 Nephi 32:5) to have revealed all things that we should do to come unto Christ, "there will be no more doctrine given until he (Christ) shall manifest himself unto you in the flesh" (2 Nephi 32:6). This is the great and last promise of the temple and it requires the gift of the Holy Ghost.

Alma the Younger, described the principle of revelation in his own life by connection with the Holy Spirit. He demonstrated the principle of prophecy by testifying of Christ:

> Do ye not suppose that I know of these things myself? Behold, I testify unto you that I do know that these things whereof I have spoken are true. And how do ye suppose that I know of their surety?
>
> Behold, I say unto you they are made known unto me by the Holy Spirit of God. Behold, I have fasted and prayed many days that I might know these things of myself. And now I do know of myself that they are true; for the Lord God hath made them manifest unto me by his Holy Spirit; and this is the spirit of revelation which is in me.

And moreover, I say unto you that it has thus been revealed unto me, that the words which have been spoken by our fathers are true, even so according to the spirit of prophecy which is in me, which is also by the manifestation of the Spirit of God.

I say unto you, that I know of myself that whatsoever I shall say unto you, concerning that which is to come, is true; and I say unto you, that I know that Jesus Christ shall come, yea, the Son, the Only Begotten of the Father, full of grace, and mercy, and truth. And behold, it is he that cometh to take away the sins of the world, yea, the sins of every man who steadfastly believeth on his name. (Alma 5:45–48)

When Alma reunited with the sons of Mosiah, he found that they also had the spirit of prophecy and revelation:

Yea, and they had waxed strong in the knowledge of the truth; for they were men of a sound understanding and they had *searched the scriptures* diligently, that they might know the word of God.

But this is not all; they had given themselves to much *prayer*, and *fasting*; therefore they had the *spirit of prophecy*, and *the spirit of revelation*, and when they taught, *they taught with power and authority of God.* (Alma 17:23; emphasis added)

Alma and the sons of Mosiah knew in their minds because they were men of sound understanding. But that was not all. They also knew in their hearts because they sought the Lord and His gift of the Spirit.

Like Nephi, Alma and the sons of Mosiah "diligently" (1 Nephi 10:19) sought God, not just mentally but also by striving to feel after Him with the spiritual discipline of a lowly heart, through fasting and prayer. Such spiritual discipline teaches the flesh and the mind that acting independently of the spirit or feelings of the heart will not produce a fulness of knowledge and joy, "for man is spirit" (D&C 93:33)! "Care not for the body, neither the life of the body; but care for the soul, and for the life of the soul" (D&C 101:37; see also D&C 88:15). For "souls are precious before thee" (D&C 109:43; compare with D&C 117:4).

Fasting and prayer discipline the will of the mind to become connected to the will of the heart. Both the mind and heart are then open to the will of God, so that we "do according to that which is in [God's] heart and in [His] mind" (1 Samuel 2:35). Then, "thy will be done, O Lord, and not ours" (D&C 109:44) and "thy will be done on earth as it is in heaven" (3 Nephi 13:10).

Since Alma and the sons of Mosiah diligently sought God, they received the power and authority of the Holy Ghost as a gift. They sought the words of Christ through scripture study. They combined their study with the spiritual discipline of fasting, or literally hungering and thirsting after righteousness, which produces the humility necessary for mighty, pleading prayer. Then His power, the spirit of prophecy and revelation, unfolded the words of Christ into a profound understanding in their minds and hearts. This power of the Holy Ghost was a real gift of the Spirit because of the power and authority with which they taught and testified of Jesus Christ throughout their missionary work (see also Mosiah 18:26). *Christ is the grand prophecy and revelation of the spirit of prophecy and revelation.* Therefore, all true messengers of God "more or less" (see Mosiah 13:33) talk, rejoice, teach, write, and prophesy of Christ because He is the source to whom "[all] may look for a remission of their sins" (see 2 Nephi 25:26).

The book of Omni reveals a powerful contrast in the writings of those who wrote without the spirit of prophecy and revelation to the writings of Amaleki who demonstrated this gift. The book of Omni is a short historical account of the succession of the plates, passed from father to son or another relative. When Abinadom received the plates, he stated, "I know of no revelation save that which has been written, neither prophecy; wherefore, that which is sufficient is written (Omni 1:11; emphasis added).

It wasn't until Amaleki, the son of Abinadom, that a testimony of Christ was reintroduced into the record. He knew that "that which is sufficient is written" was not sufficient. He affirmed the goodness of King Benjamin, then bore his testimony of Christ:

> And it came to pass that I began to be old; and, having no seed, and knowing King Benjamin to be a just man before the Lord, wherefore, I shall deliver up these plates unto him, exhorting all men to come unto God, the Holy One of Israel, and *believe in prophesying, and in revelations*, . . . and *continue in fasting and praying*, and endure to the end. (Omni 1:25–26; emphasis added)

While both the Israelites and converted Lamanites observed the law of Moses, the difference between these two groups was their ability to recognize Christ in this law. The Israelites constantly looked back to Moses and Egypt while the converted Lamanites "did look forward to the coming of Christ, considering that the law of Moses was a type of his coming," (Alma 25:15; see Mosiah 3:14–15). Instead of looking for worldly salvation, these righteous Lamanites retained a "hope through faith, unto eternal salvation, relying upon *the spirit of prophecy*" (Alma 25:16). Of course, it is righteousness not nationality that merits this gift of the Spirit.

One of the most remarkable scriptural examples of the spirit of prophecy and revelation of Jesus Christ as a gift of the Spirit, even the gift of the great and last promise of the temple, occurred in the temple eight days after the Savior's birth. Simeon, a devout and just man, seeking for the great and last promise of the temple in his own life, came by the spirit unto the temple (see Helaman 10:16–17) where "the Holy Ghost was upon him." There he held the child Jesus in his arms and bore testimony of His divinity when he said: "For mine eyes have seen thy salvation. . . . This child is set for the fall and rising again of many in Israel . . . *that the thoughts of many hearts may be revealed*" (see Luke 2:25–35). The revelation of Christ will reveal the thoughts and intents of our hearts.

If, like Simeon, we come with the Spirit to the temple and desire to be taught in the temple by the Spirit then, in the temple, we will receive the spirit of prophecy and revelation of Jesus Christ. With this spirit we will not lose focus on our lead climber as we scale Mount Zion. Then we will become the "seed of Christ" (see Mosiah 15:10–14) and be prepared for the great and last promise of the temple.

The Power of the Holy Ghost Is the Power of the Word of God

As a physician who understands the piercing power required to divide bone and joint asunder, yet seeing some pleasing results in healing the delicacies of the wounded hand, I marvel at the power of the word of God (see D&C 6:2; Hebrews 4:12) that "maketh my bones to quake" (D&C 85:6) and "healeth the wounded soul" (Jacob 4:8). The word of Christ, the healing word of God, is, indeed, powerful and pleasing. As Alma discovered, "it has more effect on the minds of people than the sword or anything else" (Alma 31:5). Sometimes "out of [God's] mouth [comes] a sharp two-edged sword" (Revelation 1:16) of judgment. More often, the word of the Lord is "sharper than a two-edged sword" (D&C 6:2) because as a still small voice, it can "prick [our] hearts" like a needle "stirring [us] up unto repentance" (see Jarom 1:12) for the gift of His mercy.

The combination of the spirit of prophecy and revelation and a righteous man makes a powerful voice (see D&C 122:4) because "great [is] the power of the language which God had given him" (see Moses 7:13; contrast with Jacob 7:4). Even the written word of God contains "the convincing power of God" (3 Nephi 28:29; see Moses 6:5). Perhaps this is why heavenly messengers often quote scripture and why the Savior expounded the scriptures to the Nephites (see 3 Nephi 23:14).

The word of God, spoken or written (see D&C 127:10) has the power to illuminate the truth that we know in our hearts because "the word" is already "in thy heart" (see Deuteronomy 30:14). Therefore, "today if ye will hear his voice, harden not your hearts" (Hebrews 3:7–8) and "resist no more my voice" (D&C 108:2). Eventually, "the voice of the Lord is unto all men, and there is none to escape; . . . neither heart that shall not be penetrated" (D&C 1:2). Like beautiful poetry, the word of God focuses our thoughts to a remembrance of the truths that we already know in our hearts. We cannot truly understand and feel the power of the word of God until we experience this personal poetry in the depth of our souls as expressed by Jeremiah: "But his word was in mine heart as a burning fire shut up in my bones" (Jeremiah 20:9).

Brigham Young, referring to the Nauvoo Covenant prior to the expulsion, to not leave anyone behind said, "let the fire of the covenant, which you made in the house of the Lord, burn in your hearts like flame unquenchable!"[11] The power of the word of God will be a burning fire in our hearts when we make and keep covenants with Him in the temple. Then the "fears in [our] hearts" (see D&C 67:3) will be replaced with a perfect brightness of burning hope. The Lord promises that "whoso treasureth up my word, shall not be deceived" (Joseph Smith—Matthew 1:37). Treasuring starts by searching the written word of God then seeking understanding in the light of the spirit of prophecy and revelation. When we understand, we should "hearken to [His] words . . . and treasure these things up in [our] hearts, and let the solemnities of eternity rest upon [our] minds" (D&C 43:34).

To experience the unique power of the words and voice of God in the heart as piercing, pleasing, and healing is to understand how the word of God "[subdues] the hearts of the children of men" (see D&C 96:5). This is a profound experience witnessed in the *scriptural temple*. On Horeb, the holy mountain of God, the word of the Lord came to Elijah, in "a manifestation from deep inside his soul."[12] He didn't feel the power of the Lord in the wind, a strong earthquake, or fire until he felt the power of "a still small voice" (see 1 Kings 19:89, 11–12). At the temple in the land Bountiful the voice of God, again a small voice, did pierce to the very center and cause the hearts of those who heard it to burn (see 3 Nephi 11:3; see also Luke 24:32).

The voice of the Spirit that can pierce the heart is heard and felt in the temple. It is the confirming response to our plea that God hear our voices as we "lift up [our voices] and declare [God's] word . . . lifting up holy hands" (D&C 60:7), "uplifted to the Most High" (see D&C 109:19).

Perhaps we are told to whisper in the temple not only for the sake of reverence, but to remind us that the pleasant voice of perfect mildness is a whisper (see Helaman 5:30, 46) that "whispereth through and pierceth all things" (D&C 85:6) and inspires us to do the will of the Spirit (see Words of Mormon 1:7). This whispering voice is "a word behind thee, saying, This is the way, walk ye in it" (Isaiah 30:21). We must "be still" (D&C 101:16) with "a meek and quiet spirit" (1 Peter 3:4) to hear it (see Psalm 107:30).

We can read or hear the word of God in our minds but to have the "still voice of perfect mildness" (Helaman 5:30) pierce to the center of the soul is to feel the power of the voice of the Spirit as burning in our hearts. By this profound experience, when our spirits are enlightened, we come to know for ourselves with "surety" (D&C 5:12), the spiritual truth of things as they really are. Therefore, to avoid "condemnation" (D&C 93:32), we are commanded to "treasure up" in our minds and hearts (see D&C 84:85; 11:26) the word of the Lord by giving diligent heed to the words of eternal life:

> And I now give unto you a commandment to beware concerning yourselves, to give diligent heed to the words of eternal life.
>
> For you shall live by every word that proceedeth forth from the mouth of God.
>
> For the word of the Lord is truth, and whatsoever is truth is light, and whatsoever is light is Spirit, even the Spirit of Jesus Christ.
>
> And the Spirit giveth light to every man that cometh into the world; and the Spirit enlighteneth every man through the world, that hearkeneth to the voice of the Spirit. (D&C 84:43–46)

The words of eternal life in the fulness of the gospel, are found in the Bible and the Book of Mormon (see D&C 42:12). They are found in all the holy scriptures "until the fulness of my scriptures (written and spoken) is given" (D&C 42:15, see 2 Peter 1:20–21). We must give diligent heed and "treasure up these things in our hearts, and let the solemnities of eternity rest upon our minds" (D&C 43:34) to be taught by the spirit of prophecy and revelation.

The Spirit, revealing and testifying of Christ, is the Holy Spirit, our teacher in the temple. It is here that we learn most about Jesus Christ and our relation to Him. It is here that the "still voice of perfect mildness" can heal us (see John 12:40) and perfect us. As Joseph Smith said, because of the spirit of revelation we become perfected in Christ Jesus.

Symbolic Jewels: Pearls of the Spirit

A teaching technique that the Holy Spirit uses to teach us in the temple is symbolism. A single scripture establishes the importance of this technique:

> The baptismal font was instituted as a similitude of the grave, . . . that all things may have their likeness, and that they may accord one with another that which is earthly conforming to that which is heavenly. (D&C 128:13)

This scripture teaches me that all things on earth are a reflection of a higher spiritual reality (see also Romans 1:20; Hebrews 8:5; D&C 77:2). We need the teaching of the Holy Spirit to help us make a connection to this spiritual reality and to escape the "prison-house" or mindset of mortality.

With symbols, even repeated words and phrases of the scriptural temple, the Holy Spirit prompts us to search for the meaning of a higher spiritual reality. Then, with the spirit of revelation, He makes the unifying connection in our minds and our hearts. This means that we need to understand the dimensions of the spiritual realm in our minds with symbols of dimension (size, shape, quality, quantity, and so on). Also, we need to "feel" truth in our hearts since many spiritual truths do not have familiar earthly dimensions but only forgotten spiritual dimensions. With this technique, we really begin to see the whole picture, the great view, "the things which are not seen [that] are eternal" (2 Corinthians 4:18).

As we learn this technique, we need to remember two other scriptural applications to symbolism. First,

> My thoughts are not your thoughts, neither are your ways my ways, saith the Lord. For as the heavens are higher than the earth, so are my ways higher than your ways, and my thoughts than your thoughts. (Isaiah 55:89)

Second:

> Verily I say unto you that all things unto me are spiritual, . . . for my commandments are spiritual. (D&C 29:34–35)

If we are to be taught spiritual truths by the Holy Spirit then we must learn to think on a spiritual level.

In *The Holiness of Everyday Life*, Joan MacDonald describes the need to think spiritually:

> Discipline, evaluation, striving for excellence, and developing personal integrity. These are common experiences of the workplace that help develop character. But developing character isn't enough . . . work can develop and reveal our souls. A soul is more than character. To develop one's soul implies a deep spiritual effort, and to be spiritual implies a connection to God. . . . We need to see, understand and experience God. We also need to know and understand ourselves. . . . We want to know that God loves and accepts us how we are, and we want to experience Him helping us to become better. . . . We are in luck, because the revealing of God, of ourselves, and of the connection between ourselves and God occurs all around us. . . . The key to seeing it is awareness. (8)

> The spirit and the body are the soul of man. (D&C 88:15) The sabbath and the workday, the sacred and the secular are the soul of our lives. . . .
>
> All things are spiritual to the Lord. If I am to become more like my Heavenly Father, then all things must be spiritual to me also. (4)[13]

Elder Orson F. Whitney once said: "The universe is built on symbols, lifting our thoughts from man to God, earth to heaven and time to eternity."[14] Joan MacDonald would agree with Elder Whitney but probably add that through symbols, the spiritual frontier that we need to probe in this life is not so much above us as it is within us.

The teaching technique of symbolism in the temple has a focal point. Two scriptures identify this point:

> All things which have been given of God . . . unto man, are the typifying of Him. (2 Nephi 11:4)

> All things are created and made to bear record of Me. (Moses 6:63)

The focal point is the Savior, Jesus Christ. It is an incredible awakening to realize the truth of these two preceding scriptures. This awakening is still occurring to me in the temple. It is one aspect of temple worship that is repeatedly exciting. We should understand the core doctrines of Christ and then explore the multiple meanings through the symbolic teachings of the Holy Spirit. Just as the forgotten symbols of the Aaronic priesthood temple of ancient Israel pointed to Christ, we should see in the symbols of our temple worship the precise and plentiful doctrines of Christ.

For instance, a circle within a square, the symbolic motif of the Bountiful Utah Temple, is very dominant. It is everywhere, even on the planter boxes in the parking lot. The square might symbolize measured time and space, the secular, or mortal man. The circle could symbolize eternity, the woman, the Spirit, or the immortal God. Therefore, the circle in the square would symbolize time and eternity, the spirit in man and woman, the Holy Spirit and God striving with man and woman, or man and woman as one. The symbol in this motif that is most revealing to me, found in a few isolated places in the temple, is the octagon: a square becoming a circle or an unpolished gem becoming a jewel.

Expanded knowledge occurs when truth is expanded in new dimensions. Concerning the circle in a square, when three dimensions are applied to both, the square can become a quadrilateral triangle that vanishes at a point where the circle, seen in some locations of the Bountiful temple and in the capstones of the Salt Lake temple, becomes a sphere. This transformation is like the Egyptian concept of a ray of light from the sun in the form of a pyramid. Interestingly, the base area of the Great Pyramid is 93,000,000 cubic feet, the same number in miles as a ray of sunlight travels to the earth. This three dimensional figure could also symbolize the temporal vanishing to the eternal. The whole figure appears as a geometric tree of life with its root in the temporal and its fruit in the eternal.

The symbol of the circle as a reflection of the eternal is a powerful symbol in all temples and in our daily lives. While the earth is described in the scriptures as having four corners (North, East, South, West), it is nevertheless a globe and in one plane a circle, suggesting the measure of its creation. The prayer circles of blessings and ordinations are symbolic of the eternal powers of heaven. In our families and in the temple we gather in prayer circles as we petition the Eternal Father. Often, in the celestial room, friends and families gather in circles of joy, reflecting the eternal nature of their relationships. These symbols of eternity help us understand that, the course of the Lord is *"one eternal round"* (1 Nephi 10:19; Alma 7:20; 37:12; D&C 3:2).

The eternal round of the Lord is symbolic of His omniscience and omnipresence (see D&C 38:2) with past, present and future continually before Him (see D&C 130:7; Moses 1:6). "From eternity to eternity he is the same" (D&C 76:4). Concerning the mortal application of His eternal plan, "the Lord [commands] and [revokes], as it seemeth [Him] good" (D&C 56:4). Therefore, some lose the eternal perspective and say "this is not the work of the Lord, for his promises are not fulfilled" (see D&C 58:32–33). A significant symbolic meaning of the "eternal round" is that if we strictly follow the eternal plan of the Eternal Father we can arrive from whence we came. This is how a straight path becomes an eternal round (see D&C 3:2).

The eternal plan is a circle of salvation based on the Atonement (see 3 Nephi 27:14; 28:11; Helaman 14:18; 2 Nephi 2:57; Alma 33:11) and conveyed through the doctrine of Christ (see 3 Nephi 11:32–39; 27:19–27; 2 Nephi 31:2–21; Hebrews 6:1–2). Faith in Christ and His Atonement, in which "He suffered the pain of all men, that all might repent and come unto him . . . that He might bring all men unto Him (to His level of holiness), on condition of repentance" (D&C 18:11–12), making them "holy without spot" (Moroni 10:33), should make us earnestly repent. True faith is "faith unto repentance" (Alma 34:16). True repentance (see D&C 58:43) with obedience to God's law is what opens the door to the full power of Christ's Atonement (see Helaman 5:11). When we repent and become obedient to the doctrine of Christ, then we obey His will to be baptized of water. This baptism opens the door to the gifts of the Holy Ghost, particularly the gift of the spirit of prophecy and revelation which reveals more of "the stature of the fulness of Christ" (Ephesians 4:13), in revealing His perfect love. Therefore, "faith and repentance bringeth a change of heart" (Helaman 15:7).

With this change of heart as a gift of the Spirit, our faith in Christ increases and we desire to repent and love our fellow men more to partake of the fulness of Christ's love or Atonement (see D&C 29:17). For those outside the circle of salvation, faith and repentance brings them within the circle through baptism by water. For disciples who have been baptized with water, faith and repentance is what keeps them moving in the circle of salvation. The Apostle Paul testified of, "repentance toward God, and faith toward our Lord Jesus Christ" (Acts 20:21). The Book of Mormon repeatedly says "baptized unto repentance" (Alma 5:62).

By seeking a change of heart through faith and repentance we are given more of the gifts of the Spirit (see 1 Nephi 10:17; D&C 1:32) until we are justified and sanctified (see Moses 6:60; 3 Nephi 27:20) or baptized with fire and the Holy Ghost. Then our love and faith in Christ will become even stronger. The Holy Ghost can be our constant companion when we are full of the pure love of Christ. Therefore, faith in Christ leads to more faith in Christ, completing a circle through the process of repentance, baptism by water and fire, and the gifts of the Holy Ghost. This circle becomes a circle of salvation when repentance is confirmed by the ordinances and directed by the commandments of Christ's church. Therefore, He commanded, "let them build up churches, inasmuch as the inhabitants of the earth will repent" (D&C 58:48).

Faith as a principle of action comes from the substance of things hoped for which are true (see Alma 32:21). A full assurance of hope comes from the evidence of things not seen (see Ether 12:6; Hebrews 6:11; 11:1) in the present (see John 7:17) when we look back in the future to see them fulfilled. Our hope in truth is confirmed in that God's decrees are always fulfilled. This cycle of present action because of hope in a future truth which is evidenced in the future by things not seen in the past is called "learning, even by study and also by faith" (D&C 88:118).

The circle of salvation moves by the power of love through the circle of charity, the pure love of God. God loved us first through the love of His Son (see 1 John 4:9–10, 19). By this atoning love we can receive forgiveness of sins (see Mosiah 4:2). This gift of love from God should cause us to repent and then receive, as an atoning gift of the Spirit, hearts purified with the ability to love one another with godly love (see 1 John 4:11–13, 20–21; 5:23). Then we will "always retain a remission of [our] sins" and "grow in the knowledge" of God (see Mosiah 4:12). This retained forgiveness and growing knowledge of God through brotherly love should increase our love for God and our faith in Him (see Matthew 25:40). The Apostle Paul simply described this circle of charity as, "faith which worketh by love" (Galatians 5:6).

In the Garden of Eden there was a tree of life and a river that watered the garden (Genesis 2:9–10). In John's vision of "the holy city, the new Jerusalem, coming down from God" (Revelation 21:2) there was "a pure river of water of life . . . and on either side of the river was there the tree of life" (Revelation 22:1–2). In Lehi's dream, the tree of life and the fountain of living waters both represented the love of God (see 1 Nephi 11:25). Since both the water and the tree are represented in terrestrial, telestial, and celestial realms, "could it be that the pure love of God given as a gift from him to us and then returned with full hearts back to him and to others is what brings us to eternal life and then sustains us and empowers us there?"[15]

The Scriptural Temple

If we endure in this circle of salvation, diligently seeking Christ, we will be protected from the circle or cycle of pride so repeatedly illustrated in the Book of Mormon. In spite of riches, there is no pride in the celestial kingdom. Endurance in the circles of salvation and love will spiral us upward to fully partake of the fruit of the tree of life (see Alma 5:62; Revelation 22:14) and to enter into the rest of the Lord. Then our faith in Christ will blossom into a perfect knowledge of Him and His perfect love. Thus, the Apostle Paul, implying this circle of salvation said, "and be found in him, not having mine own righteousness, which is of the law, but that which is through the faith of Christ, the righteousness which is of God by faith: That I may know him" (Philippians 3:9–10).

We learn and experience this circle of salvation in the temple as our baptisms of water and the Spirit are symbolically renewed by the ordinance of washing and anointing. The blessings of this temple baptism are contingent upon our faithfulness to Christ. This faithfulness is demonstrated by our repentance in keeping temple covenants. Then we will be sanctified or endowed with the gifts of the Spirit.

It is not only at the temple altar that the circle of salvation is revealed but also at the sacrament altar. The key words and phrases of the sacramental prayers (see D&C 20:77, 79) reveal the doctrine of Christ. The prayer "in remembrance of the body of thy Son" focuses on our bodily or mortal requirement to keep His commandments. Then the prayer "in remembrance of the blood of thy Son" or His Atonement, will have full effect upon us in filling us with the Holy Spirit. To ask God to bless and sanctify the bread and water is symbolic of asking God to bless and sanctify us, for we become what we eat but we shall not live by bread alone. We cannot become sanctified unless we completely partake of Christ's Atonement. To fully partake of Christ's Atonement we must partake of the fruit of the tree of life which is symbolized in partaking of the sacrament worthily (see Alma 5:34). This also occurs through endurance in the circle of salvation which is the doctrine of Christ.

To partake, drink, and always remember Him are expressions of our faith in Christ. To witness (see D&C 20:37) in always remembering Him is demonstration of repentance. To witness (see Mosiah

18:10) by taking Christ's name upon us in keeping His commandments starts with the covenant of baptism. Then we open the door
to always have His Spirit to be with us which implies constant companionship and gifts of the Holy Ghost.

The apostle John Widtsoe expressed the power of endowment
symbols when he said:

> No man or woman can come out of the temple endowed as they
> should be unless they have seen beyond the symbols, the mighty reali-
> ties for which they stand.[16]

In his book *Endowed From On High*, John Charles made this
significant observation, in a more personal interpretation of Elder
Widstoe's statement:

> The most meaningful insights occur when you begin to see how
> events and aspects of your own life function as signified [the personal
> meaning of symbols], to the endowment's signifiers [the symbols], i.e.
> how the endowment provides a symbolic representation of your daily
> life.[17]

As a hand surgeon, I love the symbolism of the hand found in
the temple and in many scriptural verses (see, for example, Galatians
2:9; Joseph Smith Translation, Genesis 24:8; Deuteronomy 5:15; Jeremiah 18:6; 1 Timothy 2:8; Acts 7:55; D&C 123:7). In fact, reference to the hand or its adjoining arm is found about every three to
four pages of the *scriptural temple*. As much as we admire and depend
on the "works which [God's] hands have made" (Abraham 3:21), He
admires "the beauty of the work of thine own hand" (D&C 42:40)
especially, "the work of our hands, which we have built unto thy name"
(D&C 109:78). The hand, His and ours, as Michelangelo painted in
The Creazione, is a symbol of the reality of the image in which we were
created (see Ether 3:6, 15) and the measure of our creation to create.

Perhaps a palm branch was used at the Feast of Tabernacles
during the Hosanna Shout because palm leaves take the cup-shaped
form of the palm of a hand and are extended on a long branch as
an arm. Therefore, the palm branch is symbolic of the outstretched
hand of the Lord. Like His outstretched hand that labors on our
behalf, we should "labor with [our] own hands that [we] may obtain
the confidence of men" (D&C 124:112). Appropriately, it is by the

"laying on of hands" (see D&C 20:41; 33:15) that the power of God is transmitted. The gentle yet powerful image of the outstretched hand of God is found in ending the drought at the time of the Prophet Elijah. When Elijah's servant looked to the Mediterranean Sea from Mount Carmel the seventh time, he saw a little cloud arise out of the sea, *"like a man's hand."* Then "the heaven was black with clouds and wind, and there was a great rain" (1 Kings 18:44–45). We cannot summit Mount Zion without helping hands, especially the omnipotent hands of the Lord.

The scripture with a hand symbol that is most meaningful to me is in Isaiah:

> Fear thou not; for I am with thee: be not dismayed; for I am thy God:
> I will strengthen thee; yea, I will help thee; Yea, I will uphold thee
> with the right hand of my righteousness. (Isaiah 41:10)

This is the scriptural basis for the words of a well-known hymn, "How Firm a Foundation" with the "hands of God" symbolizing the power of God (see Mormon 5:23)

In May of 1977, I began my final examinations in medical school. I already had a job in Detroit and my family was waiting for me there. All had to go well. Therefore, I prayed for a feeling of assurance that all would go well.

The Sunday before the examinations began, I went to church and sang the opening hymn "How Firm a Foundation." "Fear not, I am with thee; oh, be not dismayed," the third verse began. Suddenly the words stood out in bold, brazen type and penetrated me with such force that I could no longer sing. I listened, transfixed, as the remaining words were sung: "For I am thy God and will still give thee aid. I'll strengthen thee, help thee, and cause thee to stand, Upheld by my righteous, upheld by my righteous, upheld by my righteous, omnipotent hand." The experience was so powerful that I knew I had just received an answer to my prayers. I went to the exams with great confidence.

John Charles' observation, connecting the events of our own lives with the symbols and teachings of the endowment, results in making personal covenants with the Lord (see D&C 40:1). Because of my "How Firm a Foundation" experience, the symbolism of the "omnipotent hand" will always have deep, personal meaning for me. It draws me to the Lord to be bound to Him with covenants.

Repetition is a technique God uses to teach us. While there is repetitiveness in temple worship, it should never become banal to us. This is true because we symbolically climb Mount Zion and personally enter the Lord's presence, each time we receive the endowment. In this climb, we are symbolically taught by the Spirit. As the layers of meaning unfold to us, we will see personal application and meaning in our climb of Mount Zion. Then we should make personal covenants with the Lord and return and report to Him on our progress. As we keep the covenants, the climb becomes easier and more exciting because the Lord unfolds the great view and prepares us for His rest (see 1 Nephi 8:13–33).

The Savior's advice to those who listened to his temple sermon in the Book of Mormon can aptly be applied to us as we learn the teaching technique of symbolism in the temple:

> Therefore, go ye unto your homes, and ponder upon the things which I have said, and ask of the father, in my name, that ye may understand and prepare your minds for the morrow, and I come unto you again. (3 Nephi 17:3)

When pondering what we learn from symbols in the temple, we should correlate it to the scriptures, and to our daily lives. Like Mary, Nephi, and others, we should ponder these things in our hearts (see Luke 2:19; 1 Nephi 11:1; 2 Nephi 4:15; Helaman 10:2–3; Moroni 10:2; D&C 88:62, 71). Pondering in the heart is careful consideration of the feelings of the heart after "[giving] diligent heed to the words of eternal life" (D&C 84:43) and "[treasuring them] up in [our] minds continually" (D&C 84:85). If we ponder in our hearts, we will be taught with the spirit of revelation by the Holy Spirit. Then we will understand the meaning and application of these symbols in order to know all things that we should do to come unto Christ.

We should prepare our minds and our hearts by study, prayer, fasting, and righteous living, and then come again to the temple in company with the Spirit, eager to be taught. When we do this, the Savior will come again and draw near to us through our teacher the Holy Spirit, because He is eager to teach us.

We took sweet counsel together and walked unto the house of God in company. (Psalm 55:14)

A New Name for a New Birth in a New Marriage Covenant

Receiving a new name, the final act of initiation to equip us for the first ascent of Mount Zion, is a very personal expression of love from the Lord before He sends us on our way. I like to think it is as personal as the privilege that I have as a father and priesthood holder to name and bless my newborn children before they ascend through life. Perhaps we received a name and blessing at the hand of our Father in Heaven before descending to mortality (see Ephesians 3:14–15).

The act of renaming is a sign that we will personally enter into a new covenant relationship. A married woman understands that taking upon her the name of her husband is the sign of a new covenant relationship in her life. This custom is probably a residual practice from the renaming of Eve by Adam and then both of them taking the name of "Adam" (see Genesis 5:2) because they had united as one in the covenant of marriage. The practice of taking the name of the bridegroom extends to the spiritual marriage of Jehovah and the House of Israel, when all under this marriage covenant will be called "The Lord Our Righteousness" (see Jeremiah 23:6; 33:16) for "thy maker, *thy husband* , the Lord of Hosts is his name" (3 Nephi 22:5).

This covenant sign was even given to the children of Israel in the Sinai, who erred in their hearts as the Lord attempted to redeem them. "And they shall *put my name upon the children of Israel*; and I will bless them" (Numbers 6:27; emphasis added). It was a covenant sign given by King Benjamin to those who heard and understood his temple sermon (see Mosiah 5:7–8, 11). This sign was literally given to Oshea, named Joshua by Moses (see Numbers 13:16), as a symbolic Jesus (see Acts 7:45).

The full covenant meaning of this sign was given to our patriarch fathers such as Abraham and Jacob, and the Apostle Paul. It is significant that Jacob had to "wrestle" (struggle in the spirit, see Enos 1:2, 10; in mighty prayer, see Alma 8:10) with the Lord to get this sign. Perhaps the Apostle Paul was referring to our spiritual struggle in the temple when he said, "we wrestle not against flesh and blood, but . . . against spiritual wickedness in high places" (Ephesians 6:12). The covenant nature of this sign expresses that God will accept us as His spiritually begotten sons or daughters as we accept Him with an eye single to His glory as our God and our Father. We accept Him by accepting His Son as our Bridegroom in the oneness of a "marriage covenant" relationship. In his book *Our Father Abraham*, Marvin Wilson wrote: "To understand Biblical marriage is to understand the Biblical concept of covenant."[18]

This image of nuptial union in covenant with God is evident throughout the scriptural temple (see Genesis 1:28, 9:1, 17:5–6, 35:10–12; Leviticus 26:9). The first book in the Bible begins with a marriage covenant between God, Adam, and Eve. The last book in the Bible ends with a marriage covenant between Christ and His church. God's desire is to espouse us to Himself forever (see Hosea 2:19–20). The "great mystery" of this nuptial union to produce the powers of pure love was expressed by the Apostle Paul (see Ephesians 5:25–33).

In the temple, we symbolically enact a "marriage covenant" relationship with God, when we receive a new name, in anticipation of a future naming by the Lord Himself:

Even unto them will I give in mine house . . . a name . . . I will give them an everlasting name, that shall not be cut off. (Isaiah 56:5)

And the gentiles shall see thy righteousness, and all kings thy glory: and thou shalt be called by a new name which the mouth of the Lord shall name. (Isaiah 62:2)

Him that overcometh will I make a pillar in the temple of my God. . . . And I will write upon him my new name. (Revelation 3:12)

Through this temple covenant we "[obtain] a more excellent name" (Hebrews 1:4). In his great temple sermon at Zarahemla, King Benjamin gave to the people gathered by the temple a new name to distinguish them as a righteous, covenant people. As in a marriage covenant, it was a name that could only be removed by infidelity:

> And moreover, I shall give this people a name, that thereby they may be distinguished above all the people which the Lord God hath brought out of the land of Jerusalem; and this I do because they have been a diligent people in keeping the commandments of the Lord.
>
> And I give unto them a name that never shall be blotted out, except it be through transgression. (Mosiah 1:11–12)

At the end of his sermon, King Benjamin revealed the name as though he were revealing the bridegroom for whom the betrothed people were anxiously awaiting:

> Therefore, I would that ye should take upon you the name of Christ, all you that have entered into the covenant with God that ye should be obedient unto the end of your lives.
>
> And it shall come to pass that whosoever doeth this shall be found at the right hand of God, for he shall know the name by which he is called; for he shall be called by the name of Christ.
>
> And I would that ye should remember also, that this is the name that I said I should give unto you that never should be blotted out, except it be through transgression. . . .
>
> I say unto you, I would that ye should remember to retain the name written always in your hearts, . . . that ye hear and know the voice by which ye shall be called, and also, the name by which he shall call you. (Mosiah 5:8–9, 11–12)

We can get lost in our ascent of Mount Zion unless we know the voice of the Lead Climber.

When Alma, who was asked to judge the "rising generation" (Mosiah 26:1) of those children who could not understand and then who would not believe the words of King Benjamin, he inquired of the Lord. When the Lord said to Alma "they are mine" (see Mosiah 26:18; Moses 1:37), he was reminded of the close "marriage covenant" relationship that those who bear the name of Christ have with Him. When a disciple diligently pleads the cause of the Lord as His helpmeet, then the Lord "will accept of his offerings . . . for *he shall be mine*, saith the Lord" (D&C 124:75; emphasis added). This is the same possessive expression the Lord used when He established and will establish a covenant relationship as "the time of love" with the House of Israel (see Ezekiel 16:8).

In giving our hearts to Christ by accepting His covenants, He becomes our bridegroom and we become his bride. We who keep His covenants are not only the bride of Christ, but through the travail of the Atonement (see Isaiah 42:14; John 16:21; John 17:1; Alma 7:11–12) we can become his spiritually begotten children (see Isaiah 53:10; Mosiah 15:10–14). Thus, a spiritual family is created. King Benjamin taught that entering into and keeping covenants with Christ to change our hearts is how we become the children of Christ:

> And now, because of the covenant which ye have made ye shall be called the children of Christ, his sons and his daughters; for behold, this day he hath spiritually begotten you; for ye say that your hearts are changed through faith on his name; therefore, ye are born of him and have become his sons and his daughters. (Mosiah 5:7; see also D&C 5:16)

The Meaning of Taking the Name of Christ upon Us

When we become the new bride and the new sons and daughters of Christ, we receive a new name. It is His name. Weekly we are reminded of this new name as we listen to the sacrament prayer: "And witness unto thee, O God, the Eternal Father, that they are willing to take upon them the name of thy Son" (Moroni 4:3).

At the sacrament altar we make a covenant to take Christ's name upon us. This covenant is a weekly renewal of the baptismal covenant in which we willingly take upon us the name of Jesus Christ by witnessing before the church our true repentance (compare D&C 20:37, 77). For "if ye believe on his name ye will repent of all your sins, that thereby ye may have a remission of them through his merits" (Helaman 14:13).

The most significant word of the sacramental prayers and the baptismal covenant is *witness* (see Mosiah 18:9–10). This word implies action on our part by "witnessing unto the Father" (see 2 Nephi 31:13), "[witnessing] before the church" (D&C 20:37), and witnessing to the world that we carry or "bear" Christ's name (see Mosiah 26:18) in our actions. *The action required is emulation of the actions of Christ by abiding in Him* (see John 15:4). To abide in Him is to "walk the talk," as expressed in the current vernacular, "in thy daily walk even unto the end of thy life" (D&C 19:32; see also Galatians 5:25). It is "to walk, even as He walked" (1 John 2:6). It is to "walk in His ways" (Deuteronomy 30:16) and "confess Him" not fearing to be "put out of the synagogue" or desiring "the praise of men more than the praise of God" (John 12:42–43). The Lord is "well pleased" when we "abideth in [Him]" (see D&C 97:3).

It is significant that Moroni asked the very Christian world of our day the following question: "Why are ye ashamed to take upon you the name of Christ?" (Mormon 8:38). When traditions, fear, and praise of men are removed from our hearts, so is the shame that prevents us from fully taking upon us the name of Christ in the fulness of His gospel.

Regardless of environmental or social pressures, it is not sufficient to just do the expected or the customary. We must do the right thing even though it is often unexpected. Emulating the Savior is being a good Samaritan and being so "unto the least of these my brethren" (Matthew 25:40). It is being able to say "if it were not so I would have told you" (John 14:2). It is to "render therefore unto Caesar the things which are Caesar's and unto God the things that are God's" (Matthew 22:21). It is overcoming sin with both justice and mercy through repentance and forgiveness (see John 8:7, 10–11). It is to have such great love for others, "that a man lay down his life for his friends" (John 15:13).

By these actions, performed with a broken heart and contrite spirit, we keep the sacrament covenant and thus partake of it worthily. This sacrament covenant prepares and reminds us to keep temple covenants that we "do always remember Him." Witnessing such that "the name of the Lord Jesus [is] magnified" (Acts 19:17) by our righteous actions and His power, comes as a blessing for keeping temple covenants.

Bearing the Name of Christ Starts with a Seed Planted in the Heart

Before we can take the name of Christ upon us and be called "the people of The Lord" we must first "hear the word of the Lord and His will concerning [us]," listening with an "ear from afar" and with "open hearts" (see D&C 63:1) in order to understand His word.

It is no wonder then, that the Savior was disturbed at the dispute amongst the Nephites concerning the name of their church. In the great Sermon on the Temple Mount, He taught the sacramental covenant. In addition, King Benjamin's temple sermon must have been part of the scriptures these Nephites had in their possession. Therefore, the Savior reminded them that taking His name upon them is a matter of endurance with an eye single to His word and glory when He said:

> Have they not read the scriptures which say ye must take upon you the name of Christ, which is my name? For by this name shall ye be called at the last day.
>
> And whoso taketh upon him my name, and endureth to the end, the same shall be saved at the last day. (3 Nephi 27:56)

In his teachings, Alma explained that taking the name of Christ upon us is not just believing in Him, but also, it is believing on His word by understanding and believing them and acting in accordance with this belief: "And now, behold, I say unto you, and I would that ye should remember, that God is merciful unto all who *believe on his name* ; therefore he desireth, in the first place, that ye should *believe, yea, even on his word* . . . if ye will awake and arouse your faculties, even to an *experiment upon my words*" (Alma 32:22, 27; emphasis added).

The experiment or action will work if His words are mixed with our faith (see Hebrews 4:2). The measure of our faith is the willingness of our hearts to receive God's gifts of love. In order to redeem us to His presence, God desires to reveal all His knowledge and share all the power of His love with us if we diligently seek Him with "faith on the Son of God" (see 1 Nephi 9:6; 10:17–22; 15:11).

Faith on the Son of God by obedience to His word corresponds to the principles of faith as taught by the Prophet Joseph Smith. The first principle he taught is **our action**, then comes **power from God** (see Mosiah 29:19–20), and finally **faith unto life and salvation**. This final faith is tested by requiring the sacrifice of all earthly things for us to know that our action is according to God's will.[19]

In this experiment, we should remember that even if we do not have enough "faith to be healed" (D&C 46:19) to cure our physical infirmities, faith on the name of Christ by "[diligence] in keeping all [God's] commandments" (D&C 136:42) is enough to cure our spiritual infirmities (see D&C 42:52). Without simple but diligent obedience (see Exodus 15:25–26) to God's commandments, our faith will fail because our enemies will triumph over us (see D&C 136:42) in destroying our faith. We should be sensitive to the "swelling motions" (Alma 32:28) of this obedient faith as our "souls [do] expand" to loosen "the bands of death" (Alma 5:9). Then comes the "change of heart" (Alma 5:7, 26) of a spiritual rebirth.

Just believing in Christ's words is not enough. We must also receive Christ's words by doing them. "If you believe all these things see that ye do them" (Mosiah 4:10) and "remember all [God's] commandments *to execute them*" (Alma 18:10; emphasis added). As many who "prepare [their] minds . . . and their hearts to receive the word" (Alma 16:16), "and doeth it, the same [are received by Christ as] my disciple" (see D&C 41:5). "For according to that which they do they shall receive" (D&C 56:13). "Prepare the way for the commandments and revelations which are to come. Whoso readeth, let him understand and receive also" (D&C 71:4–5). When we "receive [Christ's] will concerning [us]" (D&C 88:1) and obey it out of love, we have truly received Christ. For "whosoever receiveth my word receiveth me" (D&C 112:20). While it is believing Christ's words, which often come from His disciples, that we believe in Him (see Ether 4:10, 12), *true belief on Christ's name is receiving Christ.*

We must also receive Christ's disciples to receive Him (see Matthew 10:40; Alma 8:24; 3 Nephi 28:34; D&C 75:19; 84:88; 90:5). Implied in this receiving is a relationship of caring support (see D&C 84:89). In receiving Christ's words "which are my voice" (see D&C 84:60), it is important to recognize and receive the authoritative voice that pronounces them. If Christ's voice comes to us from a true messenger of God, especially the Holy Spirit, "contend no more against the Holy Ghost, but that ye receive it, and take upon you the name of Christ;" (Alma 34:38), because "whoso receiveth not my voice is not acquainted with my voice, and is not of me (D&C 84:52; 133:71). Those who "received not the testimony of Jesus in the flesh" still must "afterwards [receive] it" (D&C 76:74) to be saved with some degree of glory. What is the difference between just believing and receiving in light of Christ's repeated statement "mine own received me not" (D&C 11:29; 88:48; 133:66; John 1:11)?

Consider Christ's discourse on how to come unto Him to receive Him (see 3 Nephi 9:13–14, 16–17, 20–22; 11:37–38; 12:23–24). Christ's initial challenge to receive Him is to change our carnal nature and become as a little child (see Matthew 18:4–5) with such an heart to receive. "And who receiveth . . . as a little child, receiveth my kingdom" (D&C 99:3). This requires the actions of humility, repentance, and "faith on the name of the Lord" (see Mosiah 3:21). Then Christ will receive us (see Alma 5:33; 3 Nephi 9:22) because in the condition of humility and faith we realize, as a little child before parents, that "a man can receive nothing except it be given him from heaven" (John 3:27).

Those who are faithfully "believing on his name" continue to receive Him by taking up His cross, following Him, and keeping His commandments (see D&C 56:2). This continued reception produces a change of heart. "These are they that shall have eternal life, and salvation cometh to none else" (Alma 11:40). For "he that receiveth [Christ] shall be saved" (D&C 49:5). The "faith on His name" to receive Christ and be called "the children of Christ" (see Mosiah 5:7), "my sons and my daughters" (see Ether 3:14), requires receiving His gospel. "The gospel is unto all who have not received it" (D&C 84:75). It is revealed to them "as fast as [they] are able to receive [it]" (D&C 111:11) or as fast as they "prepare [their] heart to receive and obey" (D&C 132:3).

Receiving the gospel requires making covenants with Christ and remaining faithful to them "unto the end of [our] lives" (see Mosiah 5:8). Receiving God by covenant is an important temple teaching. A valid covenant with God always requires priesthood authority and ordinances. The covenant in the ordinance of baptism is how we initially take Christ's name upon us (see Mosiah 25:23) in believing on His name to receive Him. The covenant of baptism starts the process of being born again because "all those who receive my gospel are sons and daughters in my kingdom" (D&C 25:1). Then, to continue the process, we must "receive the Holy Ghost" (see D&C 84:64) "whom the world cannot receive" (John 14:17). "He that receiveth my gospel receiveth me" (see D&C 39:5–6) as the father of their spiritual rebirth.

"My gospel" also means receiving the fulness of Christ's priesthood. This means to "receive the consecrations of mine house" (D&C 124:21) or "receive their endowment from on high in my house" (D&C 105:33) to receive Him (see D&C 84:35). Through the temple endowment, we receive a fulness of the Holy Ghost (see D&C 109:15) in preparation to receive the fulness of Christ. "And inasmuch as they do repent and receive the fulness of my gospel, and become sanctified . . . they that receive these things receive me;" (D&C 39:18, 22; see D&C 88:68). To receive the fulness of Christ is ultimately to receive His presence in the great and last promise of the temple. They who receive not the fulness of Christ "shall return again to their own place, to enjoy that which they are willing to receive, because they were not willing to enjoy that which they might have received" (D&C 88:32). "Wo be unto him that saith: We have received, and we need no more" (2 Nephi 28:27).

As a man and a women promise to receive each other in a state of oneness at the altar of the Holy Order of Matrimony, receiving Christ's fulness is equivalent to becoming one with Christ and the Father. "Inasmuch as ye have received me, ye are in me and I in you" (D&C 50:43). "Behold, thou art one in me, a son of God; and thus may all become my sons. Amen" (Moses 6:67; see Moses 8:13). To fully receive Christ as one in our house we must fully receive Him in His house. There we receive Him in a marriage covenant.

In this process of receiving Christ, we must "[believe] in the power of Jesus Christ" (D&C 11:10). He "taught and gave them power" (D&C 138:51) such that "as many as receive me give I power to do many miracles, and to become the sons of God; and . . . to obtain eternal life" (D&C 45:8; 39:4; John 1:12). By faith in Christ's power, we are given His gifts to help us make the mighty change of heart— "born of him . . . his sons and daughters" (Mosiah 5:7), to become exalted sons and daughters of God (see John 1:12; 3 Nephi 9:17; D&C 25:1). When Christ receives us and we continue to receive Him by keeping all His commandments and covenants, we are given the power to become like Him (see 3 Nephi 27:27; 28:10; D&C 132:23–24) because we "receive of his fulness and of his grace" (D&C 76:94). "For unto him that receiveth it shall be given more abundantly, even power" (D&C 71:6). With the power of this mighty change, we can "come unto the Father in Christ's name, and in due time receive of his fulness" (D&C 93:19; see also 93:20; 76:20), "all that [the] Father hath" (see D&C 84:37–38), as we come to know the Father. As Christ received the fulness of His Father, grace for grace (see D&C 93:12–13) while in the world (see D&C 93:5), we can receive the same fulness if we receive the commandments of Christ (see D&C 93:27). For "in nothing do [we] sin save in those things which [we] received not of [Christ]" (D&C 132:38). When we receive Christ we receive the power, path, and pitons (covenants) to reach the summit of Mount Zion.

Alma compared the word of Christ to a seed planted or received in the heart (see Alma 32:28; 33:23). This seed will then grow so that we "*feel* these swelling motions" (Alma 32:28). This growth enlightens our understanding until we can say "it beginneth to be delicious to me" (Alma 32:28). Once we experiment upon the word by keeping commandments and covenants and feel the "swelling within our breasts" and "taste the light" (Alma 32:35), then we must "press forward, feasting upon the word of Christ" (2 Nephi 31:20) and "upon his love" (see Jacob 3:2). This is "[pressing] toward the mark for the high calling of God" (Philippians 3:14).

We partake of the fruit of the tree of life by feasting upon and obeying all the words and covenants of Christ in His holy order. This is how we are received by Him (see Alma 7:22). Then His name will be written always in our hearts (see Mosiah 5:12) by the covenants of the heart that we keep with Him. Alma even reasoned that if we plant the seed of His word in our hearts and nourish it, it will "take root in you" and "become a tree springing up unto everlasting life" (see Alma 32:40–42). Therefore, we can grow a tree of life within us and ultimately become like the Savior, by taking His name upon us.

In a spiritually literal sense, the seed planted in our hearts is the Son. The Word of God is the Son of God for "he was the Word, even the messenger of salvation" (D&C 93:8). A seed will produce a tree of life within us if it is a "true seed" (Alma 32:28) of the tree of life. A true seed of the tree of life has the power to produce eternal life and continuation of the seeds of eternal lives. Because of His divine sonship and infinite Atonement, the Son is the true seed. He is the "incorruptible seed" from which we are born again (see 1 Peter 1:23). He is the "holy seed [that is] the substance" (Isaiah 6:13) of all other true seeds. He, as the true, incorruptible, and holy seed, grows a "life which is endless" by a "light that is endless" (see Mosiah 16:9). We cannot plant the philosophies of men even mingled with the word of God and expect to grow a tree of life within us. Therefore, we must find the true, incorruptible, and holy seed of the tree of life and receive or plant it within us.

In its early growth, as we experiment upon the word with patience, diligence and faith, demonstrating obedience to commandments, the young tree of life within us will "bring forth therefore, fruits worthy of repentance" (see Luke 3:8; Alma 34:30). The taste of the fruits of repentance makes us want to taste more of the tree of life. We taste more of the tree of life by doing "that which is meet in mine eyes, and which I commanded them" (D&C 121:16). This obedience "brings forth fruit and works meet for my kingdom" (D&C 101:100). Otherwise, we are "not meet for a kingdom of glory" (D&C 88:24).

We take the name of Christ upon us through baptism. The action of this baptismal covenant opens the door to baptism of fire by the Holy Spirit, which baptism produces in our personal tree of life, fruits of the Spirit (see Galatians 5:18, 22–23). Therefore, the gift for faithfully keeping the words of Christ to plant them in our hearts is "the manifestations of my Spirit" (see Ether 4:11) or the gifts of the Spirit.

We then realize that the fruits "meet" or worthy of repentance (see Moroni 6:1) and the fruits of the Spirit come from the spiritual growth we experience in keeping ordinances and covenants with the Son of God (see Alma 13:13–16). His Atonement affords the gifts of the Spirit that we might become His spiritually begotten seed in the circle of salvation through His covenants (see 2 Nephi 30:2). This is how we plant the true and holy seed or the Son of God within us. As we continue to keep more covenants, especially temple covenants, our nature changes by the sanctifying power of the Spirit until the fruit produced by the tree of life within us truly becomes "delicious" or "fruit meet for their Father's Kingdom" (D&C 84:58).

The Temple Blessings for Taking
Christ's Name upon Us

Taking the name of Christ upon us in the sacrament covenant prepares us to fully feast upon the "hidden manna" (Revelation 2:17) in
the temple. This bread of life in the temple will nourish our own tree of
life if we bind and then graft ourselves to the tree of life of the temple.
By receiving His word with joy (see Alma 16:17) through temple covenants, we bind and graft to Christ. In keeping them, we grow straight
to produce much fruit: "I am the vine," the Savior said, "ye are the
branches: He that abideth in me, and I in him, the same bringeth forth
much fruit: for without me ye can do nothing" (John 15:5).

When we are bound and grafted by covenant to Christ we become
His spiritual covenant offspring (see D&C 5:14). To be "born again"
(see 1 Peter 1:23) by Christ is to become, by His gift and power, new
creatures with His virtues of faith, hope, and charity. Without these
qualities we can do nothing (see D&C 18:19) and receive nothing
(see John 3:27) to partake of the fulness of His Atonement. Therefore, without Christ we are nothing (see Mosiah 4:11). As His spiritual "branches" we can bring forth much spiritual fruit when His
grace and power abide in us. This was symbolically witnessed in the
temple when Moses found the rod (branch) of Aaron covered with
buds, blossoms, and almonds (see Numbers 17). Today, all who graft
to Christ in His holy house can blossom with His spiritual gifts.

Through temple covenants, we first "grow" as spiritual "newborn
babes" by the "milk of the word" (1 Peter 2:2), building upon the
"living stone" (1 Peter 2:4). Then as spiritual "lively stones . . . [we]
are built up a spiritual house, an holy priesthood to offer spiritual
sacrifices" (1 Peter 2:5). Finally we are built up as a "pillar [king or
queen] in the temple" (Revelation 3:12) and in the "kingdom of
heaven to go no more out" (Alma 7:25; see also 2 Kings 11:14; 2
Kings 23:3; Alma 29:17; Helaman 3:30; 3 Nephi 28:40).

The temple is the place appointed by the Savior where He "will
plant [us]" to become His branches. As we are edified by His word
and build upon His rock, we become as temples, a "spiritual house,"
"to dwell in a place of our own," to escape "the children of wickedness,"
"[to] move no more" (see 2 Samuel 7:10) and "to not be moved out of

[our] place" (D&C 124:45). There "the devil and his armies . . . shall not have power over the saints any more at all" (D&C 88:114). In the temple we become the branches of an eternal family.

It is in the temple we truly learn how to take Christ's name upon us because His name is written in the temple: "In all places where I record my name I will come unto thee, and I will bless thee" (Exodus 20:24), "that no combination of wickedness shall have power to rise up and prevail over thy people upon whom thy name shall be put in this house" (D&C 109:26).

In the temple we can fully take the name of Christ upon us because there, both men and women can receive the powerful blessings of the fulness of the Priesthood in His Holy Order. This is what Abraham learned when he left the Chaldeans: "Behold, I will lead thee by my hand, and I will take thee, to put upon thee my name, even the Priesthood of thy father, and my power shall be over thee" (Abraham 1:18). Then Abraham's name was made great in that all who "receive this Gospel shall be called after thy name, and shall be accounted thy seed," and that all the families of the earth would be blessed through the power of the Priesthood (see Abraham 2:9–11).

In the temple we learn that the covenants we make with Christ will be valid covenants with the Father. Taking upon us the name of Christ and remaining true to His name ultimately leads to taking upon us the name of the Father with the "Father's name written" upon us (see Revelation 14:1; 22:4) through His priesthood. Elder Bruce R. McConkie exclaimed the ultimate meaning of taking upon us the name of God when he said, "To have his name written on a person is to identify that person as a god. How can it be said more plainly? Those who gain eternal life become gods!"[20]

As we become sealed to our Heavenly Father through our spiritual rebirth by His Son, the Father gives us a new name as a token of this sealing because we have become new creatures (see Isaiah 62:2; Revelation 3:12):

> Then the white stone mentioned in Revelation 2:17, will become a Urim and Thummim to each individual who receives one, whereby things pertaining to a higher order of kingdoms will be made known;
>
> And a white stone is given to each of those who come into the celestial kingdom, whereon is a new name written, which no man

knoweth save he that receiveth it. The new name is the key word. (D&C 130:10–11)

Apparently, learning how to take upon us the name of Christ is the key to that key word, a new name that will unlock the knowledge of "a higher order of kingdoms." This is why Joseph Smith said:

Knowledge through our Lord and Savior Jesus Christ is the grand key that unlocks the glories and mysteries of the kingdom of heaven.[21]

Therefore, it is critical that we "receive the word with joy and as a branch be grafted into the true vine" (Alma 16:17). We graft to Christ, the true vine, when "we come to the knowledge of the true Messiah" (see 1 Nephi 10:14) and are "converted unto the Lord" (His stature and His words), learning how to take His name upon us. This "grafting in" occurs by first binding to Christ with faith in Him demonstrated by obedience to His word. Then by continual holding fast to His word (see 1 Nephi 8:30) when our faith is tested, we will grow as His grafted offspring in the bond of charity which is the bond of perfectness (see D&C 88:125). This perfect bond, "perfect in one" (John 17:23), will be sealed as an eternal "compound in one" (see 2 Nephi 2:11). No compound becomes an eternal compound in one unless Christ is part of it (see Ephesians 2:15–16).

We learn through the naming process of the endowment that while we maintain our identity, we must enter into a new covenant relationship with God symbolized by a new name (see Isaiah 44:5). This new name is valid to receive the fulness of the Father only if we take the name of His Son upon us by grafting to Him because "God also hath highly exalted him, and given him a name which is above every name" (Philippians 2:9). Being grafted to Christ is the only way that we will "never fall away" (see Alma 23:6) nor be "hewn down" (see Jacob 5:66) as dead branches. It is the only way that we will not become dead trees with "neither root nor branch" (Malachi 4:1; D&C 109:52) meaning without ancestry or posterity. "For he remembereth the house of Israel, both roots and branches" (Jacob 6:4) to "[preserve] the roots and branches of the first fruit" (Jacob 5:60). The fruit of this grafting is that "signs [gifts of the Spirit and powers of the Priesthood] shall follow them that believe in my name" even that they "be lifted up to dwell in the kingdom prepared for [them] from the foundation of the world" (Ether 4:19; see also Mormon 9:24–25). There we will dwell in the fruits of a preserved ancestry and everlasting posterity because we are grafted to the First Fruit.

The profundity of taking the name of Christ upon us is captured in the following verses:

> Behold, Jesus Christ is the name which is given of the Father, and there is no other name which is given of the Father whereby man can be saved;
>
> Wherefore, all men must take upon them the name which is given of the Father, for in that name shall they be called at the last day;
>
> Wherefore, if they know not the name by which they are called, they cannot have place in the kingdom of my Father. (D&C 18:23–25)

"In that name," and "upon whom [that] name shall be put in this house" (D&C 109:26) is the power to realize a calling and election to exaltation.

The New and Everlasting Covenant: A Covenant of the Heart

To be equipped to climb Mount Zion and understand the great endowment we must understand the nature of covenants with the Lord. We have already learned one aspect of the nature of His covenants. They bind us to Him with a personal, trusting relationship like a marriage covenant. To be "without God in the world" is to be without His "covenants of promise" (see Ephesians 2:12). *Such covenants are necessary to protect holiness and intimacy so pure love that really binds can grow.* Therefore, because of their love for each other, Jonathan and David made a covenant (see 1 Samuel 18:3). As we learn in the temple, keeping covenants with the Lord protects us from the power of Satan. We need this protection because Satan's power depletes and destroys the power of love by depleting and destroying agency.

When our covenants with others and the Lord are such that "the Lord be between thee and me for ever" (1 Samuel 20:23), then we understand Abigail as a type of Christ between David and her husband Nabal (see 1 Samuel 25). As Abigail said to David, "the soul of my lord shall be bound in the bundle of life with the Lord thy God" (1 Samuel 25:29), it is the power of pure love from the Atonement of Christ, activated by solemn covenants with Him, that causes us to be bound in the bundle of eternal life.

The Lord taught that strict obedience to the commandments of God, by sacrifice of all earthly things, is how we must keep covenants and therefore obtain the keys to the knowledge of eternal life:

> Verily I say unto you, all among them who know their hearts are honest, and are broken, and their spirits contrite, and are willing to *observe their covenants by sacrifice*—yea, every sacrifice which I, the Lord, shall command they are accepted of me. (D&C 97:8)

Joseph Smith reaffirmed this scripture when he said, "If a man would obtain the keys of the kingdom of an endless life, he must sacrifice all things."[22]

Under the law of Moses, the main covenant principle taught was making and keeping covenants by sacrifice (see Psalm 50:5). Animal sacrifice was not only symbolic of the sacrifice of Jesus Christ, but it also symbolized the sacrifice of the beastlike or "carnal nature" (Mosiah 16:5) of each person who promised to keep the covenants in order to be sanctified. The Latin roots of the word sacrifice are *sacer* (sacred) and *facere* (to make) that together mean "to make sacred." *Sacrifice for others is the foundation of pure love.* Sacrifice of selfish individual rights for higher collective rights (such as marriage, family, and community) is the law of God. Satan's law sacrifices higher blessings for selfish, supposed individual rights. Today, the higher blessings of traditional marriage are being sacrificed for individual rights.

The eternal laws of sacrifice are intimately linked to the eternal laws of love. Therefore, Christ and "Adam fell that men might be and men are that they might have joy" (see 2 Nephi 2:25). Adam and Eve fell in love, or sacrificed for and committed to love each other, that their children might be happy. In 2 Nephi 2:25 are the principles of the plan of salvation and happiness. Sacrifice for others out of love brings salvation and happiness, even a fulness of joy in the bonds of pure love. Keeping temple covenants by sacrifice, as we will see, leads to the sacredness of pure love.

It is instructive that the covenant of circumcision given to Abraham had, as its token, a sacrifice of blood and flesh in the organ that produces seed to create physical life (see Joseph Smith Translation, Genesis 17:3–7, 11–12). As women already know that bodily sacrifice is necessary to produce the fruits of love, circumcision symbolizes this truth to men. The token of circumcision is a sign of the sacrifice that needs to happen to the organ where the seeds of spiritual rebirth germinate. This organ is the heart that must have "the circumcision made without hands in putting off the body of the sins of the flesh by the circumcision of Christ" (Colossians 2:11). By this circumcision, the hardness of the heart is sacrificed and it is broken open to spiritual rebirth (see 3 Nephi 9:20; Deuteronomy 10:16). As the Apostle Paul instructed, true circumcision is "that of the heart" meaning "in the spirit" (see Romans 2:25–29). When the heart is broken of pride and opened such that "the Holy Ghost may have place in their hearts . . . after this manner bringeth to pass the Father, the covenants which he hath made unto the children of men" (Moroni 7:32).

To those who do not sacrifice the pride in their hearts, the Prophet Nephi said, "O ye fools, ye uncircumcised of heart, ye blind, and ye stiffnecked people" (Helaman 9:21). Stiffneckedness is a physical manifestation of a proud, uncircumcised heart. A stiff neck cannot look up to God, nor down in humility, nor sideways to see others.

In reference to making covenants with the Lord by taking His name upon us, it is interesting that King Benjamin stated that we "retain the name always written in our hearts" (Mosiah 5:12). This significant statement refers to the type of temple covenants that we keep with the Lord. Except to reflect the everlasting nature of the covenant, they are not carnal covenants written on stone. They are not stone-cold business contracts. They are spiritual covenants based on the principles of pure love. They are made with our spirits—our true hearts—to be understood in this carnal world. Therefore, they are covenants written by "the spirit of the living God; in the fleshy tables of the heart" (2 Corinthians 3:3) as the Holy Spirit carries them unto our hearts (see 2 Nephi 33:1). Notice that understanding God's covenants through the scriptures is a heart to heart matter, for God said, "the scriptures shall be given, even as they are *in mine own bosom*, to the salvation of mine own elect" (D&C 35:20; emphasis added). Such was the case of the Prophet Joseph Smith who declared in reference to the old and new covenants of the Bible, "I have the oldest book in my heart, even the gift of the Holy Ghost."[23]

If our proud hearts are not sacrificed by circumcision of pride, then they are not receptive to be written on by the Holy Spirit (see Acts 7:51). To retain the name of Jesus Christ always written in our hearts is to always retain in remembrance the greatness of God (Mosiah 4:11) and to "always retain a remission [our] sins" because our hearts are "filled with the love of God" (Mosiah 4:12).

When the Prophet Abinadi asked the priests of King Noah: "Are ye priests, and pretend to teach this people, and to understand the spirit of prophesying, and yet desire to know of me what these things mean?" (Mosiah 12:25), and "If ye teach the law of Moses why do ye not keep it? Why do you set your hearts upon riches?" (Mosiah 12:29), he was confirming that they did not apply their hearts to understanding (see Mosiah 12:27). Therefore, the law of Moses was not written in their hearts (see Mosiah 13:11). To understand and properly live the law of Moses it was necessary to have this law written in one's heart or spiritual self. In order to have a spiritual understanding and perspective of this law, it was necessary to soften one's heart by sacrifice (see Mosiah 13:32). Then it could be applied to understanding by the influence and teachings of the Spirit which is "the spirit of prophesying" and revelation. This is how the laws and covenants of God are written in our hearts. Then we understand, as Abinadi said, the "types of things to come" (Mosiah 13:31) by understanding Christ with His name and covenants written in our hearts by the power of the Holy Spirit.

To those under the law of Moses, the Lord prophesied concerning "this manner" of covenants: "Behold, the days come saith the Lord, that I will make a *new covenant* with the House of Israel. . . . I will put my law in their inward parts and *write it in their hearts*" (Jeremiah 31:31, 33; emphasis added). The "days" came when Christ came to the earth, making possible the new and everlasting covenant through the Atonement. This new covenant is contained in the Sermon on the Mount and the Sermon on the Temple Mount. Their core doctrine is a transformation of the heart by making covenants with Christ through His holy ordinances that we might be prepared to meet God. Perhaps, as emphasized in all four Gospels and the Book of Mormon, this is why Christ consistently taught and performed at the temple. There He directed our attention to this holy place where we will find His sanctifying power through the Holy Spirit (see Matthew 12:6; 3 Nephi 27:20) for the mighty change of heart. This change occurs when Christ's name and covenants are written in our hearts.

Christ's message at "His Father's House" that disturbed so many meridian Jews and led to His crucifixion (see Matthew 27:40) was the same message that caused other Israelites to kill the prophets and the Saints (see 1 Nephi 1:19–20; Mosiah 7:26–28; 17:78; 24:11; 3 Nephi 1:9; Moroni 1:2). In reality, those who murdered (see Alma 36:14) became as Satan seeking to "destroy the tree with the fruit thereof . . . that [Christ's] name may be no more remembered" (Jeremiah 11:19). They fulfilled the will of Satan because:

> Satan got possession of the hearts of the people . . . insomuch that he did blind their eyes and lead them away to believe that the doctrine of Christ was a foolish and a vain thing. (3 Nephi 2:2)

The doctrine of Christ included the end of the Mosaic temple order by changing it to the "Melchizedek" temple order as His holy order. This change required not only proper priesthood authority, but also ordinances of holiness and covenants of the heart, not just outward acts of the hand (see Hosea 6:12, 67). If there are "outward ordinances" for the body such as baptism (see D&C 107:20), there are inward ordinances for the spirit or the heart. These ordinances are by "the power and authority of the higher or Melchizedek Priesthood (which) is to hold the keys of all the spiritual blessings of the church" (D&C 107:18). The fulness of these blessings is found in the ordinances of the temple when God's laws and covenants are written in our hearts. This new (original) temple order and everlasting covenant, was based on the power and grace of the Atonement. The sanctifying (see 3 Nephi 27:20) and confirming (see Mormon 9:25) power of the Holy Spirit in the temple of our body is by the power of the Atonement (see 3 Nephi 28:11; John 7:39). Therefore, the sacrifice of the temple of Christ's body was necessary to release the powers of His holy order, including the fulness of the power of the Holy Spirit in this fallen world for the salvation and exaltation of man. Thus, Christ truly came to fulfill the law of the gospel, including the law of Moses (see Alma 34:13–14) by providing the power for salvation and exaltation.

Paul and the early Christian Saints understood this new covenant and temple order.

> Now of the things which we have spoken [the new temple order] this is the sum: We have such an high priest, who is set on the right hand of the throne of the Majesty in the heavens;
>
> A minister of the sanctuary, and of the *true tabernacle*, which the Lord pitched and not man.
>
> But now hath he obtained a more excellent ministry, by how much also *he is the mediator of a better covenant*, which was established upon *better promises*.
>
> For if that first covenant had been faultless, then should no place have been sought for the second.
>
> For finding fault with them, he saith, Behold, the days come, saith the Lord, when I will make a *new covenant* with the house of Israel and with the house of Judah:
>
> Not according to the covenant that I made with their fathers in the day when I took them by the hand to lead them out of the land of Egypt; because *they continued not in my covenant*, [the first covenant] and I regarded them not, saith the Lord.
>
> *For this is the covenant* [the new covenant] that I will make with the house of Israel after those days, saith the Lord; *I will put my laws into their mind, and write them in their hearts*: and I will be to them a God, and they shall be to me a people. (Hebrews 8:12, 6–10; emphasis added)

The "new covenants" that we receive in the Melchizedek Priesthood temples today are not the schoolmaster Mosaic laws that lead us to Christ. They are the spiritual covenant laws of Christ (see Romans 7:14; D&C 29:35) with which He leads us to the Father:

> I give unto you these sayings that you may understand and know *how to worship,* and know what you worship, *that you may come unto the Father in my name,* and in due time receive of his fulness.
>
> For if you keep my commandments you shall receive of his fulness, and be *glorified in me as I am in the Father.* (D&C 93:19–20; emphasis added)

> I am the Lord thy God; and I give unto you this commandment—
> that *no man shall come unto the Father but by me or by my word*, which is
> my law, saith the Lord. (D&C 132:12; emphasis added)

As John Charles said, the covenants of the temple "penetrate to the core of how we will live our life."[24] They take our faith to the threshold of spiritual decision: *How much are we willing to sacrifice to become holy?* How much carnal are we willing to sacrifice for the spiritual? Therefore they are spiritual covenants to be understood by the mind and the heart. "I command you again to build a house to my name, even in this place, that you may prove yourselves unto me that ye are faithful in all things whatsoever I command you, that I may bless you, and crown you with honor, immortality, and eternal life" (D&C 124:55).

Our relationship with the Lord is developed through covenants. Psalm 25:14 points out: "The secret of the Lord is with them that fear him; and he will shew them his covenant." Then "[He] will prove [them] in all things, whether [they] will abide in [His] covenant, even unto death, that [they] may be found worthy" (D&C 98:14). Without covenants, God could not fulfill His promise to bless His people because a covenant "binds" God to us (see D&C 82:10) and us to Him in a marriage bond of loving commitment while maintaining the law of agency. To covenant with God is the first step in our obedience to Him with real intent. Specifically, the Lord counsels us to "prepare and organize [ourselves] by a bond or everlasting covenant that cannot be broken" (D&C 78:11) except by transgression that warrants the judgment of God (see D&C 82:11).

A covenant is a commitment to self-sacrifice for the higher principles of love. A covenant binds us together by the power of love. Keeping a covenant is the ultimate expression of our desire to live a commandment of the Lord because we love Him (see 1 John 5:3). By keeping covenants with the Lord our holiness is perfected because our fear of the Lord becomes pure love of the Lord (see 2 Corinthians 7:1). Elder Henry B. Eyring said,

> The fruit of keeping covenants is the companionship of the Holy Ghost
> and an increase in the power to love. That happens because of the
> power of the Atonement of Jesus Christ to change our very natures.[25]

The power of godliness, which is the power of pure love, is manifest in the ordinances (see D&C 84:20–21) because the focus of a priesthood ordinance is to covenant with God. Only in the confines of covenants kept are found the trust and fidelity necessary to permit the power of pure love to manifest itself.

Christ's name is always written in our hearts (see Mosiah 5:12) because His covenants are written and understood in our hearts. This is how we "take upon [us His] name with full purpose of heart" (D&C 18:27; see also 2 Nephi 31:13; Jacob 6:5). This is how we are accounted to Him as a righteous people (see Isaiah 51:7). If Christ's laws and covenants are not written in our hearts we risk becoming like King Noah and his priests who did not understand the law of Moses in their minds nor their hearts because they "[taught] with their learning, and [denied] the Holy Ghost" (2 Nephi 28:4). In this case, a sacred covenant becomes a mere contract to be broken at will. There is no "fear" of the Lord. In a form of idolatry, King Noah and his priests hid their unrighteousness behind the righteousness of the law of Moses while living it on their own terms of "Hearken unto us, and hear ye our precept; for behold *there is no God today*, . . . "Eat, drink, and be merry, for tomorrow we die; and it shall be well with us" (2 Nephi 28:5, 7; emphasis added; compare Mosiah 11:20, 27; 12:13–14).

These verses in 2 Nephi chapter 28 are specifically describing our day. Therefore, today, like King Noah and his people, those who say "Do this, or do that, and it mattereth not, for the Lord will uphold such at the last day" (Mormon 8:31), or "it is vain to serve God, and what doth it profit that we have kept his ordinances and that we have walked mournfully before the Lord of Hosts?" (3 Nephi 24:14); must answer Mormon's editorial question:

> For do ye suppose that ye can get rid of the justice of an offended God, who hath been trampled under feet of men, that thereby salvation might come? (3 Nephi 28:35)

Those who do not have the law of God written in their heart are the object of the Savior's warning to the Pharisees:

> Ye are they which justify yourselves before men; but God knoweth your hearts. (Luke 16:15)

> O fools! for you have said in your hearts, *There is no God.* (Joseph
> Smith Translation, Luke 16:21; emphasis added)

The martyrdom of Abinadi, like burnt offerings in the law of
Moses, was "a type and shadow of things which are to come" (Mosiah
13:10; see also Mosiah 16:14). The Savior stated that as the days of
the Prophet Noah were, "so shall also the coming of the Son of man
be" (see Matthew 24:37–39). The earth was suddenly cleansed of
wickedness by water at the time of the Prophet Noah. So will it be
cleansed by fire before the Second Coming (see 3 Nephi 25:1). The
Savior could have said "as the days of King Noah were, so shall the
coming of the Son of man be." This is the type and shadow that Abinadi prophesied concerning the fate of King Noah as the exact fate
of a wicked world before Christ's second coming (compare Mosiah
12:10–12 with 3 Nephi 25:1). It is fire that ultimately separates the
light from the dark, the wicked from the righteous (see 3 Nephi 1:15;
9:3, 9–11; 8:19–23) by "[trying] every man's work of what sort it
is" (1 Corinthians 3:13). The orange and red glow of a sunset is the
symbolic witness of this truth. Abinadi was implicating our day, not
just the cleansing of the earth by fire, but the cleansing of ourselves,
to have light and dark clearly separated within us by the fire of the
Holy Ghost (see 1 Corinthians 3:15). This is how we have the law
written and burned into our hearts.

The council held with the sons of Mosiah and the Anti-Nephi-
Lehi Lamanites (see Alma 24:5–18) was for "covenanting with God"
(Alma 24:18). This covenant was based on a change of heart through
repentance because of the Atonement of Christ (see Alma 24:8–13).
It was manifest by a token of love (see Alma 24:15–17; 26:31–33).
The promises of this covenant in sacrifice and consecration to work
for the benefit of others (see Alma 24:18) are similar to covenants of
pure love that we make in the temple today. To covenant with the
Lord is to enter an order of solemn ordinances, obligation and promises, instituted from before the foundation of the world. The context
of the covenant presented to the Nephites by Moroni with an ensign,
name, token, and consequence of disobedience (see Alma 46:11–21)
closely reflects the "oath and sacred ordinance" (Alma 50:39) of covenants made in the temple. Captain Moroni's important message
was that to "take upon us the name of Christ" (Alma 46:18) is to

covenant with the Lord in His sacred ordinance and then to keep the covenant.

In section 132 of the Doctrine and Covenants the "new and everlasting covenant" and specifically the Holy Order of Matrimony is taught. The new and everlasting covenant is the total of all gospel covenants,[26] "even that which was from the beginning" (D&C 49:9). In this section, the Lord used very direct terms explaining how we are bound to Him in His order through His everlasting covenants:

> For all who will have a blessing at my hands shall abide the law which was appointed for that blessing, and the conditions thereof, as were instituted from before the *foundation of the world.* And as pertaining to the *new and everlasting covenant,* it was instituted for the fulness of my glory; and he that receiveth a fulness thereof must and shall abide the law,
>
> And verily I say unto you, that the conditions of this law are these: All *covenants* . . . that are not made and entered into and *sealed by the Holy Spirit of Promise,* . . . by revelation and commandment through the medium of mine anointed, whom I have appointed on the earth to hold this power, . . . are of no efficacy, virtue, or force in and after the resurrection from the dead; for all contracts that are not made unto this end have an end when men are dead. Behold, *mine house is a house of order,* saith the Lord God, and not a house of confusion. Will I accept an offering . . . that is not made in my name?
>
> Or will I receive at your hands that which I have not appointed?
>
> And will I appoint unto you, saith the Lord, except it be by law, even as I and my Father ordained unto you, before the world was?
>
> I am the Lord thy God; and I give unto you this commandment—that *no man shall come unto the Father but by me* or by my word, which is my law, saith the Lord.
>
> For whatsoever things remain are by me; and whatsoever things are not by me shall be shaken and destroyed. (D&C 132:5–12, 14; emphasis added)

The principle of order in this new and everlasting covenant was certainly applied by the Lord concerning the dead works performed before the restoration of priesthood authority:

> Behold, I say unto you that all old covenants have I caused to be done away in this thing; and this is *a new and an everlasting covenant,* even that which was from the beginning.

> Wherefore, although a man should be baptized an hundred times it availeth him nothing, for you cannot enter in at the strait gate by the law of Moses, neither by your dead works.
>
> For it is because of your *dead works* that I have caused this last covenant and this church to be built up unto me, even as in days of old.
>
> Wherefore, enter ye in at the gate, as I have commanded, and seek not to counsel your God. Amen. (D&C 22:1–4; emphasis added; see also Moroni 8:23)

The Holy Spirit of Promise ignites the bonding reaction of us to Christ and to each other through covenant relationships of the heart. The Holy Spirit is the catalyst of this bonding because He can reveal to us "things as they really are" and "bring all things to [our] remembrance" (Jacob 4:13, John 14:26). Perhaps, one reason He is the Holy Spirit of Promise is because He can plant the promises of the Father in our hearts and make them grow to spiritual understanding in our minds. If we respond and are true to His teachings, the bond (the covenant with Christ), will be sealed by "the earnest of the Spirit" (see 2 Corinthians 1:22) and hold forever. We securely connect our carabineers to Christ's atonement rope through covenants with Him.

Covenants for the Last Time in the Fulness of Times

The Apostle Paul had a vision of our dispensation and the great covenants and sealings with the Lord that will gather all things in Christ when he said:

> That in the *dispensation of the fulness of times* he might *gather together in one all things in Christ*, both which are in heaven, and which are on earth; even in him. (Ephesians 1:10; emphasis added)

The beginning of the gathering "together in one all things, both which are in heaven, and which are on earth" (see D&C 27:13) was the restoration of the fulness of the gospel "for the last time; and for the fulness of times" (D&C 27:13). This occurred when God "committed the keys of [His] kingdom, and a dispensation of the gospel" (D&C 27:13) with its covenants and ordinances to Joseph Smith. "I the Lord . . . called upon my servant Joseph Smith Jun., . . . and gave him commandments . . . that mine everlasting covenant might be established; That the fulness of my gospel might be proclaimed"

(D&C 1:17, 22–23). In a revelation concerning the Nauvoo temple, the Lord made the connection between this dispensation of the fulness of times and the temple:

> And verily I say unto you, let this house be built unto my name, that I may reveal mine ordinances therein unto my people;
>
> For I deign to reveal unto my church things which have been kept hid from before the foundation of the world, things that pertain to the dispensation of the fulness of times. (D&C 124:40–41)

Brigham Young encouraged worthy Saints of Nauvoo to receive ordinances and covenants of the temple. He did this with great urgency not only because he knew the Nauvoo temple would be destroyed, but because of the importance of temple covenants and work in this dispensation (see D&C 112:30–31; D&C 124:47). In fact, demonstrating this focus on the temple, on May 24, 1845, most of the citizens of Nauvoo attended the capstone ceremony of the temple rather than the opening day of the trial of the accused murderers of Joseph Smith.

The dispensation of the fulness of times is the dispensation of great temple work, as defined by President Wilford Woodruff when he said: "This is the great work of the last dispensation: the redemption of the living and the dead."[27] It is the dispensation when righteous men and women understand the importance of taking upon themselves the name of Christ. In so doing they receive in the temple new names for themselves and the dead, entering into a new covenant relationship with their Redeemer and their Heavenly Father.

The Great Endowment: The Purifying Power of Mount Zion

In spite of procrastination by the Saints, the Lord persisted in endowing His people with temple ordinances and covenants hidden from the foundation of the world. Even in the midst of the afflictions of Zion's Camp, the Lord declared a great blessing, a "great endowment": "For behold, I have prepared a great endowment and blessing to be poured out upon them, inasmuch as they are faithful and continue in humility before me" (D&C 105:12).

An Endowment Is Given When We Serve God upon His Mountain

Joseph Smith may have known about the endowment as early as 1823 when Moroni appeared to him and "offered many explanations" (Joseph Smith—History 1:41) about the restoration of the gospel. The prophet of this restoration was certainly aware of an endowment of power from God by 1831, when he received a revelation concerning the "exodus" to Ohio from Fayette, New York. "Wherefore, for this cause I [give] unto you the commandment [D&C 37:1] that ye should go to the Ohio; and there I will give unto you my law; and there you shall be *endowed* with power from on high" (D&C 38:32; emphasis added).

This scripture reflects the commandment of the Lord to Moses on Mount Sinai concerning the exodus from Egypt in that: "When thou hast brought forth the people out of Egypt, ye shall serve God upon this mountain" (Exodus 3:12).

The greatness of the blessing awaiting the Saints' exodus to Ohio echoes the "holy nation" blessing promised in the Sinai exodus:

> And inasmuch as my people shall assemble themselves at the Ohio, I have kept in store *a blessing such as is not known among the children of men*, and it shall be poured forth upon their heads. And from thence men shall go forth into all nations. (D&C 39:15; emphasis added)

The commandment to build a temple or a holy mountain in which the Saints of the Ohio exodus would serve God, was given in 1832 in the "olive leaf" revelation:

> Tarry ye, tarry ye in this place, and call a solemn assembly, even of those who are the first laborers in this last kingdom.
>
> And I give unto you, who are the first laborers in this last kingdom, a commandment that you assemble yourselves together, and organize yourselves, and prepare yourselves, and *sanctify yourselves*; yea, *purify your hearts*, and cleanse your hands and your feet before me, that I may make you clean;
>
> Organize yourselves; prepare every needful thing; and establish a house, even a house of prayer, a house of fasting, a house of faith, a house of learning, a house of glory, a house of order, *a house of God*. (D&C 88:70, 74, 119; emphasis added)

This commandment to build a house of God in Kirtland was not immediately obeyed. Joseph Smith was reminded of this commandment six months later in a revelation where the connection between the temple and the endowment was established:

> Yea, verily I say unto you, I gave unto you a commandment that you should build *a house*, in the which house I design *to endow* those whom I have chosen with power from on high;
>
> For this is the promise of the Father unto you; therefore I command you to tarry, even *as mine apostles at Jerusalem*. (D&C 95:8–9; emphasis added)

The Scriptural Temple

What a marvelous reference to the companion scripture, for the apostles in Jerusalem also received a "great endowment," probably as they served God on holy mountains or places set apart for holiness:

> And, behold, I send the promise of my Father upon you: but tarry ye in the city of Jerusalem, until ye be *endued* with power from on high. (Luke 24:49; emphasis added)

Section 88 of the Doctrine and Covenants is particularly significant to the temple endowment because it contains important verses concerning the great and last promise of the temple endowment. This promise is the same great promise given to the children of Israel after the exodus from Egypt. This great promise was the rest of the Lord once the people were sanctified (see Exodus 19:10–11).

To Be Endowed Is to Be Covered with the Power of Christ

The Greek meaning of the word *enduo* is a covering of raiment or virtue.[1] Therefore, a metaphorical expression in the Savior's sermon on the Temple Mount implied an endowment of glorious clothing to the chosen twelve:

> And why take ye thought for raiment? Consider the lilies of the field how they grow; they toil not, neither do they spin;
> And yet I say unto you, that even Solomon, in all his glory, was *not arrayed like one of these.*
> Wherefore, if God so clothe the grass of the field, which today is, and tomorrow is cast into the oven, *even so will he clothe you*, if ye are not of little faith. (3 Nephi 13:28–30; emphasis added)

To be "arrayed like one of these" in the context of the temple is to be endowed with the garment of salvation and the robes of righteousness.

The endowment is a great gift of power from Christ. It is the gift for which He paid with His blood to purchase us as the Hebrew groom purchased his bride. This gift becomes *our dowry or "en-dower-ment."*[2]

To help us understand the power of the Atonement, the temple endowment teaches us about the celestial realm from which we fell and the possibility of our return to this realm because of the power of the Atonement. How could we be born innocent before God in our fallen state if it were not for the Atonement (see Moroni 8:8)? How could we return to the celestial presence of God except by the sanctifying power of the Holy Spirit? This gift also comes to us by the power of the Atonement (see 3 Nephi 28:11).

The endowment gift is not only this knowledge of the Atonement, but also, where the Atonement was accomplished and the endowment given. It is because of the agony in the Garden of Gethsemane that the Lord sent the Garden of Eden with us in our fall. As a power to entice us to return to His presence, *the temple is the Garden of Eden in our midst.* The great endowment is a great enrichment of knowledge (see 1 Corinthians 1:5) about the power of Christ to make in us a mighty change so we can return to the celestial realm. This change is symbolized in the form of holy clothing that represents the covering of righteousness or endowment of the power and graces of Christ in our personal lives. As we climb Mount Zion in making and keeping covenants with Christ, *He will provide the power to guide us through trials on the trail to the summit.* Nephi saw, in our dispensation, "the power of the Lamb of God [descend] . . . upon the covenant people of the Lord" so that "they were armed with righteousness and with the power of God in great glory" (1 Nephi 14:14).

Endowed with Power to Return to the Presence of God

Brigham Young stressed the importance of feeling or experiencing the endowment. Only a temple setting can provide this experience. He then said the purpose of the endowment is to receive everything necessary to return to the Father:

> But be assured, brethren, there are but few, very few of the Elders of Israel, now on earth, who know the meaning of the word endowment. To know, they must experience; and to experience, a temple must be built.
>
> Let me give you the definition in brief. Your endowment is to receive all the ordinances necessary to walk back to the presence of the Father. Passing the angels . . . being able to give them key words, the signs and tokens pertaining to the Holy Priesthood.[3]

The Scriptural Temple

With similar emphasis on returning to God the Father, Joseph Smith said the endowment comprises:

> All those plans and principles by which anyone is enabled to secure the fulness of those blessings which have been prepared for the Church of the Firstborn, and come up and abide in the presence of the Eloheim in the eternal worlds.[4]

The endowment is the power to return to the presence of God (see D&C 29:29). Each time we go through the temple endowment we prepare for this reality. It is real, because during its ceremonial drama, we see, hear, speak, act, and feel the realization within ourselves that through the Atonement, we can become sanctified to endure the presence of the Lord. In the mortal manifestations of the resurrected Redeemer, the reality of being in the presence of a God was witnessed by seeing, hearing, speaking with, acting with, and feeling Him. "Having therefore, . . . boldness to enter into the holiest by the blood of Jesus" (Hebrews 10:19), *we are endowed or enriched with the power of authority, truth and light,* a divine nature of pure love, key words, tokens and signs, sealings, protection, celestial law and glory. We are sanctified or made clean and pure before the Lord.

This sanctifying blessing of the temple endowment will become evident to the world when "the heathen shall know that I the Lord do sanctify Israel, when my sanctuary shall be in the midst of them for evermore" (Ezekiel 37:28). The actual reality of being in the presence of the Lord was again given to Joseph Smith and also Oliver Cowdery as He blessed them with His purifying power in the temple:

> Behold, your sins are forgiven you; you are clean before me; therefore, lift up your heads and rejoice.
>
> Yea, I will appear unto my servants, and speak unto them with mine own voice, if my people will keep my commandments, and do not pollute this holy house. Yea the hearts of thousands and tens of thousands shall greatly rejoice in consequence of the blessings which shall be poured out, and the endowment with which my servants have been endowed in this house. (D&C 110:5, 8–9)

The first reality of the Savior's presence may have occurred to Oliver Cowdery as early as 1829 (see D&C 6:20, 37).

This declaration of the Lord becomes even more significant when we comprehend what the endowment blessing of power will do to our hearts, our true spiritual selves. The endowment, according to Elder H. Burke Peterson, is not just knowledge, but also a power that brings about the mighty change of heart:

> We can talk about the process, but it is a power. The endowment is a power, and it can come to us only by revelation. We must feel the endowment to know its meaning.[5]

We can feel and see the power of the endowment, explained Elder Boyd K. Packer, as we feel the warmth and see the light of the sun:

> In the temple we face the sunlight of truth. The light of the temple, that understanding, shines upon us as does the light of the sun. And the shadows of sin, ignorance and error, of disappointment and failure, fall behind us.[6]

The warmth of pure love and the light of pure truth from the Son is the power of the endowment that brings about the mighty change of heart. Perhaps Carlos E. Asay, former president of the Salt Lake Temple, captured the power of the endowment when he said, it is "an exchange of love between God our Father and us."[7]

As the scriptural temple clearly reveals, it is not sufficient to just see. We must also feel to understand pure love and pure truth. The first time in the scriptures that a leper felt the touch of another's hand is when "Jesus put forth his hand and *touched him*" (see Matthew 8:2–4; emphasis added). As spiritual lepers, the profound truth that should irresistibly draw us to the temple is that if we want to "feel and see" (3 Nephi 18:25) the fulness of the Atonement in our lives then we need to feel and see the fulness of the temple endowment in our lives.

Endowed with Holiness through Covenants with the Lord

The Lord requires that we become holy (see Leviticus 11:44–45; 19:2, 20–26) during our climb back to the Father's presence. We become holy by becoming purified then perfected (see Matthew 5:48). Specifically, this means we are purified to be endowed with perfect love. The Jewish scriptural concept of the term *perfect* was defined as faithful observance of covenants.[8] Therefore, the power to become perfectly holy, which is the ultimate gift of the Holy Ghost and the Holy One of Israel, is given to us as we make and keep covenants with the Lord.

To "press toward the . . . high calling of God . . . as many as be perfect" (Philippians 3:14–15) is to become perfect in obedience to receive "all that my Father hath" (D&C 84:38) because "no man is possessor of all things except he be purified and cleansed from all sin" (D&C 50:28). By the power of the garment of salvation (the Atonement), we are clothed with the robes of righteousness (the divine or holy nature), as we keep covenants with our Savior.

The process of becoming holy is sacred for a consecrated or set apart people because the "secret things" of the Lord are "revealed" to them (see Deuteronomy 29:29) in a "secret place" (Ezekiel 7:22) through sacred covenants and ordinances. Just as the "sacred treasury of the Lord" (D&C 104:66) in Kirtland was for "all the sacred things . . . for sacred and holy purposes" (D&C 104:62, 65), so is the house of the Lord.

Contrast Satan's mimic of the endowment "concerning them of old, that they by their secret plans did obtain kingdoms and great glory" (Ether 8:9) and "whoso should divulge whatsoever thing . . . made known unto them, the same should lose his life" (Ether 8:14). "The Lord worketh not in secret combinations" (Ether 8:19). The *endowment is only secret in the sense that it is "kept sacred" (Alma 63:13) by God's covenant people.* Sacredness kept in the intent of our hearts is expressed in our worship. To keep the Lord's sacredness is also to protect it from those "making a mock of that which [is] sacred" (Helaman 4:12) by not delivering "that which [is] sacred, unto wickedness" (D&C 10:9). "For I, the Lord, am not to be mocked" (D&C 104:6; 63:58). "Remember that that which cometh from above is sacred, and must be spoken with care, and by constraint of the Spirit" (D&C 63:64; see also D&C 6:10). "Of [these] we cannot now speak particularly" (Hebrews 9:5). Therefore, "Trifle not with sacred things" (D&C 6:12).

Endowed with Knowledge to Understand the Gospel

When we are taught by the power of the Holy Spirit in the temple, the endowment greatly enriches our understanding of gospel principles. This is another reason why I find the endowment exciting. I wish to share gospel principles under the titles of "accountability," "sweetness of the fruit" and "true messengers," that have been enhanced in my understanding because of the endowment:

Accountability

Once a year the bishop invites me to be fiscally accountable to the Lord. I must report and declare my status concerning the law of tithing. Throughout the year I have numerous other occasions to account my stewardship directly with the Lord and through priesthood leaders. An important function of visiting and home teachers is to take account of their families. The most important and sacred account that I make to priesthood leaders is during the temple recommend interview.

Giving account is a remarkable practice in our Church that distinguishes us from most other religions. It is a necessity because we are the clergy of our church. We do not follow a professional clergy and rely on them to mediate between us and the Lord. It is interesting that the children of Israel in the Sinai wanted Moses to be the mediator between them and the Lord because they did not want to be directly accountable to the Lord. Here we see the beginning of religious intercession with mortal mediators, common in most orthodox Christian religions today. As we have seen, when the children of Israel rejected God's theocracy of righteous judges and demanded a king in order to be like other nations, this intercession extended to civil leadership (see 1 Samuel 7:5–7). While the Lord uses righteous mediators such as judges, kings, and prophets to direct and protect His people (see 2 Nephi 6:2), His desire is that all people, especially religious and civil leaders (see Deuteronomy 17:14–20), become righteous messengers, accountable to Him as the ultimate mediator. It is God's desire "that every man might speak in the name of God" (see D&C 1:19–20).

The Scriptural Temple

The Prophet Moses declared this desire when he said, "Would God that all the Lord's people were prophets, and that the Lord would put his spirit upon them!" (Numbers 11:29).

We are not only accountable to the Lord but to each other (see Daniel 6:2). This is especially true in the church where we are "accounted worthy by the voice of the church . . . to belong to the church" (D&C 51:4–5). "Let every elder who shall give an account . . . be recommended by the church or churches, in which he labors, that he may render himself and his accounts approved in all things" (D&C 72:19). By this accountability to each other, we learn how to be accountable to God. We also learn how to edify each other because we learn that we are our brothers' keepers. As the Prophet Joseph Smith taught, in order to edify others and judge righteously we must learn to govern ourselves through God's correct principles practiced "with His spirit upon [us]." Paul expressed this accountability to others and to God in writing to the Hebrews:

> Obey them that have the rule over you, and submit yourselves; for they watch for your souls, as they that must give *account*, that they may do it with joy, and not with grief. (Hebrews 13:17; emphasis added)

An account of us will be with joy if the Lord's spirit is upon us and we produce "fruit that may abound to [our] account" (Philippians 4:17). Virginia Pearce observed that, "it is very often in the act of reporting that the Holy Ghost chooses to witness and confirm the actions. And ultimately, it is the confirmation of the Spirit that provides the best motivation to keep doing good things."[9]

The Order and Age of Accountability

There is a priesthood order in this accountability. This priesthood order includes the Holy Order of Matrimony. Women have as important a role in this Holy Order as men. Both are to bring forth and sustain physical and spiritual life or in other words, "to bear the souls of men" (D&C 132:63).

We cannot declare ourselves unaccountable to those in this priesthood order and please God. Whatever we do to the least of the servants of God we do unto Him. Fathers and mothers, husbands and wives, especially in the Holy Order of Matrimony, are servants of God. Evil speaking of the Lord's anointed, men or women, is a displeasing declaration of independence to the Lord.

This priesthood order is the order of accountability between God and man as taught in the temple. The temple is a "house of order" (D&C 88:119). There we learn the law of heavenly order which states "there are last which shall be first, and there are first which shall be last" (Luke 13:30). This law inherently implies that "first" is not necessarily better than "last." It is a matter of order according to the laws and covenants of God (see 3 Nephi 20:26). God taught Adam and Eve this law when Eve was the first to yield to Satan. Therefore God first instructed Adam. Then Adam, as a true messenger of God, instructed Eve. In the end, the instruction from women to men is of great value.

A father's responsibility and accountability is not only to sustain physical life but to bring forth spiritual life to his family through the word of God (see Matthew 12:36–37). In both ways, he "nourisheth" (see Ephesians 5:29) his family as the menorah and shewbread table of the temple symbolize. Nephi's opening statement about his "goodly parents" was that he "was taught somewhat in all the learning of my father" (1 Nephi 1:1). Then he explained in detail only the spiritual learning and stature he received from his father through the word of God.

At age eight, children become accountable to their parents for the word of God. As parents, a husband and wife are accountable to each other and their priesthood leaders for the word of God. These leaders are accountable to their leaders until the earthly father of the Church, the holder of the keys of authority, the prophet, seer, and revelator of the word of God, is reached. He is accountable to the Heavenly Father for His word being taught to the kingdom of God on earth. Christ gave account to His Heavenly Father at the end of His mortal ministry (see John 17:4).

By being accountable to each other in spite of our weaknesses, we demonstrate faith in the omnipotent hand of the Lord to sustain and direct those chosen as stewards of His word (see D&C 70:34). In the Church, by uplifted hands, we do not only sustain the individual. We sustain individuals called as representatives of God as though we were sustaining God. In sustaining those chosen by God's revelations to act under His order, we demonstrate faith in the "principles of righteousness" and "love unfeigned" (see D&C 121:36, 41) upon which His order works. One reason we practice this order of accountability is to prepare to fully live the law of consecration with love unfeigned. Accountability to determine need and want is an integral part of this law (see D&C 42:32–33). The accountability will be of "their manner of life, their faith, and works" (D&C 85:2) and "accounts of their stewardships to the land of Zion" (D&C 69:5). Accountability will establish "every man according to his wants and his needs, inasmuch as his wants are just" (D&C 82:17).

The Lord has fixed the starting time of "the years of accountability" (see D&C 18:42) to be the age of eight years during our mortal probation. At this age or older, all men, women, and children are accountable before the Lord to repent and be baptized (see D&C 18:42; Moroni 8:10). Parents are accountable to the Lord to teach their children the doctrine of Christ by this age (see D&C 68:25, 27; Moses 5:12; 6:5–6, 57, 58).

The age of eight years is not an arbitrary number. It is the age at which we begin to partake of the fruit of the knowledge of good and evil with agency. At this age, we begin to understand the good of spiritual knowledge and the evil of Satan's temptations because he is permitted to tempt us (see D&C 29:46–47, 49–50). After baptism we receive the gift of the Holy Ghost to counter this temptation. Truly, at the age of accountability it is given unto us through the enticements of Satan and the Holy Ghost that we might know good from evil (see Helaman 14:31). Until that day we are accounted before God to have "no knowledge between good and evil" (Deuteronomy 1:39). This beginning of accountability starts a progression until our accountability is mature before the Lord and His forgiveness becomes more restricted.

Through life our parental dependence diminishes, but from age eight our dependence on the gifts of the Holy Spirit steadily increases as we are born again into the kingdom of God. This change in dependency as we become again sons and daughters of God makes us more and more accountable to our heavenly parents. Therefore, it is imperative that earthly parents do "great things" (D&C 29:48) to "prepare the minds of their children to hear the word" (Alma 39:16) and "bring up [their] children in light and truth" (D&C 93:40) to receive the gifts of the Holy Spirit. The Lord warned Frederick G. Williams as a warning to all parents that "you have not taught your children in light and truth, according to the commandments; and that wicked one hath power, as yet, over you" (D&C 93:42). The great things parents should do are to plant the seeds of truth in the hearts of their children, and then teach them where and how to receive the power of the Holy Ghost. The Holy Ghost will cause these seeds to grow by bringing spiritual light to their remembrance. If we as parents proceed with the light of a righteous example, our children will "learn wisdom in [their] youth; yea, . . . to keep the commandments of God" (Alma 37:35) and "grow up unto the Lord" (see Helaman 3:21). Because of parental righteousness, it may be the will of the Spirit, to "command [our] children to do good" (Alma 39:12) and repent as the father of his spiritual rebirth commanded Martin Harris (see D&C 19:13, 15, 20–21, 26, 28).

The one great thing that we as parents of the earthly kingdom of God can do is to teach our children early and often that the temple should become the most powerful spiritual motivation in their lives because this is where they will receive the fulness of the Holy Spirit. We must teach them about the great and last promise of the temple as Adam's blessing to his righteous posterity. We must teach them the beauty of holiness in their lives and that God is a "Man of Holiness" (Moses 7:35). We must teach them that to understand the power of the Atonement, they must partake of the power of the endowment by binding themselves to Christ through His priesthood covenants.

Our Final Accountability to the Savior

We become accountable to Christ when we receive the light of Christ and even more when we take His name upon us by joining His church (see D&C 20:71). When we "receive of God" we must "account it of God" (see D&C 50:34). "For it is required of the Lord, at the hand of every steward, to render an account of his stewardship, both in time and in eternity" (D&C 72:3). "Every man [a steward over earthly blessings (see D&C 104:13)] shall be made accountable unto me" (D&C 42:32) in "that every man may give an account unto me of the stewardship which is appointed unto him" (D&C 104:12).

The Scriptural Temple

Our final accountability is to the Savior. The Prophet David O. Mckay explained the order of this accountability. First will be an account of the relationship with our spouse and our children. Christ will next inquire about the use of our God-given talents and the magnifying of our church callings. Finally He will ask an account of our honesty in dealing with others and our ability to edify them in the world in which we have lived.[10] This final account will be of our forgiveness and mercy (see Matthew 18:23–35). The Savior is the one to whom we are accountable at the veil, before entering the presence of the Father. To Him who "is ready to judge the quick and the dead" (see 1 Peter 4:5) we will give account as "stewards of the mysteries of God" (see 1 Corinthians 4:1) because "I have appointed unto you to be stewards over mine house" (D&C 104:57). "An account of this stewardship will I require of them in the day of judgment" (D&C 70:4). We can prepare for this final accounting by giving Christ account in the temple of the personal stewardships and the personal covenants we make with Him.

Christ employs no servant at the veil (see 2 Nephi 9:41). He is the only true mediator (see 1 Timothy 2:5). He is the one that will plead our case with the Father and make the final accounting. In preparation for our completion of the first spiritual death when all mankind will return to God and report on their works whether they be good or evil (see Mormon 3:20), let us return and report often to those in the priesthood order who have responsibility for us. Let us return and report to prove ourselves to the Lord in His holy house:

That [you] may render [yourselves] and [your] accounts approved in all things. (D&C 72:19)

I command you again to build a house to my name, even in this place, that you may prove yourselves unto me that ye are faithful in all things whatsoever I command you, that I may bless you, and crown you with honor, immortality, and eternal life. (D&C 124:55)

The inquiries in the endowment from an omniscient God emphasize that we will be proved in accounting to Him. Since "every one of us shall give account of himself to God" (Romans 14:12), we must do so completely and honestly. In preparation for this accounting we must learn to give honest account with ourselves by being watchful

176

and prayerful continually (see Alma 13:28; Mosiah 4:30). In order climb Mount Zion, orderly accounting communication with each other and God is essential.

Sweetness of the Fruit

While living in Detroit, we eagerly anticipated Saturday. We didn't miss our Saturday morning trip to the downtown open market. Any imaginable earth product or man-embellished variation was available. We particularly enjoyed the fresh Ohio corn and tomatoes. We would impale the ears of corn on a nail driven through a board then the kernels were quickly harvested with a sharp blade. These golden kernels were frozen to be mixed later with a bottle of tomato preserves, heated gently and topped with a little cheese and pepper. I can still taste this delight.

One Saturday, there seemed to be an abundance of citrus fruit. Bartering for price was fierce. All the juice oranges looked alike but one vendor was selling a particularly sweet-tasting orange. We bought a bushel and consumed half of them the same day in a most joyous citrus feast. It wasn't the good price or the appearance. It was the exquisite sweetness of the fruit that brought the joy of this feast.

The Need for Opposition: Tasting the Bitter to Prize the Sweet

When father Lehi instructed his sons shortly before his death, he addressed his son Jacob with the great words of 2 Nephi. Here he reasoned for a need of opposition in all things. He even used the example of the two opposing fruit trees in the Garden of Eden:

> And to bring about his eternal purposes in the end of man, . . . it must needs be that there was an opposition; even the forbidden fruit in opposition to the tree of life; the one being sweet and the other bitter. (2:15)

It is interesting that Eve was enticed by a bitter fruit. Or was it really bitter? Eve's initial impression of the fruit attracted her:

> And when the woman saw that the tree was good for food, and that it became pleasant to the eyes, and a tree to be desired to make her wise, she took of the fruit thereof, and did eat, and also gave unto her husband with her, and he did eat. (Moses 4:12)

The Scriptural Temple

When Eve offered Adam the fruit she described it as "delicious to the taste." How could this fruit be bitter? Certainly it had a bitter result causing mortality compared to the fruit of the tree of life, which would result in immortality. Yet the forbidden fruit had a sweetness in the form of knowledge and remembrance of good. Depending on how we understand and apply this knowledge to remember good, the apparent bitter result of mortality can be sweet or bitter (see D&C 42:46–47). Is it possible that Eve tasted sweetness in the forbidden fruit by remembering the result of eating it would be sweet through Christ? After partaking, Eve began to "see." Then Adam partook and both began to see a difference between good and evil. They recognized the difference between God their Father and Satan their rebellious brother. Remember, Lehi compared the forbidden fruit to the fruit of the tree of life. Both were a delicious fruit surrounding a seed of life: one mortal, the other immortal. To have knowledge of the eternal fruit of the tree of life it was necessary to partake of the mortal forbidden fruit.

When Adam and Eve partook of this fruit, they began to see that the forbidden fruit, no matter how delicious it tastes, is ultimately bitter without the fruit of the tree of life. They also understood that the sweetness of the fruit of the tree of life could not be fully enjoyed in a state of sin. Therefore, God the Father revealed to them how sin could be removed from their lives through the plan of redemption.

The Meaning of the Tree of Life

Father Lehi partook of a fruit from the tree in his dream and described it as "to exceed all the whiteness," being "most sweet," "to make one happy" even with "exceedingly great joy." Therefore it was "desirable above all other fruit" (see 1 Nephi 8:10–11).

After being asked by the Spirit of the Lord: "knowest thou the condescension of God?," Nephi was shown the mortal conception (see 1 Nephi 11:16, 18–20) and the mortal ministry (see 1 Nephi 11:27–33) of the Son of God. Then he was asked: "Knowest thou the meaning of the tree which thy father saw?" (1 Nephi 11:21):

> And I answered him, saying; Yea, it is the **love of God**, which *sheddeth* itself abroad in the *hearts* of the children of men; wherefore, it is the *most desirable* above all things.
>
> And he spake unto me, saying: Yea, and the *most joyous* to the soul. (1 Nephi 11:22–23; emphasis added)

178

With the terms *most desirable* and *most joyous*, similar to those of his father, Nephi understood about the tree his father reached and the fruit of which he ate. The tree represents the love of God that sheds forth in the hearts of men when they taste or comprehend the shedding of the blood of His Son for them in the fulness of His gospel. This comprehension occurs by the power and gifts of the Holy Spirit, "because the love of God is shed abroad in our hearts by the Holy Ghost which is given unto us" (Romans 5:5).

This shedding forth "is given unto us" by true messengers who carry the love of God in the fruits of the fulness of the gospel. "Whatsoever thing [they] declare in my name, in solemnity of heart, in the spirit of meekness, . . . I give unto you this promise, that . . . the Holy Ghost shall be shed forth in bearing record unto all things whatsoever [they] shall say" (D&C 100:7–8).

> For it shall come to pass in that day, that every man shall hear the fulness of the gospel in his own tongue, and in his own language, through those who are ordained unto this power, by the administration of the Comforter, shed forth upon them for the revelation of Jesus Christ. (D&C 90:11)

The love of God is clearly demonstrated in His condescension to us: "For God so loved the world, that he gave his only begotten Son, that whosoever believeth in him should not perish, but have everlasting life" (John 3:16).

This scripture is a description of the tree of life, "the great and wonderful love" (D&C 138:3) of God. When we partake of its fruit by taking Christ's name upon us and receive the fulness of His Atonement, we do not perish but become a tree of life producing the fruit of everlasting life that is everlasting love (see John 15:5). *Therefore, the tree of life represents the love of God and the fruit of that love is His Son and our Savior.* He makes the "fruit" of everlasting life possible for all. True to Mosaic law and sacrifice, Father Lehi described Christ as the "firstfruits" (see 2 Nephi 2:9). In the mortal world, the tree of life is a "sign" or symbol of the Son of God (see 1 Nephi 11:4–8). He completely represents the love of God the Father for His children. He is the one to whom we must come for happiness and holiness to partake of the fruit of eternal life.

The Reality of Partaking of the Fruit of the Tree of Life

The Levitical temple symbol of the shewbread which means "bread of the presence of God" or the bread "set forth"[11] is reflected in Paul's teachings of Christ to the Roman Saints: "Whom God hath *set forth* to be a propitiation through faith in his blood" (Romans 3:25; emphasis added).

This concept of showing Christ set before us as sustenance to consume like fruit, the firstfruit, or bread, the bread of life, is captured in the origin of the word *lord* which derives from the old English word *hlafweard*, meaning "he who guards the loaf." Showing Christ as the guardian and giver of the bread of life was directly stated in the sacramental instructions of the Savior to the Nephites at the temple of Bountiful:

> And this shall ye do in remembrance of my body, which *I have shown unto you*. And it shall be a testimony unto the Father that ye do always remember me. And if ye do always remember me ye shall have my Spirit to be with you. (3 Nephi 18:7; emphasis added)

The body of Christ shown to the Nephites (see 3 Nephi 10:19) was the sacrificed and resurrected body of the Savior. He was sacrificed that they might live as He lives if they would partake of His saving sustenance. In the world room of the Salt Lake temple, on the upper back mural is a striking scene that symbolically depicts the sacrifice of the Lamb of God that life might live more abundantly.

The shewbread and wine on the table of the Holy Place was a symbol of Christ and a precursor of the sacrament symbols of the body and blood of Christ that we partake of today. Like His forerunner, the great high priest Melchizedek, Christ "brought forth bread and wine" (Genesis 14:18; see also Matthew 26:26–29; 3 Nephi 18:1) for the covenant meal. *We symbolically eat of the fruit of the tree of life* in the covenant meal when we physically partake of the sacrament bread and water (see Alma 5:34, 62). We partake of the "firstfruits."

This physical gesture should direct our thoughts and actions to a spiritual feast of the fruit of the tree of life. This occurs in the temple where the Holy Spirit feeds us the fulness of the firstfruits by teaching us about the Atonement and the graces of Christ. It is significant that the shewbread and the hidden manna in the ark of the covenant, both symbolic of Christ, were "hidden" in the holy places of the temple. It is there that Christ is fully shown forth to spiritually sustain those who overcome in the temple (see John 6:51; Revelation 2:17).

This spiritual feast was the feast of those who listened to King Benjamin at the temple of Zarahemla. As Lehi described, the feast began when he saw "others pressing forward, and they came . . . and caught hold of the end of the rod of iron" (1 Nephi 8:24). As Nephi envisioned, the feast continues when we, "press forward, feasting upon the word of Christ" (2 Nephi 31:20) which is a spiritual feast of the Holy Ghost (see 2 Nephi 32:3) through our own personal revelation. This is how we come to know what is "just and true" (see Mosiah 2:35; 4:12). Therefore, the terminal rod of iron is the principle of revelation in ourselves. Like the Prophet Alma (see Alma 32:35), the Prophet Joseph Smith described this feast:

> I can taste the principles of eternal life, and so can you. They are given to me by the revelations of Jesus Christ; and I know that when I tell you these words of eternal life as they are given to me, you taste them, and I know that you believe them. You say honey is sweet, and so do I. I can also taste the spirit of eternal life. I know it is good; and when I tell you of these things which were given me by inspiration of the Holy Spirit, you are bound to receive them as sweet, and rejoice more and more.[12]

Growing a tree of life within us and then feasting upon its sweet fruit is how we personally feast upon and are filled with the words of Christ. This is what Alma taught when he spoke about planting the word of God in our hearts and nourishing it with faith, patience, repentance, and diligent obedience until it becomes a mature tree of life within us (see Alma 32:41–42). Then we can say "behold the tree" (Jacob 5:16). However, if "[our] ground is barren," meaning sinful or slothful, "and [we] will not nourish the tree, therefore [we] cannot have the fruit thereof" (Alma 32:39).

Our mature tree of life will produce a fruit that will fill our spiritual hunger and thirst in this life (see Alma 32:28–43). This fruit is "the fruit of the Spirit" (Galatians 5:22) which is the fruits of pure love.

Partaking of the fruit of the tree of life during the sacrament and in the temple, and thereby learning to grow a tree of life within us, is preparation for partaking fully of the tree of life (the full blessings of the love of God) in the realm of eternal life. This will fill our spiritual hunger and thirst everlastingly. This is the sweetness of the fruit. "To him that overcometh will I give to eat of the *tree of life*, which is in the midst of the paradise of God" (Revelation 2:7; emphasis added).

Heartburn from the Forbidden Fruit

God taught Adam a great truth when He said that being "conceived in sin," meaning in the conditions of a fallen state (see Mosiah 3:16; 27:25), leads to "sin [conceiving] in their hearts" (Moses 6:55). Growing up in mortality produces a contrasting experience so that we can learn to prize the good of spiritual truth:

> And the Lord spake unto Adam, saying: Inasmuch as thy children are conceived in sin, even so when they begin to grow up, sin conceiveth in their *hearts* , and they *taste the bitter* , that they may know to *prize the good* . (Moses 6:55; emphasis added)

Just as spiritual truth must be understood in our hearts even with joyous heartburn, so it is in our hearts that sin must be understood by producing a painful feeling in our conscience. This is how we taste (recognize) the bitter to prize the sweet. This heartburn from sin, opposite to the joyous heartburn experienced at the temple of the land Bountiful (see 3 Nephi 11:3) and on the road to Emmaus (see Luke 24:32), occurs when the light of Christ burns in our conscience or the Spirit withdraws to warn us of sin (see D&C 19:20). We all have this heartburn, for example, when we tell a lie. Even a physical reaction, which can be measured by a lie detector, occurs from this heartburn. Zeezrom experienced an intense degree of this heartburn and called it "the pains of hell" (Alma 14:6). Interestingly, this pain in his conscience physically produced "a burning heat" (Alma 15:3).

When we honestly react to this type of heartburn and do not attempt to cover it up by hardening our hearts, we experience what Paul called "godly sorrow" (2 Corinthians 7:10). Godly sorrow is the first step to becoming "goodly" because godly sorrow means sorrowing unto repentance. To be repentant we must come unto Christ with a broken heart and contrite spirit (see Mormon 2:13–14) to prize the good of Christ. Then, godly sorrow invites the Spirit's return to comfort us and teach us about Christ's goodness. Therefore, godly sorrow sharply defines the difference between good and evil in our lives and helps us "prize the good."

The more we become of "full [spiritual] age, . . . by reason of use [we] have [our] senses exercised to discern both good and evil" (Hebrews 5:14). With this sharpened discernment the more we understand God. With this understanding in mortality, farther seems the reality to become like Him. This would explain why those with senses to discern good from evil such as the Prophet Nephi and the Apostle Paul could say "O wretched man that I am" (2 Nephi 4:17; Romans 7:24). As C. S. Lewis said, "Good people know about both good and evil: bad people do not know about either."[13] This latter case occurs when "mind and conscience is defiled" (see Titus 1:15). This truth about knowing good from evil is captured in the Savior's statement, "I am the light which shineth in darkness, and *the darkness comprehendeth it not*" (D&C 6:21; emphasis added). Even Satan acknowledged this truth, when he declared to Eve that gods know good and evil (see Moses 4:11). God confirmed this truth when He said, "man is become as one of us *to know* good and evil" (Moses 4:28; emphasis added).

The importance of knowing the difference between good and evil is that it provides "a state to act according to their wills" (Alma 12:31). So, "Remember, remember, . . . ye are permitted to act for yourselves; for behold, God hath given unto you a knowledge and he hath made you free. He hath given unto you that ye might know good from evil, and he hath given unto you that ye might choose life or death" (Helaman 14:30–31).

Acting in this state of opposition (see 2 Nephi 2:11) is proving contraries by being proved by God in proving by our own experience, and in proving by the light of the Holy Spirit (see Exodus 20:20; 1 Thessalonians 5:21; D&C 57:13). The Prophet Joseph Smith said, "in proving contraries is truth made manifest."[14] Choosing evil brings spiritual death, a state of captivity where one is acted upon being "led by [Satan's] will" (Alma 12:11). Alma defined spiritual death as death "to things pertaining unto righteousness, being dead unto all good works" (Alma 5:42). Contrast this state of death with the state of life when one chooses to be "led by the Holy Spirit" (Alma 13:28).

Being led by the Holy Spirit leads to a quickened state of ultimate freedom where agency still exists along with the full power of God's mercy (see Helaman 10:4–7).

When we partake of the fruit of the tree of knowledge of good and evil by being "conceived in [the state of] sin," we discover our nakedness meaning our mortal weaknesses, our vulnerability to sin, corruption, and death. This is the bitterness we taste. Satan would have us believe that through the arm of flesh and his satanic powers he can cover this nakedness. However, his covering always leads to more bitterness in that he leaves us sinfully naked and exposed to the laws of justice in the end (see Alma 30:60). If the bitterness of nakedness (when the Spirit withdraws) is tasted in our hearts with a bitter heartburn leading to godly sorrow, we can come to know of the sweetness of good.

The source of good is always God (see Ether 4:11–12; Moroni 7:12–13), and the source of every good thing to cover the nakedness of our fall is Christ (see Moroni 7:24). God, through His Son, will cover our nakedness everlastingly with the good fruit of His love in the joy of redemption to eternal life.

Exceedingly Great Joy: A Cure for the Heartburn of Sin

It is interesting that Eve desired to give the fruit of the tree of knowledge of good and evil in all sincerity to Adam just as Lehi desired to give the fruit of the tree of life to his family. Did Eve sense or savor a deeper sweetness in this fruit than first met her taste? When Eve partook of this fruit it was delicious just like most temptations from Satan. They are at first delicious and enticing but ultimately lead to sorrow, bitterness, and death.

Eve tasted of the knowledge of good in the fruit of the tree of knowledge. She tasted in part the sweetness of good. This sweetness is the light of Christ or the Spirit of Christ given to all men who enter mortality (see D&C 93:2; Moroni 7:16). It is the sweetness of the self-evident truths of natural affection found in our conscience. The sweetness of these truths is part of the sweetness we taste when we learn how to truly love and edify others in this life.

When my seventeen-year-old daughter, Leslee, returned from a stake summer youth conference, I asked her about the event. She said her favorite part of all was sharing time and love with handi-capped youth who had been invited to participate. This is the real fruit of "good" in this mortal life. It is a reflection of the love of God. To do an altruistic, benevolent act for someone else is most desirous above all things and most delicious to the soul. It is what gives us joy.

The sweetness of good we can taste in the fruit of the tree of knowledge should make us desire to taste the greater sweetness of the fruit of the tree of life and "lay hold upon every good thing" (Moroni 7:20) by hearkening to the voice of the Spirit (see D&C 84:46). The Spirit will teach us to have faith in Christ (see Moroni 7:25–26, 38), who is the fruit of the tree of life.

In the forbidden fruit, Eve savored in part the fruit of the tree of life. This is the taste of charity, the pure love of God. She knew she needed to bear the souls of men by bringing forth children in mortality to learn this love in sharing it with them. Adam knew that he would not arrive at a fulness of this love without Eve. Therefore, he fell to be with Eve so they could have a posterity that would also know this pure love. As Adam and Eve knew, *only in contrast with the taste of evil could they come to a full taste of the love of God, and a fulness of exquisite joy*: "Were it not for our transgression we never should have had seed, and never should have known good and evil, and *the joy of our redemption*" (Moses 5:11; emphasis added). Lehi taught the same concept when he said:

> Wherefore [Adam and Eve] would have remained in a state of inno-cence, *having no joy*, for they knew no misery; *doing no good*, for they *knew no sin*.
>
> Adam fell that men might be; and *men are, that they might have joy*.
> (2 Nephi 2:23, 25; emphasis added)

It is interesting that two of the first commandments that God gave Adam and Eve before they entered the Garden, in reference to having a posterity and taking care of the Garden, indicated joy as the result of obeying these commandments. Joy in the Garden of Eden seems to contradict the reasoning in 2 Nephi 2:22–23. An innocent child can have joy in the presence of its parents but it takes the experience of sacrifice in a setting of contrasted good and evil to become as the gods and arrive at a fulness of joy.

Taking care of the garden was a beginning in teaching Adam and Eve about the sacrifices of stewardship to arrive at a fulness of joy that is the pure love of Christ. They then understood that taking care of God's children in mortality would bring them even closer to this fulness of joy. However, a sacrifice was needed for this fulness of joy, even their fall from the presence of God. Adam understood the necessity of the Fall to arrive at a fulness of joy when he said: "For because of my transgression my eyes are opened, and in this life I shall have joy" (Moses 5:10).

Because of the Fall and its subsequent mortality, multiplying and replenishing the earth became a necessity. While instinct to procreate may seem the reason for "making love," more profound powers of love are at work in our sexuality. As these other sexual reasons for love are understood, marriage, family, and civilization improve. *In the reproductive necessity are all of the elements and forces that teach us about obtaining a fulness of joy through sacrifice.* Parents who master this fulness of joy are given the privilege of eternal seed.

Eve specifically related joy to redemption by sacrifice. Sacrifice brings the joy of redemption from the misery of the Fall. It brings the joy of receiving a remission of sins (see Mosiah 4:3). A fulness of this joy is to be redeemed back into the presence of God to receive the great and last promise of the temple (see Ether 3:13). This joy comes because of the pure love of Christ in His redemptive sacrifice. When Alma was "racked with all [his] sins" (Alma 36:12) and then remembered "the coming of one Jesus Christ, a Son of God, to atone for the sins of the world" (Alma 36:17), he exclaimed, "oh, what joy . . . yea, my soul was filled with joy as exceeding as was my pain!" (Alma 36:20). It is this joy we express when we sing "the song of redeeming love" (Alma 5:26) of our Savior with our fellow men because of the power of His word (see Alma 26:13). It is this "exceedingly great joy" (1 Nephi 8:12) that Lehi tasted in the fruit of the tree of life. Without a fall there never could be a redemption. Without evil there never could be good. Without sorrow or misery there never could be true joy (see John 16:20–21). *The joy of good is redemption to righteousness from the misery of evil* (see 2 Nephi 2:13).

A fulness of joy in mortality and immortality is experienced when body and spirit act "inseparably connected" (see D&C 93:33). Separation of body and spirit within us is a witness of our fall to a world of good and evil. Union of body and spirit occurs when we practice charity in redemptive ways, edifying ourselves and fellow men to righteousness, even becoming saviors on Mount Zion (see Obadiah 1:21). *It is in the temple that body and spirit learn to become inseparably connected and receive a fulness of joy.* Therefore, the commandment of the Father to be happy and have joy therein by receiving "glad tidings of great joy" (D&C 128:19) means in the temple, even the temple of our body.

Those hearing the words of King Benjamin sang the song of redeeming love when they were born again in the temple. They experienced the exquisite joy of redemption through their mighty change of hearts because of their obedience to the commandments and faith in the Atonement of Christ:

> O have mercy, and apply the atoning blood of Christ that we may receive forgiveness of our sins, and our hearts may be purified, for we believe in Jesus Christ. . . .
>
> And it came to pass that after they had spoken these words the Spirit of the Lord came upon them, and they were filled with joy, having received a remission of their sins, and having peace of conscience, because of the exceeding faith which they had in Jesus Christ. (Mosiah 4:2–3)

It was at the temple that these Saints of Zarahemla partook of the fruit of the tree of life and experienced "exceedingly great joy":

> That as ye have come to the knowledge of the glory of God, or if ye have known of his goodness and have tasted of his love, and have received a remission of your sins, which causeth such exceedingly great joy in your souls. (Mosiah 4:11)

While teaching his son Helaman about the joy he tasted in being "born of God" Alma like Ammon (see Alma 36:24) spoke of this "exceeding joy" as the "fruit" of his labors due to the power of the word of God:

> Yea, and from that time even until now, I have labored without ceasing, that I might bring souls unto repentance; that I might bring them to taste of the *exceeding joy of which I did taste*; that they might also be born of God, and be filled with the Holy Ghost.
>
> Yea, and now behold, O my son, the Lord doth give me exceedingly great joy in the fruit of my labors;
>
> For because of the word which he has imparted unto me, behold, many have been born of God, and have tasted as I have tasted, and have seen eye to eye as I have seen; therefore they do know of these things of which I have spoken, as I do know; and the knowledge which I have is of God. (Alma 36:24–26; emphasis added)

The redeeming love of Christ is a taste of exceedingly great joy which causes a mighty change of heart so that we are born of God. It is the focal point of the "great view," so we know and see as Alma and King Benjamin's people:

> And they all cried with one voice, saying: Yea, we believe all the words which thou hast spoken unto us; and also, we know of their surety and truth, because of the Spirit of the Lord Omnipotent, which has wrought a mighty change in us, or in our hearts,
>
> And we, ourselves, also, through the infinite goodness of God, and the manifestations of his Spirit, have great views. (Mosiah 5:2–3; see also Alma 19:33)

It is in the temple that we can feast upon the fruit of the tree of life, see great views of the glory of God, experience the mighty change of heart, and feel exceedingly great joy. It is therefore, in the temple, that we are born of God, becoming the spiritual offspring of Christ as "a kind of firstfruits of his creatures" (James 1:18). For "they are Christ's, the first fruits" (D&C 88:98).

Promptings and Gifts of the Spirit: A Cure for the Heartburn of Tribulation

We also gain knowledge of the difference between good and evil by experiencing adversity or tribulation. Tribulation can produce a fear, even a pain in our hearts that causes us to feel after the Lord if our hearts are not too hardened:

They were slow to hearken unto the voice of the Lord their God; therefore, the Lord their God is slow to hearken unto their prayers, to answer them in the day of their trouble.

In the day of their peace they esteemed lightly my counsel; but, in the day of their trouble, of necessity they feel after me. . . .

Notwithstanding their sins, my bowels are filled with compassion towards them (D&C 101:7–9)

Adversity and tribulation can be a stumbling block or a steppingstone in our spiritual progress depending on how we partake of the fruit of the tree of knowledge of good and evil. Because of tribulation, do we "curse God" (see Job 2:9; Mormon 2:14; D&C 45:32) then continue to yield to Satan's deceptions relying on the arm of flesh? Or does tribulation cause us to feel humility, and then the sweet comfort of the love of God by yielding to the promptings of the Spirit? The answer depends upon the hardness of our hearts as was illustrated by those who endured the long wars between the Nephites and Lamanites:

But behold, because of the exceedingly great length of the war between the Nephites and the Lamanites many had become hardened . . . and many were softened because of their afflictions, insomuch that they did humble themselves before God, even in the depth of humility. (Alma 62:41)

Paul learned how to overcome the bitter tribulations of the forbidden fruit with the sweetness of the fruit of the tree of life by yielding to the promptings of the Spirit:

But *we glory in tribulation* [see D&C 58:3] also: knowing that tribulations worketh patience;

And patience, experience; and experience, hope:

And hope maketh not ashamed; because *the love of God* is shed abroad in our hearts *by the Holy Ghost* which is given unto us. (Romans 5:3–5; emphasis added; see also D&C 127:2)

Paul witnessed his mastery over tribulation when he said: "I have learned, in whatsoever state I am, therewith to be content (Philippians 4:11) because, "I can do all things through Christ which strengtheneth me" (Philippians 4:13).

The more good (love of God) we taste in the forbidden fruit by letting adversity and tribulation purge us with patience, meekness, experience, and hope, the more our nakedness to the precarious nature of life is covered with the good fruits of the Holy Spirit. The sweetness of this fruit is the enticing taste of the fruit of the tree of life. It takes meekness from adversity and a perfect brightness of hope in the love of God to discover the sweetness of this exquisite fruit.

> Know thou, my son, that all these things shall give thee experience, and shall be for thy good. (D&C 122:7)

Everlasting fruit of the tree of life will finally grow from a tree of life within us when we are "crowned with much glory" (D&C 58:4), "immortality, and eternal life" (D&C 81:6), even "a crown of righteousness" (see 2 Timothy 4:8; D&C 25:15), "in the mansions of my Father" (see D&C 59:2). But we are not crowned without a cross. Until then, we shall "be crowned with blessings from above, yea, and with commandments not a few, and with revelations" (D&C 59:4).

As the beautiful rose blooms at the end of a thorny stem (see D&C 49:24) or sweet fruit grows at the end of a branch that has survived the winter frosts and summer heat, so are we, who are "patient in tribulation" (D&C 54:10) by being "faithful in tribulation" (D&C 58:2), crowned: "For after much *tribulation* come the blessings" (D&C 58:4; emphasis added) of the "peaceable fruit of righteousness" (see Hebrews 12:11).

Even the tribulation of aging, as we accelerate with infirmities to the fixed result of partaking of the fruit of the tree of knowledge, can be covered and crowned with sweetness. To those who die in the Lord by partaking of the fruit of the tree of life, death as a fruit of the tree of knowledge of good and evil is sweet because it has been swallowed up in victory (Alma 27:28; see also D&C 42:46–47; 1 Corinthians 15:54–57). If we are spiritually prepared (see D&C 38:30) we shall "fear none of those things which [we shall] suffer" (Revelation 2:10).

The Lord will immediately apply His redemption if we repent (see Alma 34:31; 36:19), but He will not immediately remove "a thorn in the flesh" (2 Corinthians 12:7). Tribulation is a necessary part of mortality in order to learn the difference between good and evil. It lets us experience faith and fear. We should remember that as we obey the Lord, He blesses us with the ability to endure tribulation in that we are "strengthened by the hand of the Lord" (Alma 2:28; see also 1 Nephi 17:3; Mosiah 24:14; Alma 31:38). This strengthening often occurs through the hand of our mortal friends (see 1 Samuel 23:16). Because of this blessing we can "turn away [our] hearts from affliction" (D&C 124:76).

Just as the blessings of the temple, the sweetness of the fruit of the tree of life is not immediately apparent. To discover which fruit is really sweet, it takes the enticing of the Holy Spirit. He teaches of things as they really are unlike the enticing of Satan, who deceives us with lies. Satan puts "bitter for sweet, and sweet for bitter" (Isaiah 5:20), making bad fruit taste sweet or good fruit taste bitter. Moroni warned about this deception and then eloquently explained how to judge between good and evil (see Moroni 7:14–17). The key is to taste (recognize) the light by which we may judge. This light is the light of Christ (see Moroni 7:18) enhanced by the Holy Spirit. Then we "may know with a perfect knowledge, as the daylight is from the dark night" (Moroni 7:15).

The Holy Spirit as the rod of iron will lead us to where the fruit is truly sweet. It is the fruit of the tree of life. The straight and narrow pathway to this tree passes through the sacrament altar and the altars of the temple.

The Law of Agency Continues through the Forbidden Fruit

When Satan said to Eve: "Partake of the forbidden fruit, and ye shall not die, but ye shall be as God, knowing good and evil" (2 Nephi 2:18), he was telling a lie (ye shall not die) and a half-truth (ye shall be as God). Betraying himself, Satan also told an apparent truth when he said "there is no other way" referring to the way of agency to become like God.

Eve understood that the more profound death from the forbidden fruit is spiritual. After partaking of this fruit, her first statement to Adam included her spiritual death or being "cast out" of the garden because of her choice. Then she remembered the spiritual death of

Satan. After identifying him, she remembered him being "cast out" of the presence of God because of his rebellious choice. When did she learn that spiritual death means being cast out of God's presence?

While Satan beguiled Eve with a lie, assuring her immortality and godliness in spite of agency, Eve understood that the consequences of both sorrow and sin from the forbidden fruit would be physical and spiritual death. However, Eve sensed that to become like God, her choice to partake of the forbidden fruit was better because there is no other way than allowing agency to become like God. Perhaps she recalled some understanding of death and the plan of redemption before she made her choice. However, her mistake, like Adam's (see Moses 4:23), was yielding to the beguiling of a false or unauthorized messenger instead of waiting for true messengers who would bring them "further instructions" of truth.

After the Fall, Adam and Eve learned that it takes more than mortal knowledge of good and evil to become like God. It also requires choosing to partake of the fruit of the tree of life to learn the "mysteries of God." By this fruit we really learn how "to know good and evil" (see Moses 4:28). This was something they could not do in the Garden of Eden after they chose the forbidden fruit. They needed their days prolonged, to be given sufficient time to repent in a probationary state of choice between the knowledge of good and evil until "the day of grace was passed with them, both temporally and spiritually" (Mormon 2:15).

This state of choice is given to all men by the Spirit of Christ (see Moroni 7:16) to see how they will act on this knowledge of good and evil (see D&C 19:4). With this comparative knowledge, they can judge between good and evil (see Moroni 7:15) and be "agents unto themselves" doing "many things of their own free will" (D&C 58:27–28). Then, because of agency, all men and women would hopefully respond to heartburn from sin and tribulation with godly sorrow. Then they would really experience the bitter to prize (seek after and partake of) the sweet, saving fruit of the tree of life:

> And it must needs be that the devil should tempt the children of men,
> or they could not be agents unto themselves; for if they never should
> have bitter they could not know the sweet. (D&C 29:39)

But wo unto him that has . . . all the commandments of God, . . . and that wasteth the days of his probation, for awful is his state! (2 Nephi 9:27)

We Still Must Choose between the Two Fruit Trees

As the two trees with two kinds of fruit were before Adam and Eve, so are they before us in mortality. Because of the Fall, we must partake of the fruit of the tree of knowledge of good and evil in mortality. We have fallen to a realm where Satan can still offer it to us with guile. We partake of the forbidden fruit as freely as Adam and Eve because of our agency and its apparent attraction.

The tree of life is still before us and still guarded as in the Garden of Eden. In this life it is guarded by solemn covenants. Unlike the Garden of Eden, we can pass the sentinels by keeping the covenants and then partake of the fruit of the tree of life in the temple because there we are preparing to live forever without our sins. We can even partake of the fruit of our own tree of life if we develop and keep our souls as a temple.

The great question is how will we partake of the fruit of the tree of knowledge of good and evil in this life? How sensitive are we to the feelings of our hearts? Will we continue to yield to the will of the flesh under Satan's beguiling, tasting more and more the bitterness of evil until it becomes bitter sweet or tasteless indifference? Or will we relieve bitter heartburn from sin and tribulation with the enticings of the Spirit, tasting more and more of the good until we partake of the sweetest fruit of all, the fruit of the tree of life?

Wherefore, men are free according to the flesh; and all things are given them which are expedient unto man. And they are *free to choose* liberty and eternal life, through the great Mediator of all men, or to choose captivity and death, according to the captivity and power of the devil. . . .

And now, my sons, I would that ye should look to the great Mediator, and hearken unto his great commandments; and be faithful unto his words, and *choose eternal life*, according to the *will of his Holy Spirit*;

And *not choose eternal death*, according to the *will of the flesh* and the evil which is therein, which giveth the *spirit of the devil* power to captivate. (2 Nephi 2:27–29; emphasis added; see also Helaman 14:30–31; Deuteronomy 30:15–20)

Lehi was telling his sons to partake of the fruit of the tree of life, the same fruit that he tasted in his great tree-of-life vision. He was teaching them that *unless they are taught by and follow the will of the Holy Spirit, they will never taste the sweetness of the fruit of the tree of life.* They may even loose their freedom to choose because forbidden fruit can lead to captivity by the devil.

If we do not yield to the enticings of the Holy Spirit and are not "led by the Holy Spirit, becoming humble, meek, submissive, patient, full of love and all longsuffering" (Alma 13:28), we will not desire to taste the exquisite atoning sweetness of the fruit of the tree of life. This is why Laman and Lemuel would not partake of the fruit of the tree in Lehi's dream (see 1 Nephi 8:17–18). They and many of their descendants would not believe in the Atoning Christ.

It is deeply significant that in film-assisted endowments, Satan is lurking behind dead trees without fruit (see Jude 1:12). These trees are the antithesis of the tree of life. Annually, most of the trees that surround us are stripped naked and appear dead as they lose their leaves. This fall of leaves in the Fall is symbolic of the Fall of man. Because of the Fall, our foliage is lost. We are stripped naked, exposed to death. Yet, as sure as the plan of redemption, the Spring always comes and the apparently dead trees respond to the light, resurrect with new leaves, and bear fruit.

If we learn to turn to the light of God and "taste the light," then the warmth of the love of God will cause the dormant seed (the word of God bringing all things to our spiritual remembrance) to swell within us and grow to a tree of life-producing precious fruit. If not, we will remain a dead tree, captive of Satan.

I have wondered why a white field is ready for harvest (see D&C 4:4). Green, red, or golden brown are more the harvest colors that I imagine. Perhaps the answer is found in D&C 6:3 when the Lord said of the harvest, "while the day lasts," implying that the harvest is to be done while there is light. The description of the Lord's vineyard in our dispensation found in D&C 33:4, where "all [have] corrupt minds," seems to be a field ripe for destruction. Yet many today are searching for the light that will help them grow (see D&C 123:12).

The Savior said to his disciples after penetrating the Samaritan women's heart at Jacob's well with spiritual truth, "My meat is to do the will of him that sent me, and to finish his work. Say not ye, There are yet four months, and then cometh harvest? behold, I say unto you, Lift up your eyes, and look on the fields; for they are white already to harvest" (John 4:34–35). When the white light of heaven shines with spiritual truths of Jesus Christ (see D&C 84:45), even on a corrupt vineyard, a harvest of salvation can occur.

There is no better scriptural example of the power of this light than in the conversion of Alma, the sons of Mosiah, King Lamoni, and many Lamanites (see Alma 19:6). Harvesting the white fields of the Lamanites is precisely what Ammon and his brothers did (see Alma 26:23–37).

The parable of the sower (see Mark 4:3–20) *is a wonderful teaching about responding to light.* It teaches that we can either produce a dead tree or a living tree of fruit within us. The difference depends on the environment and soil in which the seed falls. More importantly, it depends on the soil's and seed's response to light. Our hearts are the best soil for the seed (the word of God). As we respond by experimenting upon the word with faith, even if the seed is simply planted in our minds, the light of the Holy Spirit will cause the seed to grow not only in our minds but also in our hearts. The light of the Spirit penetrating the heart results in miraculous growth.

> And unto you that hear shall more be given. . . . So is the kingdom of God, as if a man should cast seed into the ground; And should sleep, and rise night and day, and the seed should spring and grow up, he knoweth not how. For the earth bringeth forth fruit of herself; first the blade, then the ear, after that the full corn in the ear. (Mark 4:24, 26–28)

The final truth of the parable of the sower (see Mark 4:20) is that in spite of the different soils there will be a harvest.

I did not understand the meaning of the phrase *full corn in the ear* until I lived in the cornfields of the Midwest. Each stalk of corn is topped with a male tassel containing pollen. Each ear of corn is topped with female silk that conducts the pollen to each cornel of corn. Unless there is sufficient rain during a brief window in July (the days of our probation) there is insufficient fertilization to produce "full corn in the ear." Thus it takes man, woman, and God (rain) to bear the souls of men to fruition. It is in the mission field that many investigators who have received the seed "spring up" over night. We know not how but by the power of the Holy Spirit penetrating their hearts. It is in the temples of the kingdom of God that the blade and the ear "grow up" with a miraculous growth to the "full corn in the ear," producing the fruit of the tree of life. This miraculous springing and growing up is the work of the Father showing forth "his own works" (3 Nephi 27:10) through the power of the Holy Spirit in the kingdom of God on earth built upon the gospel of Christ.

As we are taught by the Holy Spirit in the temple, we learn about the qualities of our Savior Jesus Christ, the fruit of the tree of life. As we follow the promptings of the Holy Spirit and are baptized by His fire, these qualities become part of our lives:

> But if ye be led of the Spirit, ye are not under the law.
>
> But the *fruit of the spirit* is love, joy, peace, long suffering, gentleness, goodness, faith,
>
> Meekness, temperance: against such there is no law. (Galatians 5:18, 22–23; emphasis added)

> For the fruit of the Spirit is in all goodness and righteousness and truth. (Ephesians 5:9)

If we continue to seek the fruits of the Spirit, we will finally be granted to taste the sweetest of His fruits. It is the taste of charity, the pure love of Christ. It is most delicious to the soul and most desirous above all fruit because it emulates the matchless love of the Father (see 1 Nephi 11:22).

In the temple we often taste the sweetness of this fruit as personal witness that Christ knows and loves us individually. We marvel and say, "how could it be?" But we do feel and know He is concerned about our trials and desires because "all things" are numbered unto God and He knows them (see Moses 1:34–35).

We marvel as Moses who heard the loving words "Moses, my son" (Moses 1:6). After feeling the love of the Lord, Moses could have expressed the words of Nephi concerning the condescension of God when he said "I know that he loveth his children" (see 1 Nephi 11:16–17). This personal knowledge that God loves us, is sweet fruit that gives us strength to overcome weakness and rise above the arm of flesh to follow His Son in a personal, loving relationship (see D&C 1:19–20).

The Holy Spirit can fill us with the sweetness of pure love and help us impart it to others. This is what happened to King Benjamin and his followers at the temple. They came there to give thanks to the Lord their God because of true messengers, just men, their teachers, and their king. They had taught them to keep the commandments of God "that they might rejoice and be filled with love towards God and all men" (Mosiah 2:4). The Lamanites (Anti-Nephi-Lehies), taught by the sons of Mosiah were converted to the Lord and filled with such great love (see Alma 26:31–33) that they were distinguished by this love as a "zeal towards God, and also towards men" (Alma 27:27).

Fruit of the Olive Tree: The Pure Oil of Charity

A different fruit tree can teach us about moving from the tree of knowledge of good and evil to the tree of life and becoming the first-fruits of Christ. This tree is not at first considered a fruit tree. It does not produce a delicious fruit spontaneously. However, with time and care, it produces a fruit that contains a pure oil.

This fruit tree is the olive tree, which the Savior often used to refer to the House of Israel (see Jacob 5). It is a perennial tree whose leaves do not change with seasons. While the tree may wither, the roots (representing the covenants of God with the house of Israel) live on, growing new, tender trees alongside the old dying tree. Therefore, the olive tree does not "[abide] alone: but if it die, it bringeth forth much fruit" (John 12:24).

The olive fruit is not produced until many years of cultivating the tree. When the olive is harvested it is bitter, requiring a purging process of salt and vinegar. Slowly the bitterness is purged and the meek and mellowed fruit is crushed under the weight of a heavy stone to force out the oil. The multiple uses of pure olive oil in Near Eastern life testify of its ability to edify lives. The anointing oil, symbolic of the Holy Spirit, and the oil for the lamps of the temple, symbolic of the light of Christ, both testify of the blessings from heaven for those who seek the pure spiritual oil of the Holy Spirit and the Savior.

Pure olive oil, the antidote for all that ails us physically and spiritually, also represents the fruit of the tree of life. This pure oil comes from the fruit of the tree of life that we can grow within us. This oil can be pressed from each of us if we let ourselves be purified by the power of Christ. It is in the temple that we learn how to become purified. Here we feel the power of Christ and His Father to purge us (see John 15:2) and press us with covenants that we might demonstrate faithfulness in sacrificing anything to be purified. Then through the power of His atoning love, we can become "the firstfruits of Christ" (Jacob 4:11; see also John 15:16; Revelation 14:4) filled with the pure "oil of joy" (Isaiah 61:3) of His pure love.

Our individual spirits, our true selves, our hearts, can become the olive oil. Purged in life with tribulation to be sweetened and purified, with the final press of death, our spirits return to the Father who made them. With resurrection they reunite with a perfected olive fruit to become fruit of eternal life. The purifying process of the olive—the cultivation from grace to grace, the purging to the sweetness of meekness, the pressing weight of trials and obedience to covenants, the sacrifice even of its own life—the Savior experienced in mortality. He leads the way for us.

We cannot become as the olive tree, submitting to pressure and sacrificing bitterness to produce a pure oil, until we partake of the fruit of the tree of knowledge of good and evil. The purging and mellowing of the experience of adversity makes real sacrifice possible. As we sacrifice all in obedience to the Savior and sacrifice all to edify others, the love within us becomes the fruit of the tree of life within us. This love is the pure oil of charity.

The profound message of the scriptural temple is that we can partake of the fruit of the tree of life in the house of the Lord and we can grow a tree of life that produces the fruit of eternal life with our own temple. This is the message taught by the Savior in the sermon on the temple mount when He combined the topics of the strait gate and narrow way, a good tree and good fruit, the will of the Father, and building upon His rock. This was contrasted with false prophets, works of iniquity, and evil fruit (see 3 Nephi 14:13–27).

In this sermon the Savior was describing Lehi's tree of life vision (see 1 Nephi 8:9–11, 19–20) and Alma's tree of life allegory (see Alma 32:28, 37, 41–42). For God, the only good fruit that can be produced comes from the tree of life because this tree obeys the will of the Father (see 3 Nephi 11:39–40; D&C 35:12) to produce His love (see 1 Nephi 11:22, 25). Therefore, we must be a branch of this tree in order to produce the purified "good fruit" of the Father (see John 15:1–16).

On our path up Mount Zion we are nourished from trial and tribulation by the sweet fruit of the tree of life. As we climb we grow a tree of life within us to become its sweet fruit.

True Messengers

One of the most important, often-repeated truths of the endowment is the principle of true messengers. This is how we are "taught of God" (John 6:45) or "taught from on high" (Ether 6:17) to receive "instruction and intelligence" (see Joseph Smith–History 1:54) that we might "be endowed with power" (see D&C 43:16).

God Calls on Men with True Messengers and Holy Works

When Adam and Eve fell from the presence of God, a most profound principle of hope was taught to them:

> I, the Lord God, gave unto Adam and unto his seed, that they should not die as to the temporal death, until I, the Lord God, should send forth angels to declare unto them repentance and redemption, through faith on the name of mine Only Begotten Son. (D&C 29:42)

> And thus the Gospel began to be preached, from the beginning, being declared by holy angels sent forth from the presence of God, and by his own voice, and by the gift of the Holy Ghost. (Moses 5:58; see also D&C 20:35)

Responding to the inquiry of Antionah, Alma explained the revelation of the plan of redemption precisely in the manner that Adam received it:

Now, if it had not been for the plan of redemption, which was laid from the foundation of the world, there could have been no resurrection of the dead. . . .

And now behold, if it were possible that our first parents could have gone forth and partaken of the tree of life they would have been forever miserable, having no preparatory state; and thus the plan of redemption would have been frustrated. . . .

But behold, it was not so; but it was appointed unto men that they must die; and after death, they must come to judgment. . . .

And after God had appointed that these things should come unto man, behold, then he saw that it was expedient that man should know concerning the things whereof he had appointed unto them;

But God did call on men, in the name of his Son [this being the plan of redemption which was laid], saying: If ye will repent, and harden not your hearts, then will I have mercy upon you, through mine Only Begotten Son;

Therefore he sent angels to converse with them, who caused men to behold of his glory.

And they began from that time forth to call on his name; therefore God conversed with men, and made known unto them the plan of redemption, which had been prepared from the foundation of the world; and this he made known unto them according to their faith and repentance and their holy works. (Alma 12:25–28, 33, 29–30)

The word of God, the gospel, the plan of redemption, the truth of things as they really are, spiritual truths and covenants would come to man by messengers. First, through heavenly messengers to holy men, the gospel would come from heaven (see Alma 13:26). But in "divers ways" (see Moroni 7:24), the true message would come from God through divers messengers even "holy men that ye know not of" (D&C 49:8).

The true message comes by His own voice, the voice of heavenly messengers, the voice of the Holy Spirit in the form of prophecy and revelation, the voice of His earthly messengers, and the voices of mother earth (see Moses 7:48) and mother nature (see D&C 43:21–25; 133:22). Unless we hear these voices "while it is called today, and harden not [our] hearts" (see D&C 45:6), "death shall overtake [us]" (see D&C 45:2).

The principle of "divers ways" or "different ways" (see Moroni 10:8) to teach us "every form of godliness" (Moroni 7:30) is what we learn in the temple endowment as we symbolically hear the voice of God and His messengers in succession. In the scriptural temple, a similar sequence is taught: "The word of the Lord came unto Alma, and Alma informed the messengers" (Alma 43:24; see Exodus 7:1–2). Whatever the medium, "whether by mine own voice or by the voice of my servants, it is the same" (D&C 1:38; see D&C 21:5). We also learn that "the voice of God . . . [will come] at sundry times, and in divers places" (D&C 128:21).

The important lesson taught in this symbolic sequence is that *we learn to recognize and hear true messengers* because they speak God's message with the power of the Holy Spirit (see 2 Peter 1:21) as though God were speaking directly to us (see Matthew 10:40). For "what I say unto one I say unto all" (D&C 61:18). Otherwise, if we reject true messengers and their heavenly gifts, we will at the same time reject the Lord. Therefore, King Noah, because his heart was hard, first rejected Abinadi then the Lord in adjoining questions (see Mosiah 11:27; see also Moses 5:16).

Joseph, the son of Jacob and Rachel, was a true messenger to his older brothers. When he "dreamed a dream" (Genesis 37:5) that offended them (see Genesis 37:7–8), he established his authority as a true messenger because he possessed the spirit of prophecy and revelation that was fulfilled (see Genesis 42:6). As we learn in the temple, the accountability of a true messenger is to his father who declares "bring me word again" (Genesis 37:14). Joseph continued as the Lord's true messenger in Egypt because "the Lord was with him" (Genesis 39:3).

The principle of recognizing and following true messengers is an important teaching in the story of Naaman, the Syrian. Because of his stature and pride, he was expecting a miraculous manifestation from the Prophet Elisha to cure his leprosy. When Elisha sent a messenger to Naaman, telling him to wash in the Jordan seven times, he at first seemed offended and refused the act. However, Naaman's servant persuaded him to comply and he was healed even becoming as "a little child" (see 2 Kings 5:10–14). Therefore, Elisha's messenger and Naaman's servant were the unlikely true messengers. While ignoring the more subtle and seemingly ordinary counsel from true messengers of the Lord, are we expecting a miraculous manifestation from the Lord before we believe? Can we recognize the still small voice within us? Do we ignore or subjugate the advice of peers, parents, priesthood leaders, and a prophet, hoping the Lord will manifest Himself to us? If so, we do not understand the Lord's principle of "divers ways" to lead us to the straight and narrow way.

Paul the chosen vessel and Cornelius the centurion both had miraculous manifestations to initiate their conversions, but both were then directed to extant priesthood authority as the next true messenger (see Acts 9:3–6; 10:3–5). Once they submitted to this authority, they entered the gate into the circle of salvation through repentance and baptism of water and the Spirit. Supposed authority, good intentions, and foreordained promises remain unrecognized and unfulfilled unless the gate to the circle of salvation is entered through true priesthood authority. "He that is ordained of me shall come in at the gate and be ordained as I have told you before" (D&C 43:7).

Recognizing a true messenger is recognizing the authority of their calling and ordination for "no man taketh this honour unto himself, but he that is called [and ordained] of God, as was Aaron" (Hebrews 5:4; see Exodus 28:1–2, 41; Numbers 27:18, 23; compare D&C 27:8; see also D&C 42:11; 20:65). The Savior said to his chosen apostles, "Ye have not chosen me, but I have chosen you, and ordained you" (John 15:16). To be chosen by the Lord as a true messenger one must be *called and ordained* by a true messenger for "if a man be called of my Father, as was Aaron, . . . I will justify him" (D&C 132:59). Recognizing a true messenger is also to recognize the truth they speak as truth from God. It is to know this truth in our minds and hearts since "he that preacheth and he that receiveth, understand one another, and both are edified" (D&C 50:22) by the "Spirit of truth" (D&C 50:17). For "he that knoweth God heareth us" (1 John 4:6) as His true messengers. When we recognize truth from true messengers by the power of the Holy Spirit, we will understand how true messengers are "ordained by the power of the Holy Ghost" (D&C 20:60). "Unto what were [they] ordained? To preach my gospel by the Spirit" (D&C 50:13–14). To be chosen by the Lord as a true messenger one must speak by the power of the Holy Ghost. This is the spirit of prophecy and revelation.

The importance of "holy works" or "an holy ordinance," meaning a priesthood or temple ordinance, to confirm (verify) the truthfulness and authenticity of the fulness of the gospel revealed in divers ways was taught to Adam:

> And thus all things were confirmed unto Adam, by an holy ordinance, and the Gospel preached, and a decree sent forth, that it should be in the world, until the end thereof; and thus it was. Amen. (Moses 5:59)

In holy ordinances, we participate in, feel, and even see the power of God (see D&C 84:20–22) to have the truthfulness of His work confirmed in our minds and hearts. The sequence of divers ways with confirmation by an holy ordinance is vividly illustrated in the missionary adventures of Alma and Amulek. They both received the plan of salvation and their calling from a heavenly messenger (see Alma 8:14–15, 20–21). Their authority as true messengers came through the spirit of prophecy and revelation which they possessed (see Alma 8:24; 11:22). Alma's calling as a true messenger of God, even though it was witnessed by the power of God (see Alma 8:31), was not recognized by the hardhearted people of Ammonihah who declared, "Who is God, that sendeth no more authority than one man among this people?" (Alma 9:6).

Yet, the meaning of "divers ways" also means more than one witness of the truth, for this is how the word of God is established (see 2 Corinthians 13:1; 2 Nephi 27:14; D&C 6:28). The three spiritual, then eight temporal witnesses of the Book of Mormon completely provided for both spiritual and temporal divers ways of witnessing the truth. After Amulek testified to them, even the people of Ammonihah felt the power of divers ways when they "began to be astonished, seeing there was more than one witness" (Alma 10:12).

The people of Gideon who accepted Alma as a true messenger had his message confirmed by a holy ordinance under the holy order of God. He taught them a temple sermon with temple teachings such as the straight path of meekness, faith, hope, and charity, the importance of becoming a holy temple, obtaining spotless garments, entering into the sanctuary of God "to go no more out," and to receive the "peace of God" (see Alma 7:19–27). The holy ordinances and doctrines of the temple must have been taught to the people of Gideon because the very first verse of the next chapter states:

> Alma . . . having taught the people of Gideon many things which cannot be written, having established the order of the church. (Alma 8:1)

We learn in the temple that we can ultimately recognize a true messenger of the Lord by "an holy ordinance" (Moses 5:59). When he asked him to "shew me a sign" (Judges 6:17), this is how Gideon finally recognized the man who sat under the oak in Ophrah as an angel of the Lord. Then the angel, with the touch of his staff, "rose up fire out of the rock, and consumed the flesh and the unleavened cakes" (Judges 6:21). Surely, this was the power of God manifest through a holy ordinance to verify His true messenger.

God will reveal His plan of redemption to men on earth through His messengers and confirm it by holy ordinances. Until the end of the world, as long as "there shall be one man upon the face thereof" (Moroni 7:36), this will be God's way of revealing Himself to man. Even today, "at the last day," when it is said that miracles and revelation from God have ceased (see Moroni 7:35–37), God calls on men in the same divers way.

These messenger mentioned in D&C 29, Moses 5, and Alma 12 aren't just any messengers. They are His "chosen vessels" (Moroni 7:31) as true messengers from the presence of God, with God's message. They are "preachers of righteousness" (Moses 6:23). We learn in the temple that Peter, James, and John were some of these holy angels or true messengers. Perhaps their postmortal calling as ministering angels is a continuation of their pre-mortal and mortal ministries (see D&C 128:20; D&C 7:5–7; D&C 130:5).

The Importance of Seeking True Messengers

After following a false messenger and experiencing a bitter fall, it is significant that Adam and Eve no longer wanted to follow any doctrine until they were sure it came from a true messenger of God. The first inquiry that Adam made after partaking of the forbidden fruit was about true messengers. Like Eve, this inquiry demonstrated that Adam was able to taste and seek good in the forbidden fruit. After partaking of the fruit they were injured spiritually, feeling bitter heartburn. Then they felt godly sorrow. Therefore, they wanted to be healed by seeking a true messenger from God while avoiding the beguiling of Satan through the philosophies of men, mingled with scripture.

This is the same patient search for truth that Moses and Joseph Smith demonstrated. It is the same patient and persistent search, with faith and repentance, that we must demonstrate to be assured that the light of Christ within us will enlighten us to be led to a true messenger from God. This is how we must seek the Lord. Therefore, we should follow the counsel of Alma and "trust no one to be [our] teacher nor [our] minister, except he be a man of God," (Mosiah 23:14; see Alma 48:18). The history of the pharaohs of Egypt seems to be a continual search for true messengers like Abraham. A symbolic yet serious search for a true messenger is demonstrated even today in the rituals of courting for marriage which often relies on spiritual feeling as the final answer.

As we have seen, a gift for seeking the Lord is the Holy Spirit, a true messenger (see Moses 5:58). This gift is important because we can neither recognize nor become true messengers without it (see D&C 14:8; 42:14, 16–17).

True Messengers with the Word of God Lead as Iron Rods

The opening scene of Lehi's dream is a striking contrast illustrating the need for a true messenger to lead us through the dark and dreary waste of life:

Methought I saw in my dream, a dark and dreary wilderness.

And it came to pass that I saw a man, and he was dressed in a white robe; and he came and stood before me.

And it came to pass that he spake unto me, and bade me follow him.

And it came to pass that as I followed him I beheld myself that I was in a dark and dreary waste. (1 Nephi 8:4–7)

The man dressed in white, a true messenger, mortal or spiritual, led Lehi to the strait and narrow path and the rod of iron leading to the tree of life. All true messengers, parents and prophets, lead their children to the rod of iron. This rod is the word of God and revelation about this word from the Holy Spirit within us. The word and the Holy Spirit are the only true messengers that can ultimately lead us along the straight and narrow path to the tree of life.

In surgery, an important modern technique uses the principle of a true messenger or guide in the form of an iron rod. With the use of modern imaging radiology, it is possible to deliver a surgical instrument to a precise target in the body with the use of a guide wire. Through x-ray visualization, the guide wire is passed through bone, blood vessels, or other body cavities to reach a specific site. Then the surgical instrument follows the guide wire until it reaches the target. This technique eliminates the need for extensive dissection and exposes parts of the body otherwise inaccessible.

Like a true messenger, the surgical guide wire is the "rod of iron" which leads safely through the fields of danger to the desired target. The surgical principle of the guide wire is the same as the scriptural principle of the iron rod. We need a true messenger (a parent, a prophet, a missionary, a true friend, the Holy Spirit) who has the iron rod which is the word of God. They will lead us to understand and help us grasp hold of this rod, which will surely guide us to the tree of life.

This gift of the Holy Ghost as a true messenger is an x-ray perspective in our lives because the Holy Spirit helps us see things not seen by the natural eye. To progress from forgetting everything to having one's eyes opened (see Genesis 3:5) is ultimately to have spiritual knowledge. With this perspective, the Holy Spirit helps us firmly grasp and follow the iron rod. The Holy Spirit secures us to the iron rod by helping us understand and personally taste the fruit of the tree of life through the gifts of the Spirit. It is significant that the "Spirit of the Lord" in 1 Nephi 11 is the Holy Spirit.[15] He led Nephi to an understanding of the tree of life and its fruit.

Christ is the ultimate word and messenger of God (see Joseph Smith Translation, John 1:1; D&C 93:8–9). The Holy Spirit speaks the words of Christ. Therefore, in a very literal sense, the iron rod is Christ. We must personally learn to "press forward" through this life "with a steadfastness in Christ" (2 Nephi 31:20), "relying wholly upon the merits of him who is mighty to save" (2 Nephi 31:19; see also Moroni 6:4). We do this by obeying Christ's words as though we were "clinging to [a] rod of iron" (1 Nephi 8:24). His rod will prevent us from falling into the mist of darkness and gulf of everlasting misery. Then with confidence, we must "press . . . forward, continually holding fast to the rod of iron" (1 Nephi 8:30).

Christ's meridian ministry was a straight path (see Mark 1:3) through strait gates. He started his ministry by entering the strait gate of baptism (see Matthew 3:16). It continued through the strait gates of the temple. His preaching started in the country of His earthly father's house but his straight path invariably led up to His Heavenly Father's house.

The rope of Christ's Atonement leads to the temple. There it becomes an iron rod. The path really becomes strait and the rope sturdy in the temple. Here we grasp hold of the word of God with the fulness of the Holy Ghost until our calling and election is sure. Through covenants, keeping solemn commitments to commandments, the Holy Ghost will secure us on the path to the tree of life. In the temple we see and taste the reality of this tree so we no more desire to wander in the dark and dreary waste of mortality. As we cling to Christ in the temple, He will lead us to "that within the veil":

> Yea, we see that whosoever will may lay hold upon the word of God, which is quick and powerful, which shall divide asunder all the cunning and the snares and the wiles of the devil, and lead the man of Christ in a strait and narrow course across that everlasting gulf of misery which is prepared to engulf the wicked—
>
> And land their souls, yea, their immortal souls, at the right hand of God in the kingdom of heaven, to sit down with Abraham, and Isaac, and with Jacob, and with all our holy fathers, to go no more out. (Helaman 3:29–30)

The Compass as an Iron Rod and a True Messenger

Lehi and his family literally traveled through the dark and dreary waste of the desert to a promised land. As with Lehi and the children of Israel in the Sinai, so it is with us. The course to the promised land is through the flesh pots of Egypt and the Sinai deserts of mortal life. A unique true messenger guided Lehi and his family through the desert. The Liahona, a compass working by faith and righteousness, pointed the way through the desert to the promised land, like a magnetic compass.

As a testament of the reality of God, the magnetic compass faithfully points to the North. The temple in Jerusalem, as God's throne, was placed on the north side of Mount Zion. This was because the Hebrew concept of the universe placed God's throne near the North Star, around which the constellations turn and where the summit of the heavenly mount is located.[16] This is the mount that is called "the mount of the congregation" located "in the sides of the north" in the description of Lucifer's desired ascent into heaven (see Isaiah 14:12–13).

In this sense, a compass is a true messenger and an iron rod. If a compass is left in our pocket unheeded, considered as "naught" (2 Nephi 33:2) or "trampled upon" (D&C 3:15; D&C 17:1), we will not know the exact direction to follow. If we do not give heed to the words of true messengers, we will not recognize that they point the way to salvation.

Alma taught Helaman this same truth about the Liahona:

And now, my son, I would that ye should understand that these things are not without a shadow; for as our fathers were slothful to give heed to this compass (now these things were temporal) they did not prosper; even so it is with things which are spiritual.

For behold, it is as easy to give heed to the word of Christ, which will point to you a straight course to eternal bliss, as it was for our fathers to give heed to this compass, which would point unto them a straight course to the promised land. . . .

O my son, do not let us be slothful because of the easiness of the way; for so was it with our fathers; for so was it prepared for them, that if they would look they might live; even so it is with us. The way is prepared, and if we will look we may live forever. (Alma 37:43–44, 46)

Alma was referring to the serpent raised by Moses to heal those stricken by fiery serpents in the Sinai (see 1 Nephi 17:41). His profound message was that it is as easy for us to look at our spiritual compass (the iron rod of personal revelation) and find the tree of life as it is to look at a magnetic compass and find the North Star. We each have a spiritual compass that is evident to us when we are diligently obedient to it.

To look is to look up and seek the light. It is to "behold a type" of Christ in what we see (see Alma 33:19) and then have faith in Him. It is to "look unto me in every thought" (D&C 6:36). It is "[seeking] those things which are above" (Colossians 3:1) by seeking the Lord in our minds and in our hearts with eyes of faith until we see with eyes of understanding. It is recognizing that the Lord as a true messenger will lead us through this world of fiery serpents. He will lead us to His holy house where He will endow us with power to "look up to God at that day [of judgment] with a pure heart and clean hands" (Alma 5:19).

A True Messenger's Mark of Authority

To look up results in seeing the light and understanding the great view that only the gift of the spirit of prophecy and revelation can bring (see Alma 17:3). From parent to prophet, this gift is the mark of authority of a true messenger in the kingdom of God. This is why it was said of the Great True Messenger in the meridian of time, that "He taught as one having authority from God, and not as having authority from the Scribes" (Joseph Smith Translation, Matthew 7:37). Even in His youth, the Great True Messenger needed not that any man should teach Him: "And he served under his father, and he spake not as other men, neither could he be taught; for he needed not that any man should teach him" (Joseph Smith Translation, Matthew 3:25) because He was "strong in spirit, filled with wisdom: and the grace of God was upon him" (Luke 2:40).

Christ knew of His divine calling as testified by the scriptures, taught by the Spirit, and confirmed by His Father in Heaven. He knew His calling for the salvation of men. His understanding was not dependent on other men (see John 2:24–25) nor blinded like the Jews of His day who sought the philosophies, traditions, and ambitions of men to interpret the Law and the scriptures. His was the message of a true messenger: Look to me (Christ) and live. Do not wander in the "forbidden paths" and "strange roads" (see 1 Nephi 8:28, 32) of the philosophies and traditions of men. "Look ye unto the revelations of God" (Mormon 8:33). Thus, Christ condemned the Pharisees for teaching "the commandments of men" (see Mark 7:7, 9).

The Pharisees, Scribes, and many Jews, with eyes blinded by pride in traditions and doctrines of men, could not look up and see the light of a true messenger:

> Then said his disciples unto him, they [the Pharisees] will say unto us, We ourselves are righteous, and need not that any man should teach us. God, we know, heard Moses and some of the prophets; but us he will not hear.
>
> And they will say, We have the law for our salvation, and that is sufficient for us. (Joseph Smith Translation, Matthew 7:14–15)

The Pharisees recognized true dead messengers in some of the prophets. They could not recognize the Savior, a living prophet, filled with the spirit of prophecy and revelation. "By denying him [as a true messenger, they] also [denied] the prophets and the law" (2 Nephi 25:28).

This truth is demonstrated in the coming forth of the Book of Mormon. Because Satan hardened the hearts of the people to stir them up against Joseph Smith, they did not believe the words of Christ in the Book of Mormon (see D&C 10:32). Yet, Nephi testified that if one believes in Christ he or she will believe in the words of the Book of Mormon for "they are the words of Christ" (see 2 Nephi 33:10). Christ affirmed that failure to recognize and understand His words is because of failure to recognize His appointed true messenger (see D&C 5:7). It is not the written word that gives authority and complete recognition of God. It is recognition and belief in the authority of His current true messengers that reveal God and His word by the spirit of prophecy and revelation.

Revelation from God was mostly a diminished or denied principle to the Christian world in 1834, as it is today. Yet in the organization of the first high council of the Church in 1834, which had almost twice as much written scripture as the rest of Christianity, the authority of revelation was the fundamental principle.

> In case of difficulty respecting doctrine or principle, if there is not a sufficiency written to make the case clear to the minds of the council,

the president may inquire and obtain the mind of the Lord by revelation. (D&C 102:23; see also D&C 120:1; consider Acts 15:25, 28)

Many doctrines and principles of Christ's gospel such as baptism, keeping the Sabbath day, grace, works, judgment, and even the nature of God do not have "a sufficiency written to make the case clear to the minds" of the professional clergy in the Christian world today. Without a true messenger who can "obtain the mind of the Lord by revelation" (D&C 102:23), the philosophies and commandments of men will continue.

Christ would not recognize or "hear" the Pharisees as true messengers because they did not have the authority of the spirit of prophecy and revelation. Looking from the court of the Gentiles across the Kidron Valley to the whited tombs at the base of the Mount of Olives, Christ said the Scribes and Pharisees where full of dead men's bones:

> Woe unto you, scribes and Pharisees, hypocrites! for ye are like unto whited sepulchres, which indeed appear beautiful outward, but are within full of dead men's bones, and of all uncleanness. (Matthew 23:27)

It is not the outward appearance or even the intellectual appearance that manifests God's authority. *It is the spirit of prophecy and revelation within a true messenger that gives the authority of truth, and the authority to teach it* (see D&C 42:14, 16–17). Therefore, at the time of the Prophet Mormon, the people "put down all power and authority which cometh from God [because] they [denied] the Holy Ghost" (Moroni 8:28).

During their ministries, Alma and the sons of Mosiah demonstrated the source of God's authority:

> And Alma went and began to declare the word of God unto the church which was established in the valley of Gideon, according to the *revelation* of the truth of the word which had been spoken by his fathers, and according to the *spirit of prophecy* which was in him, according to the testimony of Jesus Christ, the Son of God, who should come to redeem his people from their sins, and the holy order by which he was called. (Alma 6:8; emphasis added)

Therefore they had the spirit of prophecy, and the spirit of revelation, and when they taught, they taught with power and authority of God (see Alma 17:3).

Joseph Smith taught that the key to distinguishing a true messenger from a false is the spirit of prophecy and revelation:

> If any person should ask me if I were a prophet, I should not deny it, as that would give me the lie; for, according to John, the testimony of Jesus is the spirit of prophecy; therefore, if I profess to be a witness or teacher, and have not the spirit of prophecy which is the testimony of Jesus, I must be a false witness; but if I be a true teacher and witness, I must possess the spirit of prophecy, and that constitutes a prophet; and any man who says he is a teacher or preacher of righteousness, and *denies the spirit of prophecy*, is a liar, and the truth is not in him; and by this key false teachers and impostors may be detected.[17]

Simply stated, true messengers "speak as they are moved upon by the Holy Ghost" (D&C 68:3; see Matthew 10:19; D&C 84:85), while false messengers "teach with their learning, [even about Christ], and deny the Holy Ghost, which giveth utterance" (2 Nephi 28:4). The spirit of prophecy and revelation is a full testimony of Jesus Christ given to men by the Holy Spirit (see Revelation 19:10; 1 Corinthians 12:3). They have this testimony written both in their minds and their hearts. Therefore, this testimony must ultimately come by revelation given in the Holy Order of God.

Transmission of authority, prophecy, and revelation is often re-enacted directly from God through His Holy Order in the heavenly temple. His foreordained true messengers are "carried away in a vision" (1 Nephi 1:8) or "carried away in the spirit" (1 Nephi 14:30) and "[stand] in the counsel of the Lord" (Jeremiah 23:18) with "the Lord sitting upon a throne, high and lifted up, and his train [filling] the temple" (Isaiah 6:1). Such was the case of Enoch, Abraham, Micaiah, Moses, Ezekiel, Joshua, Isaiah, Lehi, Nephi, Paul, John the Revelator, and Joseph Smith.

No matter the method, the important point is "that none [receive] authority to preach or to teach except it [is] by him from God" (Mosiah 23:17). Otherwise, "there [is] none in the land that [have] authority from God" (Mosiah 21:33). Revelation from God in the spirit of prophecy and revelation is the key for God's "power and authority" (see Words of Mormon 1:17; Mosiah 13:6; 18:17; Alma 5:3; 3 Nephi 7:15, 17–18, 21). It is the same today, in the dispensation of the fulness of times, where "the voice of the Lord . . . is mine authority, and the authority of my servants" (D&C 1:2, 6).

It was by revelation that the Ethiopian recognized Philip as a true messenger:

> And Philip ran thither to him, and heard him read the prophet Esaias, and said, Understandest thou what thou readest?
> And he said, How can I, except some man [a true messenger] should guide me? And he desired Philip that he should come up and sit with him.
> Then Philip opened his mouth, and began at the same scripture, and *preached unto him Jesus.* (Acts 8:30–31, 35; emphasis added)

In the meridian of time, as today, it took a messenger with the spirit of prophecy and revelation to recognize the words of Isaiah as a testimony of Christ:

> The words of Isaiah are not plain unto you, nevertheless they are plain unto all those that are filled with *the spirit of prophecy.* (2 Nephi 25:4; emphasis added)

The message of true messengers is always complete truth and testimony about Jesus Christ and His gospel. Some Nephites, after the sign of the birth of Christ, needed a true messenger to correctly understand the scriptures about Christ's birth and Atonement in relation to the law of Moses (see 3 Nephi 1:24–25). Abinadi, who was the great "type and shadow" prophet in the Book of Mormon, taught King Noah and his priests how to recognize the importance of Christ in the law of Moses. He emphasized that unless the law of God is written or understood in the heart it will be misunderstood (see Mosiah 12:27; 13:11; see also Mosiah 26:3).

This writing in the heart by the Holy Spirit comes by the spirit of prophecy and revelation. This truth Abinadi taught when he explained who the seed of Christ is (see Mosiah 15:11–18; compare 1 Nephi 13:37). It is in the temple, through the Holy Order of God, that the writing of the laws of God in our hearts is completed. There we blossom from the seed of Christ to his spiritual offspring.

Contrast the reasoning of the Pharisees who claimed that, "we . . . need not that any man should teach us" (Joseph Smith Translation,

Matthew 7:14), with the reasoning of the Apostle John who said: "Ye need not that any man teach you" (1 John 2:27). Both declared similar words but for entirely different reasons. The Pharisees reasoned that "the law" (the written law of Moses) was sufficient for their authority and salvation. This reasoning is exactly what is heard in the religious world today: "A Bible! A Bible! We have got a Bible, and there cannot be any more Bible" (see 2 Nephi 29:3). Or in other words, we have the written law of God as our authority in the Christian world today. As the boy Joseph Smith discovered, relying only on the written word results in a "war of words and tumult of opinions" (Joseph Smith—History 1:10). He concluded that "the teachers of religion of the different sects understood the same passages of scripture so differently as to destroy all confidence in settling the question by an appeal to the Bible" (Joseph Smith—History 1:12).

In contrast, the apostle John reasoned that "the anointing," the Holy Spirit, a true messenger, who "teacheth you of all things and is truth" is the assurance of authority and salvation. Therefore, *the Holy Ghost giveth authority*" (1 Nephi 10:22; emphasis added). His authority in revealing pure truth is why no man or man's interpretation of the written law can provide that assurance. This is why the Ethiopian was converted and baptized when his spirit received a witness from the Holy Spirit through Philip. Both true messengers prophesied and revealed Jesus Christ.

How clearly this contrast is present in the religious and secular world today! There are many religious messengers today who preach Christ's divinity but deny continuing revelation and His holy order. Therefore, they do not have a fulness of the testimony of Christ. There also are many religious messengers today who deny any revelation as well as the divinity of Christ. Both deny "a more sure word of prophecy" (2 Peter 1:19) in the true principle, "ye are to be taught from on high" (D&C 43:16).

After the First Vision, Joseph Smith was surprised that a Methodist minister would say of this important event, "it was all of the devil, that there were no such things as visions or revelations in these days; that all such things had ceased with the apostles, and that there would never be any more of them" (Joseph Smith—History 1:21).

Such reasoning sounds similar to that of the Nephites and Lamanites who "[forgot] those signs and wonders" at the birth of Christ, stating that "it was wrought by men and by the power of the devil" (3 Nephi 2:1–2). Thus the Lord gave today's world the following warning:

> And when the times of the Gentiles is come in, a light shall break forth among them that sit in darkness, and it shall be the fulness of my gospel;
> But they receive it not; for they perceive not the light, and they turn their hearts from me because of the precepts of men. (D&C 45:28–29)

They "perceive not the light" because they turn their hardened hearts from the spirit of prophecy and revelation, to the precepts of men who deny the spirit of prophecy and revelation. The Savior foretold in a warning the fate of the Gentiles in this dispensation if they continue to perceive not the light in the fulness of the restored gospel (see 3 Nephi 16:8–15).

The fulness of the gospel has been revealed by true messengers from God, not by the precepts of men. One true messenger, the Holy Spirit, can really show us the light and give us the vision of this true message. Filling us with the spirit of prophecy and revelation, He removes the shades of pride and tradition from our eyes so that we look up and see the light carrying the great view of the true message. Therefore, we no longer want to follow the precepts of men "save their precepts shall be given by the power of the Holy Ghost" (2 Nephi 28:31).

Identifying a true messenger from God was an important issue in the meridian of time. I often wonder if I would have recognized the man Christ as the Savior of the world had I lived during His ministry. Christ in His glory as the great and last promise of the temple was veiled in a mortal body. Yet, in His condescension the promise was manifested for those that had eyes to see. Like the righteous Nephites who saw the resurrected Christ, it took some sanctification through discipleship, Christ's resurrection, and the power of the gift of the Holy Ghost for His disciples in Jerusalem to truly recognize and understand Him. Perhaps recognizing the Book of Mormon as the word of God and a true witness of Jesus Christ is today's test in answer to the question about recognizing Christ. Both Christ and the Book of Mormon appear among those who should recognize them as coming from God but who were and are blinded by the traditions of men.

The Savior said to the scribes and Pharisees: "Search the scriptures . . . they are they which testify of me" (John 5:39; compare 3 Nephi 23:5). How could the Scribes and Pharisees have missed Christ and His gospel even in their written law? It is because they interpreted the written law with the traditions and commandments of men (see Mark 7:7, 9) and not with the spirit of prophecy and revelation from the Holy Spirit as did the apostles and prophets (see Ephesians 3:3–5). Written scriptures are but relics of revelation. Unless they are perceived and understood in our hearts by the same spirit they were given (see 2 Peter 1:20–21), scriptures remain artifacts of antiquity in our minds. Even with a scholarly interpretation of the scriptures, are we missing a true messenger today because we follow the traditions and commandments of men? To know the truth of God, we must know both in our minds and in our hearts, which requires not only scholarly study but also the teaching of the Spirit. To be taught by the Spirit we must humbly seek Him through study, fasting, prayer, and holy ordinances. Then we must learn to recognize His voice, especially in our hearts, being present where it is spoken.

> Behold, that which you hear is as the voice of one crying in the wilderness—in the wilderness, because you cannot see him—my voice, because my voice is Spirit; my spirit is truth; truth abideth and hath no end; and if it be in you it shall abound. (D&C 88:66)

Once we hear His voice, we must obey it by "acting in the authority which [God has] given [us] (D&C 68:8). The ultimate and motivating confirmation of truth must come from God or His true spiritual messenger, the Holy Spirit. "For it is my voice which speaketh [my words] unto you; for they are given by my Spirit unto you" (D&C 18:35). This is pure knowledge that gives us unwavering conviction. If we do not have this kind of conviction then we do not experience God's and the Holy Spirit's unique role in our ability to recognize truth.

True Messengers on Both Sides and between the Veils of Birth and Death

The calling of Peter, James, and John to act as holy angels, sent to declare the gospel to Adam and Eve, portended their mortal calling as apostles of the Savior and portends their postmortal calling as ministering angels (see D&C 7:5–7; 128:20). "There are no angels who minister to this earth but those who do belong or have belonged to it" (D&C 130:5). There have been many, even Christ, who have worked on both sides and between the veils as true messengers. Christ is the ultimate true messenger as declared by His Father: "This is My Beloved Son. *Hear Him*" (Joseph Smith—History 1:17; emphasis added). On either side and between the veils, He was the "Word . . . even the messenger of salvation" (D&C 93:8) like no other messenger from God. In this life, Christ is "the messenger of the covenant" (Malachi 3:1). He has established temple covenants in every gospel dispensation. This will dramatically occur at His second coming to introduce the Millennium.

Christ's role as a true messenger of salvation and of the covenant continued beyond this life to the other side of the veil in the spirit world. There he organized His true messengers as section 138 of the Doctrine and Covenants so vividly reveals:

> But behold, from among the righteous, he organized his forces and appointed messengers, clothed with power and authority, and commissioned them to go forth and carry the light of the gospel to them that were in darkness, even to all the spirits of men; and thus was the gospel preached to the dead. (D&C 138:30)

> The faithful elders . . . when they depart from mortal life, continue their labors in the preaching of the gospel . . . in the great world of the spirits of the dead. (D&C 138:57)

Melchizedek Priesthood Holders Are Called as True Messengers

The importance of true messengers as guiding rudders to steer us on a straight course that we be not "tossed to and fro" is emphatically stated by Paul:

And he gave some, apostles; and some, prophets; and some, evan-
gelists [patriarchs]; and some, pastors [bishops] and teachers [home
teachers];

For the perfecting of the saints. . . .

Till we all come in the unity of the faith, and of the knowledge
of the Son of God, unto a perfect man. . . .

That we henceforth be no more children, tossed to and fro, and
carried about with every wind of doctrine, by the sleight of men, and
cunning craftiness, whereby they lie in wait to deceive. (Ephesians
4:11–14)

Verse 11 mentions essentially Melchizedek Priesthood offices
or messengers. It is a sobering fact that all those who hold the
Melchizedek Priesthood were foreordained to become true messengers of salvation for those on earth:

And this is the manner after which they were ordained—being called
and prepared from the foundation of the world according to the
foreknowledge of God, on account of their exceeding faith and good
works; in the first place being left to choose good or evil; therefore
they having chosen good, and exercising exceedingly great faith, are
called with a holy calling, yea, with that holy calling which was prepared, with and according to, a preparatory redemption for such.
(Alma 13:3)

The apostle Paul taught how holders of the Melchizedek Priesthood are true messengers of salvation for the preparatory redemption
of their fellow men:

For every high priest taken from among men is ordained for men in
things pertaining to God, that he may offer both gifts and sacrifices
for sins. (Hebrews 5:1)

In messianic imagery, Paul defined "high priest" as one who
offers spiritual gifts and makes sacrifice for others.[18] All ordained
high priests are to follow the example of the Great High Priest by
being a true messenger "of good things to come, by a greater and
more perfect tabernacle" (Hebrews 9:11) and by obeying the edifying doctrine of the priesthood. "He that is ordained of God . . . is
appointed to be the greatest, notwithstanding he is the least and the
servant of all" (D&C 50:26). As we will see in the Chapter 9, "The

Great and Last Promise: Seeing the Summit of Mount Zion" which discusses the pure love of Christ, *the greatest application of this pure love is sacrifice of self for the edification of others.* We will also learn in Chapter 13, "The Salt and Light of the Covenant," that all endowed members of the Church covenant to be its true messengers.

Paul's definition of high priest could likewise be the definition of a mother. Love through sacrifice is the essence of the calling in this Holy Order, even the Holy Order of Matrimony. I believe the most important calling I have in this Holy Order is that of husband and father. I am called to sacrifice in obedience to the Lord in order to lead my wife and children in the way of salvation. As a true messenger and earthly father, I am called to turn their hearts to the Heavenly Father.

We learn in the temple, that it is God's will that we follow His true messengers between the veils during our mortal probation (see 3 Nephi 12:2). The current temple endowment ceremony teaches us that as the meridian apostles Peter, James, and John were commanded to "go, stand and speak in the temple to the people all the words of this life" (Acts 5:20), so are we taught "the words of eternal life in this world" (Moses 6:59) by instruction from true messengers. These messengers are God's prophet and counselors—the current Peter, James, and John of His church. When we raise our arms to sustain true messengers we agree to support them by sustaining their arms (see Exodus 17:11–12) which point the way through this mortal desert, leading us to the iron rod and the straight path up Mount Zion. We also agree that God will sustain them as true messengers.

Becoming True Messengers: Our Imperative Duty

It is not only important that we learn how to recognize true messengers, but that we as parents, gospel teachers, church leaders, missionaries, and true friends become true messengers. As true messengers, we are expected to "be anxiously engaged in a good cause, and do many things of [our] own free will, and bring to pass much righteousness" (D&C 58:27). We are to become righteous judges of those who hear our message (see D&C 75:21).

During my tour of Israel, an enjoyable break from the sightseeing was listening to the thoughts of one who is a true messenger. After dinner, our guide Wayne Brickey selected scriptural topics and

The Scriptural Temple

discussed them with those interested. I particularly enjoyed his discussion of D&C 123:7–17.[19] These verses of scripture contain an important doctrine from the inspired mind of the Prophet Joseph, a true messenger who had languished in Liberty Jail for months. It is the doctrine of our "imperative duty" to become a true messenger of God:

> It is an imperative duty that we owe to God, to angels, with whom we shall be brought to stand, and also to ourselves, to our wives and children, who have been made to bow down with grief, sorrow, and care, under the most damning hand of murder, tyranny, and oppression, supported and urged on and upheld by the influence of that spirit which hath so strongly riveted the creeds of the fathers who have inherited the lies, upon the hearts of the children, and filled the world with confusion, and has been growing stronger and stronger, and is now the very mainspring of all corruption, and the whole earth groans under the weight of its iniquity.
>
> It is an iron yoke, it is a strong band; they are the very handcuffs, and chains, and shackles, and fetters of hell.
>
> For there are many yet on the earth among all sects, parties, and denominations, who are blinded by the subtle craftiness of men, whereby they lie in wait to deceive, and who are only kept from the truth because they know not where to find it. (D&C 123:7–8, 12)

After explaining how the creeds (traditions, philosophies, and precepts) of men, so strongly entrenched in the hearts of men by the father of lies, have become the "mainspring of corruption," the Prophet explained our "imperative duty":

> Therefore, that we should waste and wear out our lives in bringing to light all the hidden things of darkness, wherein we know them; and they are truly manifest from heaven. (D&C 123:13)

This is a passionate call for us to be true messengers of God. This is the same call that Mormon, who on the verge of seeing the destruction of his people, remarkably made to his son Moroni:

> And now, my beloved son, notwithstanding their hardness, let us labor diligently; for if we should cease to labor, we should be brought under condemnation; for we have a labor to perform whilst in this tabernacle of clay, that we may conquer the enemy of all righteousness, and rest our souls in the kingdom of God. (Moroni 9:6)

To be a true messenger we must declare the gospel like Moroni with "the voice and sound of a trump" (see D&C 24:12; D&C 29:4; D&C 42:6), serving as an instrument in the Lord's hands to save and preserve all the people (see Alma 2:30). Yet, we must be confident in the power of the still small voice of truth while suffering "all manner of afflictions" that we might be the means of "saving some soul" (Alma 26:30). Our words and actions must be ignited and constrained by the Spirit. We must become true messengers by following the doctrine of the priesthood (see D&C 121:41–43). Thus, to be a true messenger we must have the true message from the True Messenger.

While traveling in Cambridge, England, I tried "punting" on the Cam River that saunters through the college campuses. A punt is an English-style gondola, propelled by a long pole. My wife sat in the middle of the punt as I stood on the back pushing the pole off the muddy bottom of the Cam. Instead of steering a straight course, I followed a desultory path from bank to bank, much to the amusement of the local students.

Observing the true gondoliers, I noticed that the punt would steer a straight course if the pole were left in the water as a rudder after it lifted from the bottom. The ending words of Joseph Smith, following the verses declaring the imperative duty of true messengers, remind me of my punting experience:

> You know, brethren, that a very large ship is benefited very much by a very small helm in the time of a storm, by being kept workways with the wind and the waves. (D&C 123:16; see also James 3:4)

Even very small true messengers, like home and visiting teachers, are of great benefit to keep those who follow them on a straight course ("workways") through the confusion of the creeds of the world ("with the wind and the waves"). Reflecting the image of God holding the ark of Noah and the land of Zion in His hand (see Moses 7:43; D&C 63:25), a true messenger like Nephi can steady the ark on a straight course to the promised land (see 1 Nephi 18:21–22). For "behold, I, the Lord, have appointed a way for the journeying of my saints" (D&C 61:24).

Becoming True Messengers in the Temple

It is in the temple that we really learn how to become true messengers because in the temple we learn the fulness of the Lord's love and the fulness of His true message. Here we learn to submit to the will of the Lord and follow him up Mount Zion as our true messenger.

In the temple, we become true messengers of the Lord by accepting and keeping His everlasting covenant. As this covenant is a messenger preparing for Christ's return, so we who keep the covenant are prepared as true messengers for this great event:

> And even so I have sent mine *everlasting covenant* into the world, to be a light to the world, and to be a standard for my people, and for the Gentiles to seek to it, and to be a messenger before my face to prepare the way before me. (D&C 45:9; emphasis added)

We who keep the everlasting covenant are the true messengers of Christ, the salt and light to the world, because we covenant to sacrifice all we possess to build up the kingdom of God on earth and to establish Zion. The gift or endowment for keeping this covenant is further light, knowledge, and righteousness from the "Father of lights" (James 1:17; D&C 67:9) and the "Spirit of truth" (see D&C 6:15; D&C 93:9).

The words *light* and *knowledge* (see D&C 77:4) make up a repeated phrase in the endowment. It is light that is a faithful keeper and director of knowledge because light is truth (see D&C 84:45). We are not just endowed with knowledge but also with light so that we are empowered to see the great view of things as they really are in order "to move [and] to act" (D&C 77:4) in the direction and perspective of the light of God. It is a matter of first "[understanding] my will concerning you" (D&C 82:8) then following the directions of this will as to "how you may act before me" (D&C 82:9).

Thus, the true message is "light and knowledge" by the spirit of prophecy and revelation so that we "see and understand the things of God" (D&C 76:12) with "purer eyes" (D&C 131:7), the "eyes of our understandings" (D&C 76:19), in order to act in the light of God. In the temple we receive the fulness of this gift and thus become the messengers of light and salt or light and knowledge to match His message on His mountain in the dispensation of the fulness of times.

A Full View of Mount Zion

*M*oses *resisted the* honor of Egypt and endured the base camp of Midian to find a true messenger. He was rewarded with the great and last promise of the temple, given "in an exceedingly high mountain":

> The words of God, which he spake unto Moses at a time when Moses was caught up *into an exceedingly high mountain,*
>   And *he saw God face to face,* and he talked with him, and the glory of God was upon Moses; therefore Moses could endure his presence. (Moses 1:1–2)

From a Glimpse to a Full View: Parting the Veil of Clouds on Mount Zion

After God showed Moses "the world and the ends thereof," the glory of God withdrew, and Moses "being left unto himself" fell to the ground. When Moses regained his natural strength he exclaimed: "Now, for this cause I know that man is nothing, which thing I never had supposed" (Moses 1:10).

This is a remarkable statement coming from Moses, who had known the wonders of Egypt and the power of Pharaoh. On this exceedingly high mountain, Moses saw the full view of Mount Zion when he experienced the *rest* of the Lord. He tasted of the fruit of the tree of life when he heard the loving, redemptive words from God: "Moses, my son" (Moses 1:6; see also Moses 6:27; D&C 9:1; 121:7). What confirmation of love this was to a man who was unsure of his parentage and heritage. What a contrast this statement was to the declaration of Satan: "Moses, son of man, worship me" (Moses 1:12).

Moses realized that he could only behold the glory of God with his transfigured "spiritual eyes" (see Moses 1:11) but that he could look upon Satan "in the natural man" (see Moses 1:14). Therefore, he said to Satan, "where is thy glory, for it is darkness unto me? And I can judge between thee and God" (Moses 1:15). Moses realized that being "a son of God, in the similitude of his Only Begotten" (Moses 1:13) is glorious beyond description when compared to being a son of man like Pharaoh.

Moses was presented with the fruit of the tree of knowledge of good and evil when Satan appeared before him. He had heartburn from fear in opposition when Satan exclaimed: "I am the Only Begotten, worship me" (Moses 1:19). Then he tasted the bitterness of the forbidden fruit since "as he began to fear, he saw the bitterness of hell" (Moses 1:20).

Moses had to use his agency and choose a messenger, God or Satan. Just as Adam faced Satan immediately after the Fall, Moses faced Satan without the full glory of God but with some of His Spirit (see Moses 1:15). And just as Adam had done, Moses straightforwardly sought a true messenger from his Father. He recognized that Satan was not such a messenger.

The experience of Moses on this exceedingly high mountain is a similitude of our fall from the presence of God, our state of agency, and our relationship with God in mortality. In mortality, God leaves His Spirit with us to expose the difference between good and evil so we can judge (see Moses 1:15, 18). He also "[gives us] commandments when he [calls unto us] out of the burning bush" (Moses 1:17) which is our burning hearts. If we do not "cease to call upon God"

(Moses 1:18) we will "[receive] strength" (Moses 1:20) to "[behold] his glory again" (Moses 1:25) even in this life and to stand like "Moses stood in the presence of God" (Moses 1:31).

Like Moses, we must face Satan in mortality. We must choose between true and false messengers when we are "left unto [ourselves]" (see Moses 1:9) and "subjects to follow after [our] own will" (Alma 42:7), having fallen from the glory of God. It is in this seemingly solitary condition that we experience the tree of knowledge of good and evil, being left unto ourselves (responsible for our own agency). However, in this condition we are left with the light or "Spirit of Christ" by which we can know with a "perfect knowledge . . . good from evil" (see Moroni 7:15–16) if we will search with this light and listen to our conscience and the voice of God.

Usually, those who receive the light of truth are shortly thereafter left unto themselves to "behold, Satan [come] tempting [them]" (Moses 1:12). This is a necessary condition of agency. Such was the case of Joseph Smith at the First Vision, who like Moses, felt the power of Satan and found himself "lying on [his] back . . . [having] no strength" (Joseph Smith—History 1:20; compare Moses 1:9–10). Like Moses, Joseph could clearly distinguish between the "thick darkness" from Satan and the "pillar of light . . . above the brightness of the sun" from God (Joseph Smith—History 1:15–16). In varying degrees, this scenario occurs to many worldwide who hear and receive the testimony of the restored gospel from true messengers. It is in this fallen state that we must begin to part the veil of clouds covering Mount Zion in order to work out our own salvation in the light of Christ with fear and trembling before God (see Philippians 2:12; Alma 34:37; Mormon 9:27). "One man shall not build upon another's foundation, neither journey in another's track" (D&C 52:33). We must climb the path up Mount Zion left unto ourselves with the light of Christ to see the full view of this exceedingly high mountain.

The imperative need for each of us to climb the exceedingly high mountain of the Lord's house in order to know the mysteries of God for ourselves is a dominant teaching of the Book of Mormon. It is a cultural expression in the Mormon Church today to "follow the prophet." While following a true messenger of God is important, relinquishing the need to know for ourselves is dangerous. Nephi could have dutifully followed his prophet father thinking he was on the right path, but he also desired to know for himself what his father knew and had seen. He had to climb an exceedingly high mountain to obtain this self knowledge.

> And it came to pass after I, Nephi, having heard all the words of my father, concerning the things which he saw in a vision, and also the things which he spake by the power of the Holy Ghost, which power he received by faith on the Son of God—and the Son of God was the Messiah who should come—I, Nephi, was desirous also that I might see, and hear, and know of these things, by the power of the Holy Ghost, which is the gift of God unto all those who diligently seek him, as well in times of old as in the time that he should manifest himself unto the children of men.
>
> For he that diligently seeketh shall find; and the mysteries of God shall be unfolded unto them, by the power of the Holy Ghost. (1 Nephi 10:17, 19)

> For it came to pass after I had desired to know the things that my father had seen, and believing that the Lord was able to make them known unto me, as I sat pondering in mine heart I was caught away in the Spirit of the Lord, yea, into an exceedingly high mountain, which I never had before seen, and upon which I never had before set my foot. (1 Nephi 11:1)

It is in the exceedingly high mountain of the temple that we can be carried away in the fulness of the Spirit of the Lord to see, hear, and understand the mysteries of God.

All conflicts requiring choice in this life are an extension of the great war in heaven. In all of these conflicts we must ultimately answer the question, Will I follow Satan or Christ? If we listen to the promptings in our hearts from the light of Christ given to each of us, we will start to part the veil by judging correctly between good and evil to discern truth. The truth always directs us to follow Christ. The light of Christ directs us to seek and diligently follow Christ's laws because "that which . . . seeketh to become a law unto itself, . . . cannot be sanctified by law, neither by mercy, justice, nor judgment" (D&C 88:35).

In the process of becoming sanctified, experiencing the glory of

God through obedience to Christ's laws and by the mercy of His Atonement, we will taste the sweetness and see the glory of the tree of life.

With this comparative knowledge from the tree of good and evil in the light of the tree of life, we gain the ability to clearly discern like Moses who said to Satan: "I am a son of God, in the similitude of his Only Begotten; and where is thy glory, that I should worship thee?" (Moses 1:13). When Moses said, "for his glory has been upon me, wherefore I can judge between him and thee" (see Moses 1; D&C 1:18), he was teaching us the important lesson that *until we experience to some degree the glory of God we cannot fully appreciate the bitterness of hell* (see Mosiah 27:27–29). We must taste the bitter to savor the sweet, but also we must savor the sweet to really taste the bitter. Then we can distinguish like Moses and declare, "Depart from me, Satan, for this one God only will I worship, which is the *God of glory* (Moses 1:20; emphasis added).

With clear distinction between good and evil, we learn how to separate the spiritual wheat from the mortal tares. We learn how to separate the many things that cumber and trouble us from that good part of our lives which shall not be taken away (see Luke 10:38–42). We learn how to distinguish a prophet clothed modestly (see D&C 42:40) or even strangely (compare 2 Kings 1:8 and Mark 1:6 with Matthew 7:15), but full of the spirit of prophecy and revelation, from a whited sepulcher full of dead men's bones. As the distinction between good and evil becomes clearer to us, the cloudy veil covering Mount Zion will dissipate to reveal the full view of its glory.

To Know God: The Exceeding Height of Mount Zion

With the spirit of prophecy and revelation we begin to get a full view of Mount Zion as an "exceedingly high" mountain. There is no other mountain that compares because on Mount Zion the Lord reveals Himself more and more as we climb to the summit and come to understand what eternal life means.

During his glorious temple encounter with God on an exceedingly high mountain, Moses learned why God created this earth and all His other created worlds (see Moses 1:33):

For behold, this is my work and my glory—to bring to pass the immortality and eternal life of man. (Moses 1:39)

It was the Savior, during His mortal ministry, who defined "eternal life": "And this is life eternal, that they might know thee the only true God, and Jesus Christ, whom thou hast sent" (John 17:3). The Savior again defined eternal life—or in this case "eternal lives" through a revelation to the Prophet Joseph Smith: "This is eternal lives—to know the only wise and true God, and Jesus Christ, whom he hath sent. I am he. Receive ye, therefore, my law" (D&C 132:24).

In this verse, the Savior taught that to know Him and His Father, we must receive His law. His law is to know and to be part of the fulness of His Father's work and glory in bringing to pass eternal lives as explained in section 132 of the Doctrine and Covenants (see "The Seed of Abraham: Receiving the Fulness of the Melchizedek Priesthood"). To receive His law, we must receive Him. To receive and know Christ is to take not only His name but His law or word (see Alma 32:22) upon us, by "abiding in my law" (see D&C 132:21, 37) and "[abiding] in my covenant" (D&C 132:19).

> I am the Lord thy God; and I give unto you this commandment—
> that no man shall come unto the Father but by me or by my word,
> which is my law, saith the Lord. (D&C 132:12)

> For I will magnify my name upon all those who receive and abide in
> my law. (D&C 132:64)

Perhaps this is why the Savior said, in His sermon on the temple mount:

> Many will say to me in that day: Lord, Lord, have we not prophesied
> in thy name, and in thy name have cast out devils, and in thy name
> done many wonderful works?
> And then will I profess unto them: *I never knew you*; depart from
> me, ye that work iniquity. (3 Nephi 14:22–23; emphasis added; see
> also Titus 1:16)

It is not by using His name but in strict obedience to His law that we come to know Christ. By obedience to the gospel laws, all may be adopted into the house of Israel and know Christ because this is the house that the Lord knows (see Amos 3:2). Specifically, Christ will not know us unless we know Him by taking His name upon us and receiving Him. "Because ye receive me not in the world neither do ye know me. But if ye receive me in the world, then shall ye know me, and shall receive your exaltation" (D&C 132:22–23). We cannot "[profess] to know [his] name and [not have] known [Him]" (D&C 112:26). To know Him we must become His spiritually begotten sons and daughters by the power of His Atonement and the fulness of the Holy Spirit (see Matthew 25:12) through the covenants and ordinances of His Holy Order. These are His works of righteousness by which we come to know Him in His holy house. For "the key of the knowledge of God" is in the "greater priesthood" (see D&C 84:19).

Eternal life is to know God in the sense of being like God. It is to be a son or daughter of God in the similitude of His only Begotten Son. A son really "knows" his father when he grows to maturity and emulates his father. Seth "was a perfect man, and his likeness was the express likeness of his father, insomuch that he seemed to be like unto his father in all things" (D&C 107:43). This is the same likeness found between God the Father and His son Christ who "thought it not robbery to be equal with God" (Philippians 2:6). It is only in knowing the father that a son comes to know the full measure of himself. This is why Joseph Smith said: "If men do not comprehend the character of God, they do not comprehend themselves."[1] Finally, to know God is to receive Him by serving Him:

> For how *knoweth* a man the master whom he has not *served* . . . and is far from the thoughts and intents of his heart? (Mosiah 5:13; emphasis added)

> If thou *lovest* me thou shalt *serve me* and keep all my commandments. (D&C 42:29; emphasis added)

To know God is the challenge of climbing the exceeding height of Mount Zion. If we are men and women to match the challenge of this climb, we will see a full view of ourselves as God sees us.

The Full View of Mount Zion is the
Full View of Christ upon Mount Zion

While teaching investigators as a missionary in France and Belgium, I constructed on a flannel board the foundation of the church of Christ with an adhesive strip that read "apostles and prophets." The remaining structure of the church was built on this foundation. When I taught the apostasy lesson, I removed the foundation strip of apostles and prophets. Simultaneously, my companion disengaged the spring that supported the flannel board, and the whole church flew apart. I read the words of Paul to the investigators as I constructed the church of Christ on the flannel board:

> Now therefore ye are no more strangers and foreigners, but fellowcitizens with the saints, and of the household of God;
> And are built upon the foundation of the apostles and prophets, Jesus Christ himself being the chief corner stone. (Ephesians 2:19–20)

Then I explained the need for apostles and prophets and other offices in the church by again reading from Paul:

> And he gave some, apostles; and some, prophets; and some, evangelists [patriarchs]; and some, pastors [bishops] and teachers;
> For the perfecting of the saints, for the work of the ministry, for the edifying of the body of Christ:
> Till we all come in the unity of the faith, and of the knowledge of the Son of God, unto a perfect man, unto the measure of the stature of the fulness of Christ. (Ephesians 4:11–13)

I did not realize at that time the importance of true messengers as I do now. In verse 11, Paul was saying God provided us with the Melchizedek Priesthood, even the fulness of the Melchizedek Priesthood declared by true messengers, until we all come to a knowledge of the fulness of Christ. Only then can we come to a full knowledge of the Father. As Christ said, this knowledge is "eternal life."

I did not recognize this scripture as a great verse of the *scriptural temple* even though I read it many times as a missionary. It was not until I pondered a verse from the dedicatory prayer of the Kirtland temple that I understood the full meaning of the Paul's words:

For thou knowest that we have done this work through great tribulation; and out of our poverty we have given of our substance to build a house to thy name, *that the Son of Man might have a place to manifest himself to his people.* (D&C 109:5; emphasis added)

This verse is reminiscent of the declaration of the Lord to the Israelites in the Sinai:

And let them make me a sanctuary; *that I may dwell among them.* (Exodus 25:8; emphasis added)

It is also similar to the temple vision of John:

Therefore are they before the throne of God, and serve him day and night in his temple: and he that sitteth on the throne shall dwell among them. (Revelation 7:15)

It is in the temple, His holy sanctuary, that Christ manifests Himself to us as we learn of the fulness of His stature unto a perfect man. After referring to priesthood offices and quorums, the Lord said, "The above offices I have given unto you, and the keys thereof, for helps and for governments, for the work of the ministry and the perfecting of my saints" (D&C 124:143).

Then the Lord connected His priesthood with the temple when He said, "Prepare rooms for all these offices in my house" (D&C 124:145). The Lord manifests Himself unto us in the temple by "[restoring] many things to the earth, pertaining to the priesthood" (D&C 127:8). "For I have conferred upon you the keys and power of the priesthood, wherein I restore all things" (D&C 132:45). In the temple we see the great view of His stature that He promises us if we receive His priesthood and follow Him. This is the great and last promise of the temple because He "dwells among [us]" (Revelation 7:15).

To get a full view of Mount Zion we must get a full view of the Savior upon Mount Zion because "a Lamb stood on the mount Sion" (Revelation 14:1) and "the Lamb shall stand upon Mount Zion" (see D&C 133:18, 56). There, we must come to understand the fulness of the Lamb on Mount Zion through His Atonement. It is only on Mount Zion that we begin to really comprehend the Atonement. Therefore, it was in the temple that Jacob made this significant statement:

Why not speak of the *atonement* of Christ, and attain to a *perfect knowledge* of him. (Jacob 4:12; emphasis added)

The Scriptural Temple

It is in the temple that the Lord promises, to "reveal" Himself today even as literally as He promised the children of Israel on the temple mount of Sinai:

> And as your fathers [in the Sinai] were led at first, even so shall the redemption of Zion be.
>
> But I say unto you: Mine angels shall go up before you, *and also my presence*, and in time ye shall possess the goodly land. (D&C 103:18, 20; emphasis added)

The promise of "the Son of Man revealing Himself" in temples of our dispensation was first given to Joseph Smith in 1833. This revelation concerned the "beginning and foundation of the city of the stake of Zion, here in the land of Kirtland, beginning at my house" (D&C 94:1), when the Lord said "my glory shall be there, and my presence shall be there" (D&C 94:8). This promise was fulfilled the Sunday after the dedication of the Kirtland temple, when the Lord appeared to Joseph Smith and Oliver Cowdery and said to them:

> For behold, I have accepted this house, and my name shall be here. . . .
>
> Yea, I will appear unto my servants, and speak unto them with mine own voice, if my people will keep my commandments, and do not pollute this holy house. (D&C 110:7–8; emphasis added)

The promise continued in the Lord's directive to build the Nauvoo temple.

> Build a house to my name, for the Most High to dwell therein. (D&C 124:27)

The promise, as a great and last promise of the temple, continues today. It should draw us to the temple and fill us with great anticipation and desire to know the fulness of Christ so we can receive "eternal life" in this life and the life to come.

The Seed of Abraham: Receiving the Fulness of the Melchizedek Priesthood

If we are to understand the fulness of Christ and become like Him, we must understand the fulness of His Order. Therefore, we must learn the fulness of the Melchizedek Priesthood. The Apostle Paul understood this truth:

> For this Melchisedec was ordained a priest after the order of the Son of God, which order was without father, without mother, without descent, having neither beginning of days, nor end of life. And all those who are ordained unto this priesthood are *made like unto the Son of God*, abiding a priest continually. . . .
>
> If therefore *perfection* were by the Levitical priesthood, what further need was there that another priest should rise after the order of Melchisedec, and not be called after the order of Aaron? . . .
>
> And it is yet far more evident: for that after the similitude of Melchisedec there ariseth another priest,
>
> Who is made, not after the law of a carnal commandment, but after *the power of an endless life*. (Joseph Smith Translation, Hebrews 7:3, 11, 15–16; see also 1 John 3:2–3)

The truths of the "revelation on priesthood" (D&C 84) state the connection between the fulness of Christ ("the power of godliness"), the promise of His rest ("see the face of god"), and the fulness of the Melchizedek Priesthood ("the key of the knowledge of God" and "the ordinances thereof"):

> And this greater priesthood administereth the gospel and holdeth the key of the mysteries of the kingdom, even *the key of the knowledge of God*.
>
> And without the *ordinances thereof*, and the authority of the priesthood, the *power of godliness* is not manifest unto men in the flesh;
>
> For without this no man can *see the face of God*, even the Father, and live. (D&C 84:19, 21–22; emphasis added)

It is most instructive to learn that the righteous people of the Book of Mormon were taught and kept the law of Moses (see Jarom 1:11) but also they functioned under the Melchizedek Priesthood or "the high priesthood of the holy order of God" (Alma 4:20). Therefore, the doctrines of the fulness of Christ and His rest are taught and manifest in the Book of Mormon. With this combination of priesthoods, the Nephites were able to "look forward unto the Messiah, and believe in him to come as though he already was" (Jarom 1:11).

The Scriptural Temple

"For this intent [they kept] the law of Moses, it pointing [their] souls to him" (Jacob 4:5). Therefore, "it [was] sanctified unto [them] for righteousness, even as it was accounted unto Abraham in the wilderness" (Jacob 4:5) who kept the laws of the fulness of the Melchizedek Priesthood.

In D&C 124, the Lord informed Joseph Smith that we learn about and receive the fulness of the Melchizedek Priesthood in the temple:

> For there is not a place found on earth that he may come to and restore again that which was lost unto you, or which he hath taken away, even the fulness of the priesthood. (D&C 124:28)

It was the intent of the Lord to reveal the fulness of His priesthood ordinances to Moses and the children of Israel. "For, for this cause I commanded Moses that he should build a tabernacle" (D&C 124:38).

In an epistle to the Church in Nauvoo concerning baptism for the dead, and alluding to all the keys, powers, and glories of temples, Joseph Smith again stressed the importance of obtaining the keys, or powers and knowledge, of the Holy Priesthood in the temple:

> Now the great and grand secret of the whole matter, and the *summum bonum* of the whole subject that is lying before us, consists in obtaining the powers of the Holy Priesthood. For him to whom these keys are given there is no difficulty in obtaining a knowledge of facts in relation to the salvation of the children of men, both as well for the dead as for the living. (D&C 128:11)

The meaning of the "whole matter" is the whole subject of temple work and worship as implied by the statement "both as well for the dead as for the living." The keys, powers, and knowledge for this worship and work of salvation are obtained in the temple where the fulness of the Holy Priesthood is obtained. "All things pertaining to this house, and the priesthood thereof" (D&C 124:42) are the temple endowment and ordinances of salvation accomplished by the fulness of the Priesthood.

In this same epistle, an offering in righteousness as required by the Lord (see Malachi 3:3; D&C 13:1) was proposed (see D&C

234

128:24). This offering, in the form of a book of temple work done for the dead, was offered in the Nauvoo temple and "put in the archives of my holy temple" (D&C 127:9). This was the beginning of this "acceptable offering" which will be completed when the "whole work upon Mount Zion" (temple work of the dispensation of the fulness of times through the Millennium) is completed (see 2 Nephi 20:12). Through this great temple work for the living and the dead with the fulness of the Priesthood, the sons of Levi, that is both the Aaronic (sons of Aaron) and Melchizedek (sons of Moses) priesthood holders will be purified:

> Therefore, as I said concerning the sons of Moses—for the sons of Moses and also the sons of Aaron shall offer an acceptable offering and sacrifice in the house of the Lord. . . .
>
> And the sons of Moses and of Aaron shall be filled with the glory of the Lord, upon Mount Zion in the Lord's house, whose sons are ye; and also many whom I have called and sent forth to build up my church.
>
> For whoso is faithful unto the obtaining these two priesthoods of which I have spoken, and the magnifying their calling, are sanctified by the Spirit unto the renewing of their bodies.
>
> They become the sons of Moses and of Aaron and the seed of Abraham, and the church and kingdom, and the elect of God. (D&C 84:31–34)

Verse 32 notes that "also many," all those, both men and women, who magnify their calling to build the Church, will be sanctified through the fulness of the priesthood in temple ordinances and covenants to become "the seed of Abraham" that grows a tree of life.

It is significant that the term *seed* is used about fifty times in 1 Nephi. In fact the introductory verse of Lehi's tree of life visions (chapter eight) talks about "seeds of every kind" which, in fruit or outcome, are represented in his vision. "Seeds of every kind" could also mean "male and female, of every kind" (Ether 2:1). The context for most of the terms *seed* or *seeds* in 1 Nephi is literal offspring. However, the concept of offspring took on a deeper meaning when Lehi was told by the Lord "that his sons should take daughters to wife, that they might *raise up seed unto the Lord*" (1 Nephi 7:1; emphasis added) or to "raise up unto me of thy seed" (Ether 1:43). When Seth was born after the death of Abel, Adam expressed this concept of the Lord's seed when he said, "God hath appointed me another seed, instead of Abel" (Moses 6:2).

The principles and promises of the Lord's seed were revealed to Nephi. The key concept in Nephi's promise, as stated in the Book of Alma where the seed of the Lamanites is distinguished from the seed of the Nephites (see Alma 3:8–17), is "he that departeth from thee shall no more be called thy seed; and I will bless thee, and whomsoever shall be called thy seed, henceforth and forever" (Alma 3:17). This promise is like the promise made to Abraham and his seed, with the escape clause, "except they repent of their wickedness and turn to me that I may have mercy upon them" (Alma 3:14).

The Lord continued to define and bless Nephi's seed raised unto the Lord when He pronounced the often quoted and illustrated promise, "And inasmuch as ye shall keep my commandments, ye shall prosper, and shall be led to a land of promise. . . . And inasmuch as thy brethren shall rebel against thee, they shall be cut off from the presence of the Lord. . . . And they shall have no power over thy seed except they shall rebel against me also" (1 Nephi 2:20–23; see also Ether 2:7–8). Before killing Laban, Nephi remembered "the words of the Lord . . . saying that: Inasmuch as thy seed shall keep my commandments, they shall prosper in the land of promise" (1 Nephi 4:14). This promise of the Lord was literally fulfilled when Lehi and his family arrived in the promised land:

> We did put all our seeds into the earth, which we had brought from the land of Jerusalem. And it came to pass that they did grow exceedingly; wherefore, we were blessed in abundance. (1 Nephi 18:24; see also 2 Nephi 5:11)

Being planted in the promised land of the kingdom of God on earth with "goodly parents" (1 Nephi 1:1) who honor their marriage covenant and teach their children to keep the commandments of the Lord is how these parents "raise up seed unto the Lord" (1 Nephi 4:14). This is how their children "prosper in the land of promise" as "godly seed" (see Malachi 2:14–16).

The concept of the Lord's seed expanded in Nephi's vision of the Gentiles. If they "harden not their hearts against the Lamb of God, they shall be numbered among the seed of thy father; yea . . . among the house of Israel" (1 Nephi 14:2). Nephi reminded his brothers that the term *seed* did not mean only their descendants. It also meant "all the house of Israel, pointing to the covenant which should be fulfilled in the latter days; which covenant the Lord made to our father Abraham, saying: In thy seed shall all the kindreds of the earth be blessed" (1 Nephi 15:18). Nephi concluded by gathering the scattered seed of Israel, literal and adopted, in the latter days as the covenant seed of Abraham:

> After our seed is scattered the Lord God will proceed to do a marvelous work among the Gentiles, which shall be of great worth unto our seed. . . .
>
> And . . . unto the Gentiles; and . . . unto all the house of Israel, unto the making known of the covenants of the Father of heaven unto Abraham, saying: In thy seed shall all the kindreds of the earth be blessed. (1 Nephi 22:8–9)

Abraham sought his "appointment unto the Priesthood according to the appointment of God unto the fathers concerning the seed" (Abraham 1:4). "The order of this priesthood was confirmed to be handed down from father to son, and rightly belongs to the literal descendants of the chosen seed, to whom the promises were made" (D&C 107:40). The Lord then told Abraham that "in thee (that is, in thy Priesthood) and in thy seed (that is, thy Priesthood), for I give unto thee a promise that this right shall continue in thee, and in thy seed after thee (that is to say, the literal seed, or the seed of the body) shall all the families of the earth be blessed, even with the blessings of the Gospel, which are the blessings of salvation, even of life eternal" (Abraham 2:11). This is the promise of the oath and covenant of the Priesthood (see D&C 84:39) which is to receive "all that [the] Father hath" (D&C 84:38) by receiving the fulness of the Priesthood in the house of the Lord (see D&C 124:47). The order and fulness of the Priesthood was literally handed down from the Father to the sons of His chosen seed (see D&C 107:40). This is why Abraham sought to become the "seed" like his patriarchal fathers (Adam, Enoch, Noah, Melchizedek, and so on) who held the fulness of the Priesthood.

The Scriptural Temple

The first major concept about the Lord's seed, and by divine appointment the seed of Abraham, Nephi, and the house of Israel, is that *seed equals priesthood* to the Lord. "For whoso is faithful unto the obtaining these two priesthoods . . . and the magnifying their calling. . . . They become . . . the seed of Abraham" (D&C 84:33–34). There is no guaranteed promise in being literal or adopted seed of the house of Israel. "For every seed bringeth forth unto its own likeness" (Alma 32:31) and "the seed of evil-doers shall never be renowned" (Isaiah 14:20; see also Psalm 37:28). The Apostle Paul explained this principle:

> They are not all Israel, which are of Israel: Neither, because they are the seed of Abraham, are they all children: but, In Isaac shall thy seed be called.
>
> That is, They which are the children of the flesh, these are not the children of God: but *the children of the promise* are counted for the seed. (Romans 9:6–8; emphasis added)

Paul understood what it means to "raise up seed unto the Lord." In Isaac, who is the sacrificial type of Christ, shall thy seed be called. In other words, in Christ shall thy seed be called. For "when thou shalt make his soul an offering for sin he shall see his seed" (Mosiah 14:10; read John 12:24). All those who hearken unto the words of the holy prophets and receive the fulness of the Priesthood receive the Lord (see D&C 84:35) and become His seed (see Mosiah 15:10–13). This was the case of Abraham whose name became great because he bore the name of Christ through His priesthood (see Abraham 2:9–11; 1:18).

To become the seed of Christ and then His fruit as His spiritually begotten children through the fulness of His priesthood, is to become spiritually adopted seed of the house of Israel and the covenant seed of Abraham. Therefore Paul said, "And if ye be Christ's, then are ye Abraham's seed, and heirs according to the promise" (Galatians 3:29). To become Abraham's seed through the priesthood of Christ is to become "the children of the promise."

This is essential for our exaltation and glory because "he [Christ] took not on him the nature of angels; but he took on him the seed of Abraham" (Hebrews 2:16; see D&C 132:37) and "covenanted with Abraham that [He] would remember his seed forever" (2 Nephi 29:14).

The second major concept about the Lord's seed is that *seed equals Christ's spiritually begotten children* or "the children of the promise." After experimenting upon the word of Christ and planting it as a seed in our hearts (see Alma 32:28), we can be "sanctified by the Spirit" (D&C 84:33) through the fulness of the Priesthood and become one in Christ as His spiritually begotten children. In this the latter days, the Saints have been told that

> Abraham received promises concerning his seed [in the world and out of the world]. . . . This promise is yours also, because ye are of Abraham . . . and by this law is the continuation of the works of my Father, wherein he glorifieth himself. Go ye, therefore, and do the works of Abraham; enter into my law. . . . But if ye enter not into my law ye cannot receive the promise of my Father, which he made unto Abraham. (D&C 132:30–33)

The link between Abraham and Joseph Smith as seed unto the Lord is found in the same promise that each received.

> And as I said unto Abraham concerning the kindreds of the earth, even so I say unto my servant Joseph: In thee and in thy seed shall the kindred of the earth be blessed. (D&C 124:58)

The purpose of restoring the priesthood in the dispensation of the fulness of times by the hand of Elijah (read D&C 2) was to restore *eternal seed* to the earth by sealing under priesthood power eternal relationships. The promises made to the fathers mentioned in D&C 2 verse 2 are the same "multitude of the promises" made by the Lord to those entering into His Holy Order of Matrimony (see 4 Nephi 1:11) and the same promise given to Father Abraham and the Prophet Joseph Smith (see Abraham 2:11; D&C 124:58). Without this eternal seed, "the whole earth would be utterly wasted at his coming" (D&C 2:3). Just as good soil of the earth is wasted if not planted with good seed, so is the work of God if there is no "[planting] in the hearts" (D&C 2:2) of "the children of the promise" (Romans 9:8) with the good word of the great promises (see D&C 88:75; 132:31–32, 63).

The full meaning of the seed of Abraham refers to a man and women who are one under the Holy Order of Matrimony. This union of male and female, who become a compound in one under

Christ's Holy Order of Matrimony, makes the fundamental unit or seed of an eternal family. With the "everlasting covenant of marriage" (D&C 131:2), they can become an exalted, eternal, and holy seed as an eternal fruit "whose seed [shall] be in itself" (Moses 2:11). "Seed in itself yieldeth its own likeness" (see Abraham 4:11–12).

Then "they shall pass the angels and gods . . . to their exaltation and glory in all things, . . . which glory shall be a fulness and a continuation of the seeds forever and ever. "Then shall they be gods, because *they have no end* . . . [are] above all . . . [and] have all power" (D&C 132:19–20; emphasis added). This is why Abraham "sought [his] appointment unto the Priesthood according to the appointment of God unto the fathers concerning the seed" (Abraham 1:4).

"By this law (the new and everlasting covenant of marriage) is the continuation of the *works of my Father*, wherein he *glorifieth himself*" (D&C 132:31; emphasis added; see Moses 1:39). "The promise which was given by my Father before the foundation of the world, and for their exaltation in the eternal worlds, [is] that they may bear the souls of men; for herein is the work of my Father continued, that he may be glorified" (D&C 132:63). It is important to understand that the souls of men as a compound in one started when God organized the intelligences and "God saw these souls that they were good . . . for he stood among those that were spirits" (see Abraham 3:22–23). Souls as compounds in one continue in God's work and glory as we participate with God in "[bearing] the souls of men" (D&C 132:63) by combining spirit souls with physical bodies to become "living souls" (see D&C 88:15; Moses 3:7; 6:59; Abraham 5:7). This joint effort continues in making living souls eternal souls.

Bearing the souls of men continues as an eternal blessing under God's work and glory when a man and women enter into the Holy Order of Matrimony. "But if ye enter not into my law ye cannot receive the promise of my Father, which he made unto Abraham" (D&C 132:33). In our current mortal state the Lord said, "ye are not yet pure; ye can not yet bear my glory" (D&C 136:37). For "no man can behold all my works . . . [and] my glory, and afterwards remain in the flesh on the earth" (Moses 1:5). But "they who keep their second estate shall have glory added upon their heads for ever and ever (Abraham 3:26) for "in me [ye] shall have glory" (D&C 24:11; see 2 Corinthians 3:18).

Abraham's promise, made even before the foundation of the world, included a continuation of seeds that "in the world and out of the world should they continue as innumerable as the stars" (D&C 132:30). "I will multiply thee, and thy seed after thee" (Abraham 3:14). Without becoming an exalted, eternal, and holy seed, "no one can . . . be permitted to enter into my glory" (D&C 132:4) because "[they] cannot have an increase" (D&C 131:4). "For this cause, that men might be made partakers of the glories which were to be revealed, the Lord sent forth the fulness of his gospel, his everlasting covenant" (D&C 133:57).

Even as Joseph and Hyrum, we must be willing to sacrifice all in obedience to this covenant for God's glory (see D&C 78:8). "They died for glory; and glory is their eternal reward" (D&C 135:6). "The glory of God is intelligence, or, in other words, light and truth" (D&C 93:36). God said, "I am the God of glory" (Moses 1:20) and the Son said, "the glory be thine forever" (Moses 4:2). God the Father and the Son say to us, "Therefore, inherit my glory" (D&C 132:18) even "the fulness of my glory" (D&C 132:6) which is "an eternal weight of glory" (D&C 132:16).

We inherit God's glory by passing through the veil of the temple. "Enter ye in at the strait gate. . . . Strait is the gate, and narrow is the way, which leadeth unto life, and few there be that find it" (Matthew 7:13–14). "For strait is the gate, and narrow the way that leadeth unto the exaltation and continuation of the lives, and few there be that find it, because ye receive me not in the world neither do ye know me" (D&C 132:22). "You cannot enter in at the strait gate by the law of Moses, neither by your dead works" (D&C 22:2). The law of Christ (the new and everlasting covenant) which leads through His gates (baptism through the veil of the temple) will open "the gate through which the heirs" of God's glory will enter (see D&C 137:2). Christ's gates are found and entered in His church and His temple. "For my house is a house of order [My holy order], saith the Lord God" (D&C 132:18).

The third important concept about the Lord's seed is that *the exalted, eternal, holy seed is a "compound in one"* (2 Nephi 2:11) *under*

*the Holy Order of Matrimony when a married man and woman become
one with God and share in his glory.* God's glory is to exalt light with
truth such that this intelligence is inseparably connected with matter.
In this work of bearing the fruit of eternal souls is the holy seed
glorified.

Abraham and Sarah are the great example of this holy seed as
a compound in one. Ironically they were childless most of their
married life. Still, they obediently sought righteousness and lived
in love of God, each other, and their fellow men. Therefore, the
Lord said to us in the last days, "Hearken to me, ye that follow after
righteousness, ye that seek the Lord: look unto the rock whence ye
are hewn, and to the hole of the pit whence ye are digged. Look
unto Abraham your father, and unto Sarah that bare you" (Isaiah
51:1–2).

The eternal truths of the relationship between a man and a
woman are in the middle, between the virtues and vicissitudes that
each brings to the relationship. The middle is where God is because
He focuses these virtues and vicissitudes in His work and glory, clari-
fying how a couple become one. For a married man and woman to
find each other, they must find God together and remain focused on
His work and glory. If this sweet spot in the middle can be found,
then a man and a woman will not be "unequally yoked together" (2
Corinthians 6:14). They will form a "compound in one" (2 Nephi
2:11) as an eternal seed. "They twain shall be one flesh, and all this
that the earth might answer the end of its creation" (D&C 49:16).
This eternal seed is made in a temple.

Priesthood Power Is Given to
Those Who Climb Mount Zion

Joseph Smith provided further enlightening insight into the fulness of the Melchizedek Priesthood when he said:

> If a man gets a fulness of the priesthood of god he has to get it in the
> same way that Jesus Christ obtained it, and that was by keeping all
> the commandments and obeying all the ordinances of the House of
> the Lord.[2]

Brigham Young continued the teachings of the Prophet Joseph Smith when he stated, "for any person to have the fulness of that [Melchizedek] priesthood, he must be ordained a king and priest."[3]

On another occasion, President Young explained that:

> Those holding the fulness of the Melchizedek Priesthood are kings and priests of the most high god, holding the keys of power and blessings.[4] (see D&C 76:56; Revelation 1:6, 5:10, 20:6, 22:5)

The association of the terms *king* and *priest* implies that the authority of a king over a kingdom or a patriarch over his family in the Holy Order of God derives from the power of the priesthood.[5] This truth we learn at the temple veil. The reality that "God reigneth" as the King of kings and "sitteth upon the throne of his holiness" (Psalm 47:8) is extended as a reality for us. We can become kings and queens upon thrones of holiness if we receive the fulness of the Holy Order of the Son of God.

In opening a window on Enoch and his seed, we get a full view of Mount Zion by seeing the great power in the fulness of the Melchizedek Priesthood:

> For God having sworn unto Enoch and unto his seed with an oath by himself; that every one being ordained after this order and calling should have power. . . .
>
> To stand in the presence of God; to do all things according to his will, according to his command; . . . and this by the will of the Son of God which was before the foundation of the world.
>
> And men having this faith, coming up unto this order of God, were translated and taken up into heaven. (Joseph Smith Translation, Genesis 14:30–32)

In our personal lives, the great power of the fulness of the Melchizedek Priesthood is the "power to overcome all things which are not ordained of [God] (D&C 50:35). It is "through faith [in the power of this priesthood, we] shall overcome" (D&C 61:9). Collectively for the Church and for God's purposes, the great key of power of the fulness of the Melchizedek Priesthood is "power given to seal both on earth and in heaven (D&C 1:8; 132:46) and to "seal them up unto eternal life" (D&C 68:12) through the one "appointed on the earth to hold this power" (D&C 132:7). This "sealing and binding power . . . [are] the keys of the kingdom, which consist in the key of knowledge" (D&C 128:14). "Whenever the Lord has given a dispensation of the priesthood . . . this power has always been given" (D&C 128:9; see also D&C 112:31). When this binding and sealing is done and recorded on earth it is "recorded in heaven" (see D&C 127:7; 128:7–8).

As declared in a revelation on the doctrines of this Order of God, we can have the heavens opened to us and even experience a change of state in communion and relationship by priesthood power:

> The *power and authority* of the higher, or Melchizedek Priesthood, is to hold the keys of all the *spiritual blessings* of the church—
>
> To have the privilege of receiving the *mysteries of the kingdom* of heaven, to have the *heavens opened* unto them, to commune with the general assembly and church of the Firstborn, and to enjoy the communion and *presence of God the Father, and Jesus* the mediator of the new covenant. (D&C 107:18–19; emphasis added)

However, the mighty power of the Priesthood is wrapped in a soft shell. It "looks small unto the understanding of men" (see Ether 3:5) because priesthood power only works through the power of love (see D&C 107:30–31; 121:41–43, 45). Therefore, Ammon spoke of the Lord's "*great power*, and of his mercy, and of his long-suffering towards the children of men" (Alma 26:16; emphasis added).

The endowment teaches that receiving the fulness of the Holy Priesthood leads men and women from the telestial realm to the terrestrial realm and finally to a celestial existence. When do we enter the terrestrial realm in this mortal, telestial existence? It occurs when we live under the loving power of oneness in the Holy Order of the Son of God. It occurs when husband and wife become "one flesh" under the Holy Order of Matrimony. It occurs when a child is born to a couple in the Holy Order of Matrimony. It occurs when we truly worship in the temple for our own preparatory redemption. It can occur in our church assemblies, homes, and individual lives if we live the laws of the fulness of the Priesthood. By regularly experiencing in this life a change of state from telestial to terrestrial (in some degree of translation) through the power of the priesthood, we prepare for the rest of the Lord.

Those who receive and magnify towards a fulness of the priesthood receive an aura of light as a token of its power (see 3 Nephi 19:25). It changes their countenance to behold, as in a mirror, the glory of the Lord (see 2 Corinthians 3:18). "And thus they all received the light of the countenance of their lord" (D&C 88:58). Such was the case of the righteous in the world of spirits when "their countenances shone, and the radiance from the presence of the Lord rested upon them" (D&C 138:24). As a messenger from God, Moroni reflected this countenance of the Lord when "his whole person was glorious beyond description, and his countenance truly like lightning" (Joseph Smith—History 1:32).

The countenance of the Lord in us is the countenance of a perfect brightness of hope from the light of the power of love as a gift of the Spirit. It is the "light of the body" (3 Nephi 13:22) that has passed the test of light to "let your light so shine" (3 Nephi 12:16). It is "the joy of [our] countenance" (D&C 88:52) which is "full of joy with thy countenance" (Acts 2:28). By this change of countenance (to some degree of transfiguration), we literally become a light unto the world because we reflect the light of the Savior (see 3 Nephi 18:24). This light often confirms to others that we are true messengers. "Behold, he changed their hearts; . . . their souls were illuminated by the light of the everlasting word" (Alma 5:7). "And now behold, I ask of you, my brethren of the church, have ye spiritually been born of God? Have ye received his image in your countenances? Have ye experienced this mighty change in your hearts?" (Alma 5:14). Contrast this change of countenance to the change in Cain whose "countenance fell" (Moses 5:21).

The Prophet Joseph Smith described the process of obtaining the image of Christ:

> All those who keep his commandments shall grow up from grace to grace, and become heirs of the heavenly kingdom, and joint heirs with Jesus Christ; possessing the same mind, being transformed into the same image or likeness, even the express image of him who fills all in all; being filled with the fulness of his glory; and become one in him, even as the Father, Son, and Holy Spirit are one.[6]

The Scriptural Temple

This is the process of going from receiving his image in your countenance (see Alma 5:14) to having "the image of God engraven upon your countenances" (Alma 5:19).

The fulness of the power of the Melchizedek Priesthood is synonymous with temple worship. The two cannot be separated as President Joseph Fielding Smith declared:

> You cannot receive the fulness of the priesthood unless you go into the temple of the Lord and receive these ordinances of which the prophet speaks. No man can get the fulness of the priesthood outside of the temple of the Lord.[7]

Perhaps, this is why the resurrected Savior took His apostles "into a mountain where [He] had appointed them" (Matthew 28:16). The full view of Mount Zion can only be seen with the full power of the Priesthood.

The Fulness of Priesthood Power Is for Both Men and Women

A pearl of today's temple worship is that men and women participate equally in its ordinances and endowment. They are endowed to become kings and queens in God's Holy Order. They are "heirs together of the grace of life" (1 Peter 3:7). Even the priesthood pattern of the Old Testament temple revealed by the Spirit to King David (see 1 Chronicles 28:12) included women (see 1 Chronicles 25:5–6).

When men and women are sealed as one in celestial marriage, they enjoy equally the greatest blessings of the fulness of the priesthood. Men and women cannot have the fulness of the Melchizedek Priesthood without each other. Ultimate exaltation is not a singular blessing.

Like a brotherhood or sisterhood, the priesthood can be viewed as a union of priests and priestesses who perform sacrifices and ordinances in a temple to worship God. Such a priest and priestess united under the Holy Order of Matrimony equally receive the fulness of the priesthood to receive the fulness of God's power. The fulness of God's power is in "the power of the Holy Ghost" (see Moroni 2:2; 3:4; 6:4, 9). The most important temple in which a man and women unite to perform sacrifices and ordinances is in the temple of their home. There, as the eternal seed, they raise seed unto the Lord. This is why the fulness of the priesthood means "the seed" (see Abraham 1:4). The altars of the temple require both a man and a woman to kneel in covenant to receive each other in order to receive the Lord (see D&C 84:36). The altar is symbolic of the sacrifice of the Savior who sacrificed all in obedience (see Hebrews 5:8) to His Father to become one with Him. Both the man and the woman become one with the Savior as they covenant to sacrifice all in obedience to Him. We must kneel, sacrificing our independence to our spouse and to our Savior, before we can stand in God's presence (see Joseph Smith Translation, Genesis 14:31).

It is evident that there is a great satanic attack on the institution of marriage today. While the progression, stability, and happiness of all civilizations of the world have been based on the successful union of a man and a woman to create and maintain a family, few today support or understand the significance of this truth. The marriage of a man and a woman to establish a family is the reflection of a celestial order. It is how God lives and how his work and glory progresses. Therefore, God commanded the institution of marriage (see D&C 49:15) so we as His children can learn to live like He lives. Bruce Satterfield expressed this truth when he said, "ultimately it is through righteous parenthood that men and women can prove themselves worthy of godhood, for I believe that the ultimate test of godhood is parenthood!"[8] Therefore, leading brethren of the Church in 1833, including the Prophet Joseph Smith, were chastened by the Lord and commanded to be "more diligent and concerned at home" (D&C 93:50) and to "set in order [their] own house" (D&C 93:43).

> Who, then, is a faithful and wise servant, whom his lord hath made ruler over his household, to give them meat in due season? Blessed is that servant whom his lord, when he cometh, shall find so doing; and verily I say unto you, he shall make him ruler over all his goods. (Joseph Smith—Matthew 1:49–50)

The scriptural meaning of the verb "to know," when for example "Adam *knew* Eve his wife" (Genesis 4:1; emphasis added), does not just mean the sexual relation between a man and a woman (see 1

Corinthians 6:16). It means to know in the bond of marriage. This implies the whole relationship, both body and spirit, which should be expressed in the conjugal relationship. This is the meaning of the repeated "one flesh" commandment (Genesis 2:24; Matthew 19:5–6; Mark 10:8; Ephesians 5:31; D&C 49:16; Moses 3:24; Abraham 5:18) in the bond of marriage. A married man and woman are to become a "compound in one" (2 Nephi 2:11) as an eternal seed. This seed is produced under the power of the Holy Order of Matrimony when a man "[cleaves] unto his wife" (Abraham 5:18). Proper sexual intimacy of "one flesh" is an ideal marriage milieu for spiritual intimacy. Only when hearts first become entwined should bodies entwine. Then, male and female, body and spirit, inseparably connected receive the full joy of incarnated divine love. Conjugal oneness is symbolic of the intimate personal relationship of commitment and purpose that the Lord requires of us "to know" Him. To know Him, we must also become a "compound in one" with Him. To arrive at God's level of unity and love in a "celestial" marriage we must not only walk in unity and love with our spouse but also with our Savior.

The full measure of the Holy Order of the Son of God is the Holy Order of Matrimony. It is an "Holy Order," not just a marriage ceremony. As we learn in the temple, this Holy Order has laws, rights, and ordinances. I do not think that all of the laws, rights, and ordinances of this Holy Order of Matrimony have yet been revealed. However, it is the order in which men and women learn to become one with each other and with God. They learn that through this priesthood order, both can become perfected before God. This doctrine of perfection through the fulness of the priesthood is what Adam and his righteous descendants like Noah (see Moses 8:19, 27) received from God. Abraham understood this doctrine in God's commandment to "walk before me, and be thou perfect" (see Genesis 17:1–2). It is the same doctrine that the Apostles Paul and John taught the meridian Saints (compare Joseph Smith Translation, Hebrews 7:3; Hebrews 7:11, 15–16 with 1 John 3:2–3). A son (and daughter) of God, as John mentioned, is one who embraces the fulness of His priesthood (see D&C 84:32–34; Moses 6:67–68). The Savior's commandment to be perfect as our Father in Heaven (see Matthew 5:48; Luke 6:40), is only possible if we receive the fulness of His priesthood in His holy order of matrimony. This is the strait gate that leads to exaltation and eternal lives (compare Matthew 7:13 with D&C 132:22). This doctrine of perfected oneness of a man and woman with God, so beautifully taught and enacted in the temple, is the meaning of Paul's declaration to the Corinthian Saints:

> Neither is the man without the woman, neither the woman without the man, in the Lord. (1 Corinthians 11:11)

The important message in this verse is that the closer a married couple draw to the Lord the closer they draw to each other until all three become one. Paul further expressed the intimate unity of a married man and woman when he said,

> Let the husband render unto the wife due benevolence: and likewise also the wife unto the husband. The wife hath not power of her own body, but the husband: and likewise also the husband hath not power of his own body, but the wife. (1 Corinthians 7:3–4)

With this union in holy marriage, men and women learn that the whole should be greater than the sum of its parts. Therefore, as the endowment implies, the Holy Order of Matrimony in this life should be edified to a terrestrial or paradisiacal relationship. Adam and Eve were united by God in the Garden of Eden, and the endowment law of this union is given in the terrestrial world.

It is fascinating that Nephi mentioned the institution of marriage during a period of great righteousness and oneness amongst the Nephites (see 4 Nephi 1:11). Was he talking about the Holy Order of Matrimony? Perhaps "the multitude of the promises which the Lord had made unto them" (4 Nephi 1:11) refers to the promises made in the Holy Order of Matrimony.

Even more than the official titles of the Melchizedek priesthood, the titles key to eternal progression are that of husband and father, wife and mother. A father and mother are to beget physical bodies for God's spirit children. They then bring their children to Christ who will beget them anew spiritually with His word and power to return them to their Father in Heaven. A father and mother must find the true church of God to become true fathers and mothers in His kingdom on earth because the purpose of His true church is to produce eternal lives in eternal families. Together, a righteous father and mother in the true church provide not only physical insemination for their children but also spiritual. Therefore, "thy duty is unto the church forever, and this because of thy family" (D&C 23:3; see also D&C 25:9). A righteous holder of the titles of husband and father can only function in unison with a righteous wife and mother. Adam understood this truth when he gave Eve the title of "the mother of all living" before she even experienced the travail of mortal motherhood. It was as though he understood the divine nature of a mother in this Holy Order. Whether or not they have mortal offspring, the holy image of this title is reflected from each woman born into this world. The importance of women and motherhood in God's Holy Order is witnessed in the temple when all men stand in the presence of this "elect lady" (D&C 25:3), "our glorious Mother Eve" (D&C 138:39). Polite men continue, in a similar gesture, to show respect when a woman enters.

In the Holy Order of Matrimony, the fulness of the Melchizedek Priesthood becomes the Patriarchal Priesthood. At the head of the fulness of any priesthood of God is always a father figure who, with perfect love, brings the covenants and blessings of eternal life from the Eternal Father to his sons and daughters. This pattern was seen on a theological and political level in ancient Near Eastern kingdoms. In ancient Israel, a king such as David became a father figure with blessings and protection to his subjects or sons because he kept covenants with the Father in Heaven who provided protection and blessings for all in the covenant. As Avraham Gileadi observed, "In the theology of the prophets, an entire hierarchy of father-son relationships thus extended all the way from the Most High God down to the lowest telestial person; and, in an antipodal sense, even to the 'sons' of Perdition."[9] In the Book of Mormon, this theology with the fulfillment of the covenant is demonstrated in the account of the "sons" of Helaman who called their commander "father" (see Alma 56:46). Using the terms *father*, *fathers*, or *patriarchs* nineteen times (see Acts 7:2), Stephen opened and developed his witness before the Sanhedrin with this truth. Such a father, a true messenger and leader, as the fathers of Israel should have been (see Isaiah 3:4, 6–7, 12; 9:14–17), abides in the Lord's covenant with unfailing love so that his heart will turn towards his children even with the sacrifice of his own life. Then the hearts of his children will turn to him as the source of their protection and righteousness (see D&C 98:13–17).

Therefore, in the Melchizedek Priesthood order, children are born under the covenant inheriting the blessings and rights of their eternal parentage in the Abrahamic covenant of the Patriarchal Order of the Priesthood. "The keys of the patriarchal blessings" to bind on earth and in heaven are "by blessing and also by right" (see D&C 124:91–93). Parents who abide the covenant of the Holy Order of Matrimony (see D&C 132:4) should "rejoice, and lift up [their] heads forever, because of the blessings which the Lord God shall bestow upon [their] children" (2 Nephi 9:3).

Not only the righteous parents, but also their "house" (family) will stand if it is founded and built upon the rock of Christ (see Matthew 7:24–25). Such righteous parents may even be privileged to extend the power of this priesthood order for the salvation of their wayward children (see D&C 132:45–48). "God will be merciful unto many; and our children shall be restored" (2 Nephi 10:2) when "all thy children shall be taught of the Lord; and great shall be the peace of thy children" (Isaiah 54:13). "For the unbelieving husband is sanctified by the wife, and the unbelieving wife is sanctified by the husband; else were your children unclean, but now are they holy" (D&C 74:1; see also 1 Corinthians 7:14). This was a doctrine also taught by the Prophet Joseph Smith given in a discourse by Elder Orson F. Whitney:

> It may be asked, what is the advantage coming to those born under the covenant? Being heirs they have claims upon the blessings of the gospel beyond what those not so born are entitled to receive. They may receive a greater guidance, a greater protection, a greater inspiration from the Spirit of the Lord; and then there is no power that can take them from their parents. Children, on the other hand, who are born to parents who were married until death separates them, have no claim upon such parents, and such parents have no claim upon the children after the resurrection from the dead. . . . The Prophet Joseph Smith declared, and he never taught a more comforting doctrine, that the eternal sealings of faithful parents and the divine promises made to them for valiant service in the Cause of Truth, would save not only themselves, but likewise their posterity. Though some of the sheep

may wander, the eye of the Shepherd is upon them, and sooner or later they will feel the tentacles of Divine Providence reaching out after them and drawing them back to the fold. Either in this life or in the life to come, they will return. They will have to pay their debt to justice; they will suffer for their sins; and may tread a thorny path; but if it leads them at last, like the penitent Prodigal, to a loving and forgiving father's heart and home, the painful experience will not have been in vain. Pray for your careless and disobedient children; hold on to them with your faith. Hope on, trust on, till you see the salvation of God.[10]

In more specific temple terms, the Prophet Joseph Smith explained the "eternal sealings": "The servants of God are sealed in their foreheads, which signifies sealing the blessing upon their heads, meaning the everlasting covenant, thereby making their calling and election sure ['the seed of Abraham, the *elect* of God']. When a seal is put upon the father and mother, it secures their posterity, so that they cannot be lost, but will be saved by virtue of the covenant of their father and mother."[11]

The fulness of the Melchizedek Priesthood in the dispensation of the fulness of times directs its holders to the Patriarchal Priesthood through the Holy Order of Matrimony. The great blessings of the Patriarchal Priesthood are given at the veil and at the altar of celestial marriage. Now we understand the declaration of our patriarchal fathers in Adam's book of remembrance: "Now this same Priesthood, which was in the beginning, shall be in the end of the world also" (Moses 6:7).

The Spirit of Elijah: The Fulness of the Priesthood Restored on Mount Zion

The restoration of the Priesthood to Joseph Smith and Oliver Cowdery through true messengers is the sequence prophesied by Malachi when he said: "Behold, I will send my messenger, and he shall prepare the way before me: and the Lord, whom ye seek, shall suddenly come to his temple" (Malachi 3:1).

First an Elias, John the Baptist, then Peter, James, and John, then other heavenly messengers restored the fulness of the keys of the priesthood. As Joseph Smith taught, this was in preparation for the return of the ultimate Elias who would truly restore all things (see Joseph Smith Translation, John 1:21–28):

> The spirit of Elias is first, Elijah second, and Messiah last. Elias is a forerunner to prepare the way, and the spirit and power of Elijah is to come after, holding the keys of power, building the temple to the capstone, placing the seals of the Melchisedec Priesthood upon the house of Israel, and making all things ready; then Messiah comes to His temple, which is last of all.[12]

It was in the Kirtland temple, a temple in which the full endowment was not practiced, that the keys of the fulness of the Melchizedek Priesthood were restored for the first time in this dispensation of the fulness of times. This restoration was foretold by Moroni when he appeared to the boy Joseph in his bedroom, reciting the words of Malachi:

> And again, he quoted the fifth verse thus: Behold, I will reveal unto you the Priesthood, by the hand of Elijah the prophet, before the coming of the great and dreadful day of the Lord. (Joseph Smith— History 1:38)

It was in the Kirtland temple on April 3, 1836, that Elijah the prophet returned to give his keys, which comprise the keys of the fulness of the Melchizedek Priesthood, the keys of sealing power, to Joseph Smith:

> After this vision had closed, another great and glorious vision burst upon us; for Elijah the prophet, who was taken to heaven without tasting death, stood before us, and said:
> Behold, the time has fully come, which was spoken of by the mouth of Malachi—testifying that he [Elijah] should be sent, before the great and dreadful day of the Lord come—
> To turn the hearts of the fathers to the children, and the children to the fathers, lest the whole earth be smitten with a curse—
> Therefore, the keys of this dispensation are committed into your hands; and by this ye may know that the great and dreadful day of the Lord is near, even at the doors. (D&C 110:13–16)

Joseph Smith later said, "The spirit, power and calling of Elijah is that ye have power to hold the keys of the revelations, ordinance, oracles, powers and endowments of the fulness of the Melchizedek Priesthood and of the Kingdom of God on the earth."[13]

The Fulness of the Priesthood Leads to Eternal Life: A Full View of Mount Zion

The fulness of the Melchizedek priesthood is the power and authority to ascend to the presence of God through the temple. How could the temple be considered an esoteric annex? It is the gate of heaven through which we must pass to ascend the strait staircase of Mount Zion and stand in the presence of God. To stand in His presence is the great and last promise of the temple. Therefore, the temple should be the center of our lives to teach us "the way of salvation."

Can we comprehend and embrace this "full order"? Are we men and women who have enough desire to see the full view of Mount Zion to match the fulness of this spiritual mountain? The Lord warns our sense of goodness if we do not :

> And there are none that doeth good except those who are ready to receive the fulness of my gospel, which I have sent forth unto this generation. (D&C 35:12)

To see and match the fulness of the Lord's mountain, we must receive the fulness of the gospel (see 3 Nephi 16:7, 10–12; 20:28, 30). To receive the fulness of the gospel we must receive the fulness of Christ (see Ephesians 4:13) and be born of Him. Mormon said that to become the spiritually begotten offspring of Christ we must "lay hold of every good thing." This is how we receive the fulness of Christ for a mighty change.

> Search diligently in the light of Christ that ye may know good from evil; and if ye will lay hold upon *every good thing . . . ye certainly will be a child of Christ.* (Moroni 7:19; emphasis added)

To receive every good thing we must search in the light of Christ because "all things which are good cometh of Christ" (Moroni 7:24). Every good thing, meaning "every form of godliness" (Moroni 7:30) is manifest in "divers ways" (Moroni 7:24) to those who diligently search with faith in the light of Christ. To prove and perfect our faith,

God's goodness and glory is revealed "line upon line, precept upon precept" (D&C 98:12)) in the light of Christ. "Fear not, little flock; do good" because you do it in the light and with the power of Christ against which nothing can prevail (see D&C 6:34).

To receive the fulness of Christ we must receive His new and everlasting covenant. This occurs when we receive the fulness of the Holy Ghost and the fulness of The Holy Order of the Son of God, by keeping the fulness of temple covenants in the dispensation of the fulness of times (see Ephesians 1:10). After this manner, the new and everlasting covenant of the Father is written in the hearts of the children of men (see Moroni 7:32).

Receiving the fulness of the gospel brings great rewards:

> Verily I say unto you, blessed are you for receiving mine everlasting covenant, even the fulness of my gospel, sent forth unto the children of men, that they might have life and be made partakers of the glories which are to be revealed in the last days, as it was written by the prophets and apostles in days of old. (D&C 66:2; see also 133:57)

Therefore, let us, both men and women, eschew the rewards of the world and declare as the Levites "the priesthood of the Lord is [our] inheritance" (Joshua 18:7) by receiving the fulness of the priesthood in the house of the Lord.

Receiving the fulness of Christ leads to the fulness of the Father:

> I give unto you these sayings that you may understand and know how to worship, and know what you worship, that you may come unto the Father in my name, and in due time receive of his fulness.
>
> For if you keep my commandments you shall receive of his fulness, and be glorified in me as I am in the Father. (D&C 93:19–20)

The path up Mount Zion to know and become like God the Father is established in the scriptures. We must first discern true messengers of God who have the spirit of prophecy and revelation, which is the testimony and knowledge of Christ. Then we must become true messengers by receiving the gift of the Holy Ghost. As we take Christ's name and words upon us through His covenants and keep these covenants by emulating Him in our thoughts and actions in the gifts of the Spirit, we come to know Him: "For behold, *in my name are they called*; and *if they know me* they shall come forth, and shall have a place eternally at my right hand" (Mosiah 26:24; emphasis added).

As we covenant in the temple with Christ, His atoning power can make us "new creatures," His spiritually begotten sons and daughters, in His similitude. Since the Father and Son are one in likeness, we then become one with the Father, sealed to Him as a son or daughter with a new name and a new nature called "eternal life." It is only on the Father's right hand, as heirs of eternal life with Christ, that we get a full view of Mount Zion.

The Great and Last Promise:
Reaching the Summit of Mount
Zion with a Great and Last Sacrifice

To climb Mount Zion is to seek after the mysteries or richness of God. It is to seek the "unsearchable riches of Christ" (Ephesians 3:8) through the "exceeding riches of his grace" (Ephesians 2:7). As the Savior explained, if we seek the riches of the Father, we will be "the richest of all, people for [we] shall have the riches of eternity" (D&C 38:39). Eternal life is "the promise" (see 1 John 2:25) of the Father. It is the full view of Mount Zion from the summit. It is the richest and greatest gift of God:

> And, if you keep my commandments and endure to the end you shall have eternal life, which gift is the greatest of all the gifts of God. (D&C 14:7; see also 1 Nephi 15:36)

> Seek not for riches but for wisdom; and, behold, the mysteries of God shall be unfolded unto you, and then shall you be made rich. Behold, he that hath eternal life is rich. (D&C 11:7; see also 6:7)

A Glimpse of the Great and Last Promise

A glimpse of the summit, a momentary view of this great gift of eternal life—this richness—is possible in mortal life. This blessing is known by several names: it is the "promise of the fathers," the "rest of the Lord," the "Second Comforter," the "heavenly gift," the "great and last promise":

> Therefore, sanctify yourselves that your minds become single to God, and the days will come that you shall see him; for he will unveil his face unto you, and it shall be in his own time, and in his own way, and according to his own will.
>
> Remember the great and last promise which I have made unto you. (D&C 88:68–69)

If eternal life is to know God, then to see His face, is a great view of this knowledge. Many of the patriarch fathers, such as the brother of Jared, had this view:

> And there were many whose faith was so exceedingly strong, even before Christ came, who could not be kept from within the veil, but truly saw with their eyes the things which they had beheld with an eye of faith, and they were glad.
>
> And behold, we have seen in this record that one of these was the brother of Jared. (Ether 12:19–20)

The Children of Israel in the Sinai were offered this view "with their eyes" but declined to be sanctified for the privilege. They did not have "eyes of faith" in the Lord for "purer eyes" (D&C 131:7) from a pure heart because they erred in their hearts. Today we are offered this view as a great and last promise because the Lord has "prepared a way that thereby others might be partakers of the heavenly gift" (Ether 12:8). The "way" is the same as with our fathers (see Ether 12:7, 20). The reality of this great and last promise should instill within us enough faith to be men and women to match Mount Zion and find the way to the summit. We should have faith enough to sacrifice anything, if necessary, to climb to the summit and find God's presence. Even during our climb, a glimpse of this promise is possible. However, I wonder if many of us consider this promise beyond our view? If so, we walk as the Israelites in the Sinai following "foolish and blind guides" (Helaman 13:29; D&C 19:40). Even with eyes of faith in Moses, their "seeing-eye dog," they did not believe in the power of the Lord to sanctify their fallen nature and cure their blindness to be in His presence. They did not see the importance of "walking in all holiness" (D&C 21:4) for eyes of understanding.

In Paul's writings to the Hebrews, notice the connection between Christ's new covenant with the house of Israel (10) and this great and last promise (11):

> For this is the covenant that I will make with the house of Israel after those days, saith the Lord; I will put my laws into their mind, and write them in their hearts: and I will be to them a God, and they shall be to me a people;
>
> And they [all those who keep the new covenant] shall not teach every man his neighbour, and every man his brother, saying, Know the Lord: for all shall know me, from the least to the greatest. (Hebrews 8:10–11)

If we keep the new covenants of the temple, we will be endowed with the heart and holiness (see Hebrews 12:14) that will bear God's presence to know Him even in mortality.

The Other, or Second, Comforter

In June of 1978, my wife called me at work. "You will never believe what has happened," she reported excitedly. "The Blacks have been given the priesthood." This was a particularly significant announcement for us while living in Detroit because we associated with wonderful black families in our Southfield Ward. It was a joyous occasion in this ward to ordain these worthy fathers as holders of the priesthood.

The Sunday following this historic announcement, our stake conference was held. Elder David Haight was the visiting authority. There was great anticipation and standing room only at this conference. The witness of Elder Haight was so powerful that we were all frozen in spiritual rapture. As though he were an angel, a true messenger, bearing witness of a great truth, he testified of the doctrine taught by Joseph Smith that knowledge of God and his attributes is the foundation of our faith and the greatest knowledge that we can acquire.

The Scriptural Temple

As he peered upward, he said that he knew better than ever before the reality of God. The only other time I have seen such a look of assurance is when I was a deacon sitting on the front row of the chapel, looking up at Elder Hugh B. Brown as he looked into the heavens and testified of the reality of Christ during a Christmas Eve address. This is the look of unwavering assurance of the spirit of prophecy and revelation. Elder Haight did not say that he had seen Christ, but there was no doubt in my mind that he and those present in the temple at this priesthood declaration from the Lord experienced the Second Comforter.

This Other Comforter, the Second Comforter, was promised to the apostles in the meridian of time by the Savior:

> And I will pray the Father, and he shall give you another Comforter, that he may abide with you for ever;
>
> Even the Spirit of truth; whom the world cannot receive, because it seeth him not, neither knoweth him: but ye know him; for he dwelleth with you, and shall be in you.
>
> I will not leave you comfortless: I will come to you. (John 14:16–18)

Joseph Smith gave precise insight to this scripture:

> [When a man joins the church and receives the Holy Ghost] . . . then let him continue to humble himself before God, and the Lord will soon say unto him: "son, thou shalt be exalted." When the Lord has thoroughly proved him, and finds that the man is determined to serve Him at all hazards, then the man will find his calling and election made sure, then it will be his privilege to receive the other comforter . . . as is recorded in the testimony of St. John in the 14th chapter. . . . *Now what is the other comforter? It is no more nor less than the Lord Jesus Christ Himself.* When any man obtains this last comforter, he will have the personage of Jesus Christ to attend to him from time to time and even He will manifest the Father unto him, and they will take up their abode with him, and the Lord will teach him face to face, and he may have a perfect knowledge of the mysteries of the Kingdom of God.[1] [see also John 14:23; Ether 3:20; D&C 130:3]

The Great and Last Promise of the Temple

Because Adam and Eve "went to hide themselves from the presence of the Lord" (Moses 4:14) and because He finally "drove out the man" (Moses 4:31) "from the face of the Lord" (Moses 5:39), the Lord gave the plan of salvation to Adam and Eve as a great and last promise for returning to His presence. Before Adam was baptized, the Lord concluded the promise by saying:

> That ye might be sanctified from all sin, and enjoy the words of eternal life in this world, and eternal life in the world to come, even immortal glory;
>
> Therefore it is given to abide in you; the record of heaven; the Comforter; the peaceable things of immortal glory; the truth of all things; that which quickeneth all things, which maketh alive all things; that which knoweth all things, and hath all power according to wisdom, mercy, truth, justice, and judgment.
>
> And now, behold, I say unto you; This is the plan of salvation unto all men, through the blood of mine Only Begotten, who shall come in the meridian of time. (Moses 6:59, 61–62)

The great and last promise of the temple is that we may have the fulness of the first Comforter (see D&C 109:15) being baptized or sanctified with fire and the Holy Ghost (see Acts 2:1–4; Mosiah 13:5; Helaman 5:23–48; 3 Nephi 17:24; 19:13–14) enabling the visitation of the Second Comforter even "in this world" "while in the flesh" (see D&C 76:118).

By this great and last promise, we may receive "revelation upon revelation, knowledge upon knowledge . . . the mysteries and peaceable thing—that which bringeth joy, that which bringeth life eternal" (D&C 42:61) even "the words of eternal life in this world." The joy from these words and this knowledge can be as great as the joy felt by the 2500 Nephites at the temple of Bountiful and the apostles gathered in the Salt Lake temple in June of 1978.

This great and last promise of the temple is the promise that Adam left as a blessing to his posterity in Adam-ondi-Ahman and thus as a blessing to all of us:

> And in that day Adam . . . began to prophesy concerning *all the families of the earth*, saying: Blessed be the name of God, for because of my transgression my eyes are opened, and in this life I shall have joy, and *again in the flesh I shall see God*. (Moses 5:10; emphasis added)

The Scriptural Temple

Referring to the resurrection, Job again pronounced Adam's blessing which can occur "in the flesh" before physical death: "And though after my skin worms destroy this body, yet in my flesh shall I see God" (Job 19:26). Jacob also said that, "in our bodies we shall see God" (2 Nephi 9:4), and then reinforced the concept of a mortal great and last promise by stating that "in the body [God] shall show himself" (2 Nephi 9:5). Nowhere in the scriptural temple of a past dispensation is this truth more clearly demonstrated than with the brother of Jared and the Nephites when they received the great and last promise of the temple (see Ether 3:16–17; 12:7–8; 3 Nephi 11).

The dispensation of the fulness of times burst forth with the great and last promise in the First Vision because of the faith of Joseph Smith. The great and last promise of the temple is a "principle with promise" (D&C 89:3). The promise is based on the principle of faith. The operative relevancy of the First Vision in our own lives is a personal "first vision" in the great and last promise of the temple if we have the faith to diligently continue in the way prepared up Mount Zion through the great latter-day work of the gospel of Jesus Christ.

President Ezra Taft Benson asked:

> How did Adam bring his descendants into the presence of the Lord? The answer: Adam and his descendants entered into the priesthood order of God. Today we would say they went to the House of the Lord and received their blessings.[2]

This truth is taught in the scriptural temple. The fulness of the higher, or Melchizedek Priesthood, through its temple ordinances is necessary to enjoy the power of godliness and the presence of God the Father and Jesus (see D&C 107:18–19; 84:19, 21–22).

The apostle John A. Widstoe taught that for most of us the great and last promise of the temple comes by the spirit of revelation through a "wonderfully rich communion with God" in the temple that will prepare us for a face to face meeting.[3] Yet, we should not consider the great and last promise of the temple beyond our view, even in mortality. The Lord does not invite us to "tread [His] courts" as sacrificial animals, ignorant of the principle and blessings of sacrifice. He invites us to come to the temple to "appear before [Him]" which is more correctly translated from Hebrew as "when you come to see me" (see Isaiah 1:11–12). In our quest to see the Lord, we should be encouraged by His omni-presence and enticing nearness:

"I am from above, and my power lieth beneath. I am over all, and in all, and through all things" (D&C 63:59). "The Lord shall have power over his saints, and shall reign in their midst" (D&C 1:36). "Where two or three are gathered together in my name, . . . there will I be in the midst of them" (D&C 6:32). "Be of good cheer, little children; for I am in your midst" (D&C 61:36) and "am your advocate" (D&C 29:5). "But behold, verily, verily, I say unto you that mine eyes are upon you. I am in your midst and ye cannot see me; but the day soon cometh that ye shall see me, and know that I am" (D&C 38:7–8).

It is instructive to learn in the temple that God first penetrates the veil towards us with His desire that "the face of the Lord shall be unveiled" (D&C 88:95). He will accomplish this desire by "[making] bare his arm in the eyes of all the nations, in bringing about his covenants and his gospel unto those who are of the house of Israel" (1 Nephi 22:11).

The Lord walks (see Moses 7:69), talks (see Moses 1:31), and dwells (see Moses 7:16) with many righteous people on the earth. If in mortality we willfully fall a second time from the presence of the Lord as did Cain (see Moses 5:39), we will be "a fugitive and a vagabond in the earth" (Moses 5:39) for the earth will not "yield unto [us] her strength" (Moses 5:37) in revealing God. This is truly to be "without Christ and God in the world" (Mormon 5:16).

Emphasizing the mortal reality of the great and last promise, the Apostle Bruce R. McConkie once said, "We must not wrest the scriptures and suppose that the promises of seeing the Lord refer to some future day, either a Millennial or a celestial day, days in which, as we all know, the Lord will be present. The promises apply to this mortal sphere in which we now live."[4]

The principle of purification to perfection, preparing us for the great and last promise of the temple, can only be learned by the power of the Holy Spirit. When the Holy Spirit teaches us about Christ in the temple, we feel Christ's power to purify us in preparation for His rest. The mysteries of God are "not the wisdom of the world" but rather "the wisdom of God in a mystery, even this hidden wisdom, which God ordained before the world unto our glory" (1 Corinthians 2:6–7). When we learn this wisdom, in understanding "the fellowship of the mystery" (Ephesians 3:9; see 1 John 1:3–7, 2:8–11, 3:14–16) in the temple from our Spiritual Teacher, we not only begin to "see" the great and last promise of the temple but also we begin to "comprehend" its glorious power: "Nevertheless, the day shall come when you shall comprehend even God, being quickened in him and by him" (D&C 88:49). "And your glory shall be that glory by which your bodies are quickened" (D&C 88:28).

The Great and Last Promise Comes by Patiently Seeking the Lord

While the promise is to "see the Lord's face," we may have to patiently progress through the implied meanings of the word *see* such as understand with "an eye of faith" (Alma 5:15) and "having not seen" yet loving and believing (see 1 Peter 1:8) before we visually see. Thus Joseph Smith exhorted us:

> Let us here observe, that after any portion of the human family are made acquainted with the important fact that there is a God, who has created and does uphold all things, the extent of their knowledge respecting his character and glory will depend upon their diligence and faithfulness in seeking after him, until like Enoch, the brother of Jared, and Moses, they shall obtain faith in God, and power with him to behold him face to face.[5]

The Prophet also encouraged the Saints "to go on and continue to call upon God until you make your calling and election sure for yourselves, by obtaining this more sure word of prophecy, and wait patiently for the promise until you obtain it."[6]

The scriptures teach that it is with patient and diligent seeking that this promise becomes reality: "Let us run with patience the race that is set before us" (Hebrews 12:1). "Ye are not able to abide the presence of God now, neither the ministering of angels; wherefore, continue in patience until ye are perfected" (D&C 67:13), "waiting patiently on the Lord" (D&C 98:2). "But let patience have her perfect work, that ye may be perfect and entire, wanting nothing" (James 1:4). "Be patient in tribulation until I come; . . . they who have sought me early shall find rest to their souls" (D&C 54:10). "And seek the face of the Lord always, that in patience ye may possess your souls, and ye shall have eternal life" (D&C 101:38). "For he that diligently seeketh shall find; and the mysteries of God shall be unfolded unto them, by the power of the Holy Ghost" (1 Nephi 10:19). Patience and diligence are the disciplines in which pure love is learned and perfected.

Again, connecting with the Holy Ghost is imperative in our patient seeking for the great and last promise of the temple because, "he (Christ) manifesteth himself unto all those who believe in him, by the power of the Holy Ghost" (2 Nephi 26:13). The power of the Holy Ghost prepares us to become a Zion-like people in order to receive the great and last promise of the temple. A blessing to those who "seek to bring forth my Zion" is "the gift and the power of the Holy Ghost" (1 Nephi 13:37). "The Holy Ghost [falls] on many, and they [are] caught up by the powers of heaven into Zion" (Moses 7:27). "And there shall be mine abode, and it shall be Zion, which shall come forth out of all the creations which I have made" (Moses 7:64). "Zion, in process of time, [is] taken up into heaven. And the Lord said . . . Behold mine abode forever" (Moses 7:21). Therefore, "give heed to the light and glory of Zion" (D&C 124:6). "Seek to bring forth and establish the cause of Zion" (D&C 6:6), "that I may visit them in the day of visitation, when I shall unveil the face of my covering" (D&C 124:8).

Seeking the Lord is not optional if we desire eternal life (see Amos 5:4). Moroni seemed to express the imperative need to diligently seek in his statement "seek this Jesus" (Ether 12:41). The Savior, speaking and showing Himself to the Nephites, implied that seeking Him means first to find and hear his voice through written scripture and true messengers and then, after this seeking, we will see Him by serving Him as His sheep and shepherds (see 3 Nephi 15:24). If we seek Jesus persistently and patiently on His terms, we will find Him for, "He that overcometh, and keepeth my works unto the end, to him will I give power. . . . And I will give him *the morning star*" (Revelation 2:26, 28; emphasis added; see also Revelation 22:16).

A Comforting Assurance as a Great and Last Promise of the Temple

If we diligently seek the Lord, doing "the works of righteousness" (D&C 59:23), we can receive the great and last promise of the temple as a promise from "the Holy Spirit of promise" (D&C 88:3). He promises to provide us with a comforting assurance, even a peace in this world (see Alma 58:11) as a sealed promise in the more sure word of the spirit of prophecy and revelation (see 2 Peter 1:19). This more sure word is a "calling and election sure" (2 Peter 1:10). It is a "sealing [blessing] of [the] church, even the Holy Spirit of promise, whereby [we] are sealed up unto the day of redemption" (D&C 124:124) and the reality of eternal life (see D&C 131:5). Elder Bruce McConkie stated, "It is the privilege of all those who have made there calling and election sure to see God."[7]

In preparation for this comforting assurance, Christ abides with us as a comforter as the Holy Spirit teaches us of His perfect stature. We see great possibilities for ourselves as we take hold of the hand of our Guide who will edify us to His level. With His comforting assurance (see Alma 17:10), there is no tribulation or temptation of life too great to overcome. When "our hearts [are] depressed, and we [are] about to turn back, behold, the Lord [comforts] us" (Alma 26:27). For He is "touched with the feeling of our infirmities" (Hebrews 4:15). This is how he "succors" us (see Alma 7:12; Hebrew 2:17–18). This is the communion and comfort expressed by a beautiful aphorism of the *scriptural temple*: "Be still, and know that I am God" (Psalm 46:10; see also D&C 101:16).

When we "pour out our souls in prayer" (Alma 58:10) and then listen to the Lord in the reverence of quiet stillness, we can know the peace that He gives unto us (see John 14:27) in His holy house (see Haggai 2:9). There "the Comforter, which [will] teach [us] the peaceable things of the kingdom" (D&C 36:2), "even peace in this world, and eternal life in the world to come" (D&C 59:23). There He will "visit us with assurances" and "did speak peace to our souls, and did grant us great faith, and did cause us that we should hope for our deliverance in him" (Alma 58:11) because we feel the "peace and power of [His] Spirit, that shall flow unto [us]" (D&C 111:8).

This comforting assurance and peaceful communion will prepare us for the trials of mortality (see Alma 58:11) and purify us for consummation when the veil is rent (see D&C 38:8; 101:23). This spiritual communion will purify us and let our hearts be comforted (see D&C 101:16) for the redemption of Zion. "For the Lord shall comfort Zion" (Isaiah 51:3).

Be it a comforting assurance or a visual witness, it is the great and last promise of the temple that draws us to the summit of Mount Zion. It is the same promise that drew our patriarch fathers to the summit of holy mounts and made Moses declare: "Now, for this cause I know that man is nothing" (Moses 1:10). This great and last promise is as much a reality to us today as the reality of this promise was to the children of Israel in the Sinai. Therefore, the prayer in our hearts today should be, "O that thou wouldst rend the heavens, that thou wouldst come down, that the mountains [temples] might flow down at thy presence" (D&C 133:40). If we are faithful and righteous, the answer to this prayer will be, "And it shall be answered upon their heads; for the presence of the Lord shall be as the melting fire" (D&C 133:41). "Yea, when thou comest down, and the mountains flow down at thy presence, thou shalt meet him who rejoiceth and worketh righteousness, who remembereth thee in thy ways" (D&C 133:44).

In fulfilling this promise for the 2500 Nephites at the temple in Bountiful because of their exceeding faith, it is noteworthy that the Savior commanded them to "do unto the world" referring to His invitation to "come unto me, that ye might feel and see" (3 Nephi 18:25). The Savior desires to have a personal "feeling and seeing" relationship with each of us. He desires that we feel and see the wounds of His Atonement (see D&C 6:37) by feeling and seeing the power of His Atonement in our personal lives. We who have "felt and seen" must bring the power of the Atonement into the lives of others by doing "that which ye have seen me do" (3 Nephi 18:24). Christ dramatically demonstrated the power of His Atonement in the lives of His Nephite disciples when "the light of his countenance did shine upon them, and behold they were as white as the countenance and also the garments of Jesus . . . they [were] purified in [Him]" (3 Nephi 19:25, 28). Ultimately, this is Christ's white light of purification that we must hold up to the world.

The Scriptural Temple

Literally, the great and last promise of the temple to "feel and see" as the Nephites felt and saw the Savior is extended to all. To experience this promise, felt as a comfort or seen with eyes of understanding even in this life, we should strive to be purified by Him who so intently wants to purify us.

> Beloved, now are we the sons of God, and it doth not yet appear what we shall be: but we know that, when he shall appear, we shall be like him; for we shall see him as he is. (1 John 3:2)

"When the Savior shall appear we shall see him as he is. We shall see that he is a man like ourselves," who has become a perfected and glorified man (see D&C 130:1). "And every man that hath this hope in him purifieth himself, even as he is pure" (1 John 3:3).

> [To mine own elect]: for they will hear my voice, and shall see me, and shall not be asleep, and shall abide the day of my coming: for they shall be purified, even as I am pure. (D&C 35:21)

> Sanctify yourselves; yea, purify your hearts, and cleanse your hands and your feet before me, that I may make you clean;
> That I may testify unto your Father, and your God, and my God, that you are clean from the blood of this wicked generation; that I may fulfil this promise, this great and last promise, which I have made unto you. (D&C 88:74–75)

Clean hands needed to ascend the hill of the Lord are hands not "entangled in sin" but "[abiding] in the liberty wherewith [they] are made free" (see D&C 88:86). Clean feet, as we will see, are feet that are edified by and stand on the rock of Christ. Both of these cleansings precede the cleansing of the heart by the Lord. Hands and feet are cleansed before entering the temple. Then hearts are purified in the temple to make a "pure people, that will serve [God] in righteousness" (D&C 100:16).

A Great and Last Sacrifice for the Great and Last Promise

The price for this "great and last promise" has to be great enough to pay for our purification and sanctification. The ultimate price already has been paid through the atoning blood of Jesus Christ (see 1 Corinthians 6:20). This is the price that will purify and sanctify us. *It is because of the great and last sacrifice of Christ that we have the great and last promise of the temple.*

Yet for His blood to miraculously wash our garments white and purify us of all sin, we too must pay a price (see D&C 19:16). This obligation on our part is discredited by many Christian religions as heresy, but as Lehi told Jacob: "he offereth himself a sacrifice for sin, . . . unto all those who have a broken heart and a contrite spirit" (2 Nephi 2:7). As Alma told Shiblon: "none but the truly penitent are saved" (Alma 42:24; see also Mosiah 2:38–39) for "through their repentance they might be saved" (D&C 3:20). The Savior Himself proclaimed "my blood shall not cleanse them if they hear me not" (D&C 29:17). These are His words to hear:

> For, behold, the Lord your Redeemer suffered death in the flesh; wherefore he suffered the pain of all men, that all men might repent and come unto him.
>
> And he hath risen again from the dead, that he might bring all men unto him, on conditions of repentance.
>
> And how great is his joy in the soul that repenteth! (D&C 18:11–13)

Since repentance is the spark that ignites the exalting power of the Atonement on our part, Christ admonished His messengers to "say nothing but repentance" (D&C 6:9). "He commandeth all men everywhere to repent" (D&C 133:16). Repentance means not only forsaking sin but also to "[keep] the covenant and [observe] the commandment, for they shall obtain mercy" (D&C 54:6) and exaltation. "And unto him that repenteth and sanctifieth himself before the Lord shall be given eternal life" (D&C 133:62). It is only on "conditions of repentance" (see Alma 42:13; Helaman 14:11; D&C 138:19) that Christ's mercy can bring all men to His level, having cleansed them with His blood (see D&C 19:16; 29:44). God is merciful (and just); therefore, repent or suffer (see D&C 3:10; 19:4).

The necessity of our cleansing through both Christ's sacrifice and our repentance and baptism was symbolically represented in the Old

Testament temples. In the outer court, the sequential proximity of the sacrificial altar, representing the cleansing blood of Christ, and the brass laver, representing the baptismal cleansing of water through repentance and obedience were first encountered. Preceded by the combination of these cleansings, baptism of fire and the Holy Ghost occurred in the holy place to sanctify for the holy of holies. This baptism of fire was symbolized by the Menorah.

In the Mosaic ritual of cleansing leprosy, which disease was symbolic of spiritual sickness that also cuts off and casts out, we see the cleansing power of baptism by water with the purifying power of baptism by the Holy Ghost. Both of these powers are possible because of the powerful atoning blood of Christ. The leper was first pronounced clean by the priest then went through a ritual of reconciliation and fellowship with the people of God. This ritual involved the blood of a sacrificed bird mixed with water then sprinkled on the petitioner. This ritual represented the cleansing power of blood and water. After seven days, the ritual of reconciliation with God was performed. This ritual, which occurred at the temple, involved the blood of a sacrificed lamb and holy oil representing the sanctifying power of the Holy Spirit. These were placed on the right ear, thumb, and toe of the petitioner so he or she could be reconciled to God by hearing His word, doing His work, and walking in His paths. The remaining oil anointed the head of the petitioner. This ritual represented the purifying power of blood and oil. Note that both rituals of reconciliation were based on the powerful atoning blood of Christ because we can only be reconciled to each other and then to God through the Atonement of Christ (see Jacob 4:11).

It was Elijah who dramatically focused the need of Christ's sacrificial blood along with our repentance and baptism by water and fire for salvation. With twelve stones, Elijah "built an altar in the name of the Lord" (1 Kings 18:32) on which he sacrificed a bullock cut in pieces. This altar and bullock represented the atoning sacrifice of Christ for the house of Israel. Next Elijah had the sacrificed animal, the wood, and the altar drenched with twelve barrels of water (see 1 Kings 18:33–34). Then Elijah called the people to repentance by turning their hearts back to God. Finally, with a baptism of fire, "the fire of the Lord fell, and consumed the burnt sacrifice, and the wood, and the stones, and the dust, and licked up the water that was in the trench" (1 Kings 18:38).

In the *Lectures on Faith*, Joseph Smith insisted on a sacrifice to God in order to produce the kind of faith necessary to obtain the great and last promise, even in the form of a comforting assurance. It requires a sacrifice of "all things": mortal objects, precepts, actions, and wills (see Philippians 3:8) in obedience to God. The prophet explained what happens when we are unable to make this essential sacrifice:

> But those who have not made this sacrifice to God do not know that the course which they pursue is well pleasing in his sight; for whatever may be their belief or their opinion, it is a matter of doubt and uncertainty in their mind; and where doubt and uncertainty are there faith is not, nor can it be. For doubt and faith do not exist in the same person at the same time; so that persons whose minds are under doubts and fears cannot have unshaken confidence; and where unshaken confidence is not there faith is weak; and where faith is weak the persons will not be able to contend against all the opposition, tribulations, and afflictions which they will have to encounter in order to be heirs of God, and joint heirs with Christ Jesus; and they will grow weary in their minds, and the adversary will have power over them and destroy them.[8]

Many religions today discredit the importance of ordinances, and require only a sacrifice of confession in coming to Christ. Others look only to rituals as the source of purification. Neither spiritual manifestation without the Lord's ordinances nor rituals without the presence of the Spirit is the "pattern" acceptable to the Lord (see D&C 52:14–19). The Apostle Paul taught this pattern of God's power expressed through His ordinances (see D&C 84:20) when he said, "There is no power but of God. . . . Whosoever therefore resisteth the power, resisteth the ordinance of God" (Romans 13:1–2).

The Lord warned in this last dispensation "they have strayed from mine ordinances" (D&C 1:15). The power and authority of godliness comes from the gifts of the Spirit through priesthood ordinances. As ordained priesthood holders, we are to act "in the power of the ordination wherewith [we have] been ordained" (D&C 79:1). Abraham was *ordained* a "High Priest, holding the right belonging to the fathers" (see Abraham 1:2). He acted in the rights of power of this ordination. In the temple "are the keys of the holy priesthood ordained" (D&C 124:34). God's blessings for us "are ordained by the ordinance of my holy house" (D&C 124:39). There we are "ordained through the instrumentality of [God's] servants" (D&C 112:1) to "receive right [to God's power and authority] by ordination" (D&C 108:4). In His holy house, "this shall be our covenant—that we will walk in all the ordinances of the Lord" (D&C 136:4). Therefore, Joseph Smith said that "being born again comes by the Spirit of God through ordinances."[9]

Some devout Jews in Israel are seeking purification in preparation for the restoration of the temple by reviving the sacrifice of the red heifer as set forth in the law of Moses (see Numbers 19:19–20). It is fascinating that an American evangelist has arranged to provide a herd of red Angus cattle for this ritual.[10] It is not some concoction of water and ashes that will purify us today any more than that same concoction purified the Jews under the law of Moses (see Mosiah 3:15). The red heifer was symbolic of the purification afforded by the Atonement of Christ. The rituals of purification are symbolic of obedience to the words of Christ that He might purify us.

The importance that Latter-day Saints place on works (performing required ordinances and being obedient to commandments; see Luke 1:6) is the ultimate expression of obedient faith in Christ that works demonstrate (see James 2:17–26). Good works also produce a change in our habits and character. We believe not that works will save us, but our obedience to Christ and His true messengers, with the real intent of a broken heart and contrite spirit will convince Him that we are truly penitent. By works obedient to His will, we are "doers of the word, and not hearers only" (James 1:22). We therefore, take the name of Christ upon us, convincing Him that we believe on His name because the real intent of our good works convinces Him that we love Him (see John 14:15). Then His grace will save us.

They that do good, "that they be rich in good works . . . [lay] up in store for themselves a good foundation . . . that they may lay hold on eternal life" (1 Timothy 6:18–19). "Wherefore, be not weary in well-doing, for ye are laying the foundation of a great work. And out of small things proceedeth that which is great" (D&C 64:33). In other words, through good works we build a personal foundation to receive the fulness of Christ's Atonement for eternal life. Because the fulness of Christ's salvation is contingent on "every man [choosing] for himself" (D&C 37:4) to repent and do good works, He declared, "save yourselves" (D&C 36:6; see also Acts 2:40). For "there is a time appointed for every man, according as his works shall be" (D&C 121:25), "to recompense every man according as his work shall be" (D&C 112:34). God will "[judge] every man according to his works and the deeds which he hath done" (D&C 19:3).

> And behold, this is the whole meaning of the law, every whit pointing to that great and last sacrifice; and that great and last sacrifice will be the Son of God, yea, infinite and eternal
>
> And thus he shall bring salvation to all those who shall believe on his name; this being the intent of this last sacrifice, to bring about the bowels of mercy, which overpowereth justice, and bringeth about means unto men that they may have faith unto repentance.
>
> And thus mercy can satisfy the demands of justice, and encircles them in the arms of safety. (Alma 34:14–16)

"For behold, justice exerciseth all *his* demands, and also mercy claimeth all which is *her* own; and thus none but the truly penitent are saved" (Alma 42:24; emphasis added) because, "He cannot deny justice when it has its claim" (Mosiah 15:27).

The comparison of gender in verse 24 is interesting. When I was growing up, my father was justice and my mother was mercy encircling me in the arms of her safety. When mercy pled with justice, promising that I would do better, mercy usually prevailed. However, did I become "truly penitent"? The truly penitent are those who "repenteth in the sincerity of [their hearts]" (Mosiah 26:29). They "believe on His name," learning to sacrifice all in obedience to the Lord. The truly penitent are those who would sacrifice all in keeping covenants with the Lord to make a mighty change of heart because they love Him.

The father of King Lamoni, who faced physical death at the hand of Ammon said, "I will grant unto thee whatsoever thou wilt ask, even to half of the kingdom" (Alma 20:23). Later, when the father of King Lamoni heard the words of Aaron and realized he could suffer eternal spiritual death, he said, "What shall I do that I may have this eternal life . . . ? Yea, what shall I do that I may be born of God . . . ? Behold, said he, I will give up all that I possess, I will forsake my kingdom that I may have this great joy" (Alma 22:15). Ultimately, however, what it took in sacrifice for the father of King Lamoni and what it takes for all of us "that [we] may be raised from the [spiritually] dead" is to "give away all my sins to know thee" (see Alma 22:18).

The price of the great and last promise for us is that we are willing to offer our own great and last sacrifice, all our sins, and even our own mortal lives if necessary, in obedience to the Lord. To summit Mount Zion and receive the great and last promise, we must begin our great and last sacrifice with broken hearts and contrite spirits until we are sanctified with a mighty change of heart.

The Sacrifice of a Broken Heart

As the rituals of the old covenant demanded specific animal sacrifice, so the new covenant also demands a specific sacrifice. When Christ appeared to the Nephites at the temple in Bountiful, He declared an end to the Mosaic ritual of sacrifice, but the principle of sacrifice continued under the new covenant:

> And ye shall offer up unto me no more the shedding of blood; yea, your sacrifices and burnt offerings shall be done away.
> And ye shall offer for a sacrifice unto me a broken heart and a contrite spirit. (3 Nephi 9:19–20)

It was the inability of the Nephites to offer this sacrifice that ended the Book of Mormon story (see Mormon 2:14).

The enduring principle of sacrifice to the Lord is the sacrifice or change of our hearts. Rudyard Kipling expressed this principle so well in the hymn "God of Our Fathers, Known of Old," when he wrote:

> The tumult and the shouting dies; The captains and the kings depart.
> Still stands thine ancient sacrifice, An humble and a contrite heart.[11]

The righteous Nephites understood this principle of sacrifice under the law of Moses (see 2 Nephi 4:32). The Jews of the Old Testament should have understood the principle of sacrifice requiring "a broken spirit: a broken and a contrite heart" (Psalm 51:16–17; see also 34:18) to "rend your heart, and not your garments" (Joel 2:13).

The Prophet Samuel warned King Saul that acceptable expression of sacrifice to the Lord is obedience to His word: "Hath the Lord as great delight in burnt offerings and sacrifices, as in obeying the voice of the Lord? Behold, *to obey is better than sacrifice*, and to hearken than the fat of rams" (1 Samuel 15:22; emphasis added).

With strong messianic imagery, The prophet Micah taught the good elements of the sacrifice of a broken heart acceptable to the Lord. They are a perfect balance in humility of justice and mercy.

> Wherewith shall I come before the Lord, and bow myself before the high God? . . .
>
> Will the Lord be pleased with thousands of rams, or with ten thousands of rivers of oil? shall I give my firstborn for my transgression, the fruit of my body for the sin of my soul?
>
> He hath shewed thee, O man, what is good; and what doth the Lord require of thee, but to do justly, and to love mercy, and to walk humbly with thy god. (Micah 6:6–8)

A similar instruction about the spiritual gifts for the sacrifice of a broken heart was given to Hyrum Smith, as a revelation through his brother Joseph:

> And now, verily, verily, I say unto thee, put your trust in that Spirit which leadeth to do good—yea, to do justly, to walk humbly, to judge righteously; and this is my spirit. . . .
>
> I will impart unto you of my spirit, which shall enlighten your mind, which shall fill your soul with joy. (D&C 11:12–13)

This gift of "My Spirit" (D&C 11:13) is the Lord's promise in the sacramental covenant. Before we partake of the sacrament, however, and even before we are baptized, we are to offer the Lord a sacrifice of our broken hearts and contrite spirits (see D&C 59:8–13; D&C 20:37). This is our spiritual manifestation to show the Lord that we are truly penitent (see D&C 58:43 with 61:2). This is a condition of repentance for which He can offer Himself as a sacrifice for our sins (see 2 Nephi 2:7).

This is the internal or spiritual sacrifice required because the "contrite spirit" is the "contrite heart" which receives a remission of sins (see D&C 21:9). This remission of sins allows our spirits to receive the truths of righteousness from the Holy Spirit. "My Spirit" (D&C 11:13) is "my voice, because my voice is Spirit; my Spirit is truth" (D&C 88:66; see also D&C 93:26). The Spirit of the Lord is in the gift of the Holy Spirit.

It is an internal sacrifice, not a ritual sacrifice that the Lord desires. It is not so much what is in our rituals as what is in our hearts that makes an acceptable sacrifice to the Lord. Yet, "[we] must [also] keep the performances and ordinances of God" (see 2 Nephi 25:29–30) in His "church articles and covenants" (see D&C 33:14; 28:12) to be acceptable to Him. Otherwise we "pervert the right way of the Lord" (2 Nephi 28:15). "Wherefore he that prayeth, whose spirit is contrite, the same is accepted of me if he obey mine ordinances" (D&C 52:15).

Notice that the combined verses of Micah 6 and D&C 11 complete the Lord's meaning of good (see Moroni 10:6). To God, "all those who are just and true" (see D&C 76:53) are good (consider Ecclesiastes 7:20). In fact, to grow in the knowledge of the glory of God is to grow "in the knowledge of that which is just and true" (see Mosiah 4:12). The "virtue of the word of God" is that it has "a great tendency to lead the people to do that which [is] just" (Alma 31:5). The word of God teaches that "if there be one among you that doeth good, he shall work by the power and gifts of God" (Moroni 10:25) because "all things which are good cometh of Christ" (Moroni 7:12). Therefore, justification and sanctification "through the grace of our Lord and Savior Jesus Christ [are] just and true, to all those who love and serve God" (see D&C 20:30–31).

"Wherefore, let every man beware lest he do that which is not in truth and righteousness before me" (D&C 50:9). Truth is in both righteous mercy and righteous justice. One can only judge righteously with the truth from God (see Mosiah 29:12–13). The truth from God only comes to our judgment in justice and mercy through humility, a common factor in the verses of Micah 6 and D&C 11.

To "do justly," "love mercy," and "judge righteously" requires first to "walk humbly" by the sacrifice of the hard heart within us.

The hard heart must be mellowed to a broken heart that will yield to the power of Christ. Then He will heal our broken hearts with faith and hope, filling them with His perfect love so that we are "made perfect in love" (see 1 John 4:18). Then we are "made perfect in one" (John 17:23). It is this perfect love that also enables us to apply justice and mercy perfectly, so that we judge righteously and not "rashly" (see Mormon 8:19) or fearfully. Therefore, "let God rule him that judgeth" (D&C 58:20). Then it is given to abide in us "all power according to wisdom, mercy, truth, justice, and judgment" (Moses 6:61).

"I, the Lord, have made my church in these last days like unto a judge sitting on a hill, or in a high place" (D&C 64:37). This verse suggests that the truth for righteous judgment is found in Christ's church as the judge of righteousness above all other churches. It also implies that to become a perfect judge in justice and mercy, we must obtain God's perfection of justice and mercy "in a high place" meaning the temple. Those who seek to judge righteously in the earth will be filled with God's Spirit "from on high" (see Isaiah 32:15–17; 42:1–4) in a high place. With the spirit of love and truth from the Holy Spirit we become "a just, and a wise steward" (D&C 51:19), just and wise in the balance of justice and mercy. Then "all things shall work together for [our] good, if [we] walk uprightly and remember the covenant wherewith [we] have covenanted one with another" (D&C 90:24).

Those who "do justice unto the people, but not unto [them-selves]" have not learned the full meaning of the great command-ments about love. They have not remembered the covenant with the Lord. In spite of their apparent goodness, they will be "cut off from the presence of the Lord" (see Ether 10:11) because they are not just and true to themselves. Good men and women who are just and true are "sealed by the Holy Spirit of promise" (see D&C 76:53) to come forth "in the resurrection of the just" (see D&C 76:17). "The spirits of the just" (see D&C 138:12–14) are "made perfect" (see D&C 76:69) like our Father in Heaven when they acquire perfect love (see 1 John 4:17) because God is "a perfect, just God, and a

merciful God also" (Alma 42:15). "He is full of mercy, justice, grace
and truth, and peace" (D&C 84:102; see Moses 7:30–31). Notice
that because of His mercy, God is justified when "[He] shall bring
[us] unto judgment (see D&C 97:2) for "in the day of wrath I will
remember mercy" (D&C 101:9). "The Lord ordained Noah after his
own order" (Moses 8:19) and "Noah was a just man, and perfect in
his generation" (Moses 8:27). Job was a "perfect and upright" man
who feared the Lord (Job 1:1). Like them, we should "continue in
[God's] goodness" (D&C 86:11) through His holy order, until our
love is perfected.

This is the principle of purification to perfection. "Be ye therefore perfect, even as your Father which is in heaven is perfect"
(Matthew 5:48; 3 Nephi 12:48). This commandment, also given to
Father Abraham (see Genesis 17:1), is the principle of purification
to perfection. At first, this commandment, like a millstone around
our necks, seems too heavy. However, through obedience to the
holy order of the Son of God and by the power of the Atonement,
the millstone becomes a refining wheel of purification on which
we turn to perfection. After we have suffered a while in refine-
ment, God will make us perfect (see 1 Peter 5:10). "Yea, come
unto Christ, and be perfected in him, . . . that by his grace ye may
be perfect in Christ" (Moroni 10:32). Through Christ we come
"unto a perfect man, unto the measure of the stature of the fulness of Christ" (Ephesians 4:13). As Hosea turned to and accepted
wayward Gomer, his wife (see Hosea 1:2), the Lord will turn to us
and edify us if we turn to Him with a broken heart. Through the
prophet Hosea the Lord declared:

> For I desired *mercy*, and not sacrifice; and *the knowledge of God* more
> than burnt offerings. (Hosea 6:6; emphasis added)

The Hebrew word for *mercy* (*hesed*) refers to a "deep spiritual and
emotional bond in loving-kindness." It also is a synonym for covenant in that to express loving- kindness towards someone means to
keep it within a covenant.[12] The Hebrew words for *knowledge* (*yada*
and *daat*) both mean "to learn by close experience."[13] In the meaning
of these Hebrew words we see the emotional, spiritual, and physical intimacy that we all need for pure love. Such intimacy can only

develop when it is protected by trustworthy promises of a covenant. This complete intimacy corresponds to the intellectual, spiritual, and physical makeup of our souls.

Mercy and knowledge are the intended results of the sacrifices required in seeking closeness with the Lord. Only with the sacrifice of our hard hearts to broken hearts can the intimacies of a personal bonding relationship begin with Christ. Then the Holy Spirit will give us His gifts to learn by close experience the merciful graces of Jesus Christ. Then we will want to continue a close relationship with Christ, granting Him intimacy or "in-to-me-see"[14] because of the fidelity of His covenant and the purity of His love.

King David understood that having the right or "clean heart" is having the right spirit and this comes by following the Holy Spirit. He pled for the Spirit when he prayed:

> Create in me a clean heart, O God; and renew a right spirit within me.
> Cast me not away from thy presence; and take not thy holy spirit from me. (Psalm 51:10–11)

It is the Holy Spirit within the temple, be it a building or an individual, not its physical makeup, who justifies (makes right) and enlightens the structure with the right spirit. This truth of the sacrifice of a broken heart to obtain a heart enlightened and justified by the Holy Spirit is immutable in any temple dispensation. Even during the construction of the Tabernacle this sacrifice was required when "every one whose heart stirred him up, and every one whom his spirit made willing [came] to the work of the Tabernacle" (Exodus 35:21).

As we make a true change from a hard heart to a broken heart, sacrificing the selfish and consuming animal within us, our hearts stir us to receive the right and willing spirit through the justification and sanctifying gifts of the Spirit. Then we are "stirred" to the work of the temple and the discipleship of Christ (see Luke 14:26).

A Sacrifice of Sweet Savor

When Moses was given instructions about burnt offerings, an unlikely term was used by the Lord to describe the sacrifice:

> And thou shalt burn the whole ram upon the altar: it is a burnt offering unto the Lord: it is a *sweet savour*, an offering made by fire unto the Lord. (Exodus 29:18; emphasis added)

The term *sweet savor* hardly fits a burning ram until we understand how the Lord considers this burnt offering a "sweet savor." Paul helped us come to that understanding when he said:

> And walk in *love*, as Christ also hath loved us, and hath given himself for us *an offering and a sacrifice to God for a sweetsmelling savour.* (Ephesians 5:2; emphasis added)

Here, a sacrifice to God of "sweet savor" or "sweetsmelling savor" is defined. It is not the sacrifice that is sweet. It is the diligently obedient and heartfelt intent to "walk in love" by the one offering sacrifice that can find sweet acceptance with the Lord. The intent of sacrifice must be love of God and fellow man, sacrificing for their benefit. "This thing [sacrifice] is a similitude of the sacrifice of the Only Begotten of the Father" (Moses 5:7). Even if our sacrifices to the Lord do not result in a completed work, He will "accept of [our] offerings" if we "cease not [our] diligence" in obeying the Lord (see D&C 124:49).

There are notable examples in the scriptural temple of this sweetsmelling sacrifice even when the desired result seemed elusive. Oliver Granger was physically handicapped. He helped construct the Kirtland temple then returned to Kirtland as an emissary of the prophet in order to help rectify financial problems. How we would like to hear these few sweet words of the Lord to describe our sacrifices:

> I remember my servant Oliver Granger; behold . . . his name shall be had in sacred remembrance. . . . for *his sacrifice shall be more sacred unto me than his increase*, saith the Lord. (D&C 117:12–13; emphasis added)

Just as sweet to our ears would be the words of assurance that Joseph Smith received from the Lord because of his sacrifices:

> I seal upon you your exaltation, and prepare a throne for you in the kingdom of my Father, with Abraham your father.
>
> Behold, I have seen your sacrifices, and will forgive all your sins;
> I have seen your sacrifices in obedience to that which I have told you.

Go, therefore, and I make a way for your escape, as I accepted the offering of Abraham of his son Isaac. (D&C 132:49–50)

Abraham had such love for the Lord that he would sacrifice his own son to be obedient. Joseph Smith sacrificed his own life with the same Abrahamic love and obedience. He was "chastened and tried, even as Abraham" (see D&C 101:3–5). The Lord will "prove [us] all, as [He] did Abraham," and that "[He] might require an offering at your hand, by covenant and sacrifice" (D&C 132:51). For this is "a day of sacrifice" (D&C 64:23). In the temple, we covenant to sacrifice with this demonstration of love and obedience that our sacrifices will be a sweet savor to the Lord.

Specific Sacrifices of the Broken Heart

A sacrifice of sweet savor to the Lord is the broken heart. The broken heart is broken or tamed because it sacrifices the ungodly and consuming animal of the natural man. The natural heart, thus broken of pride and ungodliness, becomes a meek heart, willing, learning, and forgiving. It can then be taught and trained by the Holy Spirit. We, who are broken, can then receive a new heart even a "might change of heart" for God "healeth the broken in heart" (Psalm 147:3). The Lord has told us specifically what the sacrifices of the broken heart should be in order that He might heal us with a mighty change of heart:

And again, verily I say unto you that it is your privilege, and a promise I give unto you that have been ordained unto this ministry, that inasmuch as you strip yourselves from jealousies and fears, and humble yourselves before me, for ye are not sufficiently humble, the veil shall be rent and you shall see me and know that I am—not with the carnal neither natural mind, but with the spiritual. (D&C 67:10)

Notice again the great and last promise of the temple in this verse. The price for this promise is to sacrifice our jealousies and fears, as well as pride.

Because of Christ, there is no place for comparison, and its resulting jealousy, between us as human beings. We need only compare our own stature and will to God's (see D&C 124:69). Since we have all disobeyed God's will and fallen short of His stature, self-esteem

The Scriptural Temple

on either side of pride, jealousy or conceit, is self-deceit (see 1 John 1:59). If, as Paul said, we live and move and have our being in Him (see Acts 17:27), then only understanding, edification, and love should be the "fellowship" (1 John 1:7) between each other since this is how God relates to us. Standing in the middle of every human relationship is the Savior. Our relationship to His stature and Atonement determines the nature of all our other relationships.

Fear is a natural human reaction but it takes the place of lost faith (see Mark 4:40; D&C 63:16). More importantly, "He that feareth is not made perfect in love" (1 John 4:18). We can begin to "[hush our] fears" if we "cry unto the Lord" (see Mosiah 23:27–28). We have nothing humanly possible to fear if we have complete faith in Christ. All we really need to fear is disobedience. "And if ye have no hope ye must need be in despair [fear]; and despair cometh because of iniquity [disobedience]" (Moroni 10:22).

Since Christ is "the way . . . prepared for all men from the foundation of the world" (1 Nephi 10:18), "there is none other way" (2 Nephi 9:41) because He is "the right way" (see 2 Nephi 25:28–29). For all men, "the right way is to believe in Christ" (2 Nephi 25:28). If we go "out of the way" (2 Nephi 28:11) or "pervert the right way of the Lord" (2 Nephi 28:15), our way will not be the right way. Therefore, in each life, "prepare ye the way of the Lord, and make his paths straight" (1 Nephi 10:8). Preparing for the right way will dispel fear, for "if ye are prepared ye shall not fear" (D&C 38:30). This is because fear will be replaced with the peace of Christ so that our hearts are not troubled or afraid (see John 14:27).

As the Hebrew bride prepared and watched in anticipation for her bridegroom's coming, so should we as the Lord's bride prepare: "Prepare ye, prepare ye, O my people" (D&C 133:4). "Let all things be prepared before you" (D&C 133:15). "Prepare ye the way of the Lord, and make his paths straight" (D&C 133:17). "Prepare ye for the coming of the Bridegroom" (D&C 133:19).

Hope in Christ, even a perfect brightness of hope, comes through preparation on our part. Preparation on our part specifically means being "faithful in keeping the commandments of God" (1 Nephi 3:15, 21; 4:1). "For if you will that I give unto you a place in the celestial world, you must prepare yourselves by doing the things which I have commanded you and required of you" (D&C 78:7; see D&C 101:69). We are faithful in keeping the Lord's commandments when we act on the belief that "the Lord giveth no commandments . . . save he shall prepare a way for them" (1 Nephi 3:7; see 1 Nephi 14:17; 16:16; 17:3, 5, 13, 41; 22:20; 2 Nephi 9:10, 41). "The Lord is able to do all things according to his will, for the children of men, if it so be that they exercise faith in him" (1 Nephi 7:12).

Preparation also means faithfully enduring trial and tribulation for "My people must be tried in all things, that they may be prepared to receive the glory that I have for them, even the glory of Zion" (D&C 136:31). Other specifics of the preparation for our redemption are found in multiple verses of the *scriptural temple* (see Alma 2:13; 5:27–32; 16:16; 34:32; Ether 12:33–34; D&C 78:67, 11–13, 17–18; D&C 105:9–13; 109:38, 46). As the five foolish virgins discovered, the ultimate result of being unprepared with the Lord is, "verily I say unto you, *I know you not*" (Matthew 25:12; emphasis added).

Standing on the roof of the house of Simon the Tanner in the old seaport of Joppa, I looked at the rock-protected enclosure of the port and the vanishing expanse of the blue Mediterranean beyond. I thought of the two scriptural men of Joppa. Jonah feared the Assyrians and had little faith in the Lord. He boarded a ship at Joppa to escape, only to find himself in the belly of hell. The other, a man who also stood on the roof of Simon the tanner, had not yet comprehended the extent of his calling until he understood the great vision of the sheet descending from heaven (see Acts 11:5–7). At that moment the protected port of Joppa, which finally was not for Jonah, was no longer a refuge for Peter. Now he saw beyond the horizon of the blue Mediterranean to the waiting Nineveh.

In the ports of our lives we may find protection and refuge but unless we venture into open water, we limit our horizons because of apathy or fear. An important challenge of this life is to leave our ports of Joppa and go through tribulation—and let tribulation go through us—in order to discover what kind of men and women holding the hand of Christ we can become.[15] We should sail out of our ports without fear, like a great ship, because our exposure to peril is covered by the Atonement as "an anchor of the soul" (Hebrews 6:19).

With "perfect brightness of hope" (2 Nephi 31:20) in our Savior, Jesus Christ who steers our ship (compare Mormon 5:18), we should "submit cheerfully and with patience to all the will [wind] of the Lord" (Mosiah 24:15) billowing our sails. "In the world ye shall have tribulation;" Christ said, "but be of good cheer; I have overcome the world" (John 16:33). To follow Him, we must do likewise. If we do not have His anchor and His hope, then we are "tossed to and fro, and carried about with every wind of doctrine" (Ephesians 4:14) as we venture into open sea.

Like a sailing ship, we must move about even in open and dangerous water to be effective true messengers "in proclaiming the gospel in the land of the living" (D&C 81:3). Like a buoy, however, unless we are tethered to a solid foundation with the rope (hope) of the anchor of our soul, we will be at the mercy of any wind and soon lose our effectiveness and our souls. We must look to the horizon, beyond our weakness and fears, with a perfect brightness of hope to the rising sun, believing that all is possible through the Atonement of the Son of God. We must hope, even as we fail, because the reality is, as the story of Jonah teaches, even in great sin and fear we can have hope through simple obedience to Christ. As we grasp His rope, He will clean us off and make us whole and fearless.

Humility is the basic quality of the heart broken of pride. This attribute opens the door to all other spiritual qualities. It is the heart broken of pride that invites the Holy Spirit (see D&C 136:32–33) to teach and train in the qualities which permit us to be sanctified by sacrificing ("submitting") all in obedience to the Lord. This was the temple teaching of King Benjamin:

> Unless he yields to the enticings of the Holy Spirit, and putteth off the natural man and becometh a saint through the atonement of Christ the Lord, and becometh as a child, submissive, meek, humble, patient, full of love, willing to submit to all things which the Lord seeth fit to inflict upon him, even as a child doth submit to his father. (Mosiah 3:19)

The Book of Mormon teaches that "the loftiness of the vineyard" is the branch that overcomes the roots because such prideful branches "[take] strength unto themselves" (see Jacob 5:48) and "lift themselves up in the pride of their hearts" (Mormon 8:36). Then the tree becomes top heavy and corrupted, disconnected from its roots. Pride of the natural man is the most difficult to sacrifice. Therefore, sufficient humility (see Ether 9:35) is the most difficult to obtain. God requires that we "repent in sackcloth and ashes" (Mosiah 11:25) by humbling ourselves "in the depths of humility" (Mosiah 21:14), "even to the dust" (Mosiah 21:13).

> Could ye say, if ye were called to die at this time, within yourselves, that ye have been sufficiently humble? . . .
>
> Behold, are ye stripped of pride? I say unto you, if ye are not ye are not prepared to meet God. (Alma 5:27–28; see also Alma 34:32)

We are not prepared to meet God unless we are stripped of pride because, as C. S. Lewis said, "Pride is spiritual cancer: it eats up the very possibility of love."[16]

When we "labor much in the spirit" (see Alma 8:10) to humble ourselves sufficiently before the Lord, we can "cry mightily to the Lord" (Mosiah 11:25; 21:14) because humility is the paradoxical key to mighty prayer. Therefore, "humble [yourself] in mighty prayer" (D&C 5:24; 29:2) and "pray always" (see D&C 19:38) because "ye receive the Spirit through prayer" (D&C 63:64; see 3 Nephi 19:9) and "are taught through prayer by the Spirit" (D&C 63:65).

With sufficient humility and mighty prayer, the door is truly opened to all other qualities and gifts of the Spirit. We cannot climb the straight and narrow path up Mount Zion without these gifts. Therefore, "be thou humble; and the Lord thy God shall lead thee by the hand, and give thee answers to thy prayers" (D&C 112:10). The greatness of Abraham started with his humility, for he knew he needed to be led by the Lord's hand: "I will lead thee by my hand . . . and my power shall be over thee" (Abraham 1:18).

Our Great and Last Sacrifice for the Great and Last Promise

Once we have sacrificed jealousy, fear, and pride to obtain a broken heart, we must make a final sacrifice of sweet savor to the Lord in order to obtain a pure heart necessary for the great and last promise of the temple:

> Verily, thus saith the Lord: It shall come to pass that every soul who forsaketh his sins and cometh unto me, and calleth on my name, and

obeyeth my voice, and keepeth my commandments, shall see my face and know that I am. (D&C 93:1)

Again the great and last promise is the result of this sacrifice and it is for "every soul." The sacrifice talked about in this verse is the sacrifice made by the father of King Lamoni—to forsake all our sins and worldliness, and come unto Christ. The essence of this great and last sacrifice for the prize of eternal life, the great and last promise of the temple, is captured in the dialogue between Christ and the rich man:

> And when he was gone forth into the way, there came one running, and kneeled to him, and asked him, Good Master, what shall I do that I may inherit eternal life?
>
> Thou knowest the commandments. . . .
>
> And he answered and said unto him, Master, all these have I observed from my youth.
>
> Then Jesus beholding him loved him, and said unto him, One thing thou lackest: go thy way, sell whatsoever thou hast, and give to the poor, and thou shalt have treasure in heaven: and come, take up the cross, and follow me.
>
> It is easier for the camel to go through the eye of a needle, than for a rich man to enter into the kingdom of God. (Mark 10:17, 19–21, 25)

The image of the camel going through the narrow gate (the eye of a needle) is the camel shedding all excess baggage in order to pass. We are all "rich men" if we have excess baggage. Death is a sudden shedding of our excess baggage as though the loaded camel suddenly ran through the narrow gate. If we are not prepared, death—like birth—can strip us naked (see 1 Timothy 6:7), unworthy for the promise. This is why the father of King Lamoni was finally willing to sacrifice all he possessed, even his sins.

We need the baggage or covering that will pass through the eye of the needle. We need "bags which wax not old" (see Luke 12:33). We need the garment of salvation, and the robes of righteousness. Sacrificing whatsoever we have that is excess, even all that we have (see Mark 12:44; 1 Kings 17:10–14), as a witness of our faith to acquire the gifts of the Spirit that He provides in the temple, is the final sacrifice in preparation to pass the narrow gate. Be it material wealth, idleness, pride, sin, or even our own lives (see Luke 14:26; D&C 103:27–28), we must be willing to sacrifice all that is excess and unnecessary to pass through the narrow gate and claim eternal life.

It is not sufficient to just rid ourselves of the excess. We must do it in a way that edifies others ("give to the poor"), including ourselves (see Daniel 4:27). Shedding excess baggage is an act of edification to ourselves if we repent. To rid ourselves of sin is only half the cleansing. We must also cleanse ourselves with righteousness (see D&C 66:1). We must "repent and return unto thee, and find favor in thy sight, and be restored to the blessings" (D&C 109:21). Shedding excess baggage can also edify others with material needs and with devotion of time to their needs. To give material wealth and time to the poor is only half the giving. We must also cover them with righteousness, giving blessings "both temporal and spiritual" (see Mosiah 2:41; 4:26; 18:29).

To take up the cross is to cross ourselves (see Alma 39:9) in crucifying or putting off our natural man (see Mosiah 3:19) in order to "deny [ourselves] of these [worldly] things" (see 3 Nephi 12:30) to keep [Jesus'] commandments (see Joseph Smith Translation, Matthew 16:24). It is to abandon the false messengers of the precepts of men to take upon us and bear the name of Christ. "For it is better that ye should deny yourselves of these thing, wherein ye will take up your cross" (3 Nephi 12:30). It is to take upon us Christ's cross in the form of worldly suffering, rejection, and sacrifice for the sake of bringing forth and establishing the cause of Zion (see D&C 6:6; 11:6; 14:6). When we "take up [our] cross daily" (Luke 9:23), we practice a daily discipline (see Alma 58:40) of sacrificing our wills in obedience to His will.

In the end, to "take up the cross" is to be totally committed to Christ even unto death, since the price for keeping the gospel treasure is to sell (sacrifice) all that we have (see Matthew 13:44–46). "What is property unto me? saith the Lord" (D&C 117:4). "Let no man be afraid to lay down his life for my sake; for whoso layeth down his life for my sake shall find it again. And whoso is not willing to lay down his life for my sake is not my disciple" (D&C 103:27–28; see also D&C 98:13).

The Scriptural Temple

To follow the Savior is to take up our cross (see Matthew 10:38) while doing the will and works of Christ. It is to remain obedient to the True Messenger through mortal tribulation by obeying and keeping His covenants with a perfect brightness of hope. To be "perfect" in this life is to keep His covenants with diligence (see Mosiah 1:11; Alma 7:23; 12:9) and exactness, having a joyful brightness in doing so (see 1 Kings 8:61). This joy comes when we realize that in taking up our cross we not only bear the Savior's cross but He also bears ours.

To endure to the end is not just hanging on until death. The command to endure transcends physical death. It is to "endure, whether in life or in death" (D&C 50:5) to "abide the day of his coming, whether in life or in death" (D&C 61:39; see also D&C 63:49–50). It is to "continue in patience until [we] are perfected" to "abide the presence of God" (D&C 67:13). Enduring is to "endure it well" (D&C 121:8) even "valiantly" (D&C 121:29) by "[enduring] in faith on his name to the end" (D&C 20:29; 63:20; 101:35). It is to "[endure] of my church to the end" (D&C 10:69). This means to endure in Christ's circle of salvation under His Order until His fulness is received. "Wo unto them who are cut off from my church, for the same are overcome of the world" (D&C 50:8), but "he that is faithful and endureth shall overcome the world" (D&C 63:47). God wills "that [we] should overcome the world" (D&C 64:2) as He did (see John 16:33). To endure is to "[abide] in me" (D&C 97:3). To abide in Christ is to follow Him to the end in "[pressing] forward with a steadfastness in Christ . . . feasting upon the word of Christ" (2 Nephi 31:20) and "[serving Him] in righteousness and in truth unto the end" (D&C 76:5). The end is eternal life (see 2 Nephi 33:4) when "God shall exalt thee on high" (see D&C 121:8). In the end, "[he who] is steadfast and is not overcome . . . shall be saved" (Joseph Smith—Matthew 1:11) because "he only is saved who endureth unto the end" (D&C 53:7).

To take up the cross, follow, and endure in the circle of salvation is "a great and the last commandment" (see D&C 19:31–32) in order to make the great and last sacrifice through temple covenants to have the great and last promise of the temple. In sum, it is the sacrifice of all forms of pride and idolatry (excess baggage) in our lives so that we are able to turn completely to the one true God. It is being able to "circumcise therefore the foreskin of your heart" (Deuteronomy 10:16). Then we will have sacrificed for a "free heart" (free of excess baggage), enabling it to be "consecrated . . . unto the Lord" (2 Chronicles 29:31). In Book of Mormon terms, this sacrifice is called "yielding [our] hearts unto God" (see Helaman 3:33–35).

Notice in this scriptural account of Helaman that those with a broken heart (the more humble part of the people) continued to sacrifice in obedience to the Lord because they became "firmer and firmer" in their faith in Christ. This firmness of faith is a gift for sacrifice in obedience to the Lord. It is the gift of the spirit of prophecy and revelation and its comforting assurance. Then these broken hearted people became a pure hearted people because they "yielded their hearts unto God." They yielded completely their will to God's will. This is the great and last sacrifice of the temple for those who are willing to "overcome" as John the Revelator said (see Revelation 2:11) by sacrificing all, yielding their hearts to God. This is the ultimate sacrifice required for the great and last promise of the temple. It was the sacrifice required by the Lord in the sermon on the temple mount when He said, "Therefore, if ye shall come unto me, . . . then come unto me with full purpose of heart, and I will receive you" (3 Nephi 12:23–24). Full purpose of heart is one of the "conditions of repentance" (Helaman 14:11; D&C 138:19) because, "if ye will repent . . . return unto me with full purpose of heart" (3 Nephi 10:6).

Sacrifice to full purpose of heart was the same sacrifice required by the Lord in "straitening" the children of Israel whose fathers rejected the great and last promise of the temple because they "err in their heart." Therefore the Lord lamented, "O that there were such an heart in them, that they would fear me, and keep all my commandments always" (Deuteronomy 5:29).

Full purpose of heart occurs by yielding our hearts to God in obeying His covenants with "exactness" (Alma 57:21), a term which is used in the endowment. It comes by making a great and last sacrifice of the many facets of stubborn pride of the natural man. It is to "deny [ourselves] of all ungodliness" (Moroni 10:32) by shedding all forms of idolatry, even the human beings that we idolize (see Luke 14:26). By completely taking Christ's name upon us in emulating Him with full purpose of heart (see D&C 18:27–28), He is the only one we idolize because His name is written always in our hearts (see Mosiah 5:12). Then the Lord will "receive" us, which implies the blessing of His presence.

Since one of Christ's titles or names is "the Bridegroom" (see D&C 33:17) there is an interesting correlation to the gift of sacrifice given to the Jewish bridegroom by the bride. It is her heart.[17] It is dedication to her husband with full purpose of heart. This is how the woman "gives herself" to the man in the Holy Order of Matrimony. The Bridegroom "[requires] the hearts of the children of men" (D&C 64:22). Just like the Savior, the man must "receive" this sacrificial gift of his bride with full love and devotion to her as his most prized and holy possession. Before giving of himself as a gift to her, the man first receives his bride as a gift from God. Receiving her must be with "the integrity of his heart" (D&C 124:20). In this giving and receiving (see D&C 88:33), man and women truly discover themselves in the other because the fulness of pure love is revealed in the giving and receiving of their masculinity and femininity.

This great and last sacrifice begins with a broken heart and continues until a sacrifice of the full heart is made. This is "such an heart" acceptable to the Lord. We sacrifice our full hearts when we "offer [our] whole souls" (see Omni 1:26; 2 Nephi 25:29) to God on the altars of the temple. Then we truly keep the first and great commandment (see Matthew 22:37) through the "great and last commandment" (see D&C 19:31–32).

Before we can offer our whole souls, body, mind, and heart, as this gift of total obedience, yielding our own wills to His on the temple altar, we must first understand "the ministry [and] the word" of reconciliation (2 Corinthians 5:18–19). This requires that we first be reconciled with our "brother" (the priesthood authorities to whom we are accountable as well as all those with whom we have "ought") so that Christ can reconcile us to God. "Therefore if thou bring thy gift to the altar, and there rememberest that thy brother hath ought against thee; Leave there thy gift before the altar, and go thy way; first be reconciled to thy brother, and then come and offer thy gift" (Matthew 5:23–24).

The greatest expression of a broken heart is the ability to completely forgive others. The word *forgive*, meaning "given (the price) before," implies the Atonement gift. When we refuse to forgive, we deny the healing and forgiving power of the Atonement. Then "there remaineth in [us] the greater sin" (see D&C 64:9) of the inability to freely give the gift of mercy (see Matthew 18:23–35). As innocent Abigail pled with David "upon me let this iniquity be . . . forgive the trespass of thine handmaid (1 Samuel 25:24, 28), so the innocent Redeemer shows the way, leaving no excuse in failure to forgive.

The object and desired result of complete forgiveness is reconciliation. This requires confession and forgiveness on both sides (see D&C 42:88). It requires making "proposals for peace . . . according to the voice of the Spirit" (D&C 105:40). The power of pure love from a heart without guile (see D&C 41:11) is usually needed to produce this kind of reconciliation. Irreconcilable differences result in being "cast out" form each others presence and possibly from the presence of the Lord. This is the gift, the reconciled heart, which is full sacrifice of the proud heart to a pure heart without guile, that we must bring to the mercy seat, the altar of the temple. This is the gift that we must bring even to the sacrament altar before partaking of the sacred emblems worthily (see D&C 46:4). Because of our "peaceable walk with the children of men" (Moroni 7:4), and our "daily walk" (D&C 19:32) in God's commandments, we can be reconciled to God (see 2 Nephi 10:24; 25:23) and obtain His mercy through the pure love of His Son (see Jacob 4:11).

The importance of being reconciled to men and God is taught in the temple. We are invited to withdraw from the circle of reconciliation if we have enmity. The source of enmity is pride. It was the pride and enmity of Laman and Lemuel that caused Nephi to exclaim to them, "I fear lest ye shall be cast off forever" (1 Nephi 17:47). Pride and enmity are what caused Satan to be cast out forever from the circle of God. Pride and its subsequent enmity are the major faults that will keep us out of celestial circles. For in that celestial day "enmity of all flesh, shall cease" (see D&C 101:25–26). The ultimate meaning of the ubiquitous scriptural temple phrases *cut off* and *cast out* is "if ye do not remember to be charitable, ye are as dross, which the refiners do cast out" (Alma 34:29).

The Mighty Change of Heart on Mount Zion: The Pure Love of Christ

King Benjamin taught that from the "depths of humility" of a broken heart, we can "[stand] steadfastly in the faith" until we are "filled with the love of God" (see Mosiah 4:11–12). By this edifying process in which "faith and repentance bringeth a change of heart" (Helaman 15:7), our faith in Christ becomes hope in Christ (see Alma 58:11). Hope in Christ is a change of heart which is "filled with desire" (3 Nephi 19:24) for continual righteousness to do good. It is a spiritual confidence (see Mosiah 5:2–3; Alma 36:28) from revealed knowledge as a "surety" of hope (see Ether 12:4) that comes of faith and repentance. Hope is "an anchor of the souls of men, which would make them sure and steadfast always abounding in good works" (Ether 12:4) in order to be "partakers of the heavenly gift" (see Ether 12:8–9) of charity. This is an important message of Jacob's temple sermon (see Jacob 2:19). Therefore, the result of true faith (see Alma 32:21) is hope and charity or a change of heart that receives the heavenly gift and gives pure love in return.

Standing steadfastly in the faith to be filled with the love of God means we must bridle our passions (see Alma 38:12) in the covenants of God. We must humble ourselves, pray continually, and follow the Spirit (see Alma 13:28) as just and merciful men and women of God who keep His covenants and commandments (see Mosiah 2:4). "Fulfilling the commandments" brings a "remission of sins" which brings "meekness and lowliness of heart" (see Moroni 8:25–26). In this condition of the depths of obedience and humility comes the "visitation of the Holy Ghost, which Comforter filleth with hope and perfect love" (Moroni 8:26; see Romans 5:5).

King Benjamin's heavenly warning is that unless we are "filled with love towards God and all men" (Mosiah 2:4), we have not found "the thing wherewith [we] have been made free" (Helaman 15:8) and are still enemies to the God (see Mosiah 3:19). Mormon called perfect love "charity" and defined its source as "the pure love of Christ":

> But charity is the pure love of Christ, and it endureth forever; and whoso is found possessed of it at the last day, it shall be well with him. (Moroni 7:47)

Mormon further exhorted us to obtain this pure love by "[praying] unto the Father with all the energy of heart, that ye may be filled with this love" (Moroni 7:48). "All the energy of heart" is equivalent to "full purpose of heart." Mormon was telling us to make a great and last sacrifice to the Lord, yielding our hearts to God in keeping all of His commandments, to obtain as a gift of God this pure love of Christ in which all the graces of holiness are found. In making a great and last sacrifice to the Lord, our broken hearts become pure hearts because they are filled with pure love. Therefore, the Savior taught, "If ye keep my commandments, ye shall abide in my love" (John 15:10).

Our great and last sacrifice to the Lord is possible when we understand the powers of pure love. Only with the power of pure love is all fear dispelled (see 1 John 4:18; Moroni 8:16). Then pure wisdom appears because pure hearts are applied to understanding (see Mosiah 12:27). With this understanding we can judge righteously, applying the power of pure love in both justice and mercy (see Philippians 1:9). Only then can we be reconciled with our brother and with God because with love comes forgiveness of sins (see Luke 7:47).

The words of Mormon about being purified (see Moroni 7:48) are similar to the words of the Apostle John (see 1 John 3:2–3). Mormon said that to be like Christ, we must fill our hearts with charity, the pure love of Christ. Seeing Christ as He is (see 1 John 3:2) and being in the world as He is (see 1 John 4:17) is to "be like him . . . purified [with His pure love] even as he is pure" (see Moroni 7:48). This pure love is "the power of godliness" in the priesthood (see D&C 84:21). This is the great and last blessing of the temple. It is required for the great and last promise of the temple (see D&C 84:22). This promise was given at the temple to the Savior's Nephite disciples and others who were purified (see 3 Nephi 19:28) with pure hearts because of the "love of God which did dwell in the hearts of the people" (4 Nephi 1:15).

When we follow the way prepared (see Ether 12:8) to receive Christ's pure love, we become "true followers" of Christ (Moroni 7:48). As His true followers, receiving Christ by taking His name upon us in keeping all His commandments, His pure love becomes our nature through the power of the Atonement. This "bond of charity" (D&C

88:125) with Christ is a birthing bond. "To as many as [receive] me, [give] I power [of pure love] to become my sons" (D&C 39:4). Spiritually begotten of Christ, we make the mighty change of heart (Alma 5:12) to become the sons and daughters of God (see 3 Nephi 9:17). A pure heart filled with God's love is "such an heart" (Deuteronomy 5:29) that God requires of us in order to stand in His presence as "a pure people before [Him]" (D&C 43:14).

The Lord connected the temple with the quality of charity and the great and last promise: "And inasmuch as my people build a house unto me in the name of the Lord, and do not suffer any unclean thing to come into it, that it be not defiled, my glory shall rest upon it. Yea, and my presence shall be there, for I will come into it, and all the pure in heart that shall come into it shall see God" (D&C 97:15–16).

Acquiring a pure heart, filled with the pure love of Christ, is the holiness required for the great and last promise of the temple for "without [this holiness] no man shall see the Lord" (Hebrews 12:14). In mortality we may not literally see the face of the Lord but a pure heart enables us to see as God sees. Seeing with eyes of His understanding is part of the great and last promise of the temple. The great and last promise of the temple, mentioned both by Mormon and John, can be our view of the summit of Mount Zion even as we climb, when, as the Apostle Paul counseled, we let "the Lord direct [our] hearts into the love of God" (2 Thessalonians 3:5). Then our hearts will become "such an heart" filled with the love of God and we will "put on the new man, which after God is created in righteousness and true holiness" (Ephesians 4:24). Doctrine and Covenants 97:16 recalls the words of the Savior in the sermon on the Temple Mount when He said: "And blessed are all the pure in heart, for they shall see God" (3 Nephi 12:8).

The setting of these beatitudes was the temple and the sermon was what John Welch calls a "temple text."[18] Such a text contains sacred ordinances and teachings of the fulness of the gospel which lead men and women to covenant with the Lord. Unlike the information provided in the New Testament "Sermon on the Mount," the "Sermon on the Temple Mount" is prefaced with two beatitudes that provide the context for the subsequent beatitudes:

Blessed are ye if ye shall *give heed unto the words* of these twelve whom
I have chosen . . . blessed are ye if ye shall *believe in me and be baptized.*
(3 Nephi 12:1; emphasis added)

In other words, blessed are ye if you give heed to the words of
true messengers and follow My words. We cannot reject His messengers and expect to come unto Christ. This is an extremely important
temple doctrine. It is how we come to know about God. Then we
are truly blessed if we give heed to the words of true messengers by
taking Christ's name upon us in joining His church.

Just like the Nephites at the temple in Zarahemla who heard
King Benjamin, the Nephites who heard this sermon were prepared
to make temple covenants with the Lord. It is not surprising then,
that in the beatitudes of this great temple sermon are the steps, the
basic and advanced principles of the gospel, leading to the great and
last promise of the temple[19] (compare Moroni 8:25–26).

1. "Poor in spirit who come unto me": Only in comparison to
   Christ do we learn how poor in spirit we are. We are all spiritual orphans who should be seeking our spiritual parents.
   Only by coming to Christ with humility and *faith* in Him to
   spiritually beget us can we find them.

2. "They that mourn": This means godly sorrow that worketh
   repentance (see 2 Corinthians 7:10; compare Mormon 2:13).
   This is the kind of sorrow that produces fruit meet for *repentance* because it not only empties us of unrighteousness (the
   comfort of confession), but fills us with righteousness (the
   miracle of forgiveness). The defining characteristic of godly
   sorrow is "godly fear" (Hebrews 12:28) that produces a heart
   broken of pride and envy (see Alma 5:28–29) by an awful
   awareness of sin (see Mosiah 3:25). It produces a contrite
   spirit totally submissive to God's will (see Mosiah 3:19). This
   reverence toward God requires not only a change of action
   but also a change of attitude. Then God's forgiveness by the
   power of the Atonement (see 2 Nephi 2:7) produces the fruits
   of the Spirit that comfort and give the joy of righteousness
   (see Alma 36:12–20).

3. "Meek": This term means having enough spiritual confidence and control to go beyond a respecting to a receiving relationship with the Savior through *baptism*. Meekness is key to having faith and hope in Christ (see Moroni 7:39, 43) to become like Him (see Moroni 7:44–45, 48), "filled with charity, which is everlasting love" (Moroni 8:17). It is key to excelling with the Lord (see D&C 58:41) for "I, the Lord, show mercy unto all the meek" (D&C 97:2). Thus "Moses was very meek" (Numbers 12:3). The meek seek the Lord because they have faith in Him and "their joy shall be in the Lord" (2 Nephi 27:30). In the Lord alone is found justice and righteousness. Therefore, the meek can go through tribulations in full control with a perfect brightness of hope. They have a craving for an emulating relationship with Christ. This relationship is built by obeying all His covenants and ordinances: first *baptism* then the higher laws and ordinances. When the meek obey the everlasting covenant, the Abrahamic covenant, they shall inherit the earth.

4. "Hunger and thirst after righteousness": This is the definition of fasting with the right heart. Then our hunger will be filled by the *Holy Ghost*. The Holy Ghost is the one who teaches us about the qualities of a little child who hungers and thirsts after righteousness. These qualities are necessary to obtain a pure heart, pass the final judgment, and enter the celestial kingdom (see Mosiah 27:25–26).

Remember who is the greatest in the kingdom of heaven (see Matthew 18:3–4). "Little children are holy, being sanctified through the atonement of Jesus Christ" (D&C 74:7). In this one verse is the key and paradox of our salvation. The key is becoming as a little child then partaking of the fulness of Christ's Atonement. The paradox in this life is that we must grow up from children to adults. In so doing, we seemingly lose our childlike innocence and natural righteousness. Yet, the Savior expressed this paradox with the inclusive term *and*: "Be ye therefore wise as serpents, *and* harmless as doves" (Matthew 10:16) or, "Therefore, be ye as wise as serpents *and* yet without sin" (D&C 111:11; emphasis added). The answer to this paradox is that we must grow up in Christ as "calves in the stall" (see 3 Nephi 25:2), remaining hungry and thirsty for His righteousness to become His sanctified, spiritually begotten children. Then we are both wise serpents *and* doves without sin or "wise, yet harmless" (Alma 18:22).

An infant has a natural attraction to adults with its unfeigned, loving appeal. As adults we have a desire for this natural loving relationship with each other. Developing unfeigned relationships of love with others is the challenge in becoming a little child as adults. John Pontius captured the truth of this challenge when he said, "It isn't natural for any person to be as a child—submissive, meek, humble, and patient, let alone full of love—but it is spiritual."[20] The importance of becoming as a little child was declared by the Savior to the spared multitude (see 3 Nephi 9:20–22). He then reinforced this doctrine in His temple sermon by stating that we must repent and come unto Him before baptism as a little child, and then become a sanctified little child after baptism if we are to inherit the kingdom of God (see 3 Nephi 11:37–38).

The Savior dramatically illustrated this truth when He formed concentric rings of righteousness while ministering to the people of Nephi (see 3 Nephi 17:12–13). He, the most righteous of all, was the center surrounded by a ring of little children who were encircled by angels and a ring of fire. Finally there was an outer ring of the faithful adult multitude. The children were blessed by the Savior and sanctified by receiving a fulness of the Holy Ghost (see 3 Nephi 17:21, 24). This sanctification was manifest by the gifts of the Spirit given even to babes who did speak marvelous things that could not be written (see 3 Nephi 26:14–16; compare Helaman 5:23, 33, 45).

When the Savior said "Behold your little ones" (3 Nephi 17:23), He taught the adult multitude that had just been healed physically but who still needed sanctification, how they were to be healed spiritually (see 3 Nephi 9:13). They must become as little children to come unto Him and they must become sanctified little children to become like Him. This adult sanctification was soon demonstrated when the twelve disciples were all baptized with water, the Holy Ghost fell upon them, they were encircled by fire, angels came down and ministered to them, and Jesus stood in the midst of them (see 3 Nephi 19:12–15).

Mormon emphasized the doctrine of an adult becoming as a little child when he said: "Teach parents that they must repent and be baptized, and humble themselves as their little children, and they shall all be saved with their little children" (Moroni 8:10). This was also King Benjamin's conclusion when there is "knowledge of a Savior" (see Mosiah 3:20–21).

A great travesty of our culture today is the belief that adults can understand and tolerate immorality labeled inappropriate for children. When we as adults comprehend the doctrine of hungering and thirsting for the righteousness of a child, we will grasp the profound meaning in Doctrine and Covenants 74:7: "But little children are holy, being sanctifed through the Atonement of Jesus Christ."

If we do not understand the importance of becoming as a little child and persecute those who have become as a little child to the Lord, we risk the fate of the Missourians who unjustly arrested and persecuted the spiritual "little ones" of the Lord. These "little children" (D&C 50:40; 61:36) were incarcerated in prison houses and had their homes destroyed under the pretext of the laws of men. Therefore, the Lord decreed, "Wo unto them; because they have offended my little ones *they shall be severed from the ordinances of mine house.* They shall not have right to the priesthood, not their posterity after them from generation to generation" (D&C 121:19, 21; emphasis added). "And the iniquity and transgression of my holy laws and commandments I will visit upon the heads of those who hindered my work, unto the third and fourth generation, so long as they repent not, and hate me, saith the Lord God" (D&C 124:50). To be severed from the knowledge, laws, and priesthood power of God in the ordinances of the temple is to be cut off from true freedom and cast off to prison forever.

To become a little child is to have childlike humility and faith (a broken heart and contrite spirit) in order to covenant with the Lord and build upon His rock (see 3 Nephi 11:39) or His Atonement through His temple covenants. It is to become a justified and sanctified spiritually begotten innocent child of Christ. It is to become a "Holy Child" (Moroni 8:3) like Christ by growing up in "his holy work" (Moroni 8:2).

Rock is another word for atonement through gospel covenants (see 1 Nephi 13:36; D&C 18:4–5). When we build upon His rock we are not just any little children (see Ephesians 4:14–15), we are the children of light (see John 12:36) encircled with fire, radiating the full light of Christ (see 3 Nephi 19:25). This means we become the children of Christ, His justified sons and daughters because of the covenants we make and keep with Him (see Mosiah 5:7). We become the spiritually begotten children of Christ by the sanctifying power of the Holy Spirit because of the fulness of the power of the Atonement (see 3 Nephi 28:11). We are then baptized with fire and the Holy Ghost as were the children who surrounded Christ and as were His chosen disciples (see 3 Nephi 19:13–14). Then our hearts are changed to pure hearts, filled with pure love, having no more disposition to do evil, but to keep covenants based on love with Christ. Then we are prepared for the great and last promise of the temple:

5. "Blessed are all the *pure in heart,* for they shall see God:" It is in the temple that we covenant to sacrifice all, yielding our hearts unto God, that we may learn how to obtain charity, the pure love of Christ. This mighty change of heart, from a proud to a broken and then to a pure heart, is the process of obtaining the pure love of Christ and the "love of the Father" (D&C 95:12; emphasis added). It is the sacrificial path to the summit of Mount Zion. The Lord warns us if we follow any other path:

> Wo unto you rich men, that will not give your substance to the poor. . . . Wo unto you poor men, whose hearts are not broken, whose spirits are not contrite . . . whose eyes are full of greediness, and who will not labor with your own hands! But blessed are the poor [in spirit] who are pure in heart, whose hearts are broken, and whose spirits are contrite, for they shall see the kingdom of God. (D&C 56:16–18)

Charity is the pinnacle of the spiritual Mount Zion. President Howard W. Hunter, who diligently directed the Church to the temple, said that charity, the pure love of Christ, "is the highest pinnacle the human soul can reach and the deepest expression of the human heart."[21]

Charity is the greatest of all spiritual qualities that will permit us to receive the great and last promise of the temple. Paul captured the essence of charity in one word when he said, "Now as touching things offered unto idols, we know that we all have knowledge. Knowledge puffeth up, but charity **edifieth**" (1 Corinthians 8:1).

The connection between charity and edification is also captured in the second of the two great commandments about love: "Thou shalt love thy neighbour as thyself" (Matthew 22:39). We truly love ourselves if we only do that which "nourisheth and cherisheth" (see Ephesians 5:29) or edifies ourselves. We truly edify ourselves if we obey the first great commandment about love. We can only keep this commandment if we "edify one another" (1 Thessalonians 5:11; see also 1 John 4:11; 5:2–3) by "[loving our] wives [and others] as [our] own bodies" (Ephesians 5:28). For Paul, doing the expedient act that edifies is greater than doing only what the law requires (see 1 Corinthians 10:23). For God, on the edifying love of Christ hangs all the law and the prophets (see Matthew 7:12; 22:40; 3 Nephi 15:10). Therefore, "the Lord God hath given a commandment that all men should have charity, which charity is love" (2 Nephi 26:30).

Charity is not the show of giving alms, being a self-righteous martyr, or boasting in knowledge (see 1 Corinthians 13:3). It is not just being kind but being kind with "loving kindness" (D&C 133:52) because love is the real intent behind the action. Charity is the ability to edify others and ourselves having mastered all its qualities enumerated by Paul:

Charity suffereth long, and is kind; charity envieth not; charity vaunteth not itself, is not puffed up,
Doth not behave itself unseemly, seeketh not her own, is not easily provoked, thinketh no evil;
Rejoiceth not in iniquity, but rejoiceth in the truth;
Beareth all things, believeth all things, hopeth all things, endureth all things.
Charity never faileth. (1 Corinthians 13:4–8)

The antithesis of charity is captured in one telling verse of the Old Testament. When the Philistine multitude "melted away" before the watchmen of Saul, "they went on beating down one another" (1 Samuel 14:16). Contrast this result to the effect on those who joined the unified Saints under the direction of the Apostle Peter when "the people [the Saints] magnified them" (Acts 5:13). Beating down the dignity of love for self gratification is lust (see 1 Nephi 3:25). Lust is the antithesis of love.

Using the words of his father, Moroni repeated the qualities of charity listed by Paul (see Moroni 7:45). Michael Wilcox, a well known author and teacher, offered his own version of Moroni's verse, substituting the word *Christ* for the word *charity*:

> And Christ suffereth long, and is kind, and envieth not. Christ is not puffed up, seeketh not his own, is not easily provoked, thinketh no evil, and rejoiceth not in iniquity but rejoiceth in the truth. Christ beareth all things, believeth all things, hopeth all things, endureth all things.[22]

Christ never faileth! When we comprehend the fulness of charity as "everlasting love" (Moroni 8:17), we comprehend the "stature of the fulness of Christ" (Ephesians 4:13). He is full of grace because He is full of charity (see Ether 12:36). We then understand the meaning of the Savior's parting commandment to his apostles: "A new commandment I give unto you, That ye love one another; as I have loved you" (John 13:34; see also Philippians 2:1–2).

We understand His words by the example He showed:

> You call me Master and Lord: and ye say well; for so I am.
>
> If I then, your Lord and Master, have washed your feet; ye also ought to wash one another's feet.
>
> For I have given you an example, that ye should do as I have done to you. (John 13:13–15)

The condescension of God is truly remarkable. In His condescension, He set the example for pure love. If we are to learn how to love like He loves, we too must condescend to our neighbors and "to men of low estate" (Romans 12:16). We must learn to "succor" (see Mosiah 4:16) as the Savior (see Alma 7:12). We must even descend below our fellow men (see D&C 88:6; 122:8), "abasing [ourselves], succoring those who [stand] in need of [our] succor" (Alma 4:13), in order to wash their feet (see 1 Samuel 25:41). Washing their feet means we must help them excavate the frail and fragmenting foundation of their mortal mindedness and worldly weaknesses.

We must lay a solid foundation on which to place their "clean feet" in order to "build up again a broken people" (Ether 10:1) and plant their feet (see Jeremiah 1:10, 31:28) by edifying them (see Romans 14:19; 15:2) "in all meekness" (see D&C 84:106). With this "godly edifying" (1 Timothy 1:4) of "compassion, making a difference" (Jude 1:22), "the brother of low degree [will] rejoice in that he is exalted" (James 1:9).

Interestingly, those who reject this washing of their feet may receive a symbolic dusting and washing of feet as a witness against them (see D&C 60:15; 84:92; 99:4). Contrast this washing of those who don't receive true messengers of the Lord with the washing of those who "shall be received [in the house of the Lord], by the ordinance of the washing of feet" (D&C 88:139).

King David expressed the need for excavation and a solid foundation in his own life:

> I waited patiently for the Lord; and he inclined unto me, and heard my cry.
>
> He brought me up also out of an horrible pit, out of the miry clay and set my feet upon a rock, and established my goings. (Psalm 40:1–2)

It was the Holy One of Zion who "established [the] feet" of Michael and "set him upon high" (D&C 78:16). We become "a wise masterbuilder" (1 Corinthians 3:10), when we excavate below our fellow men to establish the foundation of the rock of Christ on which they are "rooted and built up in him" (Colossians 2:7). Then an exalted edifice that endures can be built.

Endurance is an attribute of charity because the pure love of Christ is "everlasting love" (Moroni 8:17) which "endureth forever" (Moroni 7:47). Charity is "that meat which endureth unto everlasting life" (see John 6:26–27). Unless we seek the Savior with the intent of the first and great commandment and the one like unto it (see Matthew 22:38–39), we will not have enough faith to even fast for that enduring meat.

The Apostle Paul stated that an enduring, exalted edification comes from "the word of [God's] grace, which is able to build you up, and to give you an inheritance among all them which are sanctified" (Acts 20:32). Therefore, Christ declared in our dispensation His intentions of charity:

> I bring this part of my gospel to the knowledge of my people. Behold, I do not bring it to destroy that which they have received, but to build it up.
>
> And for this cause have I said: . . . I will establish my church among them. (D&C 10:52–53)

Christ's church edifies others with the power of His pure love unlike those who "build up churches unto themselves to get gain" (D&C 10:56). The doctrine of "stewardship" in the Church (see D&C 42:53; 64:40; 104:11–13) is how the Lord expects us to use our initiative, talents, and wealth for the edification of others. It is precisely in the organizations of the Church that we are built up and learn to build up others. We cannot separate the gospel from the Church. We must "[endure] of my church to the end" (D&C 10:69) and then "render an account of [our] stewardship, both in time and in eternity" (D&C 72:3).

Climbing Mount Zion: Building an Edifice of Pure Love on a Sure Foundation

The word *edify* comes from *edifice* suggesting a structure built upon a solid, sure foundation. The Latin roots are *aedificare* which means to construct spiritually and aedes which means a temple. To edify therefore means to "build up" a spiritual temple upon a solid foundation. We should follow the example of Nephi and "build a temple" (2 Nephi 5:16) with our lives. We are edified or built up as temples upon the foundation of the whole rock of Jesus Christ. This foundation is found in the temple for "His foundation is in the holy mountains" (Psalm 87:1).

> Build upon my rock, which is my gospel. (D&C 11:24; see also D&C 76:40–42; 10:53–55, 62; 39:6)

The Scriptural Temple

> Build up my church, upon the foundation of my gospel and my rock.
> (D&C 18:5)

> And if it so be that the church is built upon my gospel then will the
> Father show forth his own works in it. (3 Nephi 27:10)

In Helaman's supplication to his sons Nephi and Lehi, he declared that the rock of Christ is "a sure foundation, . . . whereon if men build they cannot fall" (Helaman 5:12). This rock is the fulness of Christ's gospel. It is the fulness of the Priesthood of Aaron or "the gospel of repentance, and of baptism" (D&C 13:1; see D&C 84:27). It is the fulness of the Priesthood of Melchizedek which is the "fulness of the everlasting gospel" (see D&C 109:65; 101:39; 107:18; 77:8) from the everlasting covenant of the temple. It is the fulness of the stature of Christ's love and power expressed through His infinite Atonement. With His love and power, built upon His foundation, we can build a structure of perfect love within us. To build up this structure of perfect love, we must precisely follow His perfect plan (see Psalm 127:1).

Isaiah prophesied that this sure foundation is the foundation of Zion: "Therefore thus saith the Lord God, Behold, *I lay in Zion for a foundation a stone*, a tried stone, a precious corner stone, *a sure foundation*" (Isaiah 28:16; emphasis added). The foundation stone of Zion is the "rock" of Christ. He is also the chief cornerstone stone that makes one out of two opposing walls because He is "the cornerstone . . . appointed for Zion" (D&C 124:23). Christ and His gospel are the rock upon which the structures of Zion are built. The foundation of Zion is "for the building of mine house, . . . and for the priesthood" (D&C 119:2).

Paul alluded to Abraham and "the heirs with him of the same promise" looking for such a foundation when he said, "for he looked for *a city* which hath *foundations*, whose builder and maker is God" (Hebrews 11:9–10; emphasis added). The city mentioned in this verse is "the Zion of Enoch" (D&C 38:4).

> Wherefore, hearken ye together and let me show unto you even my
> wisdom—the wisdom of him whom ye say is the God of Enoch, and
> his brethren,

Who were separated from the earth, and were received unto myself—a city reserved until a day of righteousness shall come—a day which was sought for by all holy men, and they found it not because of wickedness and abominations. (D&C 45:11–12)

The foundation of Zion was laid by the Lord "who hath established the foundations of Adam-ondi-Ahman" (D&C 78:15) when He "laid the foundation of the earth" (D&C 45:1). He said of the temple, "Thy foundation shall be laid" (Isaiah 44:28), and "founded Zion" (Isaiah 14:32). Having dwelt with Adam, Enoch probably patterned his city after Adam-ondi-Ahman. Zion, the New Jerusalem, will be built on these same foundations of the Lord by "laying the foundations of the great latter-day work, including the building of the temples" (D&C 138:53–54). A "laying out and preparing a beginning and foundation of the city of the stake of Zion, . . . beginning at my house" was revealed to the Saints of Kirtland (see D&C 94:1–2). The Saints of this dispensation will finally be appointed by the Lord "to make a commencement to lay the foundation of the city" where we will be "gathered with our families" (D&C 48:6), "which city shall be built, beginning at the temple" (D&C 84:3). As we seek to establish Zion, we must learn the sure foundation of the Lord, and "[lay] the foundation" of "the Zion of God" (D&C 58:7).

If we are to become a Zion-like people with pure hearts filled with pure love, we need to look for the structures built on the sure foundation of the gospel of Christ that will edify us to become such a people. When our hearts respond to the Holy Spirit and we build our lives on the spirit of prophecy and revelation which is the rock of the testimony of Christ, we become such a structure as true messengers. The Church of Jesus Christ of Latter-day Saints is such a structure, built on a foundation of true messengers: the apostles and prophets, with Christ the chief cornerstone. Our homes, built on the foundation of the gospel with parents who live the Holy Order of Matrimony, are such structures. The House of the Lord is such a structure, built on the foundation of the fulness of the Melchizedek Priesthood, with Christ leading the way to the presence of God. Interestingly, all these "structures" built on the rock of Christ are the temples in our lives (see 1 Corinthians 6:19; Isaiah 4:56).

The Scriptural Temple

Becoming "fitly framed and joined together" on this foundation and cornerstone means that we build upon the rock of Christ's Atonement by making covenants with Him through priesthood ordinances. When we keep these covenants, we as Saints become collectively and individually temples where God and His Spirit can dwell:

> Now therefore ye are no more strangers and foreigners, but fellowcitizens with the saints, and of the household of God;
> And are built upon *the foundation* of the apostles and prophets, Jesus Christ himself being the chief cornerstone;
> In whom all the building *fitly framed together groweth unto an holy temple* in the Lord:
> In whom ye also are builded together *for an habitation of God through the Spirit.* (Ephesians 2:19–22; emphasis added)

Paul said that we become part of the structure "fitly joined together" as we learn to edify others:

> From whom the whole body *fitly joined together* and compacted by that which *every joint supplieth,* according to the effectual working in the measure of every part, maketh increases of the body unto the *edifying of itself in love.* (Ephesians 4:16; emphasis added)

Being a physician familiar with muscles, bones, and joints, I interpret Paul beautifully describing the edifying function of a joint as a symbol of our relationships with each other. For as a bone supports a muscle, whose edifying action is conveyed across a joint to another bone, so must our relationships be with others. The joint is the interface of our relationships. It may be constrained or free as needed but it must have smooth interactions, being well lubricated with the pure oil of charity. Then our efforts are well received to the edification of others. The whole relationship is then edified; the whole, being greater than the sum of its parts. The whole body then moves with the grace of a holy temple.

A rebuke from the Lord to the Kirtland Saints, for a "very grievous sin" (D&C 95:3) was the result of contentions (see D&C 95:10; 3 Nephi 11:29) that arose in the school of the prophets and the failure to build a house of the Lord. Without a temple, the Lord was unable to prepare His apostles for the final pruning of His vineyard, even a "mighty pruning" (D&C 24:19), and bring about His "strange act" and "strange work" that would clearly distinguish good from evil in the world (see D&C 101:95).

It is the knowledge and power of perfect love as a promised endowment of power from the Father (see D&C 95:8–9; Luke 24:49; Acts 1:4–5) that will make this clear distinction. Only on the foundation of pure love from a pure and understanding heart can we judge righteously between good and evil (see 1 Kings 3:9; Philippians 1:9), discerning "the spirit of truth" from "the spirit of error" (1 John 4:6). This temple sanctification (see 3 Nephi 27:20) and endowment of the power of pure love will occur as a promise of God the Father to all those who believe on His Son and learn to love one another (see 1 John 3:23; 4:12), "for he will visit [them] with fire and with the Holy Ghost" (3 Nephi 11:35; see also 1 John 3:24). Then the "called" will be "chosen."

> For ye have sinned against me a very grievous sin, in that ye have not considered the great commandment in all things, that I have given unto you concerning the building of mine house;
>
> For the preparation wherewith I design to prepare mine apostles to prune my vineyard for the last time, that I may bring to pass my strange act, that I may pour out my Spirit upon all flesh—
>
> But behold, verily I say unto you, that there are many who have been ordained among you, whom I have called but few of them are chosen.
>
> They who are not chosen have sinned a very grievous sin, in that, they are walking in darkness at noon-day. . . .
>
> Yea, verily I say unto you, I gave unto you a commandment that you should build a house, in the which house I design to endow those whom I have chosen with power from on high.
>
> For this is the promise of the Father unto you. . . .
>
> Verily I say unto you, it is my will that you should build a house. If you keep my commandments you shall have power to build it.
>
> If you keep not my commandments, the love of the Father shall not continue with you, therefore you shall walk in darkness. (D&C 95:3–6, 8, 11–12; compare 1 John 2:11 with D&C 95:10)

The message in these verses is a powerful message about the temple. A temple is needed in the world and in our own lives so that the fulness of the love of the Father can be endowed to us as a gift (see 1 John 2:15–16, 3:1, compare with D&C 95:13, consider Ephesians 3:19; Mosiah 4:12; D&C 93:19–20). Temple worship is the great commandment in all things because the great commandment is to love perfectly (see Matthew 22:36–40). It is in temple worship that we learn perfect love by first learning to love God as King Benjamin described (see Mosiah 3:19). When we come to know and love the fatherhood of God, we will want His love for the brotherhood of man. Without a temple, "the love of the Father shall not continue with [us]" and we shall "walk in [the] darkness" of the world as unendowed, unchosen, unrighteous judges. "There has been a day of calling, but the time has come for a day of choosing" (D&C 105:35).

If the Lord prepares us in the temple by the pouring out of His Spirit, we will not walk in darkness at noonday even if there is a cloud cover. Rather we will be "clothed with light" (D&C 85:7) which is the light of perfect love. We "grow unto a holy temple" (Ephesians 2:21), when we are clothed with the garments of salvation and the robes of righteousness as an "armour of light" (see Romans 13:8–12), keeping ourselves as a temple. Then we will be clothed with light, the "marvelous light of His goodness" (Alma 19:6), because the Holy Spirit will dwell with us and enlighten us about the marvelous light and joy of Christ's perfect love (see D&C 6:15; D&C 11:11–13). Then we become the chosen "children of light and the children of the day" (1 Thessalonians 5:5; see also D&C 106:5). Then we "walk in light as he is in the light" (1 John 1:7) even the "light in the Lord" (Ephesians 5:8).

There is an intimate relation between light, love, and life (see 1 John 1:2, 5, 7; 2:8, 10; 3:1, 11, 14–16, 18; 4:7–9, 11, 16; 5:11–13, 16; then read John 1:4–5, 9; 13:34; 15:10; 2 Timothy 1:10; James 1:17). Spiritual light is the truth that enlightens us about the power of perfect love. The fulness of the light of Christ is the power to love perfectly. The power of this love produces eternal life. Light and knowledge from the Holy Spirit provides the truth and power we need to construct an edifice of pure love on the rock of Christ as we climb Mount Zion to life eternal. "And that which doth not edify is not of God, and is darkness. That which is of God is light; and he that receiveth light, and continueth in God, receiveth more light; and that light groweth brighter and brighter until the perfect day" (D&C 50:23–24). The perfect day in our lives is the day we acquire perfect love.

Our Lead Climber: The Master of Grace and Truth

Christ's ability to edify through love is declared with a particular description in the scriptures. "And I John, bear record that I beheld his glory, as the glory of the Only Begotten of the Father, full of grace and truth" (D&C 93:11). Christ is like "[his] Father, who is full of grace and truth" (D&C 66:12).

The teachers I admire the most are those who are full of grace and truth. They are full of knowledge, but they are most gracious to me as a student, considering my needs and ability to learn. I want to learn from them because I feel they respect me as an individual and love me as a student. The Savior's grace, His ability to edify us with His love, is what draws us to Him (see 2 Nephi 26:24–25) as the Great Teacher. Therefore, we follow Him as the lead climber in our ascent of Mount Zion because He is the Master of Grace and Truth. He commanded that we in His church be likewise when He said "ye shall instruct and edify each other that you may know how to act and direct my church" (D&C 43:8). Now I understand why Paul and Mormon taught that knowledge (truth) without charity (grace) is nothing (see 1 Corinthians 8:1; Moroni 7:44).

The greatest application of a pure heart that we make in this life is the sacrifice of self for the edification of others. According to President Hinckley, "the greatest selfless act of Christian service that we can perform in this mortal life"[23] occurs in temple service. We desire consistently to make a sacrifice of self when our hearts are filled with this pure grace, the pure love of Christ. This transformation in our hearts occurs in the temple as we keep the covenants of our Savior receiving grace for grace:

> For if you keep my commandments you shall receive of his fulness, and be glorified in me as I am in the Father; therefore, I say unto you, you shall receive grace for grace. (D&C 93:20)

Perhaps this is another reason why Christ spent so much time in His Father's House during His mortal ministry, because it was there He "continued from grace to grace" (D&C 93:13) receiving the fulness of the gifts of grace from His Father. The grace of pure love is a gift from God (see Ether 12:36). As the Apostle Paul indicated in his benediction, "the grace of our Lord Jesus Christ be with your spirit" (Galatians 6:18), spiritual reception is required for the gifts of grace. Therefore, we should "seek this Jesus" as Moroni said, that the graces of the Godhood "may be and abide in [us] forever" (see Ether 12:41).

A Contrast Between Priestcraft and Charity

The Book of Mormon offers a striking contrast between priestcraft and charity. *Priestcraft sacrifices others for oneself.* This is the great secret of Satan: to get material gain and power (see Moses 5:31, 6:15; Alma 30:17). *Charity sacrifices the interests of oneself for the edification of others.* This is the great secret of God: to obtain His honor and power (see D&C 29:36).

Those who practiced priestcraft such as Nehor (see Alma 1:12–16), were contrasted with priests and other true messengers preaching the word of God to edify the people of God:

> And when the priests left their labor to impart the word of God unto the people, the people also left their labors to hear the word of God . . . *for the preacher was no better than the hearer, . . . and thus they were all equal.* (Alma 1:26; emphasis added)

In the following verses we see that the people of God learned the value of charity:

> And they did impart of their substance, every man according to that which he had, . . . and they did not wear costly apparel, yet they were neat and comely.
>
> And now, because of the steadfastness of the church they became exceedingly rich. . . . They did not set their hearts upon riches; therefore they were liberal to all . . . having no respect to persons as to those who stood in need. (Alma 1:27, 29, 30)

In contrast, Nephi, prophesying of the last days and time of the Gentiles, described the pride of priestcraft as their great stumbling block:

> And the Gentiles are lifted in the pride of their eyes, and have stumbled, because of the greatness of their stumbling block, that they have built up many churches; nevertheless, they put down the power and

miracles of God, and preach up unto themselves their own wisdom and their own learning, that they may *get gain* and grind upon the face of the poor. . . .

For, behold, *priestcrafts* are that men preach and set themselves up for a light unto the world, that they may *get gain* and praise of the world; but they seek not the welfare of Zion. . . .

Wherefore, the Lord God hath given that *all men should have charity*, which charity is love. (See 2 Nephi 26:20, 29–30; emphasis added)

Nephi contrasted the pride and priestcraft of the Gentiles with the Savior's charity when he wrote:

For behold, my beloved brethren, I say unto you that the Lord God worketh not in darkness.

He doeth not anything save it be for the benefit of the world; for he loveth the world, even that he layeth down his own life that he may draw all men unto him. (2 Nephi 26:23–24)

A revealing characteristic of supposed messengers of God practicing priestcraft, such as the Zoramites and many Gentiles today, is that "they [are] angry because of the [revealed] word, for it [destroys] their craft; therefore they [do] not harken unto the words" (Alma 35:3) of God. Since priestcraft is an expression of pride, even in the true church of God it exists as the Book of Mormon witnessed. Even without monetary reward, using the word of God to lift oneself up in the pride of his heart is a form of priestcraft. Therefore, the Lord warned in our dispensation,

There is none which doeth good save it be a few; and they err in many instances because of priestcrafts. (D&C 33:4)

Perhaps there is no more conspicuous contrast between priestcraft and charity than with the value of the golden plates as prophesied by Moroni:

And I am the same who hideth up this record unto the Lord; the plates thereof are of no worth, because of the commandment of the Lord, For he truly saith that no one shall have them to get gain; but the record thereof is of great worth. (Mormon 8:14)

Then, recalling the Lord's prophecy, Moroni warned Joseph Smith before he obtained the plates:

> I beheld the same messenger at my bedside, and heard him rehearse or repeat over again to me the same things as before; and added a caution to me, telling me that Satan would try to tempt me . . . to get the plates for the purpose of getting rich. This he forbade me, saying that I must have no other object in view in getting the plates but to glorify God, and must not be influenced by any other motive than that of building his kingdom; otherwise I could not get them. (Joseph Smith—History 1:46)

When Joseph Smith received the plates on September 22, 1827, he also received a charge from the Angel Moroni that "he should be responsible for them; that if [he] should let them go carelessly, or through any neglect . . . [he] should be cut off;" (Joseph Smith—History 1:59). The Prophet was cut off from the gift of translating the plates when he "set at naught the counsels of God" and "[went] on in the persuasions of men" concerning the 116 pages of lost manuscript (see D&C 3).

Do we receive "golden plates" from the Lord with the same responsibility for them? Do we receive the oracles of God as a "light thing" (see D&C 90:5). Certainly in the form of true messengers, personal and written revelation, priesthood power, gifts of the Spirit, children, spouses, ordinances and covenants with the Lord, and especially in the power of the Atonement, we receive His oracles and gifts of gold. With these precious gifts we must have no other object in view than the glory of God by obedience to His will. If not, we will be cut off, temporarily or permanently, from these gifts and from the presence of God.

In the temple, the contrast between priestcraft and charity is taught. Satan entices us with money (see Ether 9:11) preaching that "for your money you shall be forgiven of your sins" (Mormon 8:32). As Amulek said to Zeezrom "the righteous yieldeth to no such temptations" (Alma 11:23). However, we all must choose between Satan's selfish, carnal desires and the word of true messengers. Will we sacrifice others to get gain or will we hold the gifts of God sacred while acting with charity to edify the lives of others? Money may advance us in this life, for "behold here is money" (see Helaman 9:20), but it is the sacred gifts and ordinances of God which cannot be purchased with money (see Acts 8:20) that advance us to God's presence. For "[we] shall be redeemed without money" (3 Nephi 20:38).

The Price to Summit Mount Zion: A Sacrifice for the Oneness of Pure Love

We also learn in the temple that we cannot reach the summit of Mount Zion alone. We must learn to edify others in our climb so that we all acquire the oneness of pure love at the summit.

Moroni was concerned about the weakness in writing of his people that the Gentiles might "mock at these things" (Ether 12:23) or "have not charity" (see Ether 12:35). Nevertheless, he said the Lord will show the weakness or pride of the Gentiles in that faith, hope, and charity is the fountain of all righteousness (see Ether 12:28). It is charity, the love of God and neighbors, that makes faith and hope endure. Therefore, it is the source of all righteousness. Even though all of us have weaknesses and have "sold [ourselves] for naught" (3 Nephi 20:38), we may "buy milk and honey, without money and without price" (2 Nephi 26:25) through Christ's charitable Atonement. Therein is our faith and hope.

Similar to Nephi (see 2 Nephi 26:24), Moroni also used great words in describing the charity of Christ:

> And again, I remember that thou hast said that thou hast loved the world, even unto the laying down of thy life for the world, that thou mightest take it again to prepare a place for the children of men.
>
> And now I know that this love which thou hast had for the children of men is charity; wherefore, except men shall have charity they cannot inherit that place which thou hast prepared in the mansions of thy Father. (Ether 12:33–34; see also 1 John 3:16)

The Apostle John expressed the depth of Christ's love for us when he wrote:

> Greater love hath no man than this, that a man lay down his life for his friends. (John 15:13)

The sacrifice of self for the edification of others is the essence of charity. When we acquire this God-given grace, then it can be said of us that "[we] doeth not anything save it be for the benefit of the world [our fellow men]; for [we] loveth the world" (2 Nephi 26:24).

Richard L. Evans, a former apostle and neighbor, described charity as a sacrifice: "Sincere love is something that sacrifices—not something that indulges itself. Sincere love is responsible. It would never knowingly hurt, but would heal."[24]

I like to think that a physician who loves to fully heal his patients understands this kind of love. I imagine Jonathan and David knew this kind of love because, "the soul of Jonathan was knit with the soul of David" (1 Samuel 18:1). A marriage where husband and wife are one knows this kind of love. Then, "[their] prayers be not hindered" (see 1 Peter 3:7).

This kind of love is the love of edification, lifelong and beyond, with the partners sustaining and affirming one another so that such love forges one flesh in that the whole is greater than the sum of its parts as described in Ecclesiastes:

> Two are better than one; because they have a good reward for their labour.
> For if they fall the one will lift up his fellow: but woe to him that is alone when he falleth; for he hath not another to help him up.
> Again, if two lie together, then they have heat: but how can one be warm alone? (Ecclesiastes 4:9–11)

Now I understand, especially in grafting to Christ, what Lehi meant when he said: "all things must needs be a compound in one; wherefore, if it should be one body it must needs remain as dead" (2 Nephi 2:11). The Hebrew word *echad* means a composite oneness. This is the essence of the "at-one-ment" principle of the Atonement taught in Zenos's allegory of grafting to the olive trees (see Jacob 5). The tame or natural olive tree also represents Christ who persistently tries to get all of God's children to graft to and grow up in Him, upon his roots or covenants according to His will (see Jacob 5:48). Then, as Nephi asked his brethren concerning their descendants of the latter days, "at that day [the day of grafting to the true vine], will they [all who graft to Christ] not receive the strength and nourishment from the true vine?" (1 Nephi 15:15).

All who graft to Christ will be "like unto one body" (Jacob 5:74). This is not the "one body" spoken of by Lehi that is "a law unto itself" (D&C 88:35). The "one body" spoken of by Zenos is the body of Christ and all his spiritually begotten children who have grafted to and grown up in Him forming a perfect, preserved olive tree or tree of life in which "the fruits [are] equal" (Jacob 5:74) because of pure love (see D&C 38:22, 24–27). This is the essence of the power of the Atonement or at-one-ment with Christ: "one body," which is a "compound in one" held together to endure eternal life with the pure love of Christ which "endureth forever" (Moroni 7:47). As a compound in one with Christ, we "become the sons of God, even one in me as I am one in the Father, as the Father is one in me, that we may be one" (D&C 35:2; 34:2).

The important teaching of John, chapters 13 through 15 and 17, is not the "transfigured . . . holy word of God" (see Mormon 8:33) or the misinterpreted ontological oneness of the Father and the Son. Rather, it is the pure love between the Father and the Son that makes them one. The concepts of pure love (see John 13:1, 15, 34, 35; 14:15, 21, 23, 28, 31; 15:9–10, 12, 13, 14–15, 17; 17:23–24, 26) are beautifully intertwined with the concepts of oneness between the Father, the Son, and their disciples (see John 13:20; 14:10–11, 13; 15:1–8; 17:11, 21–22). It is in keeping the commandments of the Father and the Son (John 14:15, 31; 15:10, 14; 17:6–8) and being sanctified by the "Spirit of Truth" (see John 14:17; 16:7; 17:17, 19) that the oneness of pure love comes. This is the "fellowship of the mystery" (Ephesians 3:9). Contrast the love and oneness of the Father and the Son with the hate of the "prince of the world" that "hath nothing in me" (John 14:30).

Viktor Frankl, describing a poignant moment in his German concentration camp experience, painted with his pen a scene of pure love and oneness with his wife. The separation of husbands, wives, and families in these camps was sudden, brutal, and usually final. While being marched to a work site early one morning, the man in front of Frankl said:

> "If our wives could see us now! I do hope they are better off in their camps and don't know what is happening to us." That brought

315

thoughts of my own wife to mind. And as we stumbled on for miles, slipping on icy spots, supporting each other time and again, dragging one another up and onward, nothing was said, but we both knew: each of us was thinking of his wife.

Occasionally, I looked at the sky, where the stars were fading and the pink light of the morning was beginning to spread behind a dark bank of clouds. But my mind clung to my wife's image, imagining it with an uncanny acuteness. I heard her answering me, saw her smile, her frank and encouraging look. Real or not, her look was then more luminous than the sun which was beginning to rise. A thought transfixed me: for the first time in my life, I saw the truth as it is set into song by so many poets, proclaimed as the final wisdom by so many thinkers. The truth that love is the ultimate and highest goal to which man can aspire. Then I grasped the meaning of the greatest secret that human poetry and human thought and belief have to impart: the salvation of man is through love and in love. I understood how a man who has nothing left in this world may know bliss, be it only for a brief moment, in the contemplation of his beloved.[25]

One of my favorite hymns, "O Love That Glorifies the Son," describes the sincere love of charity that should fill our souls. It is the love of the Son in obedience to the Father, making them one. It is the love that comes from the Savior to us, to bind our families as one. It is His pure love that fills our hearts and makes us like Him. It is this love that overcomes adversity and edifies our lives and those around us to make us one. It is His love that makes within us the mighty change of heart and sustains us to the end:

> O love that glorifies the Son, O love that says, "Thy will be done!"
> Pure love whose spirit makes us one Come, fill my soul today;
> Come, fill my soul today.
> O love that binds our family, O love that brings my heart to thee,
> Pure love that lasts eternally Come, fill my soul today;
> Come, fill my soul today.
> O love that overcomes defeat, O love that turns the bitter sweet,
> Pure love that makes our lives complete Come, fill my soul today;
> Come, fill my soul today.
> O lord, give me the will to mend; O lord, change me from foe
> to friend;

Dear Lord, sustain me to the end Come, fill my soul today;
Come, fill my soul today.[26]

When we seek the pure love of Christ in being founded and built on the rock of Christ which is His atonement and doctrine (see 3 Nephi 11:39; 27:8), we can say as Paul that we are "rooted and grounded in love" until we "know the love of Christ" and are "filled with all the fulness of God" (see Ephesians 3:17–19). These verses describe the growth and fruition of the love of God within us, thus our own tree of life, as we work out our own salvation on Christ's rock. "May God grant, in his fulness, that men might be brought unto repentance and good works, that they might be restored unto grace for grace, according to their works" (Helaman 12:24; see also D&C 93:19–20).

After dedicating the temple, King Solomon said to his people: "Let your heart therefore be perfect with the Lord our God, to walk in his statutes, and to keep his commandments" (1 Kings 8:61). When we make the ultimate sacrifice of yielding our hearts to God, then they will be filled with the grace or pure love of Christ thus "all the fulness of God." Then we can say they are perfect. When our hearts are perfect, we have made the sacrifice to climb to the summit of Mount Zion and receive its great and last promise as did those of Enoch's Zion:

> But *the Lord came and dwelt with his people,* and they dwelt in right-eousness. (Moses 7:16; emphasis added)

Climbing Up to the Summit of
Mount Zion: Lord, How Is It Done?

While struggling to sacrifice our pride, fears, jealousy and disobedience, desiring to yield our hearts to God, that we might have the pure love of Christ, we often say as Enos said: "Lord, how is it done?" (Enos 1:7).

This is the question I asked myself concerning the "mighty change." Is it possible in this life? Can I make the great and last sacrifice for this mighty change? Am I a man to match Mount Zion? Many of us are content to answer that "we are what we are." This is the mistaken precept of men that is used to justify any behavior.

The important question is: What are we to the creator God? Until this question is answered, we can not say "we are what we are." We can only say "by the grace of God I am what I am" (1 Corinthians 15:10). We cannot honestly rationalize any human behavior as a normal and acceptable part of our intrinsic nature until we answer the question of the reality of our intrinsic nature. What is our true nature? What is "the measure of man, according to his creation before the world was made" (D&C 49:17)?

Volumes have been and are being written attempting to answer the question of our true nature. Yes, we are individually different but have we discovered how individually important we are? I prefer to believe in the importance that I learned in Primary: I am a child of God. I was taught this truth by true messengers of God who learned it from other true messengers who ultimately learned it from God. This truth is confirmed to my heart, my spiritual self, in such unwavering conviction that I would be under condemnation to deny it.

Another true messenger, the apostle Paul, along with the Holy Spirit, confirmed what I learned in Primary: "The Spirit itself beareth witness to our spirit that we are the children of God" (Romans 8:16; see also Numbers 16:22). Notice how we learn this truth. It is by spiritual recall of pure knowledge of things as they really are, when we let the Spirit of prophecy and revelation teach us. This is also how we learn of the spiritual qualities that we inherited as spirit children of our Father in Heaven: "For God hath not given us the spirit of fear; but of power, and of love, and of a sound mind" (2 Timothy 1:7).

The true answer to the question of our identity automatically leads to an even more important question: What is the measure of the stature of the fulness of man's creation (compare Ephesians 4:13 with D&C 49:16–17)? Verse 16 implies that a full measure of the creation of a man and woman is to become greater than themselves alone in becoming "one flesh" together. It is to become individually "wise yet harmless" (Alma 18:22) together. This oneness is part of the great gathering in one, all things in Christ (see D&C 27:13).

The full measure of our creation is that of the very earth upon which we stand. "The earth abideth the law of a celestial kingdom, for it filleth the measure of its creation" (D&C 88:25). When we have "filled the measure of [our] creation, [we] shall be crowned with glory, even with the presence of God the Father" (D&C 88:19). This is the great and last promise of the temple.

What can we really become? When we master the power of love within us, then "[we] may be the children of [our] Father which is in heaven" (see Matthew 5:44–45). "And if children, then heirs; heirs of God, and joint-heirs with Christ" (Romans 8:17; see also Psalm 82:6). We become "heirs according to the covenant" (D&C 52:2), meaning according to our obedience to the covenants made with the Lord. The Prophet Joseph Smith stated that "all those who keep his commandments, shall grow up from grace to grace, and become heirs of the heavenly kingdom, and joint heirs with Jesus Christ; possessing the same mind, being transformed into the same image or likeness, even the express image of Him who fills all in all; being filled with the fulness of his glory, and becoming one in him, even as the Father, Son, and Holy Spirit are one."[1]

President George Q. Cannon taught that no sin or weakness need be permanent because God can give gifts (see D&C 46:11) to correct any imperfection.[2] The great gift that God gave to all men is the Atonement of His Son. With this gift, "old things are done away, and all things have become new" (3 Nephi 12:47). The new creation began in the middle of mortality with the resurrection of Christ. With a first resurrection we can move beyond salvation from sin to that within the veil, meaning exaltation within the kingdom of God. *Therefore, with this gift of Christ, we can become perfect.* When perfected, we become heirs with Christ and inherit eternal life.

Both of these questions about our true nature must be examined and answered in light of thanatology. Life is hard, then we die. Yet Amulek said to live well is to prepare to die (see Alma 34:32–34). In the words of the Savior, to live well is to believe in Him and not "die in [our] sins" (see John 8:22). Christ has told us and promised us that He has overcome the tribulations of the world and mortality (see John 16:33). If we have faith in Him and follow Him, then we also can overcome the world (see 1 John 5:5) so that death, physical and spiritual, is swallowed up "by the victory of Christ over it" (Alma 27:28). To live in Christ by following Him is to prepare to die and meet God (see Galatians 2:20). Ultimately, preparation to meet God and live with Him means becoming like Christ (see 3 Nephi 28:10). The peace of His assurance to overcome the world and death and to become like Him is pure knowledge and joy of things as they really are. In Climbing Mount Zion it is not just following our Lead Climber but becoming like Him that is required to reach the summit.

Climbing Up to the Summit
by Growing Up in the Lord

As we grow up in mortality, most of us struggle to answer these questions in our own lives. At 16 we are given permission to drive a car. We think we are grown up until the first accident or citation reminds us of our responsibility to others. Between the ages of 18 and 21, we gain a new sense of being grown up when we decide for ourselves at the ballot box or leave our parents for matrimony, matriculation, or missions. This sense of independence quickly faces reality as we feel the responsibility for ourselves and others.

Within the question: *Can I really change?* is the question: *Can I really grow up?* It is in the *scriptural temple* that I found the Lord asking me, an adult who has passed the maturity markers of 16 and 21, to "grow up"!

> That we henceforth *be no more children*, tossed to and fro, and carried about with every wind of doctrine, by the sleight of men, and cunning craftiness, whereby they lie in wait to deceive;
> But speaking the truth in love, may *grow up into Him in all things*, which is the head, even Christ. (Ephesians 4:14–15; emphasis added)

Paul was telling the Ephesian Saints not to be vulnerable children "like a wave of the sea driven with the wind and tossed" (James 1:6). Instead, Paul urged his followers to become the children of Christ and obtain His unwavering stature by growing up in Him.

Again, I did not recognize this scripture as a great truth of the *scriptural temple* until I began to "grow up" and see the temple in the scriptures. Then for me, the following scripture came alive:

> And that they may *grow up in thee*, and receive a fulness of the Holy Ghost, and be organized according to thy laws, and be prepared to obtain every needful thing. (D&C 109:15; emphasis added)

Joseph Smith prayed for this growing-up blessing in the dedication of the Kirtland temple. It is in the temple that we can receive a fulness of the Holy Ghost. With this fulness we are taught how to become the children of Christ and are given the power to "grow up" in Him. This verse is the answer to Enos's question and to my question. The growing up process of the temple is how we can really change in this life. As Enos learned, this mighty change is based on faith in Christ (see Enos 1:8). He also learned that coming to a knowledge of spiritual truth requires being taught by both an earthly father (see Enos 1:1, 3) and especially a Heavenly Father (see Enos 1:4–5, 10).

The apostle Paul taught us about growing up in the Lord when he said: "Furthermore, we have had fathers of our flesh which corrected us, and we gave them reverence: shall we not much rather be in subjection unto the Father of spirits, and live?" (Hebrews 12:9). The growing-up corrections from our mortal fathers are preliminary to the real growing-up corrections from the Father of spirits (see Proverbs 3:12).

Mormon taught his son Moroni that growing up in the Lord starts with the first four principles of the gospel and ultimately leads to "perfect love":

> And the firstfruits of repentance is baptism; and baptism cometh by faith unto the fulfilling the commandments; and the fulfilling the commandments bringeth remission of sins;
>
> And the remissions of sins bringeth meekness and lowliness of heart; and because of meekness and lowliness of heart cometh the visitation of the Holy Ghost, which comforter filleth with hope and perfect love, which love endureth by diligence unto prayer, until . . . all the saints shall dwell with God. (Moroni 8:25–26)

This perfect love is the sweet fruit of the tree of life, of which we can partake if we follow the commandment to be baptized unto repentance (see Alma 5:62).

If we grow up by the Father of spirits and are corrected by Him, we will have "eternal life" and dwell with Him. Elder Henry B. Eyring described growing up in the Lord as an "upward pull" requiring a "mighty change":

> That upward pull we have felt is far more than a desire for self-improvement. It is a longing for home, to be again with the Heavenly Father . . . feeling the love we felt there and which we can taste here. . . . And all of us sense the mighty change that must come in us for us to be able to dwell with Him. The exchange is all He has for all we have.[3]

Growing up in the Lord is to climb up to the summit of Mount Zion.

Growing Up in Grace and Truth

The Lord tenderly invited us to grow up in Him when He said: "Behold, ye are little children and ye cannot bear all things now; ye must grow in grace and in the knowledge of the truth" (D&C 50:40).

This is precisely how Luke described the mortal growing up of the Savior. "And the child grew, and waxed strong in spirit, filled with wisdom and the grace of God was upon him" (Luke 2:40). I believe that because Jesus "waxed strong in spirit" his growing up was complete, not only spiritually but also mentally, physically, and socially. "And Jesus increased in wisdom and stature, and in favor with God and man" (Luke 2:52).

This growing-up process of the Lord in "grace and truth" is found in His holy temple where we learn from the Master of "grace and truth." This is what King Benjamin taught at the temple of Zara- hemla: "And ye shall grow in the knowledge of the glory of him that created you, or in the knowledge of that which is just and true" (Mosiah 4:12).

An important part of this growing-up process is the endowment of the temple. *The purpose of the endowment is to endow us with the graces of pure love and the truths of eternal life.* In the temple we are led to grasp all the qualities (graces) of charity as listed by Paul and Mormon. As we make these graces part of our lives we become justi- fied and sanctified by the power of the Atonement before the laws of God. Then we will be given the keys which unlock the truths of eternal life.

The lyrics of the Psalms reflect the growing-up process of the temple endowment where we are gathered as Saints before the Lord to make covenants with Him. When we obey these covenants through the sacrifice of our proud hearts, then "the heavens shall declare his righteousness" (see Psalm 50:5–6). By obedience, sacrifice, and living the covenant laws of the gospel, we shall dwell in God's "holy hill" and "shall never be moved" (see Psalm 15:1–5), because we are endowed with the fulness of His Atonement and His gift of pure love. Those who learn to "worship the Father in [Christ's] name, with pure hearts and clean hands" (see 2 Nephi 25:16) are those who learn to worship the Father and the Son in the temple. "Who shall stand in His holy place? He that hath clean hands and a pure heart" (Psalm 24:3–4).

The Sermon on the Mount, which is the temple mount in the Book of Mormon, contains the higher laws of pure love that fulfill the lesser laws ultimately given on Mount Sinai. *In teaching obedience, sacrifice, the law of the gospel through reconciliation, chastity in marriage, and even the higher laws of consecration* (see 3 Nephi 12:1–48; 13:19–34), *the sermon of sermons eloquently reveals the stature of the fulness of Christ to which we are expected to grow through the temple endowment.*

The Apostles Paul and James described growing up in faith tested by tribulation that works patience or endurance. Then, as James said, "let patience have her perfect work, that ye may be perfect and entire, wanting nothing" (James 1:4). Paul explained that the perfect work of patience brings and is sustained by perfect love. He said, "Being justified by faith. . . . We have access by faith into this grace . . . and rejoice in hope of the glory of God. We glory in tribulations . . . tribulation worketh patience; And patience, experience; and experience, hope; And hope maketh not ashamed; because the love of God is shed abroad in our hearts by the Holy Ghost" (Romans 5:1–5). Therefore, the Lord counseled Oliver Cowdery to "have patience, faith, hope, and charity" (D&C 6:19). The Lord insisted that all those who "bring forth and establish the cause of Zion" must "be humble and full of love, having faith, hope, and charity, being temperate in all things" (D&C 12:6, 8).

The Apostle Peter described growing up to a "divine nature" by a process similar to Paul and James. He also taught that this divine nature is reached when we obtain the quality of charity:

Whereby are given unto us exceeding great and precious promises: That by these ye might be partakers of the divine nature. . . .

And beside this, giving all diligence, add to your faith virtue; and to virtue knowledge;

And to knowledge temperance; and to temperance patience; and to patience godliness;

And to godliness brotherly kindness; and to brotherly kindness charity. (2 Peter 1:47)

A revelation on the priesthood through the Prophet Joseph Smith teaches the attributes of the doctrine of the priesthood (see D&C 121:36–42) in connection with the same growing-up qualities taught by Peter (see D&C 107:30). Then the Prophet Joseph Smith told us, using tree of life imagery, about the ultimate blessing of Peter's "promises," received when we have these divine qualities. It is the great and last promise of the temple, the promise of eternal life or knowing the Lord: "Because the promise is, if these things abound in them they shall not be unfruitful in the knowledge of the Lord" (D&C 107:31; see also 2 Peter 1:8).

The sequence of graces listed in the Psalms, the Sermon on the Mount, the writings of Paul, James, Peter, and Joseph Smith, closely reflect the spiritual qualities obtained when we keep the major covenants of the temple endowment. The sequence of covenants we make in the law of obedience, the law of sacrifice, the law of the gospel (the laws of reconciliation), the law of chastity, and the law of consecration is the growing-up process of the endowment. It is through this "growing up" that we become men and women to match His mountain and "climb up" Mount Zion.

As we climb, we are endowed with virtue through the **law of obedience** to the moral, ethical, and celestial principles of the laws of the Lord. As we "walk in the paths of virtue" (D&C 25:2), we live the **law of sacrifice** of our pride and selfishness. By these laws we are endowed with patience and temperance because of the moderation and self-restraint we learn from obedience and sacrifice. Then we are prepared to learn the graces of charity as taught in the Sermon on the Mount. With these graces, we are endowed with more godliness or holiness of the divine nature because we live the **law of the gospel** (see D&C 88:78; 104:18). Essentially, this law is "to learn to impart one to another as the gospel requires" (D&C 88:123). "Cease drunkenness; and let your words tend to edifying one another" (D&C 136:24). "If thou art merry, praise the Lord" (D&C 136:28). "If thou art sorrowful, call on the Lord . . . that your souls may be joyful" (D&C 136:29). "Be not partial . . . in love . . . let thy love be for [others] as for thyself" (D&C 112:11). We are to "esteem [our] brother as [ourself]" and practice this law with virtue and holiness before the Lord (see D&C 38:24). As we live the principles of the law of the gospel, we are endowed with the "love of God and all men" (2 Nephi 31:20). Because of this love, we would do nothing to destroy relationships with others, even enemies. We strive only to "esteem" then edify. This love is especially intended in the **law of chastity** as we apply it to our marriage relationship. Literally the law of chastity will be fulfilled in the Lord's definition of a "legal and lawful marriage." It is for those who have become one in love in the Holy Order of Matrimony.

Finally, "after all we can do" (2 Nephi 25:23), we are endowed with the celestial quality of charity. This pure love of Christ comes to us as an atonement gift because we have kept the preceding covenants. Then we can "practice virtue and holiness before [the Lord] continually" (D&C 46:33) with "holiness of heart" (D&C 46:7). The power of the love of Christ makes a mighty change in our hearts, even to "the consuming of [our] flesh" (see 2 Nephi 4:21) as we become "new creatures." We are then prepared to fully live the **law of consecration**, which is a law of the celestial kingdom. The law of consecration is a sure covenant in a sure place.

We are not asked by the Lord to fully live the law of consecration at the present time. We are asked to accept it by living the law of sacrifice and the law of the gospel in preparation to one day establish Zion. We must first learn to sacrifice our envy and avarice, then edify others with pure love before we can fully live the law of consecration. In preparation for the celestial law of consecration, today we live a law of sacrifice by living the law of tithing and fast offering along with fasting. Through these practices the rich man and poor man learn to become one. The law of tithing and offerings will "prepare us against the day of vengeance and burning" (see D&C 85:3) and "sanctify the land of Zion" (see D&C 119:6) as we grow up and fully live the law of consecration.

In his book, *Temples in the Last Days,* Elder Royden Derrick described the "growing-up" transformation in the temple:

> In the temple, through the power of the Holy Spirit, knowledge is transformed into virtues. A person who attends the temple regularly grows more patient, more longsuffering, and more charitable. . . . In the temple knowledge is transformed into feelings of the heart resulting in actions that build character.[4]

The character built in the temple is that of a divine nature: the perfect man or woman in "the measure of the stature of the fulness of Christ" (Ephesians 4:13). This is the measure of the stature of the fulness of man's creation when he attains the "great grace" (Acts 4:33) of pure love.

Growing Up on Mount Zion of the Old Testament

The growing-up message of the book of Leviticus can be hidden by the tedious rituals and carnal commandments of the Levitical laws given to Moses for those who rejected the "rest" of the Lord. *Yet the dominant theme of the Book of Leviticus is holiness through sacrifice and atonement.* "Be [ye] holy, for I am holy" is repeated four times in Leviticus (see 11:44–45; 19:2; 20:26). In fact, in the Book of Leviticus, the sum of the words *sacrifice* and *atonement* equals the total use of the word *holy*. The formula of Leviticus is sacrifice plus atonement equals holiness. Near the middle of Leviticus, perhaps suggesting the Atonement in the meridian of time, the laws of the rituals of the Day of Atonement are described (see Leviticus 16:30–34). Contrasting synonyms of holy and unholy such as circumcised-uncircumcised, pure-profane, clean-unclean, sanctified-defiled, righteous-unrighteous, redeemed-not redeemed are used in Leviticus. The term *nakedness*, as used in Leviticus, can be holy or unholy depending on how it is discovered.

The Lord was anxiously trying to separate this group of people in the Sinai who "err in their hearts" and make them holy (see Leviticus 10:10, 11:45, 20:24). To "put difference between holy and unholy" is still the work of the Lord in our day. In the context of the law of Moses, the laws of the Lord found in Leviticus reflect the growing-up process of the endowment. These laws focused on rituals and worship in the holy place, the tabernacle of the congregation:

- worship of the Lord through sacrifice (Leviticus 17)
- holy living, loving one's neighbor (Leviticus 19)
- avoiding blasphemy (Leviticus 24)
- living the law of chastity (Leviticus 18, 20)
- living the law of consecration (Leviticus 25, 27)

The Scriptural Temple

On the plains of Moab, before crossing Jordan, Moses revealed the contents of Deuteronomy to the children of Israel. Deuteronomy means the law repeated or the second law implying that the law of the Lord is to be repeated and not forgotten. In fact, the specific law of repetition in Deuteronomy was a gathering of the people every seven years in consecration to the Lord and to each other to hear again the words of this great book (see Deuteronomy 31:10–13). Specifically, the words of the law of Deuteronomy, which is the first and great commandment (see Mark 12:29–30), were to be kept in the hearts of the people (see Deuteronomy 6:5–6). These words contained in detail the rules of successful relationships in this life so the people, as a people set apart by the Lord, would obey the first and great commandment with full purpose of heart. Deuteronomy contains the rules of application of the law of consecration in this life. They are based on this truth: As God has freely consecrated all for our well being, so we should freely share His gifts for the well being of our fellow men. This we must do out of love for God and all men. We would do well to liken the laws of the Lord in Deuteronomy to our own lives. Then we should apply them as best we can so that one day we will be prepared to observe and keep the law of consecration.

Concerning this Old Testament foundation of our growing up in the Lord, John Welch draws our attention to its value:

> Not being steeped in the ethical and spiritual dimensions of the law of Moses, modern LDS readers tend to overlook the profound religious legacy of these underlying purposes of the law that have enduring relevance to the temple.[5]

Just like those who worshiped at the tabernacle under the law of Moses, we become separate and holy by growing up in the grace and truth of the Lord in His holy house: "Do ye not know that they which minister about holy things live of the things of the temple?" (1 Corinthians 9:13).

Growing Up on Mount Zion: Endowed with Charity

The laws and covenants of the endowment will prepare us to one day fully live "the law of the celestial kingdom" (D&C 105:4), because charity will have become the crowning quality of our divine, holy nature. Therefore, *the purpose of the endowment is to endow us with the celestial quality of charity.*

The apostle Paul concluded that "if there be any other commandment, it is briefly comprehended [in the law of love]," for "love is the fulfilling of the law" (Romans 13:9–10). He captured this truth in one verse of scripture: "Now the end of the commandment is charity out of a pure heart" (1 Timothy 1:5).

Charity is the result of keeping God's commandments because "whoso keepeth his word, in him verily is the love of God perfected" (1 John 2:5). The end result of growing up in the Lord by keeping His word is a divine nature. The quintessential quality of this divine nature is "charity out of a pure heart," the "manner of love the Father hath bestowed upon us, that we should be called the sons of God" (1 John 3:1).

Alma instructed his son Shiblon how to grow up in the Lord when he said: "Use boldness, but not overbearance; and see that ye bridle all your passions that ye may be filled with love" (Alma 38:12). This is the counsel that all parents raising "seed unto the Lord" (1 Nephi 7:1) should give the "rising generations that shall grow up on the land of Zion" (D&C 69:8). The Lord bridles passions with commandments and covenants.

The rape of Tamar is a powerful Old Testament story revealing the difference between the love of selfish passion and the love of charity. Amnon, Tamar's half brother who loved her, lured her to his sick bed, "took hold of her," and said "come lie with me" (2 Samuel 13:11). Tamar answered saying, "Nay, . . . do not force me; . . . do not thou this folly" (2 Samuel 13:12). But Amnon "forced her, and lay with her" (2 Samuel 13:14). Then the revealing verse shows that Amnon's pride changed his passion of love to the passion of hate in "that the hatred wherewith he hated her was greater than the love wherewith he had loved her." So, he "said unto her, Arise, be gone" (2 Samuel 13:15). Truly, Amnon hated himself but his selfish pride projected this hate on Tamar. Then, reminiscent of the coat of many colors and symbolic of the virtue of her virginity, Tamar rent her "garment of divers colors," and "went on crying" and "remained desolate" (2 Samuel 13:18–20), because the holiness which was most precious to her had been desecrated. How often the same scenario is played out in today's world when the passion of love turns to hate and desolation because it is not bridled in the bounds the Lord has set.

Charity is the arena and boundary of true love because it keeps out the hate and desolation of selfish pride. A kiss of passion is outside this boundary if it is not also "a kiss of charity" (1 Peter 5:14). Charity never hurts. It only edifies.

The words of the tongue are a particular passion, even a "world of iniquity" (James 3:6) when untamed (see James 1:26; 3:8). When we understand the Lord's question, "Who hath made man's mouth? . . . have not I the Lord? (Exodus 4:11), we want to use our mouth only to reflect godliness. We can "bridle the whole body" (James 3:2) to show that we are filled with love when we bridle our tongue because not only what we say but how we say it can express sincere love that edifies (see D&C 52:16). Edifying words can lift "the spirit of heaviness" by covering our fellow men with "the garment of praise" (Isaiah 61:3) and sustaining them with the "fruits of praise" (D&C 52:17).

The Apostle Paul taught that seeking charity is to seek the gifts of the Spirit, especially the gift of prophecy since this is the gift of the tongue that edifies others:

> Follow after charity, and desire spiritual gifts, but rather that ye may prophesy. . . .
> But he that prophesieth speaketh unto men to edification, and exhortation, and comfort. . . .
> He that prophesieth edifieth the church. (1 Corinthians 14:1, 3–4)

When we speak by the power of the Holy Spirit with the gift of prophecy, we "speak with the tongue of angels" (2 Nephi 31:13). Then our speech will "be always with grace, seasoned with salt" (Colossians 4:6).

The laws and covenants of the endowment teach us how to bridle our passions that we may be filled with the love of charity. In an article titled "Bridle All Your Passions," Bruce and Marie Hafen beautifully explained why the Lord wants us to grow up and bridle our passions:

The truth is not that worldly gratifications are too satisfying, but they are not satisfying enough. . . . The Lord desires that we find fulfillment to the height of human capacity. . . . The Lord seeks to satisfy everlastingly our deepest human longings. . . . If [we] accept the disciplined yoke of the Gospel, one day we will have a divine nature and a fulness of joy.[6]

The disciplined yoke is the commandments and covenants of the gospel in the iron rod. Particularly, it is the growing-up covenants of the temple that result in a divine nature with the full joy of charitable love.

When we show our love to God by keeping His commandments and covenants, He shows His love to us through the gifts of the Spirit. As Parley P. Pratt testified, pure love can be ours as a gift of the Holy Spirit:

The gift of the Holy Ghost . . . quickens all the intellectual faculties, increases, enlarges, expands, and *purifies all the natural passions and affections*, and adopts them by the gift of wisdom to their lawful use.[7]

I have loved before, but I knew not why. But now I love with a pureness, an intensity of elevated, exalted feeling. . . . In short I could now love with the Spirit and with understanding also.[8]

Growing Up in the Lord is Preparing to Meet God

When Amulek said, "now is the time for men to prepare to meet God," (see Alma 34:34), he didn't have last-minute preparation in mind. Amulek was not warning of an impending return of the Savior, even though this return was implied in his warning. The world continues to be warned that the Savior will return to earth. Similar to the anticipation of many Jews in the meridian of time, many today look forward to this event as a solution to the world's and their problems. However, most people don't understand that prophetic warnings like those of Amulek and Alma (see Alma 13:21) usually warn about how we use the time of our mortal probation in preparation to meet God (see D&C 78:7). The Nephites under the direction of Captain Moroni certainly had an understanding of the prophetic warning voice to prepare since "They were sorry to take up arms against the Lamanites . . . and be the means of sending so many of their brethren out of this world into an eternal world, *unprepared to meet their God*" (Alma 48:23; emphasis added).

Brigham Young focused Amulek's warning, emphasizing the growing-up process of the temple as the preparation to meet God.

> Do not be too anxious for the Lord to hasten His work. Let our anxi-
> ety be centered upon one thing: The sanctification of our own hearts.
> The purifying of our own affections.[9]

To "be prepared against the day of burning" and "not faint in the day of trouble" requires "[preparing] the hearts of [the] saints." This preparation occurs, as we will learn in Chapter Eleven, when "the testimony of the covenant" and the laws of God are written, bound, and sealed in our hearts (see D&C 109:38, 46). Then we will be prepared to "gather together . . . upon the land of Zion" (see D&C 133:4).

The temple is where we learn to "grow up" in the Lord. It is where we learn to "climb up" the spiritual Mount Zion in order to "stand up" before the Lord. The temple is were we learn the qualities of a divine nature and acquire pure hearts filled with pure love. With this mighty change of heart, we are prepared for the great and last promise of the temple and all that eternal life means. Therefore, the temple should be the center of our lives, teaching us the way of salvation.

Growing Up in the Preparatory Redemption of Zion

Brigham Young had a great understanding of the redemption of Zion which began with his Zion's Camp experience. Therefore he must have understood the meaning of D&C 105:5:

> And Zion cannot be built up unless it is by the principles of the law
> of the celestial kingdom; otherwise I cannot receive her unto myself.

Brigham Young knew, as Moses knew, that a Zion society requires the celestial law of consecration. *In order to live this law on a celestial level, we must have pure hearts filled with the pure love of charity.* The failure to establish a holy nation of Zion in both the Sinai and Missouri was because the Saints "erred in their hearts." Whether rich man or poor man, greed is an impurity of the heart (see D&C 56:16–18). When the Lord's people have impure hearts, they will fail to completely keep the law of consecration. They will not be "gathered in one" at His coming (see D&C 42:36).

The law of consecration was introduced to the Latter-day Saints as early as 1831 before the exodus to the Ohio (see D&C 38:16, 25–27, 34–35), and then fulfilled in working application for a brief period, one month later in Kirtland (see D&C 42:2, 30–39; 53–55). One of the reasons that some of the Kirtland Saints were sent to Missouri to establish the foundation of Zion was that their "hearts might be prepared" for "the things which are to come" (see D&C 58:6). This is why Brigham Young called for "the sanctification of our hearts, the purification of our affections." This sanctification and purification of hearts produces a unity and equality that is required of a Zion people on the celestial level (see D&C 105:34; D&C 78:67).

Worshiping in the temple prepares us for this unity and equality. Susan Savage captured this feeling of unity in her poem *Temple Snow*:

To one who loves winter this pilgrimage is so white.
    Gone the cut and color of difference, the clatter of humanity that wars with birdsong and gentle thought.
    Hearts toward heaven, voices hushed to sacredness focus in unity.
We are one all alike before Him, as snow shapes line to line,
    White truth sifting softly, drink for our seasons.[10]

"It is not given that one man should possess that which is above another" (D&C 49:20). "It is not right that any man should be in bondage one to another" (D&C 101:79). We are to be "equal in the bonds of heavenly things, yea, and earthly things also, for the obtaining of heavenly things" (D&C 78:5). "In your temporal things you shall be equal, and this not grudgingly, otherwise the abundance of the manifestations of the Spirit shall be withheld" (D&C 70:14). When we willingly strive for temporal equality and unity, the display of spiritual gifts enhancing white truth increases. In the temple, when we learn that we are "all beggars" (Mosiah 4:19) before the Lord, He [pours] out his Spirit . . . [causing our] hearts [to] be filled with joy" (see Mosiah 4:20). This is the white truth that overcomes the "inequality of man because of sin and transgression, and the power of the devil" (Alma 28:13). It is this white truth we drink in the temple that makes us one with each other and with the Lord.

I love the expression of the unity that existed with Alma and his followers:

> And he commanded them that there should be no contention one with another, but that they should look forward with one eye, having one faith and one baptism, having their *hearts knit together in unity* and in love one towards another. . . .
>
> They should impart of their substance of their own free will . . . imparting to one another both temporally and spiritually. (Mosiah 18:21, 28–29)

The Apostle Paul used the same terms in addressing the Saints of Colosse:

> That their hearts might be comforted, being knit together in love and unto all riches of the full assurance of understanding, to the acknowledgment of the mystery of God, and of the Father, and of Christ. (Colossians 2:2)

The power of the pure love of Christ to change behavior was manifest in a remarkable state of unity of the Nephites and Lamanites. For nearly 200 years after the appearance of Christ to these people, they were unified in peace and love:

> And it came to pass that there was no contention in the land, because of the love of God which did dwell in the hearts of the people. . . .
>
> There were no robbers, nor murderers, neither were there Lamanites, nor any manner of -ites; but they were in one, the children of Christ, and heirs to the kingdom of God. (4 Nephi 1:15, 17)

It is a powerful message to recall that this pure love of the Savior was shown and taught to these people when He appeared to them at the temple of the land Bountiful. How profound and long lasting His marvelous love was! How profoundly changing His love is as we learn of it in the temple and practice it in our own lives keeping "church covenants" to "establish" us now and in the New Jerusalem (see D&C 42:67) as His "covenant people" (see D&C 42:36).

In order to bring His Latter-day Saints to this state of pure hearts with pure love, knit together in unity, the Lord promised the Missouri Saints, who failed in their attempt for a Zion society, the redemption of Zion:

> Therefore, in consequence of the transgressions of my people it is expedient in me that mine elders should wait for a little season for the redemption of Zion. (D&C 105:9)

> Zion shall be redeemed, although she is chastened for a little season. (D&C 100:13)

It is interesting that these revelations came through a prophet who led Zion's Camp. The formation of Zion's Camp in Kirtland was the beginning of an attempt to immediately redeem Zion in Missouri. However, the Prophet Joseph Smith must have known that Zion and "the regions round about" (see D&C 133:9) would truly be redeemed in the future after much tribulation and preparation (see D&C 58:3–14; 63:31; 103;12–13; 105:9–10). While this thousand-mile march of tender mercies and hardships from Ohio to Missouri did not achieve its intended purpose, it did provide a foundation of valuable experience in the power of love for Brigham Young and other future Church leaders. It remains as a great witness to the importance of the temple for "the strength of mine house" (D&C 105:17) who form Zion's Camp today. Zion's Camp was a camp where unity was learned since the welfare of Zion was sought. After the loss of the Zions in Missouri and Illinois, the Saints still had the concept of Zion's redemption in their minds and hearts because in Winter Quarters the Lord said, "Zion shall be redeemed in mine own due time" (D&C 136:18).

The Lord compared the redemption of Zion in the latter days to His attempt at creating a holy nation, a Zion in the Sinai:

> The redemption of Zion must needs come by power. Therefore, I will raise up unto my people a man, who shall lead them like as Moses led the children of Israel.
>
> For ye are the children of Israel, and of the seed of Abraham, and ye must needs be led out of bondage by power, and with a stretched-out arm.

The Scriptural Temple

> And as your fathers were led at the first, even so shall the redemp-
> tion of Zion be. . . .
>
> Mine angels shall go up before you, and also my presence, and in
> time ye shall possess the goodly land. (D&C 103:15–18, 20)

The Lord specifically said in these verses that Zion will be
redeemed as the children of Israel were led at first (before the provocation) with power and an outstretched arm, with the Lord Himself
going before them and His eyes upon them.

> And verily mine eyes are upon those who have not as yet gone up unto
> the land of Zion; wherefore your mission is not yet full. (D&C 62:2)

The Lord explained to those of Zion's Camp why He would
"wait for a little season" (D&C 105:13) before redeeming Zion (see
D&C 105:9–10). What He meant by power and an outstretched
arm with His presence before them is explained in the following
verses: The redemption of Zion "cannot be brought to pass until
mine elders are endowed with power from on high. For behold, I
have prepared a great endowment and blessing to be poured out
upon them" (D&C 105:11–12). *The power, the outstretched arm of
the Lord in His presence, is the endowment of the temple with its great
and last promise.*

It is in the temple that we receive the power and are prepared,
that we may be "taught more perfectly and have experience" (D&C
105:10; see D&C 97:12–14) until "[our] redemption shall be perfected" (D&C 45:46), for the redemption of Zion. Unlike the children of Israel in the Sinai, the Lord continues to go before us with
the fulness of the Melchizedek priesthood in His holy house and
with the great and last promise of the temple. Therefore, "continue
your journey. Assemble yourselves upon the land of Zion" (D&C
62:4) by assembling in the temple for "I am he who led the children
of Israel out of the land of Egypt" (D&C 136:22). "Israel's God is
[our] God" (D&C 127:3)! As with them, He wants to redeem Zion
by purifying us in the temple.

> Verily this is the word of the Lord, that the city New Jerusalem shall
> be built by the gathering of the saints, beginning at this place, even
> the place of the temple. (D&C 84:4)

Because as President Kimball said, "Creating Zion 'commences in the heart of each person.'"[11]

The Savior's parable about the redemption of Zion (See D&C 101:43–62) emphasizes the importance of building a watchtower even in "a time of peace" (D&C 101:48) because,

> If the good man of the house had known in what watch the thief would come, he would have watched. (Joseph Smith—Matthew 1:47)

> Watch, therefore, for you know not at what hour your Lord doth come. (Joseph Smith—Matthew 1:46)

The underlying principle of this parable is, "All who are founded upon the watch-tower . . . shall be saved" (D&C 101:12).

The equivalence of the watch-tower and the temple is strongly suggested when the Savior said, "That the work of the gathering together of my saints may continue, that I may build them up unto my name upon holy places" (D&C 101:64). This gathering is in the context of the parable of the wheat and the tares when "the wheat may be secured in the garners (temples, consider the carved symbolism of the new Nauvoo Temple) to possess eternal life" (D&C 101:65).

It seems that in the in the parable of the watchtower, an obedient servant or watchman who has not "fallen asleep" (D&C 101:53) on the watchtower is one who is faithful and wise in the temple. "And this shall be my seal and blessing upon you—a faithful and wise steward in the midst of mine house" (D&C 101:61). Perhaps, this is one reason we are instructed in the temple to be alert and attentive. If we are alert on temple watchtowers, we will be prepared for the salvation of Zion, for God "hath sworn by the power of his might to be her salvation and her high tower" (D&C 97:20).

If we do not understand the meaning of the parable of the watchtower in a time of peace, then we are like the "many who will say: Where is their God? Behold, he will deliver them in time of trouble, otherwise we will not go up unto Zion (or upon the watch-tower) and will keep our moneys" (D&C 105:8).

Nestled in a rather long verse about temple ordinances, the redemption of Zion is the focal point of D&C 124:39.

The Scriptural Temple

> Therefore, verily I say unto you, that your anointings, and your wash-
> ings, and your baptisms for the dead, and your solemn assemblies,
> and your memorials for your sacrifices by the sons of Levi, and for
> your oracles in your most holy places wherein you receive conver-
> sations, and your statutes and judgments, for the beginning of the
> revelations and foundation of Zion, and for the glory, honor, and
> endowment of all her municipals, are ordained by the ordinance of
> my holy house, which my people are always commanded to build
> unto my holy name.

The beginning of the revelations and foundation of Zion, therefore the beginning of the redemption of Zion as promised by the
Lord, comes to pass through the ordinances and endowment of the
temple. This is the Lord's expedient course through tribulation to
Zion. The Prophet Joseph Smith first taught this truth to the church
in Kirtland:

> The Lord has commanded us to build a house, in which to receive
> an endowment, previous to the redemption of Zion; and that Zion
> could not be redeemed until this takes place.[12]

In the dedicatory prayer of the Kirtland Temple, the Prophet
Joseph Smith prayed for the redemption of Zion (see D&C 109:51).
Then, after the failure to establish Zion in Missouri, D&C 124:39
was given in reference to the Nauvoo Temple. In the dedicatory
prayer of the Manti Temple, given May 21, 1888, Lorenzo Snow
prayed for freedom from persecution so that temple worship could
be a "purpose" of the Lord for the redemption of Zion:

> We ask thee, Righteous Father, to so control this present persecu-
> tion that thy purposes may be accomplished in the redemption of
> thy Zion.[13]

Elder Bruce R. McConkie noted that:

> All subsequent temples (to Nauvoo) are for the express purpose of
> preparing and purifying the Lord's people, freeing them from the
> blood and sins of the world, so they will be ready in due course to
> build the New Jerusalem and the temple on that center place.[14]

As the Missouri Saints and the Nauvoo Saints were led by
Moseslike prophets, Joseph and Brigham, so are we led today by a

living prophet. If we will obey his voice and become a temple loving people, then shall we possess the goodly land and enter into the rest of the Lord through the temple endowment. The endowment or "preparatory redemption" (see Alma 13:3) will be accomplished in the temple by growing up in the Lord to a "holy calling" through His holy order.

How does the endowment of the temple prepare us for the redemption of Zion? The scriptural definition of Zion gives the answer: "Therefore, verily, thus saith the Lord, let Zion rejoice, for this is Zion—the pure in heart" (D&C 97:21).

The ultimate purpose of the endowment is to endow us with the quality of charity, the pure love of Christ, which changes a broken heart to a pure heart. With this celestial quality, we are prepared to be a Zion people. The pure heart permits us to live in unity and equality required by celestial law (see D&C 105:4).

The formula for the redemption of Zion is straightforward:

- Zion is the pure in heart.
- The endowment produces a pure heart.
- The endowment is the preparatory redemption of Zion.

The temple endowment will prepare the hearts (see D&C 58:6) of His people for the redemption of Zion. "They that remain [from the scattering "who have been scattered upon the mountains" (see D&C 109:61)] *and are pure in heart,* shall return . . . to build up the waste places of Zion" (see D&C 101:17–18 emphasis added; 103:11). For "not many years hence they [mine enemies] shall not be left to pollute mine heritage, and to blaspheme my name upon the lands which I have consecrated for the gathering together of my saints. The strength of my house [will] gather together for the redemption of my people, and throw down the towers of mine enemies, and scatter their watchmen" (D&C 105:15–16). They will "go up to the land of Zion . . . upright in heart" (D&C 61:16) and "gathered in one" as His "covenant people" when He comes to His temple (see D&C 42:36). For "the kingdom of Zion is in very deed the kingdom of our God and his Christ; therefore, let us become subject unto her laws" (D&C 105:32).

The Scriptural Temple

Zion's Redemption: The Rainbow Connection

The *scriptural temple* informs us that unity of heart and mind was the essence of Enoch's Zion: "And the Lord called his people Zion, because they were of *one heart and one mind*, and dwelt in righteousness: and there was no poor among them" (Moses 7:18; emphasis added).

The scriptures also indicate that Enoch and the people of this former Zion knew of the redemption of Zion in the fulness of times:

> And righteousness will I send down out of heaven; and truth will I send forth out of the earth, to bear testimony of mine Only Begotten. . . . And righteousness and truth will I cause to sweep the earth as with a flood, to gather out mine elect from the four quarters of the earth, unto a place which I shall prepare, an Holy City, that my people may gird up their loins, and be looking forth for the time of my coming; for there shall be my tabernacle, and it shall be called Zion, a New Jerusalem. (Moses 7:62)

The beginning of this scripture was fulfilled in the First Vision of Joseph Smith when God the Father, the most righteous of all, descended from heaven to bear testimony of His son. Righteousness continues to descend from heaven in the form of heavenly manifestations of "every form of godliness" (Moroni 7:30) with "the power thereof" (Joseph Smith—History 1:19), such as holy ordinances of the temple. It continues in the form of revelations, such as those compiled in the Doctrine and Covenants, from heavenly messengers and "chosen vessels of the Lord" (Moroni 7:31).

Truth ascended from the earth in the form of faith in God (compare Joseph Smith—History 1:11–12 with Moroni 7:36–38; 10:47) from those seeking the truth under the influence of the Holy Ghost (see Jarom 1:4). It literally ascended in the coming forth of the Book of Mormon and other ancient records bearing testimony of Christ. It was also by faith that these records came forth (see D&C 10:46–52).

Perhaps Joseph Smith went to a grove of trees to pray because there he found a most symbolic place where heaven and earth meet. Trees are the staples that bind heaven and earth. While their roots are in the earth, their branches must grow towards the light of heaven to produce foliage and fruit. They are symbolic of the binding power of the truth on earth and righteousness in heaven (see D&C 127:7). They start from a seed that, with faith, bursts through the dark weight of the earth to the light of heaven. Then with nourishment (truth) from the earth and light (righteousness) from heaven the seed will grow to the full measure of its creation.

Joseph Smith spoke of the Book of Mormon in the setting of the Savior's mustard seed parable (see Mark 4:31–32) where heaven and earth met:

> Let us take the book of Mormon, which a man took and hid in his field, securing it by his faith, to spring up in the last days, or in due time; let us behold it coming forth out of the ground, which is indeed accounted the least of all seeds, but behold it branching forth, yea, even towering, with lofty branches, and God-like majesty, until it, like the mustard seed, becomes the greatest of all herbs; And it is truth, and it has sprouted and come forth out of the earth, and righteousness begins to look down from heaven; and God is sending down His powers, gifts and angels, to lodge in the branches thereof.[15]

The trees of the sacred grove are symbolic of the boy prophet who knelt on the earth, then, with faith in the seed of truth planted in his heart (see Joseph Smith—History 1:12), he burst from the darkness surrounding him (see Joseph Smith—History 1:15) and looked up to be enlightened by the righteous Gods of heaven. He then grew up in the truth of the sacred records from the earth and continuing righteous light from heaven to bring forth the fruits of the fulness of the restored gospel and the full measure of his creation. Like a tree and a prophet, we, "with all the precious trees of the earth" (D&C 124:26), can "take root downward, and bear fruit upward" (2 Kings 19:30). The strength of a tree by receiving the light to bear fruit depends on how deeply it takes root in the covenants of the Lord.

The Prophet Joseph Smith is the "root of Jesse" (Isaiah 11:10; D&C 113:5–6) who "set up an ensign for the nations" (Isaiah 11:12) in the restoration of the fulness of the gospel of Christ. On April 3 1836, at the hand of Moses, Joseph Smith received "the keys of the gathering of Israel" when heaven and earth again met (see D&C 110:11). Then the Lord "set his hand again the second time" (Isaiah 11:11) to "assemble the outcasts of Israel, and gather together the dispersed of Judah" (Isaiah 11:12). For, "by the keys which I have given shall [Israel] be led" (D&C 35:25). This was the beginning of the "root of Jesse" meeting a "branch" of Jesse (see Isaiah 11:1; D&C 113:3–4), the future Davidic king of Judah. With both root and branch attached to Christ, "the stem of Jesse" (Isaiah 11:1; D&C 113:1–2), Israel will again be united. Then "the envy of Ephraim also shall depart, and the adversaries of Judah shall be cut off; Ephraim shall not envy Judah, and Judah shall not vex Ephraim" (Isaiah 11:13). "Thy watchmen shall lift up the voice; with the voice together shall they sing, for they shall see eye to eye when the Lord shall bring again Zion" (3 Nephi 16:18).

The hallmark of the restoration of the fulness of the gospel is when heaven and earth met in 1820 and continue to meet in right-eousness and truth as a testimony of the Savior, Jesus Christ, and as a preparation for the ultimate witness of the Savior, the Second Coming. This testimony and witness will be given first to the jewels of the Lord, His elect, who have been prepared as were the people of Enoch to live in a Zion society, the New Jerusalem. There the Savior will appear in His tabernacle fulfilling the great and last promise of the temple for all present.

In reference to the blessings of Enoch's Zion, Joseph Smith said of our preparation to become like Enoch's elect people, "yet if we are . . . called with the same calling . . . and *embrace the same covenant* . . . we can . . . obtain the same promises . . . because we, ourselves, have faith . . . even as they did."[16]

In preparation to be gathered to the millennial Zion we must first be gathered on Mount Zion to Christ, the Master of pure love, who can make us a Zion people. He will do this by the sanctifying power of the Holy Spirit, "which Comforter filleth with hope and perfect love" (Moroni 8:26) making us a beautiful people on the temple mounts. Then we will publish the peace and great joy of the Lord in seeking to bring forth Zion: "And blessed are they who shall seek to bring forth my Zion at that day, for they shall have the gift and the power of the Holy Ghost; and if they endure unto the end they shall be lifted up at the last day, and shall be saved in the ever-lasting kingdom of the Lamb; and whoso shall publish peace, yea, tidings of great joy, how beautiful upon the mountains shall they be" (1 Nephi 13:37; see Moses 7:27). Therefore, let us who seek to bring forth Zion fulfill Lehi's prophecy and admonition for this the promised land to become the promised Zion. Let us "be men, determined in one mind and one heart, united in all things" (2 Nephi 1:21) by "[putting] on the armor of righteousness" (2 Nephi 1:23) with the temple robes of righteousness.

While I was driving over Big Mountain from East Canyon recently, a severe rainstorm lifted. I saw the setting sun in the west refract through the mist in the atmosphere. Then, a full, brilliant rainbow spanned the air from Big Mountain to Wyoming. This glorious wonder of nature reminded me of a special witness that I had in the temple.

While sitting in the celestial room of the Bountiful Temple, the sun broke from behind a cloud and penetrated an upper window. Like a laser beam, it pierced the crystal jewels of the chandelier. The whole celestial room was filled with miniature rainbows. As I contemplated this wondrous show of light, I realized that the rainbow is more than the sign of the end of the earth's baptism. *It is also the sign of the redemption of Zion.*

In connection with this sign of the rainbow, Noah was reminded of the "everlasting covenant" given to Enoch, who wept when he saw Noah's day. Perhaps Enoch was also given the sign of the rainbow:

> And *the bow* shall be in the cloud, that I may remember the *everlasting covenant* which I made unto thy father Enoch: That, when men should keep all my commandments, *Zion should again come on the earth, the city of Enoch.* (Joseph Smith Translation, Genesis 9:21; emphasis added)

The reality of the return to the earth of Zion, the city of Enoch, is confirmed in a revelation given in our dispensation as "a city reserved until a day of righteousness" (see D&C 45:11–12).

While I sat in the celestial room flooded with rainbows, recalling the promise given to Enoch, I understood the real meaning of the rainbow. For, as the full rainbow rises from the earth and then returns to the earth in the distance, so Enoch and his Zion people were taken from the earth and will return to the earth in the future. This will be similar to the New Jerusalem and the holy sanctuary of the Lord which "should come down out of heaven" (Ether 13:3).

I no longer look at a rainbow, and think only of Noah and the great flood. I think of Enoch and the great event of the redemption of Zion that he and the people of the city of Enoch are anticipating.

I think of how I want to be there to meet them, for it will be a joyous meeting as though there were a pot of gold at the end of the rainbow:

> And the Lord said unto Enoch: Then shalt thou and all thy city meet them there, and we will receive them into our bosom, and they shall see us; and we will fall upon their necks, and they shall fall upon our necks and we will kiss each other. (Moses 7:63)

> The Lord hath gathered all things in one. The Lord hath brought down Zion from above. The Lord hath brought up Zion from beneath. (D&C 84:100)

At that marvelous moment in the celestial room, when I made the rainbow connection, I really began to glimpse the importance of the temple. It was becoming the center of my life to teach me the way of salvation and prepare me for the redemption of Zion. I wanted to grow up and become a man who could match Mount Zion in order to receive its great and last promise.

The Bond of Perfectness:
The Only Way to the
Summit of Mount Zion

On Mother's Day, while talking long distance with my daughter Lys-An who was serving a mission in Poland, I asked what scripture had become a favorite to her. She said she found comfort in D&C 50:40–43:

> Behold, ye are little children and ye cannot bear all things now; ye must grow in grace and in the knowledge of the truth.
>
> Fear not, little children, for you are mine, and I have overcome the world, and you are of them that my Father hath given me;
>
> And none of them that my Father hath given me shall be lost.

After quoting this scripture, Lys-An expressed her love for the Polish people. She so much wanted to share her joy, being a true messenger of the true message. At that time, only a precious few had seen the great view with the courage to change. Others had glimpsed the light, but not enough to embrace it. These she considered the "little children" who somehow, sometime, would grow in grace and knowledge of the truth to become the children of Christ. These, she hoped, because of her love for them, would be given by the Father that none would be lost.

The Scriptural Temple

I was greatly moved by her love and desire to bind her Polish friends to Christ, that none would be lost. I feel that same concern for those who are like I once was—temple dropouts and temple inactives. I desire that we as members of His church understand the importance of diligently following our Savior, and literally become as the "generation" of Nephites who bound themselves to Christ at the temple that none were lost (see 3 Nephi 27:30).

> Verily, verily, I say unto you, ye are little children, and ye have not as yet understood how great blessings the Father hath in his own hands and prepared for you;
>
> And ye cannot bear all things now; nevertheless, be of good cheer, for I will lead you along. The kingdom is yours and the blessings thereof are yours, and the riches of eternity are yours. (D&C 78:17–18)

It is our guide and Savior, Jesus Christ, who will lead us along a sure path to the summit of Mount Zion. If, with faith, we grasp and graft to the rope of His Atonement, by obediently following Him, none will be lost.

Sealing of Hearts: The Great Welding Link of Mount Zion

I often look at a cherished portrait of my family and think that these are the people I love and want to be with. The pose in this portrait is a pyramid shape with us all linked together pointing towards heaven. I see in this family that is linked together the image of the temple, the mountain of the Lord. Perhaps this is why King Benjamin had the people of Zarahemla and Mosiah arranged in families in front of the temple so its image would reflect on them and they would understand that families should focus on the temple (see Mosiah 2:56).

The symbolism of this portrait projects backward and forward through infinity like the mirrors of a sealing room. We are gathered as a family on the foundation of our ancestors. We will be remembered by many as their ancestral family. The double helix of DNA is a welding link of individuals but this welding link is not just genetic.

Hopefully, we can all be bound or linked together with hearts turned to eternal relationships.

As a parent and husband, I desire that none of my family will be lost. I see us all bound together in eternal relationships with the rope of our Savior's Atonement, following Him to the summit of Mount Zion. This is the image in my mind of the great welding link, the whole and complete and perfect union envisioned by Joseph Smith (see D&C 128:18). This is the vision in portrait of the prophecy of Malachi (see Malachi 4:5–6; D&C 2; D&C 110:14–15; Joseph Smith—History 1:39) concerning the "turning of hearts."

Once I turn my attention from my immediate family to those of my ancestors, I realize I want to be sealed to them in eternal relationships. Because my identity is fixed to my ancestors, and I desire that none of them be lost, *I seek to turn my heart to God—to perfect it with pure love.* Then with this love, I seek to turn my heart to my ancestors and seal them in the eternal relationships of the temple.

Joseph Smith explained that the word *turn* in Malachi's prophecy (see Malachi 4:5–6) is correctly translated to mean bind or seal.[1] As we turn our hearts to our fathers and they turn their hearts to us we can be bound or sealed together. Therefore, the turning of hearts leads to the sealing of hearts. "And seek diligently to turn the hearts of the children to their fathers, and the hearts of the fathers to the children" (D&C 98:16). Ultimately we can be bound or sealed to our Eternal Father. This great binding or sealing occurs in the temple as our hearts become purified in binding to our Savior. *Temple binding is true bonding!*

The Great Sealing of Mount Zion: Birth into the Kingdom of God

The fundamental unit of exaltation is not an individual but rather a family defined as a husband and wife married in the Holy Order of Matrimony. As in the Davidic Covenant (see 1 Chronicles 17:1, 4, 10–14), the Lord's work and glory is to build a house that binds all the houses or families of men into the house or family of Christ (see 1 Corinthians 3:9–11; Hebrews 3:6). The history of the families of the house of Israel is a history of each family's relationship to the House of the Lord.

The Scriptural Temple

The temple has a great attraction for families because in it they can bind or seal the relationships developed in this life and the pre-earth life for time and eternity. In the temple we can receive a promise to be "[exalted], with all [our] families" (D&C 109:71). The promise, through worthiness, that none will be lost through this temple sealing is a great blessing and comfort. It is a promise like the promise of the resurrection that takes the sting out of death. This is especially true when our children die young, voiding the privilege to raise them in mortality.

As much as we talk about and desire the sealing of families that occurs in the temple, little do we consider the most profound sealing that occurs as we become faithful and wise stewards in His holy house (see D&C 101:61). It is the sealing of us, spirit children, to our Heavenly Parents. In the temple we make great progress in finding our spiritual parents, filling the void of spiritual orphans. Perhaps the Prophet Elijah best represents the spiritual orphan who is finally sealed to his Heavenly Father. No mention is made of Elijah's earthly family ties. He wandered throughout Israel like an orphan seeking to turn the hearts of his kinsmen back to God. After the miraculous events of Mount Carmel, he retreated to the Negeb Wilderness in some despair because he thought he was "not better than [his] fathers" in turning hearts to righteousness. He requested that God "take away [his} life" (1 Kings 19:4).

Then the Lord revealed to Elijah why He called him to the wilderness. He was to make a great journey to the summit of the temple, the holy Mount Horeb. This journey required the sacrifice of fasting forty days and nights, sustained only by a meal of cake and water (see 1 Kings 19:6). The Atonement sacrifice of the body and blood of Christ, represented by the sacrament bread and water, sustains us in the wilderness of the world on the great journey to eternal life. When we grow spiritually in the trials of life by maintaining faith in Christ's Atonement, the "endurance of faith on his name" (Moroni 8:3) occurs in the "bread of adversity, and the water of affliction" (Isaiah 30:20). If we lose obedience and faith in the Lord while in the wilderness, he will "take away . . . the whole staff of bread and the whole stay of water" (Isaiah 3:1; compare Alma 5:34).

When Elijah came to the temple mount, the Lord asked him "What doest thou here, Elijah?" (1 Kings 18:9). Burdened by the trials and loneliness of the world, this same question could be asked to each of us as we go to the temple. Do we only go to the temple to escape the world? Yet the temple endowment offers us more than escape from the world. Its invitation is to find joy in serving there (see Joel 1:16).

Again, Elijah expressed his despair, stating the feelings of an orphan when he said, "I, even I only, am left" (1 Kings 19:10). The answer to the Lord's question about Elijah coming to the temple mount came to him when the Lord said, "stand upon the mount before the Lord" (1 Kings 19:11). This is the temple challenge to all of us. To stand before the Lord upon His mount is to find Him in the temple and ultimately be worthy to be sealed to Him. Elijah was then taught that this relationship with God the Father does not come through external forces but rather it comes through the Atonement of His Son by following the powerful internal force of a "still small voice" (1 Kings 19:12).

Elijah was again asked the question "What doest thou here, Elijah? (1 Kings 19:13). But now this spiritual and perhaps earthly orphan "wrapped his face in his mantle" to cover his joy for having been sealed to his Father in Heaven through the great and last promise of the temple. Now his mantle signaled a newfound resolve and joy when Elijah declared, "I, even I only am left" (1 Kings 19:14) but "I, even I only, remain a prophet of the Lord" (1 Kings 18:22).

In his temple sermon, King Benjamin explained the truth taught to Elijah that being sealed to God occurs through the mediation of Christ by being spiritually born of Him:

> And now, because of the covenant which ye have made ye shall be called the children of Christ, His sons, and His daughters; for behold, this day He hath *spiritually begotten you*; for ye say that *your hearts are changed* through faith on his name; therefore, *ye are born of Him* and have become his sons and his daughters. (Mosiah 5:7; emphasis added)

We are born of Christ through His Atonement when we are bound to His everlasting covenants. When we follow the words of

Christ through our teacher, the Holy Spirit (see 2 Nephi 32:3–5) and climb to the summit of the temple mount, Christ will "deliver" us to His Father's kingdom.

The process of being born into the celestial kingdom of God through the temple has a beautiful correlation to being born into the earthly kingdom of God. Into both kingdoms we are born by "water, and blood, and the spirit" (see Moses 6:59; D&C 5:16). The unborn child is cleansed in the living water of the womb and survives by the blood of its mother. As the unborn child's heart starts beating, it is animated and becomes a new and living creature by its own spirit. Likewise, we are "born of the Spirit" and "quickened in the inner man" (Moses 6:65). We all must be cleansed by the living water of the womb of baptism to witness that we keep the commandment, are sanctified by the blood of Jesus Christ, and justified by the power of the Holy Spirit (see Moses 6:60–61) renewing our spirits.

As we enter the Kingdom of God on earth through baptism and the subsequent gift of the Holy Ghost, the cleansing power of water baptism and spirit baptism (the Holy Ghost) come together (see Mormon 7:10). Their cleansing power is made possible by the atoning blood are the "three that bear witness in earth" (see 1 John 5:68) and heaven of Jesus Christ. Truly, He is the foundation of salvation. Therefore, Christ's final expression of our spiritual destiny, that comes by obedience to the will of the Father, is found in his dying words, "Father, into thy hands I commend my *spirit*" (Luke 23:46; emphasis added). Perhaps dying suddenly of a broken heart, from which "came there out *blood* and *water*" (John 19:34; emphasis added), Christ left us a dramatic, final witness of the path we must follow in order to commend our renewed spirits to the Father.

We are born through a temple into the kingdom of God on earth when we are born through a woman bound to the everlasting covenant of marriage. Part of the ancient Hebrew concept of a betrothed woman was that she represented a holy temple. This is why she was veiled. A veiled woman in the temple represents the glory of God. Since the glory of God is the glory of man and a woman is the glory of man, then to man a woman should represent the glory of God (see 1 Corinthians 11:7, 10, 12, 15; see also Micah 2:9).

The grand finale of God's creations was a temple. As a temple, woman was created from man and for man as a symbol of their intended oneness. Like a holy angel or true messenger, the woman was created for the man (see 1 Corinthians 11:9) as a holy temple to whom he can go for the refuge of her love and the counsel of her heart (see D&C 25:5). She will not be defiled if he treats her with holiness. Now we understand why the Lord said: "I, the Lord God, delight in the chastity [holiness from chastening] of women" (Jacob 2:28). A woman should be considered as sacred space. Her chastity and virtue are "most dear and precious above all things" (see Moroni 9:9). She is a "holy woman" (1 Peter 3:5) like a temple because of pure love in "chaste conversation" (1 Peter 3:2) from "a meek and quiet spirit" (1 Peter 3:4).

The great secret of women is that they are holy temples. The great secret of men is that they can hold the holy priesthood of God. A woman is not a completed temple without binding the powers of pure love to the powers of the fulness of the priesthood. A man cannot fully bring the powers of the priesthood to the temple of a woman without practicing the doctrine of the priesthood. This doctrine brings the priesthood power of pure love. A man cannot fully learn this doctrine without the temple of a woman. A man and a woman cannot fully acquire pure love without the power of the priesthood in the temple. It was only a righteous high priest who could officiate with authority from God in the holy of holies (see Hebrews 2:17–18). The great secret of a happily married couple in the Holy Order of Matrimony is that they are powerful as a compound in one when they equally share the power of the priesthood in God's love.

Satan is intently working to destroy the binding powers of love. From all his devices and enticings, the greatest sin and atrocity in the world today by both men and women is desecration of the temple (see Ezekiel 5:11). "Her gates shall lament and mourn; and she being desolate shall sit upon the ground" (Isaiah 3:26). This is "the abomination that maketh desolate" (Daniel 11:31; see also Luke 13:35). Then "your houses will be left unto you desolate" (Helaman 15:1; D&C 84:115) "because of the loss of [your] kindred and friends" (3 Nephi 10:8).

To his betrothed bride the Hebrew groom would say: "Thou art set apart for me according to the law of Moses and Israel." *The woman was like a temple in being set apart for holiness.* Mary expressed the importance of her calling and completion of her holiness when she said: "For he that is mighty hath done to me great things; and holy is his name" (Luke 1:49).

God's calling for a woman is the great holiness of making a new life and bringing it to the earthly kingdom of God.[2] To "bear the souls of men . . . is the work of [the] Father continued, that he may be glorified" (D&C 132:63). This holy work is started and completed in a temple. To desecrate the temple of a woman is to profane the holy name of God (see Amos 2:7). Anatomically, a woman is constructed like a temple with an outer court, a holy place, and a holy of holies. She is a temple garden and fountain (see Song of Solomon 4:12–14). Physiologically, with a menstrual bleed from her temple fountain (see Leviticus 20:18) which provides for life and birth from her holy of holies, she symbolically enacts the Atonement of Christ. Likewise, through the temple, a new creature with a mighty change of heart is made and delivered to the presence of God by the travail and power of the Atonement (see Isaiah 46:3–4). Appropriately, a woman first witnessed mortal life and a woman first witnessed immortal life on this earth.

It takes two in both the earthly kingdom (a man and a woman) and heavenly kingdom (The Son of Man and mankind) to make a new life. In both kingdoms this new life is made in a temple. A most wonderful description of a temple is Adam's description of Eve when he called her "the Mother of all living." *Truly in a temple all living, mortal and eternal beings, are created.*

Catherine Thomas has beautifully expressed our birth through the strait gait and narrow way (see Matthew 7:14; 1 Nephi 8:20) or "narrow channel" of the temple into the celestial kingdom of God by the travail and power of the Atonement. This is the sealing power of perfection that occurs in the temple so we will be delivered in perfection to our Father in Heaven:

> The temple is the narrow channel through which we must pass to reenter the Lord's presence. A mighty power pulls us through that channel, and it is the sealing power of the atonement of the Lord Jesus

Christ. The Savior's atonement is another word for sealing power. By the power of the atonement, the Lord draws and seals his children to himself in the holy temples.[3]

The final words of King Benjamin's temple sermon expressed the great sealing to our Heavenly Father that occurs through our sealing to His Only Begotten Son, being born of Him and "brought to heaven":

> Therefore, I would that ye should be steadfast and immovable, always abounding in good works, that Christ, the Lord God Omnipotent, *may seal you His, that you may be brought to heaven,* that ye may have everlasting salvation and eternal life. (Mosiah 5:15; emphasis added; compare Alma 34:35; see also D&C 77:12)

The declaration of the resurrected Christ to the Nephites must have recalled the great words of King Benjamin in their minds:

> And as many as have received me, to them have I given to become the sons of God; and even so will I to as many as shall believe on my name. (3 Nephi 9:17)

Binding to Christ and Following Him to the Summit of Mount Zion

In binding through obedience to Christ's covenants of grace and truth we grow up straight to a fulness of perfection and reach the summit of Mount Zion. This is why the Savior gave the following commandments to the Ohio Saints in 1831 and 1832 in preparation for the binding that would occur in temples:

> And thus ye shall become instructed in the law of my church, and be sanctified by that which ye have received, and ye shall bind yourselves to act in all holiness before me
>
> That inasmuch as ye do this glory shall be added to the kingdom which ye have received (D&C 43:9–10)

> Wherefore, a commandment I give unto you, to prepare and organize yourselves by a bond or everlasting covenant that cannot be broken.
>
> Behold, this is the preparation wherewith I prepare you, and the foundation, and the ensample which I give unto you, whereby you

may accomplish the commandments which are given you. (D&C 78:11, 13)

As an orthopedic surgeon, I see practical application of binding a crooked limb to a sturdy, straight device. The term *orthopedic* means straight child. I have straightened many broken bones by binding them to a straight rod or other fixation device. Sometimes this must be done in stages by gentle persuasion so the soft tissues around the bone will tolerate the straightening. The principle of binding to something straight is engraved in the "Tree of Andry," a symbol of orthopedics.

The image of a crooked tree bound to a straight rod, or a crooked child bound to a fixation device, that they might grow straight and tall is the perfect image for the growing-up process of the temple. This image gives new meaning to Nephi's expression about the Israelites in the Sinai and the straight rod of the Lord that straitens:

And he did straiten them in the wilderness with his rod; for they hardened their hearts, even as ye have; and the Lord straitened them because of their iniquity. (1 Nephi 17:41)

The term *rod* gives the image of an instrument that physically gets our attention as a sign of authority or a tool of correction (see 2 Samuel 7:14). The "rod" of the Lord is His "word," like the iron rod. It is the rod of His mouth (see D&C 19:15) that demands our attention and corrects us with His commandments and covenants. His rod is a straight rod because it tells us all that we must do to grow straight (see 2 Nephi 32:3).

The term *straiten* means to confine or limit. Our wandering, disobedient nature becomes confined or limited as we are bound to the straight rod or word of the Lord. We can at first lean on His "rod" for support, but we must ultimately take His yoke upon us and do His work in keeping His commandments and covenants to be straightened. The straitening that makes us straight is with gentle persuasion and chastisement.

We should remember that the Lord chastens or straitens those He loves (see D&C 95:1; Hebrews 12:6; Helaman 15:3) "until they learn obedience, if it needs be, by the things which they suffer" (D&C 105:6). He "will contend with Zion, and plead with her strong ones, and chasten her until she overcomes and is clean before me" (D&C 90:36). Even in times of prosperity, "the Lord seeth fit to chasten his people, yea, he trieth their patience and their faith" (Mosiah 23:21). The Lord's chastening starts with feelings and understandings in the heart. If we respond honestly to these feelings and understandings, in order to "chasten thyself before thy God" (see Daniel 10:12), He will prepare for us a way of deliverance from temptation through chastening (see D&C 95:1). Finally if we cannot bear the Lord's chastening we cannot be sanctified (see D&C 101:5). If we are not sanctified we are not "chastened from all [our] sins, that [we] might be one" (D&C 61:8) to be worthy of His kingdom (see D&C 136:31).

Hopefully the result of chastening or straitening is repentance (see D&C 1:27) and meekness. Then we can be straightened or grow straight as we are taught by the Spirit and obey the words of Christ (see 2 Nephi 32:5). This obedience gives us a fulness of freedom because we grow straight to a fulness of God's powerful love. Of course we have our agency in deciding to bind ourselves to our Savior and to be straitened and straightened by His rod.

In making and keeping righteous covenants (see Mosiah 5:6) as we do in the temple, we are bound to Christ. If we want to "cleave unto the Lord" (Helaman 4:25), we should "cleave unto every good thing" (Moroni 7:28) "[living] by every word which proceedeth forth out of the mouth of God" (see D&C 98:11). Since all good things come from and lead to Christ, we should "cleave unto the covenants" (D&C 25:13) of Christ which will lead us to "cleave unto charity" because "charity never faileth" (see Moroni 7:46). In cleaving to the covenants we are bound to Christ in the sense that we take His name upon us in a marriage-type covenant. We become His helpmeet in trying to emulate Him and follow His will. This is how we keep His commandment to "take hold of my covenant" (Isaiah 56:4) and "cleave unto me with all your heart" (D&C 11:19). This is how we "cleave unto God as he cleaveth unto [us]" (Jacob 6:5). It is "in thy temples we'll bend"[4] in binding to Christ so He can straiten and straighten our wills to His until we cleave to each other and are grafted to Him as a compound in one.

Christ has many names or titles suggesting the various ways in which we must bind to Him and emulate Him. He warns that when we take His name upon us, we must use His name with reverent sincerity and proper authority (see D&C 63:61–62; 136:21; Exodus 20:7). It is not only how the name of the Lord passes through our lips but also how it passes through our hearts, expressed in our actions, that may condemn us. Unless we keep the covenants of the Lord in His Holy House by authority of His Holy Order with "full purpose of heart and real intent" (2 Nephi 31:13), we use His name in vain.

The message of the hymn "Come Thou Fount of Every Blessing" beautifully expresses the desire and need to be bound (fettered) and sealed to the Lord.

> Come thou fount of every blessing. Tune my heart to sing thy grace.
> Streams of mercy never ceasing, call for songs of loudest praise.
> Teach me some melodious sonnet, sung by flaming tongues above.
> Praise the mount, I'm fixed upon it, mount of thy redeeming love.
> Here I raise my Ebenezer. Hither by thy help I'm come.
> And I hope by thy good pleasure, safely to arrive at home.
> Prone to wander, Lord, I feel it. Prone to leave the God I love.
> Here's my heart, O take and seal it. Seal it for thy courts above.
> Jesus sought me when a stranger, wandering from the fold of God.
> He to rescue me from danger. Interposed his precious blood.
> Prone to wander, Lord I feel it. Prone to leave the God I love.
> Here's my heart, O take and seal it. Seal it for thy courts above.
> O to grace how great a debtor, daily I'm constrained to be.
> Let thy goodness, like a fetter, bind my wandering heart to thee.
> Prone to wander, Lord, I feel it. Prone to leave the God I love.
> Here's my heart, O take and seal it, seal it for thy courts above.[5]

Being fixed upon the mount of the Atonement, we realize what debt to Christ's grace we owe. We then want to be bound to Him and have His seal of approval upon us. This will only occur if we fetter or straiten our wandering by keeping His covenants. In taking the name of Christ upon us through these covenants we promise to grow straight by emulating Him. As we keep this promise we will receive His power (see D&C 39:4) to perfect us and imbue us with a "new spirit" and a "new heart" filled with His perfect love (see Ezekiel 36:25–27). By this power, He will seal or preserve our pure hearts for the courts of His Father above if we are obedient to Him "unto the end of our lives."

> Therefore, I would that ye should take upon you the name of Christ, all you that have entered into the covenant with God, that ye should be obedient unto the end of your lives.
>
> And it shall come to pass that whosoever doeth this shall be found at the right hand of God, for he shall know the name by which he is called; for he shall be called by the name of Christ. (Mosiah 5:8–9)

Knowing the name by which we are called, we as His sheep are led by the power of Christ to the right hand of God, perfected for celestial glory in the fold of the Father.

The Power of Christ to Heal Us and Make Us Holy on Mount Zion

The Savior has the "holy hands" (see D&C 60:7) of a holy "potter" (see Jeremiah 18:6; Isaiah 64:8) with "all power unto the fulfilling of his words" (1 Nephi 9:6). Out of "vessels of wrath" He can make of us "vessels of mercy" (see Romans 9:21–23). Then when He "makes known the riches of His glory on the vessels of mercy" like He did to Paul, we can become "chosen vessels" (see Acts 9:15; Ephesians 1:4; Moroni 7:31). Therefore, Christ will cleanse our inward vessel first, and then our outer vessel (see Alma 60:23). This He does by endowing us with power from on high (see D&C 38:32) and molding us as clay if we will bind ourselves to act in all holiness before Him (see D&C 43:9).

The Savior can truly make us whole by making us holy. This is what He taught the infirm man at the pool of Bethesda:

> And a certain man was there, which had an infirmity thirty and eight years.
>
> When Jesus saw him lie, and knew that he had been now a long time in that case, he saith unto him, Wilt thou be made whole ? . . .
>
> And immediately the man was made whole, and took up his bed, and walked. . . .

> Afterward Jesus findeth him in the temple, and said unto him, Behold, thou art made whole: sin no more lest a worse thing come unto thee.
>
> The man departed, and told the Jews that it was Jesus, which had made him whole. (John 5:5–6, 9, 14–15)

It is in the holy temple that we hear the Savior say to us "be whole by being holy and sin no more." It is in the temple that we can say "it was Jesus that made us whole." It is in the temple that we come to understand and feel the power of Christ to make us whole by purifying and perfecting our hearts, that we "[obey] from the heart" (Romans 6:17) and do all in "holiness of heart" (D&C 46:7). For the temple is "a place of thy holiness" (D&C 109:13). In His Holy House and by His Holy Order we are made whole as a little child (see Moroni 8:8), "sanctified by the Spirit unto the renewing of [our] bodies" (see D&C 84:33).

During his great temple sermon, King Benjamin described the power of Christ to maintain and even renew the mortal body as a "matchless and marvelous power" (see Mosiah 1:13; 2:11). Even though Moses was "an hundred and twenty years old when he died: his eye was not dim, nor his natural force abated" (Deuteronomy 34:7). It is also by the matchless and marvelous power of the Atonement, through His Holy Order, that Christ can physically and spiritually renew us by making us holy. He tenderly and enticingly invites us to Him, to understand His purifying power:

> Learn of me, and listen to my words; walk in the meekness of my Spirit, and you shall have peace in me. (D&C 19:23)

As we listen to Christ's words, He desires that we reason with Him "that [we] may understand" (see D&C 50:11–12).

> For after this manner doth the Lord God work among the children of men, For the Lord God giveth light unto the understanding; for he speaketh unto men according to their language, unto their understanding. (2 Nephi 31:3; see also D&C 1:24; Matthew 13:23)

In reasoning with the Lord or His true messengers in humility, those who "bring forth their strong reasons against the Lord" (D&C 71:8) come to understand His power to make them holy:

> Come now, and let us reason together, saith the Lord: though your sins be as scarlet, they shall be as white as snow; though they be red like crimson, they shall be as wool. (Isaiah 1:18)

We must reason the words of Christ not only in our minds but also in our hearts. "By the Spirit" (D&C 50:10), His and ours, is how the Lord finally reasons with us to our understanding. It is only "by the Spirit" that we can truly reason to understanding with each other. Therefore, the type of reconciled relationship that we want to develop with God and with others is one in which understanding and love come "by the Spirit." The wisdom of God can only be fully understood if it comes by the Spirit and is received by the spirit (see D&C 50:17–22). When we accept the everlasting covenant and come unto Christ in the temple we receive through the spirit of prophecy and revelation the "strong reasoning" and "wisdom" of the Lord about the power of pure love (see D&C 45:9–12). Then we will come to understand the power of the redemption of Christ, and see ourselves with an eye of faith raised to immortality and incorruption:

> Do ye exercise faith in the redemption of him who created you? Do you look forward with an eye of faith, and view this mortal body raised in immortality, and this corruption raised in incorruption, to stand before God? (Alma 5:15)

If we keep an eye of faith single to the glory of God, one day the veil will be lifted from our minds and we will see the great and last promise of the temple with eyes of understanding (see D&C 110:1).

Those who cannot understand Christ's matchless power in their hearts, with an eye of faith, should at least acknowledge it in their minds. The creation of this earth, from matter unorganized to a sphere glorious and beautiful is an evident reality. There is no place like it in the known solar system or near galaxy. All forces of the universe seem to be concentrated on this speck of organized matter to maintain life and to "be for signs" (see Moses 2:14). And for what purpose? To testify that there is a God and by the matchless power of His Son He can take us, His banished dust, from matter unorganized to a state glorious and beautiful if we will bind ourselves to the Son and sin no more.

> For we must needs die, and are as water spilt on the ground, which cannot be gathered up again . . . yet doth he devise means, that his banished be not expelled from him. (2 Samuel 14:14)

> Forasmuch as I exalted thee out of the dust. (1 Kings 16:2)

The world still believes in the geocentric theory. From the surface of the earth, it appears the sun revolves around us every day. However, Copernicus, one who sought the truth, was right. *Everything revolves around the Son!* (see D&C 88:7). As C. S. Lewis said, "I believe in Christ as I believe in the rising sun. Not only because I can see it, but because of it, I can see everything else more clearly."[6] We all should believe in the risen Son because He fell at noon (compare Amos 8:9 with Matthew 27:45) for us all. Even the sun will one day "hide his face in shame" to the glory of the Son (see D&C 133:49).

Joseph Smith expressed the need to "revolve around the Son" in our daily lives when he said, "we need the temple more than anything else."[7] Why? Because we need Christ more than anything else. For the "living deaths" of everyday life we need the healing and sealing power of the Atonement through Jesus Christ (see Isaiah 53:36; 61:13) that only the temple can fully provide. This truth was expressed by Truman Madsen when he wrote:

> All "living deaths" require atonement and healing. The atonement of Christ through ordinances of the temple "reverses the blows of death." If his healing the wounds is the beginning then His sealing of families [and us to Him] is the end.[8]

It is a marvelous healing of "living deaths" as the wounds of resentment, rejection, and conflict disappear in the temple when we can draw near to the Savior and emulate Him. The Savior assures those who draw near to Him that He will draw near to them (see D&C 88:63; 3 Nephi 24:7).

When we begin to comprehend the magnificence of the stature of Christ, and understand the will of the Father (see John 6:29, 44–45), Christ becomes a force that draws us to Him (see John 12:32; 3 Nephi 27:14). This drawing force is the power of His and His Father's love. Because of this love, Christ makes an offer that should irresistibly draw us to Him:

He loveth the world, even that he layeth down his own life that he may draw all men unto him. Wherefore, he commandeth none that they shall not partake of his salvation.

Behold, doth he cry unto any saying: Depart from me? Behold, I say unto you, Nay; but he saith: Come unto me all ye ends of the earth, buy milk and honey, without money and without price. (2 Nephi 26:24–25)

Christ literally has the ability to lift up and draw all men to Him because of the power of the resurrection. We are raised because He is risen. He also has the power to save us from spiritual death and perfect us in both body and spirit if we will draw near to Him and become like Him. The righteous shall be lifted up because "the Righteous is lifted up" (Moses 7:47). For "he shall rise from the dead, with healing in his wings" (2 Nephi 25:13). Christ's ability to heal both physically and spiritually is manifest in his ministry on earth (see Matthew 4:23). What it takes from us for His healing is a broken heart then full purpose of heart (see Isaiah 61:1 & Luke 4:18; read 3 Nephi 9:13; 17:7–9; 18:32; James 4:10).

If we put our "trust in God . . . [we] shall be delivered out of [our] trials, and [our] troubles, and [our] afflictions and [we] shall be lifted up at the last day" (Alma 38:5). Christ's healing salvation, this lifting and saving power, is not just for the future. Even in this life, Christ has the power that we "be lifted up" (Mosiah 23:22) above the "depressions" of mortality (see D&C 24:1). We are lifted with a peace (see John 14:27; D&C 19:23) and a "perfect brightness of hope" (2 Nephi 31:20) in the love of God and all men that will save us from ourselves and help us endure to the end. Therefore, as Mormon wrote to his beset but believing son Moroni, "May Christ lift thee up" (see Moroni 9:25).

The keys to being lifted up by Christ now and in eternal life are to "humble yourselves in the sight of the Lord" (see James 4:10), and then "trust in him" (see Mosiah 23:22) and finally to have "the love of god always in your hearts" (see Alma 13:29). Such was the case of Enoch who, in a great and last promise of the temple, was "lifted up, even in the bosom of the Father, and of the son of Man" (Moses 7:24). Contrast those who are lifted up by Christ to those who "lift themselves up in the pride of their hearts" (Mormon 8:36).

The Scriptural Temple

As a physician, I wish I could lift my patients in healing their physical and spiritual wounds so well. Unfortunately, as Francis Bacon said, many do not want to be healed because they prefer to keep "deaths" living: "This is certain, that a man that studieth revenge keeps his own wounds green, which otherwise would heal and do well."[9]

The wounds of "living deaths" must be healed if we are to be sealed to each other and to our Heavenly Parents (see 3 Nephi 12:23; Matthew 5:23–24). *We must be reconciled to each other if we are to be reconciled to God.* These wounds are healed by the power of the Atonement through temple covenants. Christ calls Latter-day Saints today who consider themselves to be righteous as He called the righteous Nephites to "return unto me . . . that I may heal you" (see 3 Nephi 9:13). It was at the temple that these Nephites were healed and lifted to the stature of Christ as we are healed and lifted in temples today.

The healing of "living deaths" in telestial temples is a reflection of the ultimate healing that will occur when the earth becomes a celestial temple and "God himself" shall be there.

> And I heard a great voice out of heaven saying, Behold, the tabernacle of God is with men, and he will dwell with them, and they shall be his people, and God himself shall be with them, and be their God.
>
> And God shall wipe away all tears from their eyes; and there shall be no more death, neither sorrow, nor crying, neither shall there be any more pain: for the former things are passed away. (Revelation 21:34)

Notice the great and last promise of the temple in these verses. The temples of mortality, extensions of the celestial temple, are the healing hospitals for our souls.

Once we understand the healing and elevating power of the Atonement through temple covenants, we then want to cry for joy as those covenant people at the temple with King Benjamin who "all cried aloud with one voice," saying:

> O have mercy, and apply the atoning blood of Christ that we may receive forgiveness of our sins, and our hearts may be purified. (Mosiah 4:2)

A Full Moon over Mount Zion

When we cry like the people of King Benjamin, we have finally understood the message of the heralding music that Moroni is trumpeting from the temple. It is the music of a full moonlight sonata captured in Don Busath's most beautifully significant picture of the Salt Lake Temple with a full moon silhouetting the angel Moroni. The symbolic meaning of the full moon is the fulness of Christ's love which is the fulness of the power of the Atonement. The message of Moroni's full moonlight sonata is the gospel in his own words "as with the voice of a trump" (D&C 24:12):

> Yea, come unto Christ, and be perfected in Him, and deny yourselves of all ungodliness; and if ye shall deny yourselves of all ungodliness, and love god with all your might, mind and strength, then is His grace sufficient for you, that by His grace ye may be perfect in Christ. (Moroni 10:32)

Then the real secret of the mighty change in this life comes to our understanding as Moroni further explained how the grace of Christ can perfect us in the second verse of his full moonlight sonata:

> And if men come unto me I will show unto them their weakness. I give unto men weakness that they may be humble; and my grace is sufficient for all men that humble themselves before me; for if they humble themselves before me, and have faith in me, then will I make weak things become strong unto them. (Ether 12:27; see also 2 Corinthians 12:9)

In the finale of Moroni's trumpet solo, the power of the full moon, the Savior's perfect love in His perfect Atonement, shines in all its glory. By this power we can again become the holy sons and daughters of God:

> And again, if ye by the grace of God are perfect in Christ, and deny not his power, then are ye sanctified in Christ by the grace of God, through the shedding of the blood of Christ, which is in the covenant of the Father unto the remission of your sins, that ye become holy without spot. (Moroni 10:33)

Christ loves us and is our advocate because He "knoweth the weakness of man and how to succor them" (D&C 62:1; Alma 7:12). "In all [our] afflictions he was afflicted" (D&C 133:53). If we search diligently in the full moonlight of Christ and receive every good thing from Christ, He will give us the power to make the mighty change in our weak hearts to become His sons and daughters (see Moroni 7:19; D&C 39:4). Like a full moon, this power is "held in reserve for them that love him" (D&C 138:52).

The Binding Power of Love

While love binds us to our mortal parents, so it is love that will bind us to our Heavenly parents—their love for us and our love for them. However, to be sealed or bound to our Heavenly Father we must have within us the kind of love that He has. It is the pure love of His only begotten Son. Paul expressed this truth in one precise verse: "And above all these things put on charity, which is the bond of perfectness" (Colossians 3:14; see also D&C 88:125).

This is the kind of bonding love that exists between the Father and the Son. It is the same love that the Father has for all His children in the world. It is a love of perfect justice and mercy. To those who believe on His Son becoming "one in [Him]" (see D&C 35:2), He gives the fulness of His love expressed in perfect oneness, the unity that the Father and Son have. This unity, even as the Father and Son are one, is beautifully expressed in the Son's prayer to His Father (see John 17:5, 20–26).

Notice the great and last promise of the temple when the Son said "that they may behold my glory" (John 17:24) in these deeply moving words of His prayer to the Father. The Son desired to reveal His glory (His rest), which is the glory of the Father. This promise can come to us when we seek the Son (see D&C 76:19). It will most certainly come when "the love wherewith thou hast loved me may be in them" (John 17:26), and we develop the kind of celestial love that the Father and Son have. We can develop and acquire within us the celestial love and unity required as we are bound to Christ, keeping His covenants. This is because He knows the love of the Father and has offered the gift of this pure love through baptism of fire and the Holy Ghost to those who are obedient to Him. Therefore, with the power of love through Christ's Atonement, we can be sealed to our Heavenly Parents with the "bond of perfectness." Parley P. Pratt captured this truth in his hymn "Father in Heaven, We Do Believe" when he wrote, "Baptize us with the Holy Ghost and seal us as thine own."[10]

Jacob described the power of the Atonement as "infinite" (see 2 Nephi 9:7–10, 12). *The power of the Atonement is the power of love, an infinite love that is the "bond of perfectness."* In his dedicatory prayer of the Kirtland temple, Joseph Smith described the Lord God Almighty as having "an infinity of fulness" (D&C 109:77). The fulness of God is the infinite measure of His perfect love "for he is full of mercy, justice, grace and truth, and peace, forever and ever" (D&C 84:102). The fulness of the Father's love is "the measure of the stature of the fulness of Christ" (Ephesians 4:13; see Ephesians 3:19). The Lord God Almighty and His Son are infinitely full of the power to love perfectly. Therefore, John the Beloved wrote:

> Beloved, let us love one another: for love is of God; and every one that loveth is born of God, and knoweth God. He that loveth not knoweth not God; for God is love. (1 John 4:78)

The greatness of God through His love, His "great and wonderful love" (D&C 138:3), is extended to us in the expression "for his love he shall be great" (D&C 124:17). "For the love which he has to my testimony, I the Lord, love him" (D&C 124:20). God's powerful bond of love binds us to Him and to each other, bringing all things to a perfected state never again to be corrupted. It is the ultimate power to overcome the force of telestial entropy that, as Jacob stated, causes all mortal matter to "rot and crumble" (2 Nephi 9:7).

Often, unfortunate mortals, born with handicapped bodies and minds, demonstrate the power of spontaneous love as their greatest asset. During a fast and testimony meeting that I attended, a woman bearing her testimony was overcome with emotion. A beloved young man with Down's syndrome spontaneously got up from his seat in the congregation, walked to the podium, and embraced this woman to comfort her. This spontaneous expression of love drew our affections towards this young man, erasing his handicap in our minds and illuminating our own weakness to love. This expression of pure love was a witness of the pure love of God that can shine through and heal any mortal situation which seemingly could "rot and crumble."

We learn to a degree in mortality that with great love comes great oneness. Growing up in mortality, hopefully we pass from a stage of entropy to a state of edification. Without the temple and the Atonement we cannot fully arrive at this state. We however, should learn in mortality that the love that edifies is a power that elevates unorganized matter and relationships to a creative, organized, lasting state of oneness.

As curious toddlers, we succumb to the forces of entropy. Everything seems to crumble in our hands. Later, when we are given responsibility for material possessions, respect for maintenance and even love of ownership develops. When this responsibility includes others, we can learn of the powerful, lasting bond that edification through love creates.

We can only fully learn the power of love with our agency to choose between good and evil in a world of trial and triumph. The best part of a skinned knee is a mother's love. Jesus Christ, who possessed the power of a god, patiently submitted Himself to mortal trials in order to perfect His love of all mankind. Such will be our triumph if, on wounded knees, we kneel obediently before Him .

After reading Moses chapter four verse one, where Satan proposed his plan to "redeem all mankind, that one soul shall not be lost," I wondered about the details of his plan. How was he going to force spirit beings, who seem to respond best to the power of love "without compulsory means" (D&C 121:46), to all be saved? Like many of his followers talked about in the Book of Mormon, he must have had a powerful rhetoric because he "turned away a third part of the hosts of heaven because of their agency" (D&C 29:36). The only way Satan's plan could be implemented would be through the elimination of the law of agency. Therefore, Satan "sought to destroy the agency of man, which I the Lord God, had given him" (Moses 4:3). Besides their mortal bodies, these "hosts of heaven" who followed Satan also lost their agency because he would "lead them captive at his will" (Moses 4:4).

In all dispensations of man on earth, Satan's plan under varying philosophies has been presented. Unlike the Lord's law of consecration, all of these philosophies have a basic element: the elimination to some degree of agency. Like the intimate relation between light, love, and life, the power of love is intimately related to the law of agency. No accountable spirit can be forced by the power of love! Yet it is precisely the power of love that creates a unity of thought and action out of obedience by choice. When there is "a variance one with another" from all forms of pride that diminish or destroy love, there is "slothfulness" expressed in all forms, from forgetfulness to feigning. To the Lord this "slothfulness" is disobedience (see D&C 101:50).

There are many inspiring stories, written and personal, that verify the power of love. A favorite story of mine that demonstrates the binding power of love is *Cry, the Beloved Country* by Alan Paton. In South Africa, during the 1940s, a prominent white man and a black minister both lost their sons. The white man's son was shot to death by the minister's son. The minister's son was executed because of this crime which occurred out of fear. Eventually, the white man's heart turned from prejudice and hate and the minister's heart turned from fear and grief to the point that they began to respect, edify, and then love each other. Their sincerity was witnessed by their love (see Alma 26:31). Finally the white man built a new church for the black minister.

A sacrifice was necessary for both of these fathers to come together in love. It was a sacrifice not only of their sons but of their proud hearts—changed first to broken hearts, then to hearts filled with pure love. This change of heart necessary to produce the binding oneness of pure love is based on the infinite sacrifice and pure love of Jesus Christ (see Galatians 3:28). The glory of God's love is fully expressed in love for enemies. It is the victory of divine love over the powers of evil by patient suffering and sacrifice until evil quells itself (see Matthew 5:38–48; Romans 12:17–21).

Pure love is a will to act on behalf of others. Therefore it is a power. It is not only the power of knowledge, but the graces of edification such as self-discipline, sacrifice, patience, long-suffering, faith, and hope.[11] It is the power that repels the forces that cause all matter and relationships to rot and crumble. Jacob said the power of the infinite Atonement, this infinite love, not only overcomes our physical but also our spiritual degradation. Therefore by the Atonement, "this corruption [can] put on incorruption" (2 Nephi 9:7) overcoming "the death of the body, and also the death of the spirit" (2 Nephi 9:10).

Connecting with the powers of heaven through faith and love is the doctrine of the priesthood (see 2 Nephi 1:10; Moroni 10:7; D&C 121:36–46; D&C 107:30–31). Our faith becomes righteous enough to draw on the powers of heaven if it is motivated by pure love. Christ is the perfect example of the powers of heaven manifest through the powers of faith and love (see Alma 26:16; Ether 12:29, 31). It is with love unfeigned, our bowels full of charity towards all men, that the rights of the priesthood we hold become inseparably connected with the powers of heaven.

The fact that God desires to bestow upon his children the powers of heaven through the rights and doctrine of the priesthood that we might wax strong in His presence (see Isaiah 40:28–31), is ample proof that He wants us to become like Him. Because the promise is if "these things" (the virtues of the doctrine of the Priesthood) are part of us, then by the power of the Atonement we shall have eternal life which is to know and become like God (see D&C 107:31). The promise for having the power of the Atonement and the doctrine of the priesthood distill upon our souls is "all that my Father hath" (D&C 84:38) which includes the binding power of His love. As the Apostle Paul said, the binding power of the love of God is so great that "[nothing] shall be able to separate us from the love of God" (Romans 8:39).

At the Summit Veil: The Mercy Seat of Mount Zion

Within the Holy of Holies of the early Old Testament temples was the mercy seat, the throne of God. The Hebrew word for the *gold* covering of this seat is *kapporeth,* which, as we have seen, means a covering of acceptance through atonement and forgiveness. Therefore, this seat was appropriately called a "mercy seat." Paul directed us to this throne, calling it "the throne of grace," that we might obtain the grace and mercy of Christ (see Hebrews 4:16).

The Lord accepted the Kirtland temple with a promise of His manifesting "in mercy in this house" (see D&C 110:7). *Nephi taught that "the tender mercies" of Christ are sufficient to make the faithful "mighty," with "the power of deliverance" from the Fall and the bitter results of the forbidden fruit (see 1 Nephi 1:20).* The real deliverance is from our weaknesses that we may be made strong (see D&C 50:16), even with the "power to overcome all things which are not ordained of God" (see D&C 50:35). When we fatigue in climbing Mount Zion we can rest upon the Savior's tender mercy seat with full confidence that the power of His infinite love will faithfully belay us.

> The soul that on Jesus hath leaned for repose
> I will not, I cannot, desert to his foes;
> That soul, though all hell should endeavor to shake,
> I'll never, no never, I'll never, no never,
> I'll never, no never, no never forsake! [12]

As we are delivered from things not ordained of God, we appear to the world as "strangers and pilgrims" (see Hebrews 11:13; 1 Peter 2:11; D&C 45:13) traveling through mortality in search of a life of righteousness like the patriarchs of old. With images of "kappo-reth," Catherine Thomas has expressed our search as "strangers and pilgrims":

> This was the very search for which they [and we] were put on earth: to rend the veil of unbelief, to yield to the pull of the Savior's sealing power, to stand in the Lord's presence, encircled about in the arms of his love. [13] (see also Acts 17:27–28)

With faith and hope in Christ, Joseph Smith taught that Christ's mercy enables us to endure the deserts and fleshpots of mortality during our pilgrimage to the promises:

> They are enabled by faith to lay hold on the promises. . . . And wade through all the tribulations and afflictions. . . . Believing that the mercy of God will . . . lay hold of them and secure them in the arms of His love. [14]

Christ's mercy expressed as the "arms of His love" is what ena-bled Father Lehi to exclaim at his mortal parting the assurance of his deliverance, having seen and felt the great and last promise of the temple (see 2 Nephi 1:15).

The fruit of the tree of life is the love and mercy of Christ. Jacob taught that as our hearts become purified, we feast upon this fruit. It is this fruit that kept Job (see Job 19:21–27) and Jacob (see Jacob 3:12) steadfast in their afflictions with "firmness of mind." Christ's love and mercy will also console us in our afflictions and plead our cause.

The hymn "I Stand All Amazed" mentions the mercy seat and teaches us that worshiping in the temple will lay hold and secure us in the love of God at His glorified throne: "I will praise and adore at the mercy seat, until at the glorified throne I kneel at His feet."[15]

Then, if we have "overcome" (Revelation 3:21) by the power and mercy of Christ, we will not only kneel at the glorified throne but "sit upon thrones" (D&C 132:37) and "have power over many kingdoms" (Joseph Smith Translation, Revelation 2:26).

Two remarkable witnesses of the great and last promise of the temple are found in the words of Orson F. Whitney and Melvin J. Ballard respectively, latter-day apostles who literally felt Christ's love and mercy:

> I ran [to meet Him] . . . fell at his feet, clasped Him around the knees, and begged Him to take me with him. I shall never forget the kind and gentle manner in which He stooped, raised me up, and embraced me. It was so vivid, so real. I felt the very warmth of His body, as He held me in His arms.[16]

> I found myself one evening on the dreams of the night in that sacred building, the temple. After a season of prayer and rejoicing, I was informed that I should have the privilege of entering into one of those rooms to meet a glorious personage, and, as I entered the door, I saw, seated on a raised platform, the most glorious Being my eyes had ever beheld or that I ever conceived existed in all the eternal worlds.

> As I approached to be introduced, he arose and stepped towards me with arms extended, and he smiled as he softly spoke my name. If I shall live to be a million years old, I shall never forget that smile. He took me into His arms and kissed me, pressed me to his bosom and blessed me, until the marrow of my bones seemed to melt! When He had finished, I fell at His feet and, as I bathed them with my tears and kisses, I saw the prints of the nails in the feet of the Redeemer of the World. (Compare 3 Nephi 11:19; 17:10).

> The feelings that I had in the presence of Him who hath all things in His hands, to have His love, His affections, and His blessings was such that if I ever receive that of which I had but a foretaste, I would give all that I am, all that I ever hope to be to feel what I have felt![17]

Mark H. Greene III

The physical symbol of the power of love in the Atonement is the embrace. It is the gesture of reconciliation or atonement between God and man.[18] The bond of the embrace of love is the consummation of reconciliation. This truth is taught in the temple as we move through hand gestures of increasing commitment and love (see Isaiah 13:2; 44:5) until we are reconciled with God at the veil and "go into the gates of the nobles" (Isaiah 13:2) as "sanctified ones . . . [rejoicing] in [God's] highness" (Isaiah 13:3). For "[His] arm [and hands are] lengthened out all the day long" (2 Nephi 28:32; Jacob 5:47, 6:4) that we may "cleave unto God as he cleaveth unto [us]" (Jacob 6:5). The ultimate goal of the Atonement is not just to bring us to Christ but to reconcile us to God the Father (see 2 Nephi 10:24; 25:23) that we might rejoice in an embrace.

In mortal life we experience the difference between the joined hands of agreement and the enveloping arms of endearment as degrees of commitment and love. The Apostle Paul testified of the power of love behind an embrace when first he embraced the disciples of Ephesus and then embraced Eutychus to raise him from the dead (see Acts 20:1, 10). Mormon lamented that his people had not repented to receive the ultimate embrace of love, "that they might have been clasped in the arms of Jesus" (Mormon 5:11) "who stood with open arms to receive [them]" (Mormon 6:17).

As we return to the temple, worshiping at the mercy seat, we lay hold of the healing and sealing power of the Atonement. We feast upon the love and mercy of God. We learn that Christ is the one who reconciles us with and leads us to the glorified throne of the Father, because He is sealed to the Father (see John 6:27). Therefore we must ultimately report to the Savior and be sealed or bound to Him by the power of His love in His outstretched arms that will embrace us. How joyous that the father of our spiritual rebirth is the only one at the gate!

> *The keeper of the gate is the Holy One of Israel*; and He employeth no servant there; and there is none other way save it be by the gate; for he cannot be deceived. . . .
>
> And whoso knocketh, to him will he open. . . . And save they shall cast these things away [things of pride] and consider themselves fools before God, and come down in the depths of humility, He will not open unto them. (2 Nephi 9:41–42)

371

The Scriptural Temple

The temple veil is the gait to the summit veil of Mount Zion. It is the final strait and narrow gate. The Savior is the gatekeeper because of the fulness and power of His love that will reconcile and seal us to the Father. Christ can then lead us through the veil to the presence of the Father if we will first knock in respectfully seeking Him.

In a Church Education Week address, Michael Wilcox revealed a vision of his own judgment. He entered a waiting room and saw about 20 people seated. When he looked closely, they were all Michael Wilcox. There was Michael Wilcox the husband, and Michael Wilcox the father, and teacher, and priesthood holder, and so forth. All of these seemed to go through judgment without incident. In the last seat was a trembling, wretched man. It was Michael Wilcox the man, stripped of all titles. As he fearfully made his way to the door of judgment, the Savior put an arm of love about him saying: "Michael, do not fear. I am your advocate with the Father because you have believed on my name."[19]

This same love and mercy of the Savior experienced by Brother Wilcox is expressed in the *scriptural temple*:

> Listen to Him who is the advocate with the Father, who is pleading your cause before Him
>
> Saying: Father, behold the sufferings and death of Him who did no sin, in whom thou wast well pleased; behold the blood of thy Son which was shed, the blood of Him whom thou gavest that thyself might be glorified;
>
> Wherefore; Father, spare these my brethren that believe on my name, that they may come unto me and have everlasting life. (D&C 45:35)

Christ invites us to plead with Him. "Let us plead together," He says, because He can blot out our transgressions (see Isaiah 43:25–26) if we permit Him. It is at the veil that we really see the mercy and power of the Atonement as "the matchless bounty of [Christ's] love" (Alma 26:15). Even if we must finally cry like Nephi and Paul "O wretched man that I am!" (2 Nephi 4:17; Romans 7:24), we who believe on His name have the greatest advocate of all that is pleading our cause because of His Atonement (Moroni 7:28; D&C 38:4) and because "He delighteth in mercy" (Micah 7:18). If in us, He finds the fruits of the Spirit by taking His name upon us, He will joyfully plead because against such there is no law (see Galatians 5:18, 22–23). His Father will then embrace us with the arms of His love and say,

> Well done, thou good and faithful servant: thou hast been faithful over a few things, I will make thee ruler over many things: enter thou into the joy of thy Lord. (Matthew 25:21)

If the Savior finds in us a pure heart and devotion to Him that is required, then a preliminary type of sealing to the Father or embrace can occur even in this life. It is the seal of assurance, the stamp of approval from the Holy Spirit of Promise, a calling and election made sure, "shed forth upon all those who are just and true" (see Ephesians 1:13; D&C 76:53).

The Bond of Perfectness: A Sure Way to Stand in the Presence of God

The bond of perfectness is the infinite power of a "perfect Atonement" that can perfect us: "These are they who are *just men made perfect* through Jesus the mediator of the new covenant, who wrought out this *perfect Atonement* through the shedding of his own blood" (D&C 76:69; emphasis added).

The bond of perfectness, the bonding and equalizing power of perfect love, is a requirement even in this life to live the laws of the celestial kingdom, that we "may be equal in the bonds of heavenly things" (see D&C 78:5). For this bond of perfectness, we must make a great and last sacrifice, yielding our hearts to God by keeping temple covenants. We must keep the everlasting covenant which is the everlasting bond (see D&C 78:11). Then the Savior will encircle us with the arms of His love and clothe us with the robes of righteousness by filling our hearts with His perfect love. This is the ultimate expression of "kippur" as we are clothed with the bond of perfect charity, becoming His spiritually begotten children:

> And above all things, *clothe yourselves* with the *bond of charity*, as with a mantle, which is the *bond of perfectness* and peace. (D&C 88:125; emphasis added)

The covering mantle of the bond of charity was described by the Prophet Joseph Smith: "If you will throw a cloak of charity over my sins, I will over yours—for charity covereth a multitude of sins."[20] (see 1 Peter 4:8). This thought is reflected in wonderful verses of instruction for the ambiance of the "school of the prophets" held in the house of God. They mention an "everlasting covenant, in which covenant," we receive each other "to fellowship in determination that is fixed, immovable, and unchangeable, to be your friend and brother through the grace of God in bonds of love" (see D&C 88:130–133). We bind to each other by giving account to each other that we might learn to edify each other. "Let us consider one another to provoke unto love and to good works: Not forsaking the assembling of ourselves together . . . but exhorting one another" (Hebrews 10:24–25).

The bond of perfectness is the bond of perfect love that binds us to our Savior and to each other, that "in life [we are] not divided, and in death [we are] not separated" (D&C 135:3). It is the bond required to live the celestial law, becoming truly equal in preparation for the redemption of Zion and the great and last promise of the temple.

May we return often to the house of God where we receive the bond of perfectness through the everlasting covenant from our friend and brother, Jesus Christ. This bond comes to us by the power of a perfect love expressed in a perfect Atonement that can spiritually beget us as the children of Christ. As we become the children of Christ (see Mosiah 5:7), we can become again the sons and daughters of God (see Mosiah 27:25; 3 Nephi 9:17; Moroni 7:48; D&C 25:1; Moses 6:68).

"To prepare to meet god" (Alma 34:32) as His sons and daughters is to prepare to "be counted worthy to stand" (D&C 107:100) and then "prepare to stand" (Mormon 3:22) in His presence. "For God hath made man upright" (Ecclesiastes 7:29). Joseph Smith prayed to know his "state and standing before [God]" (Joseph Smith—History 1:29). Standing in the presence of God is not so much a matter of muscular strength as it is a matter of our "spiritual standing" (D&C 108:2). The mighty people at the time of Enoch "could not stand in his presence" (Moses 6:47) as he spoke the word of God. Through temple worship we become "the people . . . [who] honorably hold a name and standing in this thy house" (D&C 109:24). By the powers of heaven through temple ordinances and the endowment of the doctrine of the priesthood, our spiritual confidence will wax strong to stand, like Gabriel (see Luke 1:19), in the presence of God.

In the Garden, Adam and Eve stood in the presence of God. After the Fall, they knelt at the altars of sacrifice. As the plan of redemption was revealed to them and they obeyed it, their confidence waxed strong so they could again stand in God's presence. This confidence came by the power of the Priesthood, the Order of the Son of God (see Joseph Smith Translation, Genesis 14:30–31). This is the same sequence we enact in the temple being frequently reminded that we, like the Prophets Moses (see Moses 1:31), Elijah (see 1 Kings 19:11), and Daniel (see Daniel 1:4) can stand in the presence of the King of Kings on His temple mount. This sequence is symbolic of our heavenly birth, our fall, and our redemption.

To mimic the true doctrine of standing in the presence of God, Satan encourages "a place for standing" (see Alma 31:13). But "the wicked shall not stand" (see D&C 29:11–12). Only those who "stand in [their] office" (D&C 81:50) as "standing ministers" (D&C 84:111) and "humble [themselves] before me" (see D&C 124:103) to "succor the weak, lift up the hands which hang down and strengthen the feeble knees" (D&C 81:50) "that all may be edified" (D&C 84:110), will stand in the presence of God. "For without the feet [that edify] how shall the body be able to stand?" (see D&C 84:109–110). The feet are the foundation on which the body stands because they represent the "more feeble," "less honorable," "uncomely parts" of the body. These parts need the pure love of edification through "more abundant honor" from the "comely parts" of the body "that the members should have the same care one for another." With this pure love of edification there is "no schism in the body." It stands as "many members, yet one body" (see 1 Corinthians 12:14–26).

What a contrasting image of standing this is to those who are "thrust down" (D&C 76:25), whose own guilt "doth cause [them] to shrink from the presence of the Lord" (Mosiah 2:38) because they "rebelled against the Only Begotten Son" (D&C 76:25). When men reject the power of God's love, they eventually "shall fall upon the ground and shall not be able to stand" (D&C 88:89). As our confidence grows with the power and bonds of God's holy order to perfect our love, even in great tribulation, we will learn to "stand fast" and "steadfast" (see Alma 1:25) as "witnesses" for Christ (see Mosiah 24:14). We will answer the questions, "who shall be able to stand?" (Revelation 6:17) and "who shall stand when he appeareth?" (Malachi 3:2). If we pass through the "refiner's fire" and the "fuller's soap," being baptized with fire and water, we will "stand upright" (Daniel 10:11) as "two olive trees, and the two candlesticks, standing before the God of the earth" (Revelation 11:4).

Herein is our love made perfect, that we may have boldness in the day of judgment; because as he is, so are we in this world (see 1 John 4:17; see also 1 John 2:28, 3:2, 3:21, 5:14). And I rejoice in the day when my mortal shall put on immortality, and shall stand before him; then shall I see his face (see Enos 1:27).

Returning often to the temple, we will desire to return to our Father in Heaven, standing in His presence, "for the Lord hath chosen you [his covenant people] to stand before him" (2 Chronicles 29:11). To stand before God is to be "exalted in [His] presence" (D&C 109:69). Our Father in Heaven desires to return to us, as He did to Adam and Eve before the fall, to give us "a new heaven and new earth" (Ether 13:9) to stand on.

> I have made the earth rich, and behold it is my footstool, wherefore, again I will stand upon it. And I hold forth and deign to give unto you greater riches, even a land of promise, a land flowing with milk and honey, upon which there will be no curse when the Lord cometh. (D&C 38:17–18)

> But go thou thy way till the end be: for thou shalt *rest and stand* in thy lot at the end of thy days. (Daniel 12:13; emphasis added)

To climb Mount Zion we must learn to maintain our balance standing upright because to stand in the presence of the Lord is the great and last promise of the temple.

The Wells of Salvation: Sustaining the Ascent of Mount Zion

Feeling my way along the chiseled walls of Hezekiah's tunnel and wading through the knee-deep cool water of the Gihon Spring to the Pool of Siloam, I recalled the miracles of the rocks at Horeb and Meribah (see Exodus 17; Numbers 20). Moses smote these rocks with his rod and water gushed forth to satisfy the thirst of the Israelites. *Giha* in Hebrew means "gush forth."

The spring of Gihon in the Kidron Valley and the springs of the Jordan valley such as En Gedi, seem to gush out of desolate ground or rocks as reminders of the water miracles of Moses. This image of water gushing from rock reminds those who drink the water that in this land precious water flows because the Lord said:

> It shall come to pass, if ye shall hearken diligently unto my commandments . . . I will give you the rain of your land in his due season. (See Deuteronomy 11:11–14)

The annual rainfall of Jerusalem is equivalent to the rainfall of London, but in Jerusalem, rain falls in winter months.[1] The remainder of the year is relatively arid. Therefore stored water from the ground that supplies springs is important. Even the water that feeds the Jordan River comes from a rock—the aquifers of Mount Hermon. The precarious edge between wet and drought on which Judea balances is evidenced by the many cisterns around Jerusalem. There are 37 cisterns under the Temple Mount courtyards capable of holding 10 million gallons of water.[2]

The threat of drought in Judea is symbolic of the threat of drought in our own lives. If we forsake "the fountain of living waters" (see Jeremiah 17:13) it is because we have hewn out "broken cisterns, that can hold no water" (Jeremiah 2:13). As we have seen, unless we hew out a temple within us, we cannot hold the Holy Spirit who brings the fountain of living waters.

The Nourishing Word of God

The water that gushed from the rocks struck by the rod of Moses was a type of Christ symbolizing the Atonement and the spiritual truths that would flow from the "rock of Israel" to everlastingly quench the spiritual thirst of those that follow Him. This truth was frequently taught by the Savior during His mortal ministry. After Christ fed the five thousand and was sought by those receiving this miracle, He taught them the truth about nourishment from God:

> And Jesus said unto them I am the bread of life; he that cometh to me shall never hunger; and he that believeth on me shall never thirst. (John 6:35)

The prophets of old have compared lack of the knowledge of God to famine and drought:

> Therefore, my people are gone into captivity, because they have no knowledge; and their honorable men are famished, and their multitude dried up with thirst. (2 Nephi 15:13; Isaiah 5:13)

The prophet Amos foretold that the worst drought and famine of all, even for the young and the strong, is a drought and famine of the word of God:

> Behold, the days come, saith the Lord God, that I will send a famine in the land, not a famine of bread, nor a thirst for water, but of hearing the words of the Lord. . . . In that day shall the fair virgins and young men faint for thirst. (Amos 8:11, 13)

The words and works of Christ are what nourish us everlastingly. He is a spring of pure water that will never dry up because His works and words "never cease" (see Moses 1:4; Joseph Smith—Matthew 1:35). This is the pure water that quenches our thirst in climbing Mount Zion.

A Well of Living Water within Us

A beautiful base relief on a front court wall of the Cardston Alberta Temple shows the scene of Christ with the Samaritan woman at Jacob's well. Christ's profound scriptural message is inscribed below this scene:

> But whosoever drinketh of the water that I shall give him shall never thirst; but the water that I shall give him shall be in him a well of water springing up into everlasting life. (John 4:14)

The Savior explained the source of this well of water within us:

> Jesus stood and cried, saying, If any man thirst, let him come unto me, and drink.
>
> He that believeth on me, as the scripture hath said, *out of his belly shall flow rivers of living water* .
>
> But this spake he of *the Spirit*, which they that believe on him should receive. (John 7:37–39; emphasis added)

The Spirit, the fulness of the Holy Ghost, the spirit of prophecy and revelation, is the source of this well of living water within us. This personal well of living water was further defined by the Lord, through a revelation to the Prophet Joseph Smith:

> But unto him that keepeth my commandments I will give the mysteries of my kingdom, and the same shall be in him a well of living water springing up unto everlasting life. (D&C 63:23)

The location of the source of the well of living water is the Mountain of the House of the Lord for "a fountain shall come forth of the house of the Lord" (Joel 3:18). It is from His house that His living waters will flow like the waters flowing from the aquifers of Mt. Hermon, symbolizing the celestial temple. It is in the temple that we receive a fulness of testimony and knowledge of Jesus Christ, because in the temple we receive a fulness of the Holy Ghost (see D&C 109:15).

The Scriptural Temple

As we are taught by the Holy Ghost and covenant in the fulness of the Melchizedek Priesthood through temple ordinances, we learn of the mysteries (the spiritually revealed truths) of God's celestial kingdom. This knowledge, this great view, becomes in us a well of living water that gushes forth quenching our thirst for eternal life. It then gushes forth, out of our bellies, as our "bowels shall be a fountain of truth" (see D&C 85:7).

We will become fountains of truth when we "feast upon the words of Christ" (2 Nephi 32:3) by eating the sweet scriptures (see Ezekiel 2:3) and drinking from the deep well of the Lord in Mount Zion. Then we will become mouths of righteousness to quench the thirst of our fellow men from the well of life within us, since "the mouth of a righteous man is a well of life" (Proverbs 11:10). For "counsel in the heart of man [is like] deep water; [and] a man of understanding will draw it out" (Proverbs 20:5).

On a wall of a hospital in which I worked are framed the following words of Tennyson:

> More things are wrought by prayer than the world dreams of.
> Wherefore, let thy voice rise like a fountain night and day.[3]

Not only should we testify eternal words to our fellow men but our bowels should be a fountain of prayer for them. This is especially true for our enemies (see Matthew 5:44) and those who know not God (see Alma 6:6). Deitrich Bonhoffer said by praying for our enemies we vicariously edify them with love:

> For if we pray for them, we are taking their distress and poverty, their guilt and perdition upon ourselves, and pleading to God for them. We are doing vicariously for them what they cannot do for themselves.[4]

Mount Zion Has the Fountain of Truth

Isaiah's vivid description of the righteousness of the Millennial Era seems to center at the temple: "They shall not hurt nor destroy in all my holy mountain; for the earth shall be full of the knowledge of the Lord, as the waters cover the sea" (Isaiah 11:9; 2 Nephi 30:15).

As we wonder how waters can cover a sea, the superlative nature of this Millennial righteousness is perhaps expressed metaphorically.

It is from the temple, the holy mountain, that the knowledge of the Lord will flow. This knowledge will cover the earth with truth and salvation during the Millennium as water covered the earth during the Great Flood. It is from the temple that we draw living water from the well of salvation because there we learn of the truths of eternal life that gush forth from the One Who Saves. When we understand this truth we understand what Isaiah meant when he declared, "Therefore with joy shall ye draw water out of the wells of salvation" (Isaiah 12:3).

A traditional Irish melody, entitled "Take Time to be Holy," describes the well of salvation. To be holy is to be with and to emulate the Savior. It is to be led to His "fountains of love":

> Take time to be holy, speak oft with thy Lord;
>> Abide in Him always, And feed on His word,
>> Make friends of God's children, Help those who are weak,
>> Forgetting in nothing His blessing to seek.
>> Take time to be holy. The world rushes on;
>> Spend much time in secret with Jesus alone;
>> By looking to Jesus, Like Him thou shalt be;
>> Thy friends in thy conduct His likeness shall see.
>> Take time to by holy. Let Him be thy guide,
>> And run not before Him, whatever betide;
>> In joy or in sorrow, still follow thy Lord,
>> And looking to Jesus, still trust in his word.
>> Take time to be holy. Be calm in thy soul,
>> Each thought and each motive beneath His control;
>> Thus led by His Spirit to fountains of love,
>> Thou soon shall be fitted for service above.
>> Thou soon shall be fitted for service above.[5]

Temples are "fountains of waters" made by God (see D&C 133:39). They are a fountain of truth from the well of salvation. The water of the temple well is the mysteries of God in the truth of things as they really are, the covenants of eternal life, and the power of the Atonement. It is in sum, the testimony of Jesus Christ.

The well of salvation is a fountain of love with "living" water because by the love of God, the Atonement, we can become forever "living." *Therefore, the well of salvation is the real fountain of youth because by drinking its spiritual water we obtain eternal lives.* In contrast to the fountain of truth in a true messenger (see D&C 85:7), false prophets are called a "bitter fountain" (Moroni 7:11) and "wells without water" (see 2 Peter 2:1, 17–18). But "a fountain . . . wherein there is plenty of water, shall be clean [holy and true]" (Leviticus 11:36).

A favorite movie of mine, *Jean de Florette,* tells the tragedy of greed from the "bitter fountain" of a man named Sobeyrand. Its incredible sequel, *Manon of the Spring,* exposes Sobeyrand whose greed for a water source results in a "well without water." Then we learn that his greed unknowingly caused the death of his own son, Jean de Florette, in the first movie. The remarkable story in *Jean de Florette* and *Manon of the Spring* vividly portray man's ability to destroy his greatest possessions out of pride and greed.

Charity, the ability to edify others out of love and sacrifice, could have been the source of a happy ending to this story. If the invitation of Jacob to come to the wells of salvation and drink freely were the attitude of Sobeyrand and his neighbors, then all would have found a well of salvation and none would have perished:

> Come, my brethren, every one that thirsteth, come ye to the waters ; and he that hath no money, come buy and eat; yea, come buy wine and milk without money and without price.
>
> Wherefore, do not spend money for that which is of no worth, nor your labor for that which cannot satisfy. Hearken diligently unto me, and remember the words which I have spoken; and come unto the Holy One of Israel, and feast upon that which perisheth not, neither can be corrupted, and let your soul delight in fatness. (2 Nephi 9:50–51; see also D&C 10:66)

"The fountain of the water of life" from the well of salvation is free for all who are "athirst" (see Revelation 21:6). The water from this well will eventually provide "a feast of fat things" through the laws of consecration so that poverty and inequality will be abolished (see D&C 58:8; Isaiah 25:6). This feast is the feast of the fruit of the tree of life, the bread and waters of life, which can be enjoyed freely (see Alma 5:34).

The well of salvation is a well that does not deplete nor depend on another source. It fills the meek and lowly heart that has faith and hope in Christ with His virtues of charity (see Moroni 7:43–44). It is the fountain of all righteousness because with faith and hope in our Savior, we desire to attain all His righteousness.

> And I will show unto them that faith, hope and charity bringeth unto me *the fountain of all righteousness*. (Ether 12:28; emphasis added)

Faith, hope, and charity summarily describe our climb to the summit of Mount Zion through temple worship. There with eternal lives we will find the fountain of all righteousness that will forever quench our thirst for righteousness and holiness.

The Healing Water Flowing from the Well of Salvation

The water of the well of salvation is not contained by its walls. The power and blessings of the temple are not confined by its walls. King Benjamin had to build a tower outside the temple to accommodate those gathered to hear him (see Mosiah 2:7).

Ezekiel had a marvelous vision of water flowing from a future temple built on Mount Moriah. It is reminiscent of the river flowing from the Garden of Eden to the four corners of the earth, and the knowledge of the Lord flowing from the millennial temple covering the earth like a sea. This vision teaches us of the cleansing and healing power of the water of the well of salvation. Even as it made the Judean desert flourish and healed the waters of the Dead Sea, His water must flow through our everyday lives to heal us and make us grow:

> Afterward he brought me again unto the door of the house; and, behold, *waters issued out from under the threshold of the house* eastward. . . . At the banks of the river were very many trees on the one side and on the other.
>
> These waters issue out toward the east country, and go down into the desert, and go into the sea: which being brought forth into the sea, *the waters shall be healed*. . . . And there shall be a very great multitude of fish, and *every thing shall live wither the river cometh*. (Ezekiel 47:1, 79; emphasis added; see also Joel 3:18)

Having traveled the route from the temple mount eastward through the barren Judean hills to the Dead Sea, I picture the imagery in Ezekiel's vision to be miraculous. I can see his vision literally fulfilled as Joseph Smith prophesied.[6] The message for me in this vision is that wherever the waters of salvation flow from the well of salvation (the temple), there is healing and growth.[7] The power of the temple prevents and cures the weaknesses and hurts of our lives and makes us grow spiritually.

The image of the "many trees" on both sides of the river is a vivid image in an arid geographic setting. The tallest, greenest trees grow near the riverbank because the river brings goodly land to the banks. Likewise, by being "planted in the house of the Lord" (Psalm 92:13), we are planted where a seed (the word of God and posterity raised up unto the Lord) can be nourished in mind and heart with water from the wells of salvation. There we can become "as plants of renown, and as watchmen upon her walls" (D&C 124:61). Then we "shall be like a tree planted by the rivers of water" (see Psalm 1:13). If we learn to worship in the temple we shall become "a very fruitful tree which is planted in "the goodly land" (D&C 99:7) of Zion by a pure stream that [yields] much precious fruit" (see D&C 97:9). As Alma taught, we can grow a tree of life within us (see Alma 32:23) producing a most delicious fruit even in this spiritually arid world. If we grow this tree within us, we will be "planted in the land of [our] inheritance" (D&C 55:5) which is to be "planted in the land of Zion . . . with [our] families" (D&C 57:14; see also D&C 58:13).

It takes some time before the fruit of a tree matures and is sweetened to holiness (see Leviticus 19:23). Therefore, before we can be planted in the goodly land of the temple as "goodly trees" (Leviticus 23:40) we must mature to obtain a temple recommend. Then we must practice temple worship to become holy and "yield unto [us] the increase thereof" (see Leviticus 19:24–25) by growing a tree of life and its fruit within us.

Alma, the converted priest of King Noah, and his followers sought refuge in a natural temple since the temple of the city of Lehi-Nephi was defiled and occupied by wicked men (see Mosiah 11:10–12). This natural temple was described as having "a fountain of pure water" and a "thicket of small trees" (Mosiah 18:5).

There are interesting similarities between the events at this natural temple and the events that occurred at the temple in Zarahemla during and after King Benjamin's speech. These include the appointing of priests to teach the people (Mosiah 6:3, compare Mosiah 18:18), teachings about Christ's Atonement and His gospel (Mosiah 3:15, 17, compare Mosiah 18:7, 19–20), covenants with the Lord (Mosiah 5:5 compare Mosiah 18:10), a desire for and a change of heart by the Spirit of God (Mosiah 4:2; 5:2 compare Mosiah 18:11–12), becoming the children of God (Mosiah 5:7 compare Mosiah 18:22), being called by the name of Christ (Mosiah 5:8 compare Mosiah 18:17), growth in the knowledge of God (Mosiah 4:12; 5:34 compare Mosiah 18:18, 26), and an apparent unity of the people (Mosiah 6:1; 7:1 compare Mosiah 18:21, 29).

The mighty change that occurred to the 204 souls at the waters and forest of Mormon was a temple event described in their fondness of this holy place as we would describe the temples that we love:

> And now it came to pass that all this was done in Mormon, . . . yea, the place of Mormon, the waters of Mormon, the forest of Mormon, how beautiful are they to the eyes of them who there come to the knowledge of their Redeemer; yea, and how blessed are they, for they shall sing to his praise forever. (Mosiah 18:30)

The temple image in mortality of the association of nourishing water and a growth of trees is a reflection of this association in the celestial realm:

> And he shewed me *a pure river of water of life*, clear as crystal, proceeding out of the throne of God and of the Lamb.
>
> In the midst of the street of it, and on either side of the river, was there *the tree of life*, which bare twelve manner of fruits, and yielded her fruit every month: and the leaves of the tree were for the healing of the nations. (Revelation 22:12; emphasis added)

The healing water of life (knowledge of God's power and love) and the healing leaves of the tree of life (the power of the Atonement) are found in earthly temples. They cast a reflection of the ultimate healing of our suffering and weaknesses, which will occur in the celestial temple where "The Lamb . . . shall feed them, and shall lead them unto living fountains of waters" (see Revelation 7:14–17).

Because of this ultimate healing promise of the temple, we should not be so concerned with tribulation surrounding us, hoping, like the Jews, for the overthrow of our oppressors. Rather, we should be more concerned about the faults within us that can be healed by water from the well of salvation. Through temple ordinances and covenants we drink pure, living water from the well of salvation. This water is the power of an infinite Atonement and the pureness of Christ. With this pure water we become "the trees of righteousness, the planted of the Lord" (see Isaiah 61:3). Like the close association of the greenest trees and rivers, in the temple we can grow a tree of life within us alongside a stream of living water.

To Be Healed: Flowing to the Well of Salvation

In imagery reverse to that of healing waters flowing from the temple, Lehi exhorted his son Laman to flow to the temple:

> And when my father saw that the waters of the river emptied into the fountain of the Red Sea, he spake unto Laman, saying: O that thou mightest be like unto this river, continually running into the fountain of all righteousness. (1 Nephi 2:9)

It is interesting that Lehi saw this same image of a river running to the "fountain of living waters" (1 Nephi 11:25) in his tree of life vision:

> And as I cast my eyes round about, that perhaps I might discover my family also, I beheld a river of water and it ran along, and it was near the tree of which I was partaking the fruit. (1 Nephi 8:13)

This river of water was accompanied by a "rod of iron" and a "strait and narrow path" which also led to the tree of life (see 1 Nephi 8:19–20).

In Nephi's vision and interpretation of his father's dream, the fountain of living waters was contrasted to a fountain of filthy water (see 1 Nephi 11:25; 12:16). There is a contrast between a river of filthy water that flows into a fountain of filthy water representing the depths of hell and a river of living water flowing into a fountain of living water representing the love of God. It is not clear in Lehi's dream how many rivers are represented. Perhaps there is one river that divides. If it divides, this occurs when we choose between the forbidden fruit and the fruit of the tree of life.

The river of living water represents the Atonement. Without the Atonement, holding the iron rod and walking the strait and narrow path would not get us to the tree of life. The healing and cleansing water of the Atonement is the only water that can bypass the flaming sword that guards the tree of life. This flaming sword as a "flaming fire" represents the justice of God (see 1 Nephi 15:30). Therefore, the Prophet Zenos said: "Thou hast turned away thy judgments because of thy Son" (Alma 33:13).

Only the Atonement extinguishes or appeases the demands of justice:

> And now the plan of mercy could not be brought about except an *atonement* should be made; therefore God himself atoneth for the sins of the world, to bring about the plan of mercy, *to appease the demands of justice*, that God might be a perfect, just God, and a merciful God also. (Alma 42:15; emphasis added)

Only the Atonement of Christ can open the way that we might fully partake of the fruit of the tree of life.

The full effect of the Atonement can be realized in our lives if we take hold of the rod of iron in following true messengers and walk the strait and narrow path in obeying the Lord's covenants. These acts of holding fast to the word and strictly following the path make the difference between filthy and living water in our lives. They distinguish the difference between good and evil in our lives as a consequence of partaking of the fruit of the tree of knowledge of good and evil. If we hold to the words of true messengers and are obedient to the covenants we make with the Lord, then His Atonement will wash us clean of all sin with healing and living water (see Ezekiel 36:25).

Just as waves roll from and recede back to the ocean, the river of living water comes from and leads to the fountain of living water and all righteousness in God's temple. When we are healed and grow because of living water from the temple, tasting the sweetness of the love of God, we want to become rivers of living water continually "running" to the temple. If like the five foolish virgins we do not fill our water bottle with some living water from the Spirit before climbing Mount Zion and replenish it during the climb, we will thirst and wither in the climb. It is in the temple that the living water within us from the spirit of prophecy and revelation is renewed.

Wells of Salvation from Heaven and Earth

Those doing and receiving the great missionary work in the world of spirits have great interest in temple activity on earth because redemption of the dead as well as the living comes through temple ordinances (see D&C 138:58). These may be the unseen sentinels and beings mentioned by Elder Featherstone. There are many reports, some personal and sacred, which verify the reality of these beings.

A good friend of mine shared a special experience with me when an ancestor spent a weekend with him in close communion because my friend had started to do temple work for hundreds of his Moravian ancestors. Promises of help in my friend's personal life came from this visitor of a higher realm as my friend promised to continue the temple work. These angelic visitors have great interest in our temple activity because of their salvation and our salvation:

> For we without them cannot be made perfect, neither can they without us be made perfect. Neither can they nor we be made perfect without those who have died in the Gospel also; for it is necessary . . . that a whole and complete and perfect union, and welding together of dispensations . . . the dispensation of the fulness of times. (D&C 128:18)

Concerning the work of "those who have died in the Gospel," Brigham Young said:

> The names of those who have received the Gospel in the spirit will be revealed by the angels of God and the spirits of just men made perfect; also the place of their birth, the age in which they lived, and everything regarding them that is necessary to be recorded on earth, and they will then be saved so as to find admittance into the presence of God.[8]

Commenting on this statement, President Joseph Fielding Smith said:

> President Brigham Young has said that during the Millennium those on the other side will work hand in hand with those in mortality and will furnish the names of the dead which we are unable to obtain through our research . . . I fully believe that many among the dead, those who are worthy, are even now engaged in compiling records

and arranging information, if it has not already been done, for this very purpose.[9]

On both sides of the veil, this temple work of a "complete and perfect union" of all dispensations and generations is now occurring in this premillennial dispensation of the fulness of times. From Paul's statement "that they without us should not be made perfect" (see Hebrews 11:40), in the meridian dispensation after the resurrection of the Savior, this great work began again on earth. It will continue throughout the Millennium to its completion.

The Shepherds of Mount Zion Drink from the Well of Salvation

In my Church callings, I had the opportunity to prepare newly called missionaries for their own temple endowment. In this capacity, I told these new elders that an important preparation for the mission field is going to the temple. There they will receive a special blessing of power and protection from the Lord. It is like filling their spiritual bowels with the protecting and healing water from the well of salvation before they go into the world as the Lord's shepherds:

> That thy servants may go forth from this house armed with thy power, and that thy name may be upon them, and thy glory be round about them, and thine angels have charge over them;
>
> And from this place they may bear exceedingly great and glorious tidings, in truth, unto the ends of the earth, that they may know that this is thy work, and that thou hast put forth they hand, to fulfil that which thou hast spoken by the mouths of the prophets, concerning the last days. (D&C 109:22–23; see also 1 Nephi 14:14)

In the temple, these new shepherds of the Lord learn that they will be taught from on high as true messengers of the true message:

> Again I say, hearken ye elders of my church, whom I have appointed: Ye are not sent forth to be taught, but to teach the children of men the things which I have put into your hands by the power of my Spirit;
>
> And ye are to be taught from on high. Sanctify yourselves and ye shall be endowed with power, that ye may give even as I have spoken. (D&C 43:15–16)

Then the Lord completed the blessing with a promise of companionship and protection:

> And whoso receiveth you, there I will be also, for I will go before your face. I will be on your right hand and on your left, and my spirit shall be in your hearts, and mine angels round about you, to bear you up. (D&C 84:88)

When missionaries replace fear of men with faith in the Lord this blessing is fulfilled (see D&C 3:78). The Lord commanded those who carry His gospel to the world to become His friends even as He becomes their most important companion (see D&C 84:77). They are His friends when they faithfully carry His testimony with the spirit of prophecy and revelation. Then, "ye are they whom my Father hath given me; ye are my friends" (D&C 84:63).

I had the great privilege to travel to Poland when my daughter Lys-An finished her mission. When I passed the border control and cleared customs in Warsaw, I walked between two packed columns of waiting Poles. At the end of this walk was an angel named Lys-An. After we embraced, I stepped back and looked at her from head to foot. On her feet were the most pathetic shoes I had ever seen. It was as though she had yielded to the ubiquitous European cobblestones, and latched two of them about her feet. All the dirt and dust of 16 months in Poland had collected upon them. Then I wept as I recalled scriptures about beautiful feet:

> How beautiful upon the mountains are the feet of him that bringeth good tidings, that publisheth peace; that bringeth good tidings of good, that publisheth salvation; that saith unto Zion, Thy God reigneth! (Isaiah 52:7; see also Romans 10:14–15; Mosiah 15:14; D&C 128:19)

> And O how beautiful upon the mountains were their feet!
> And again, how beautiful upon the mountains are the feet of those that are still publishing peace!
> And behold, I say unto you, this is not all. For O how beautiful upon the mountains are the feet of him that bringeth good tidings, that is the founder of peace, yea, even the Lord, who has redeemed his people; yea, him who has granted salvation unto his people. (Mosiah 15:15–16, 18)

I then understood that feet of true messengers are beautiful not because of the shoes they wear but because their feet carry the testimony of Jesus Christ. It is the spirit of prophecy and revelation within true messengers that makes them beautiful. This is why my missionary daughter was beautiful beyond her natural beauty. It was witnessed by her well-worn shoes covering feet that carried the testimony of Jesus Christ and brought "glad tidings of good things" (Romans 10:15) to the Polish people.

The testimony of Jesus Christ is the living water of salvation that will gush forth from us as we become true messengers of the Lord. This is the glorious calling of my young missionary friends who were about to receive their temple endowment and drink from the well of salvation. For out of their bellies "shall flow rivers of living water." That is to say "the Spirit" (see John 7:38–39), the spirit of prophecy and revelation. These beautiful missionaries were about to have well worn but beautiful feet that will carry the testimony of Jesus Christ:

> And again, how beautiful upon the mountains are the feet of those who shall hereafter publish peace, yea from this time henceforth and forever! (Mosiah 15:17)

When full-time missionaries are released, the full-time nature of this blessing is released. However, some of the best missionary work a returned missionary can do, maintaining the spirit of this blessing, is to return to temple worship and do the work needed in the world of spirits. In doing this worship and work, they refill their spiritual bowels with the living waters of the spirit of prophecy and revelation. President Kimball extended the missionary calling when he said:

> I feel the same sense of urgency about temple work for the dead as I do about missionary work for the living, since they are basically one and the same.[10]

Whether we are returned missionaries or not, regardless of where we live or what we do, the blessings, protection, and power of the temple can be ours if we learn to climb Mount Zion by worshiping in the temple. There, in drinking from the well of salvation, the Lord declares, "blessed are they whose feet stand upon the land of Zion, who have obeyed my gospel" (D&C 59:3) in climbing Mount Zion.

The Scriptural Temple

In the temple we covenant to build the kingdom of God on earth as shepherds who lead His sheep to the well of salvation. Endowed members who keep this covenant are the real missionary force of the Church. Therefore, a full-time missionary calling extends well beyond two years. It is a permanent calling through the temple covenant as it was with Moses:

> And in very deed for this cause have I raised thee up, for to shew in thee my power; and that my name may be declared throughout all the earth. (Exodus 9:16)

The Distilling Dews of Mount Zion

We drink of the water of the wells of salvation as the water of the firmament comes to the land of Israel. For a short season it comes in great bursts of rain, and then gushes forth from dry ground. For the rest of the year it distills upon the land as dew. In the temple, sometimes spiritual truths will gush forth to our understanding. More often, keeping pace with our growing up, these truths will slowly distill upon us like "the dew that descended upon the mountains [temples] of Zion" (see Psalm 133:3).

Standing on the summit of Mount Carmel, overlooking the great view of the fertile Jezreel Valley below and the misty Mediterranean to the west, I read a scripture that refers to this sacred natural temple with imagery of the distilling dews of eternal life:

> Now, what do we hear in the gospel which we have received? . . . A voice of gladness for the living and the dead; glad tidings of great joy. How beautiful upon the mountains are the feet of those that bring glad tidings of good things, and that say unto Zion: Behold, thy God reigneth! As the dews of Carmel, so shall the knowledge of God descend upon them! (D&C 128:19)

What distills upon us in the temple, as we come to understand the holy virtues of the endowment, is the "doctrine of the priesthood" which is the endowment of the quality of charity:

> Let thy bowels also be full of charity towards all men, and to the household of faith, and let virtue garnish thy thoughts unceasingly; then shall thy confidence wax strong in the presence of God; and the

doctrine of the priesthood shall distil upon thy soul as the dews from heaven. (D&C 121:45; see also verse 46)

Notice in these verses, that the virtue of charity, the great doctrine of the fulness of the priesthood, leads to constant companionship of the Holy Ghost and confidence in the presence of God. This is the great and last promise of the temple.

The Power of the Lamb: A River of Love

In the temple, whether missionary or regular Church member, we continue to be taught from on high and endowed with power. This "power of the Lamb of God, descending upon the saints" in the dispensation of the fulness of times was foreseen by the prophet Nephi:

> And it came to pass that I, Nephi, beheld the power of the Lamb of God, that it descended upon the saints of the church of the Lamb, and upon the covenant people of the Lord, who were scattered upon all the face of the earth; and they were armed with righteousness and with the power of God in great glory. (1 Nephi 14:14)

As we drink from the well of salvation in the temple and are healed by its living water flowing into our lives, our parched minds and hearts become refreshed with the words and blessings of the fulness of the gospel. This is why Peter, foretelling our dispensation, said:

> Repent ye therefore, and be converted, that your sins may be blotted out, when the times of refreshing shall come from the presence of the Lord. (Acts 3:19)

In his book *House of Glory*, Michael Wilcox described the refreshing river of the temple:

> Latter-day temples are the source of a powerful, deeply refreshing river. It is a river of peace, revelation, truth, light and priesthood power. But above all else, it is a river of love.[11]

As we flow with this river of love, "how long can rolling waters remain impure?" (D&C 121:33). The power of the Lamb of God that distills upon and flows into us from the wells and dews of Mount Zion is the power of the Savior's love. This is the power that will sustain us as we ascend to the summit.

Stand in Holy Places: Safety in Ascending Mount Zion

*C*uriously *in* the midst of the Missouri persecution, the Lord commanded the Saints to build a temple. The Lord explained the necessity of this commandment:

Verily I say unto you, that it is my will that a house should be built unto me in the land of Zion, like unto the pattern which I have given you.

Yea, let it be built speedily, by the tithing of my people.

Behold, this is the tithing and sacrifice which I, the Lord, require at their hands, that there may be a house built unto me for the salvation of Zion.

And, now, behold, if Zion do these things she shall prosper, and spread herself and become very glorious, very great, and very terrible. (D&C 97:10–12, 18)

It seems evident that the fate of the Saints in Missouri would have been different had they heeded this commandment. It is as though the Lord was using the same reasoning found in the movie *Field of Dreams*: build it (the temple) and I (the Lord) will come, for "in mount Zion . . . shall be deliverance" (Joel 2:32).

"Verily I say unto you, it is my will that you should build a house. If you keep my commandments you shall have power to build it" (D&C 95:12). Then God will come with His priesthood power when it is built (see D&C 97:15–16; 103:15; 105:11–12).

The fate of the Northern Kingdom which was carried away by Assyria in the fourth year of King Hezekiah would have been different had they heeded the invitation of King Hezekiah to go to the temple and "enter into his sanctuary" (see 2 Chronicles 30:8). When the Assyrian army besieged the Southern Kingdom, the people of Jerusalem renewed their worship of the Lord. Hezekiah went into the House of the Lord and prayed for his people. The Lord responded with the miraculous decimation of the Assyrian army (see 2 Kings 19:32–36).

Later, the Samaritans, a remnant of the Northern house of Israel mixed with other nations, opposed the building of the temple of Zerubbabel. The Lord reminded the Jews returning from Babylon that if they would "consider from this day" and compare, they would see that a temple of the Lord protects and blesses their lives (see Haggai 2:15–19).

The Lord's message to the Missouri Saints and the Israelites of the northern and southern kingdoms was that faith in building a temple and worshiping in the temple would be a great protection to them. This protection was dramatically seen in the life of Joash in order to preserve the lineage of King David on the throne of Judah. The high priest Jehoiada hid Joash in the house of the Lord for six years to protect him from destruction by Athaliah (see 2 Kings 11). The Lord is sending us, collectively and personally, the same message of temple protection today:[1]

> Behold it is my will, that all they who call on my name, and worship me according to mine everlasting Gospel, should gather together and *stand in holy places.* (D&C 101:22; see also 2 Chronicles 35:5)

> Wherefore, stand ye in holy places, and be not moved, until the day of the Lord come. (D&C 87:8)

> When you, therefore, shall see the abomination of desolation, spoken of by Daniel the prophet, concerning the destruction of

Jerusalem, then you shall stand in the holy place; whoso readeth let him understand.

And again shall the abomination of desolation, spoken of by Daniel the prophet, be fulfilled. (Joseph Smith—Matthew 1:12, 32)

The pattern set in the Book of Mormon to "be gathered together in their place" (Alma 26:6) or "unto one place" (3 Nephi 3:13, 25) "in one body" (Mormon 2:7), with the "more righteous" spared yet called to return to Christ "that [He] might heal [them]" (see 3 Nephi 9:13), is a harbinger of the "gathering of mine elect" in preparation for the Second Coming of Christ (see D&C 29:7–8) and the Judgment. Those who receive the fulness of Christ "shall be gathered unto me in time and eternity" (D&C 39:22).

It was, is, and will be at the temple (see 3 Nephi 11:1; D&C 49:25; 84:24) "that my covenant people may be gathered in one in that day when I shall come to my temple. And I do this for the salvation of my people" (D&C 42:36). Therefore, in preparation for Christ's final healing we must "watch steadfastly for that day" (3 Nephi 1:8) and "save [ourselves]" by going "out from among the wicked" (D&C 38:42) and "stand in holy places."

Allusions to future conspiracies and calamities in the United States are found in the revelation to the Prophet Joseph Smith concerning the move from New York to Ohio. The purpose for this move was to gather the Saints to the temple where they would be protected because "ye know not the hearts of men in your own land." To "go to the Ohio" today, is synonymous with "gathering unto me a righteous people" at the temple to be "endowed with power from on high" to protect them from the "power of the enemy" (see D&C 38:13, 28–32) and "from wrath when it shall be poured out without mixture upon the whole earth" (see D&C 115:6). Are not the Saints today and will they not continue to "gather themselves together to the temple" (Mosiah 7:17) to hear the words of deliverance such as those given by King Benjamin and King Limhi (see Mosiah 7:18–33)? In a letter to the Missouri Saints, Joseph Smith reinforced the Lord's commandment to go to "holy places" for deliverance:

Hold fast that which you have received. Trust in God. Consider Elijah when he prayed for rain. Go often to your holy places and look for a cloud of light to appear to your help.[2]

Isaiah has told us what these holy places are and why we should stand in them and for them "and be not moved" (see D&C 45:32; 87:8):

> And the Lord will create upon every dwelling place of Mount Zion, and upon her assemblies, a cloud and smoke by day, and the shining of a flaming fire by night; for upon all the glory shall be a defense.
>
> And there shall be a tabernacle for a shadow in the daytime from the heat, and for a place of refuge, and for a covert from storm and from rain. (Isaiah 4:5–6)

The holy places are our homes (dwelling places), our churches (assemblies), and our temples (tabernacle). Perhaps these holy places are equivalent to temples, sanctuaries, and synagogues mentioned in the Book of Mormon (see Alma 16:13). Now and more in the future, "gathering together upon the land of Zion," upon her stakes, and upon Mount Zion may be for a defense, and for a refuge from the storm, and from wrath when it shall "be poured out without mixture upon the whole earth" (D&C 115:6). Collectively, Zion is these holy places for with pure hearts, "surely Zion shall dwell in safety forever" (Moses 7:20).

Holy places are "heavenly places" as stated by the Apostle Paul. They are places where "all spiritual blessings" (Ephesians 1:3) are given, where we are "raised up together" and "sit together" (Ephesians 2:6), and where "the manifold wisdom of God" (Ephesians 3:10) is revealed. A holy place is also within us as we become holy like a temple (see Alma 34:36) and "[walk] in holiness before the Lord" (Moses 5:26). To the Jew, the place where he stands is holy if he is righteous (see D&C 115:7; 124:44) because "in the fear of the Lord is strong confidence: and His children shall have a place of refuge" (Proverbs 14:26). Therefore, we must learn to "[dwell] in tabernacles" (see Hebrews 11:9) like Abraham, Isaac, and Jacob while sojourning to the promised land. From all of these holy places can flow living waters of growth and healing if we keep them holy and righteous like a temple. Therefore, they can be a defense, a refuge, and a covert against the doctrines of men and the temptations of Satan for "them that worship therein" (see Revelation 11:1).

The Scriptural Temple

In a special temple address, Elder Vaughn Featherstone expressed the power and protection of the temple:

> Just as this is the dispensation of the fulness of times, so it is also the dispensation of the fulness of evil.
>
> As the evil night darkens upon this generation, we must come to the temple for light and safety. In our temples we find quiet, sacred havens where the storm cannot penetrate to us. There are hosts of unseen sentinels watching over and guarding our temples. Angels attend every door. . . .
>
> Before the Savior comes the world will darken. There will come a period of time when even the elect will lose hope if they do not come to the temples. . . .
>
> There will be greater hosts of unseen beings in the temple. Prophets of old as well as those in this dispensation will visit the temples. Those who attend will feel their strength and feel their companionship. . . .
>
> The Savior will come and will honor his people. Those who are spared and prepared will be a temple loving people. They will know Him. They will cry out "blessed be the name of him that cometh in the name of the Lord, thou art my God and I will bless thee, thou art my God and I will exalt thee." . . .
>
> Come, come, oh come up to the temples of the Lord and abide in His presence.[3]

The scriptural text for a well known painting by Greg Olsen of Christ overlooking the Jerusalem Temple Mount is "O Jerusalem, Jerusalem, . . . how often would I have gathered thy children together, even as a hen gathereth her chickens under her wings, and ye would not" (Matthew 23:37). Psalm 61:4 suggests that the temple is the wings: "I will abide in they tabernacle for ever: I will trust in the covert of thy wings." In time of trial the song in our hearts should be as the hymn "Guide Us, O thou Great Jehovah" says: "When thy judgments spread destruction, Keep us safe on Zion's hill."[4]

Protection from the Power of Satan while Ascending Mount Zion

A dramatic scene from the endowment is a warning from Satan. It is a warning of bad news but hidden in the bad news is good news.

The good news is that we are protected from the power of Satan if we will worship in the temple and keep temple covenants. Satan knows the power of temple protection as evidenced by his mimic in protecting the Gadianton robbers as they would "retreat back into the mountains and into the wilderness and secret places" (Helaman 11:25). To put on the robes of righteousness is to put on the whole protecting armor of righteousness (see 2 Nephi 1:23) in order to "put on thy strength" (Isaiah 52:1) through the fulness of priesthood power. Elder John A. Widtsoe expressed the protective power of the temple with the following words: "Men grow mighty under the results of temple service; women grow strong under it; the community increases in power; until the devil has less influence than he ever had before."[5]

One reason King David had the Ark of God moved to Jerusalem was because of its power to bless the lives of those where it resided (see 2 Samuel 6:12). The arc of fire from heaven, as a divine manifestation upon the altar that David built on Mount Moriah to stay the three days of pestilence (see 1 Chronicles 21:26), caused him to declare: "This is the house of the Lord God" (1 Chronicles 22:1). In this future temple of Solomon, the Ark of the Covenant finally came to rest. The power of the Ark of the Covenant is the arc of power and protection from God to those who keep His covenants in the His holy house.

The protection of the Lord as an arc of power was also demonstrated when David sought refuge with the Prophet Samuel in his school of the prophets at Naioth. This was a holy sanctuary because the power of the Lord through the spirit of prophecy was there to protect the righteous. Seeking to kill David, King Saul was overcome by this power when he came to the holy sanctuary (see 1 Samuel 19:18–24). This is in ironic contrast to the time that he righteously held the power to prophesy (see 1 Samuel 10:11). The Lord promises to those who have made "a covenant of peace" in His sanctuary (see Ezekiel 34:25; see also Ezekiel 37:26) "and the places round about [His] hill a blessing" even "showers of blessing" (see Ezekiel 34:26).

Adam and some of his righteous posterity received a special blessing from the Lord. It was the blessing of having Satan cast out of their lives. This blessing was dramatically demonstrated by Moses when Satan began to tremble, and the earth shook; and Moses received strength, and called upon God, saying: "In the name of the Only Begotten, depart hence, Satan. And it came to pass that Satan cried with a loud voice, with weeping, and wailing, and gnashing of teeth; and he departed hence, even from the presence of Moses, that he beheld him not" (Moses 1:21–22).

Certainly this blessing removes a great barrier in tasting the good in the fruit of the tree of knowledge of good and evil to "judge" (see Moses 1:15, 18) or clearly distinguish between the two and, ultimately, grow a tree of life within us. Perhaps this is why Enoch and his people could so completely live the celestial law. They must have been a temple-loving people because as Enoch, who [stood] upon the hills and the high places" (Moses 6:37), "they were blessed upon the mountains, and upon the high places" (see Moses 7:17). Because of true temple worship today, "Satan shall tremble and Zion shall rejoice upon the hills and flourish" (D&C 35:24; see also D&C 49:25).

The many years of peace and love experienced by the Nephites after the appearance of the Savior was possibly the result of having Satan cast out. This is implied in the Savior's sermon on the temple mount when He said: "He that hath the spirit of contention . . . is of the devil. Behold . . . this is my doctrine that such things should by done away" (see 3 Nephi 11:29–30). If the spirit of contention is done away in our lives then Satan, the source of that spirit, is also removed.

To receive this blessing of having Satan removed from our lives starts with obedience to the Lord and His prophets as the Savior emphasized to the Nephites (see 3 Nephi 23:5). We must be actively obedient in casting Satan out of our lives, especially in our own homes, by not permitting Satan or any of his agents to "creep into [our] houses" (2 Timothy 3:6). We must "resist the Devil, and he will flee from [us]" (James 4:7) because the Lord will "rebuke the devourer" (Malachi 3:11) and "disperse the powers of darkness from before [us]" (see D&C 21:56) if we keep His commandments: "He that is begotten of God keepeth himself, and that wicked one toucheth him not" (1 John 5:18). One important daily practice of "keeping" ourselves is to obey the commandment to "pray always lest that wicked one have power in you and remove you out of your place" (D&C 93:49). We may have to pray mightily to have Satan removed from our lives but the Lord will hear our prayers if we stand in holy places. Notice that Moses commanded Satan to leave three times (see Moses 1:16, 18, 20) before he finally cast Satan out by the power of God in the name of the Only Begotten (see Moses 1:21–22).

One of the great endowment blessings taught in the temple is that man can receive and exercise God's power if he is authorized to do so under the Holy Order of the Son of God. This blessing specifically refers to the power that will cast Satan out. The blessing or power to cast out Satan may ultimately be a temple blessing or endowment as implied by the sanctifying power of the Priesthood (see Exodus 28:41) given to the meridian apostles (see John 17:17) to "keep them from evil" (John 17:15). Evil in this verse is more correctly translated as "the Evil One."[6]

The Savior's great message in His temple sermon at Galilee and Bountiful was the message of the great commandment: to love perfectly even with love of enemies. The power of love is the power that removes Satan from our lives. Our expression of love to God is obedience to Him and His messengers (see John 14:15). This expression of love through obedience leads to perfection of our love (see 1 John 2:5; 4:12). The process of perfecting our love brings the mighty change of heart and even a change in our physical nature being "sanctified in the flesh" (3 Nephi 28:39) as were the Nephite disciples. Then we will live in continual righteousness and Satan will have no influence upon us (see 1 Nephi 22:26; 3 Nephi 28:39).

If we are to prepare for the redemption of Zion, we must acquire pure hearts and live the celestial law of perfect love as did Enoch's Zion. They grew up in the Lord "upon the high places," having Satan cast out of their lives. So it is with us today:

> But before the great day of the Lord shall come . . . Zion shall flourish upon the hills and rejoice upon the mountains , and shall be assembled together unto the place which I have appointed. (D&C 49:24–25)

Literally, Satan can be cast out of our lives, that we have no more disposition to do evil, if we learn how to love perfectly by drinking from the fountain of all righteousness while standing in holy places and rejoicing upon the temple mountains. If we reject this temple blessing then "inasmuch as [we] are cut off for transgression, [we] cannot escape the buffetings of Satan until the day of redemption" (D&C 104:9). The ascent of Mount Zion is facilitated if we learn to cast Satan out of our lives. Then we are protected from the winds and storms.

> Wherefore, I, Moroni, am commanded to write these things that evil may be done away, and that the time may come that Satan may have no power upon the hearts of the children of men, but that they may be persuaded to do good continually, that they may come unto the fountain of all righteousness and be saved. (Ether 8:26)

The Salt and Light of the Covenant: Preserving the Endowment of Mount Zion

Not far from the city of Krakow in southern Poland is a large salt deposit under the town of Wieliczka. For centuries this salt was mined from deep subterranean caverns. The mining was begun in the fourteenth century under the direction of King Kazimierz the Great. He permitted the miners to take a small, personal portion of salt when they came to the surface. This made the miners wealthy because salt, being an important preservative, was an expensive commodity.

Today the salt mine is a tourist attraction with scenes from Polish history and the history of the mine preserved in salt carved by the miners. The grand carving is an entire cathedral. Even the chandeliers are salt crystals. The walls are carved with scenes from the life of Christ. Past and current use of part of the mine is a sanatorium for respiratory illnesses due to the medicinal effects of the salt.

After visiting this mine I reflected on the purging, preserving, healing, and flavoring qualities of salt. I recalled the scriptural uses of salt and include them in the scriptural temple because the temple purges and preserves, by healing and flavoring then sealing like salt.

Salt was often used in Levitical rituals as a symbol of purging, preserving, healing and flavoring through covenants with the Lord:

> All the heave offerings of the holy things, which the children of Israel offer unto the Lord, have I given thee, and thy sons and thy daughters with thee, by a statute for ever; it is a *covenant of salt* for ever before the Lord unto thee and to thy seed with thee. (Numbers 18:19; emphasis added)

Berith, the Hebrew word for *covenant*, is derived from the word meaning "to eat with salt." As salt softens hard water, in making and keeping covenants with the Lord our hard hearts are purged and softened as it were with salt, to become meek and lowly of heart.

The Abrahamic Covenant: An Everlasting Covenant of Salt

The Abrahamic Covenant, which has been preserved as a covenant between God and those who are obedient to His gospel, as an everlasting covenant (see Genesis 17:7), is a covenant of salt. This covenant has four main parts. The first three are blessings from the Lord. The last part is our obligation in order to receive and preserve the stated blessings.

To remember the parts of this covenant, I use pneumonic "P" words:

- Property (Genesis 13:14–15)
- Posterity (Genesis 22:17)
- Priesthood (Genesis 17:7; Abraham 2:9, 11)
- Proselyte (Genesis 22:18; Abraham 2:9, 11)

I take liberty with the word *proselyte*, using it to reveal a deeper meaning. The word *proselyte* can be considered a composite of three words: Pro-Sel-Light. *Sel* is the French word for "salt," so in my mind, *proselyte* means "for salt and light." The scriptural temple states the obligation of those accepting the "everlasting covenant" to be for salt and light:

> When men are called unto mine everlasting gospel, and covenant with an *everlasting covenant*, they are *accounted* as the *salt of the earth* and the *savor of men*. (D&C 101:39; emphasis added)

In the sermon on the mount, the Savior said:

Ye are the *salt* of the earth. . . .
Ye are the *light* of the world. (Matthew 5:13–14)

Salt only loses its savor when it becomes contaminated by other elements. Therefore, we keep our savor as long as God is our God and we yield our hearts to Him. We who keep the everlasting covenants of the temple are the pure salt that flavors the earth because we preserve through our obedience the everlasting gospel in its purity and fulness. Referring to the importance of covenants that are to be preserved and obeyed and the type of relationship they require, the Savior said: "Have salt in yourselves and have peace one with another" (see Mark 9:50; see also Colossians 4:6).

When we take the everlasting gospel and its everlasting covenants to the world, teaching the love of God, those who feel and accept it savor the sweet flavor of the fruit of the tree of life. Symbolic of sweet fruit surrounding a seed of new life, those who eat the entire fruit will plant a seed within them to grow a new tree of life. This fruit was never meant to be hidden under a bushel. Therefore, we must keep our part of the Abrahamic covenant and let the love of God shed forth (see Romans 5:5) and be savored because we have a covenant of salt and light within us.

Those who hear and feel our testimonies of Christ "as a lamp that burneth" (see Isaiah 62:1), taste the light (see Alma 32:35) and feel the power (see 2 Nephi 33:1) of the Holy Spirit as His witness sheds forth (see Romans 5:5) in their hearts. As the salt and light of the everlasting covenant we are to be like the planets that "give light to each other" (D&C 88:44). In His sermon on the temple mount the Savior directed us to hold up His light to the world. His light is the light of the planets (see D&C 88:7–12).

Therefore, hold up your light that it may shine unto the world. Behold I am the light which ye shall hold up—that which ye have seen me do. (3 Nephi 18:24)

Arise and shine forth, that thy light may be a standard for the nations. (D&C 115:5)

The Scriptural Temple

Christ's Shepherds: The Savor and Saviors of Men

The Lord counseled Joseph Smith, Lyman Wight, and Parley Pratt with the following advice concerning the salvation and redemption of the Saints in Missouri:

> Verily I say unto you, my friends, behold, I will give unto you a revelation and commandment, that you may know how to act in the discharge of your duties concerning the salvation and redemption of your brethren, who have been scattered on the land of Zion.
>
> And by hearkening to observe all the words which I, the Lord their God, shall speak unto them, they shall never cease to prevail until the kingdoms of the world are subdued under my feet, and the earth is given unto the saints, to possess it forever and ever.
>
> For they [the obedient Saints] were set to be a light unto the world, and to be the saviors of men. (D&C 103:1, 7, 9)

While this revelation was directed to a specific need in Missouri, it has general application as we learn our duty concerning the salvation and redemption of our brethren. When we let the love of Christ and His gospel shine from us by sacrificing our own interests to edify others, then we become the savor of men by becoming the saviors of men. "Inasmuch as they are not the saviors of men, they are as salt that has lost its savor (D&C 103:10). Being saviors of men has direct application when we perform the temple saving and exalting ordinances for the dead. "Therefore, blessed are ye if ye continue in my goodness, a light unto the Gentiles, and through this priesthood, a savior unto my people Israel" (D&C 86:11).

During His meridian ministry, the Savior taught the truth about our role in being saviors of men:

> But he that entereth by the door is the shepherd of the sheep.
>
> Verily, verily, I say unto you, I am the door of the sheep.
>
> I am the door: by me if any man enter in, he shall be saved, and shall go in and out, and find pasture.
>
> I am the good shepherd: the good shepherd giveth his life for the sheep. (John 10:2, 7, 9, 11)

In calling us to be saviors of men, Christ is calling us to be shepherds as "[we have] Christ for [our] shepherd" (Mormon 5:17). We

406

need to "take up [our] cross, follow [Him] and feed [His] sheep" (D&C 112:14). The calling to be good "shepherds of Israel" (Ezekiel 34:2) is what Christ desires most of His disciples (see Matthew 9:35–38; John 21:17).

The shepherd stays with the flock. He knows all the sheep by name and loves them. He feeds them by leading them gently to the green pastures of the gospel and finally to "the high mountains of Israel" (see Ezekiel 34:13–14) which means to the temple as their fold. He will "both search [the] sheep and seek them out" (Ezekiel 34:11) and bring the lost sheep back to the fold. Instead of fleeing from wolves he gives his life for the sheep. The "good shepherd" was defined by the Savior as one who ultimately gives his life for the sheep (see John 10:11).

The shepherd leads the sheep with a mighty staff. It is an iron rod, a mighty sword, even the word of God (see Ephesians 6:17). Therefore, a shepherd of Israel is a watchman of Israel called to speak the words and warnings of the Lord (see Ezekiel 3:17). The good shepherd does not stop calling the sheep for, "A shepherd hath called after you and is still calling after you" (Alma 5:37). The word of God protects the sheep from wolves and touches the hearts of the sheep, moving them to righteousness by the power of the Holy Spirit. To be a good shepherd (a true messenger, the savor and savior of men, the salt and light of the everlasting covenant), the shepherd must have compassion for the sheep and lead them with a gentle iron rod. His staff is a scepter of authority and "power in his hand" (see D&C 85:7) even the "sceptre" of Jesus Christ (see Numbers 24:17). However, it must be used with the doctrine of the priesthood and the power of the Holy Spirit, the spirit of prophecy and revelation (see 2 Peter 1:21). A good shepherd knows how to edify.

If we don't "hearken unto the voice of the good shepherd, to the name by which we are called, behold, [we] are not the sheep of the good shepherd" (Alma 5:38). The Lord's sheep are those who have "heard my voice, and seen me" (3 Nephi 15:24). Therefore, ultimately to be a sheep of the Good Shepherd is to receive the great and last promise of the temple.

The Burden Is Light in Climbing Mount Zion

Oliver Cowdery received the call to Pro-Sel-Light in the following revelation:

> Now, as you have asked, behold, I say unto you, keep my commandments, and seek to bring forth and establish the cause of Zion. . . .
>
> And if you desire, you shall be the means of doing much good in this generation.
>
> Say nothing but repentance unto this generation; keep my commandments, and assist to bring forth my work, according to my commandments, and you shall be blessed. . . .
>
> And if thou wilt inquire, thou shalt know mysteries which are great and marvelous; . . . that thou mayest bring many to the knowledge of the truth, yea, convince them of the error of their ways. (D&C 6:6, 8–9, 11)

This revelation evokes the Prophet Joseph Smith's call to be true messengers as our imperative duty (see D&C 123:11–13).

When we covenant in the temple to accept the law of consecration, we covenant to become the salt, the preservers, of the Abrahamic covenant. We covenant to sacrifice all to establish the cause of Zion that the great view of the kingdom of God will shine as a great saving light, for "a great benefit" (see Mosiah 8:18) to the world. The greatest benefit and greatest miracle of all is that by the power of Christ we and all our fellow beings can become the sons and daughters of God with eternal life (see D&C 45:9).

Since being a true messenger is not always easy or comfortable (ask any missionary), perhaps there is a deeper message for those who labor to climb Mount Zion when the Lord said:

> Come unto me, all ye that labour and are heavy laden, and I will give you rest.
>
> Take my yoke upon you, and learn of me; for I am meek and lowly in heart: and ye shall find rest unto your souls.
>
> For my yoke is easy, and my burden is light. (Matthew 11:28–30)

Our burden in the Abrahamic covenant is to be the salt (savor) and light (saviors) of the world by emulating the Savior. In so doing we "bear one another's burdens, that they may be light" (Mosiah 18:8).

Heavy laden, laboring to rid ourselves of excess baggage in climbing Mount Zion, we find our rest in the Savior. For His rest or fulness, the burden we must continue to carry is to be the salt that preserves the full savor of the covenant and the light that shines as the Savior of the covenant. This burden we learned in Primary when we enthusiastically sang, "I'll be a sunbeam for Him."

The burden to be a true messenger of the true message is a great responsibility. However, it is a responsibility that is joyfully carried because of the exquisite savor of joy and the taste of light (see Alma 32:35) that dissolves all the discomfort and disappointment as we labor to save our fellow men (see Alma 36:24–26). As he and his brethren had been "instruments in His hands of doing this great and marvelous work" (see Alma 26:15–16), Ammon expressed this exquisite savor of joy even to the point that his joy was "full." Ammon's burden for this full joy was to bring the Lamanites from "everlasting darkness" to "everlasting light," freeing them from the darkness of the pains and chains of hell (see Alma 26:15).

The "instrument in His hand" is a trump similar to the trump in the hand of the angel Moroni. The trump is God's true messengers sounding the true message "both day and night" (D&C 24:12) and "long and loud" (D&C 43:18). This trump heralds "with the sound of rejoicing, as with the voice of a trump" (D&C 29:4), lifting up "voices as with the sound of a trump" (D&C 42:6), even "the trump of God" (D&C 88:92) saying "Ye saints arise and live" (D&C 43:18).

Elder John A. Widtsoe said that not only in the mission field but in temple work we can savor exquisite joy in the great and marvelous works of redemption:

> Men may rise through temple work to high levels of character and spiritual joy. Once only may a person receive the temple endowment for himself, but innumerable times may he receive it for those gone from the earth. Whenever he does so, he performs an unselfish act for which no earthly recompense is available. He tastes in part the sweet joy of saviorhood. He rises toward the stature of the Lord Jesus Christ who died for all.[1]

Part of the sweet joy of redemption that Adam and Eve tasted was the same sweet joy of charity that we taste as saviors to our fellow men, when we offer them the joy of their redemption by our works.

The Scriptural Temple

As the Savior saw His seed as His spiritually begotten sons and daughters in working His Atonement (see Mosiah 15:10), let us who are His seed work to declare His generation and become with the Savior the saviors of men. Therefore, that our joy be full, let us become the "seed of Abraham" who are the seed of Christ. Let us keep and preserve the everlasting covenant by doing the works of Abraham that are the works of Christ and His Father. Let us enter into covenants with the Lord to receive the promise of the Father unto Abraham:

> This promise is yours also, because ye are of Abraham, and the promise was made unto Abraham; and by this law is the continuation of the works of my Father, wherein he glorifieth himself.
>
> Go ye, therefore, and do the works of Abraham; enter ye into my law and ye shall be saved.
>
> But if ye enter not into my law ye cannot receive the promise of my Father, which he made unto Abraham. (D&C 132:31–33)

Preserving the Covenant: The Turning of Hearts

It is deeply significant that Malachi 4:5–6, the last recorded revelation in the Old Testament dispensation, became the first recorded revelation in the dispensation of the fulness of times (see D&C 2:1–3). Moroni's words to Joseph Smith, declaring the coming of Elijah, portended the restoration of this everlasting covenant in our dispensation:

> And he shall plant in the hearts of the children the promises made to the fathers, and the hearts of the children shall turn to their fathers. (D&C 2:2)

Because, unto Elijah, "I have committed the keys of the power of turning the hearts" (D&C 27:9).

These verses reflect Adam seeking messengers from his Father. His heart was turned to the Father for truth and salvation. So should our hearts be turned to the Father and His true messengers, who have received the promises, for one is your Father, which is in heaven. "The fathers" who received the promises are the patriarchal fathers (see Abraham 1:31) such as Adam the "first father" (Abraham 1:3), Abraham, and others who received the promises from "the fathers (the god fathers) . . . from before the foundation of the earth" (Abraham 1:3; see Alma 13:3). They are "my servants, thy fathers" (Moses 6:30). To these fathers were "committed the keys" (see D&C 27:9–13) and "the power of this priesthood given" (see D&C 112:30–32) to "unlock the door of the kingdom in all places" (D&C 112:17). The kingdom of God is where the keys of His priesthood are found that open the doors of the kingdom on earth that connect with the kingdom in heaven.

> Lift up your hearts and rejoice, for unto you the kingdom, or in other words, the keys of the church have been given. (D&C 42:69)

The fathers are the prophets to whom the hearts of the Jews should turn (see D&C 98:17) because the prophets' hearts turn to the house of Israel. The fathers are "your fathers, by whom the promises remain" (D&C 27:10) because "the priesthood hath continued through the lineage of your fathers" (see D&C 86:8). When we hear and respond to the voice of the Father and "the fathers" in our hearts, these promises will be written or planted in our hearts through spiritual, everlasting covenants with the Father (see Jeremiah 31:31, 33; Hebrews 8:10) made in His holy house.

The importance of Malachi's prophecy concerning Elijah and the turning of hearts in the scriptural temple cannot be overemphasized. On Mount Carmel, in confrontation with the priests of Baal, Elijah took twelve stones and built an altar in the name of the Lord (see 1 Kings 18:32). Then he came near to the altar and said:

> Hear me, O Lord, hear me, that this people may know that thou art the Lord God, and that thou hast *turned their heart back again*. (1 Kings 18:37; emphasis added)

The principle of turning hearts to God at the altar of sacrifice (the temple altar) was dominant in Old Testament temples. This is why Rehoboam feared losing the tribes of Israel (see 1 Kings 12:27). This important principle is the foundation for turning hearts of fathers and children in order "to come to the knowledge of [our] fathers" (see Mormon 7:5–10). We cannot turn our hearts in covenant to our earthly fathers until we have turned it in covenant to our Heavenly Father. This is because of "the influence of that spirit which hath so strongly riveted the creeds of the fathers, who have inherited lies, upon the hearts of the children" (D&C 123:7). We must learn the truth about our Father in Heaven in order to turn our hearts to Him. Abraham turned his heart from his "father's house . . . because they [turned] their hearts away from [the true God]" (see Abraham 1:16–17).

In the end, hearts of fathers and children shall turn to each other by turning to the Lord. "If the children shall repent, . . . and turn to the Lord their God, with all their hearts . . . and restore four-fold all their trespasses . . . or wherewith their fathers have trespassed, . . . then thine indignation shall be turned away" (D&C 98:47). If the sins of the fathers can fall on their children's heads (see Joseph Smith Translation, Matthew 23:36), and the sins of the children can fall on their fathers' heads (see 2 Nephi 4:6; Jacob 3:10), then a great responsibility lies within each of us to do the work that reunites families in turning hearts to God the Father through repentance (see Jacob 1:10).

The principle of turning hearts is found in the last words of the Old Testament. It continued with John the Baptist, the last prophet of the Old Testament and first prophet of the New Testament. Foreshadowing the Melchizedek Priesthood temple order of the New Testament, he, "in the spirit and power of Elias" was "to turn the hearts of the fathers to the children" (Luke 1:17). The same principle was found in the spirit world also foreshadowing temple work in the meridian dispensation and the great temple work in the dispensation of the fulness of times.

In his great vision of the redemption of the dead, the Prophet Joseph F. Smith saw the faithful spirits of the prophets and elect of God organized to continue pronouncing the Abrahamic covenant in the world of spirits. Elijah had at this time and perhaps still has an important role proselyting in the world of spirits:

> The Prophet Elijah was to plant in the hearts of the children [in spirit prison] the promises made to their fathers [the patriarchs],
>
> Foreshadowing the great work to be done in the temples of the Lord in the dispensation of the fulness of times, for the redemption of the dead, and the sealing of the children to their parents, lest the whole earth be smitten with a curse and utterly wasted at his coming. (D&C 138:47–48)

Therefore, the hearts of many of our fathers had already turned to us in the "foreshadowing," long before our hearts began to turn to them.

Part of Christ's teachings during the forty-day ministry to the meridian Saints after His visit to the spirit world, for He spoke "of things pertaining to the kingdom of God" (Acts 1:3), must have been the importance of turning the hearts or the great sealing work of temples He initiated while in the world of spirits. For, if "the dead who repent will be redeemed, through obedience to the ordinances of the house of God" (D&C 138:58) is it not the same for the living? Therefore, we find hints in the writings of Peter (see 1 Peter 3:18–20; 4:6) who, like Joseph Smith, received the "keys of the kingdom" (Matthew 16:19) from Elijah and other patriarch fathers (see D&C 110:16; 112:32) to bind or seal on earth to be sealed in heaven (compare Matthew 16:19 with D&C 1:8). These hints also appear in the writings of Paul (see 1 Corinthians 15:29; Hebrews 11:40) concerning the importance of temple work in this binding.

To the scriptures of the more righteous Nephites the Savior added the prophecies of Malachi. These started with Christ's final appearance at the temple (see 3 Nephi 24:1) and concluded with the turning of hearts (see 3 Nephi 25:6). Then, "he did expound all things unto them, both great and small . . . even from the beginning until the time he should come in his glory" (3 Nephi 26:1, 3). No doubt, Christ expounded the importance of temple work to these Nephites.

Therefore, it is not surprising that the first written prophetic declaration of the dispensation of the fulness of temples is the prophecy of Malachi concerning the coming of Elijah and the turning of hearts. This prophecy was fulfilled in the Kirtland temple when "the time [had] fully come, which was spoken of by the mouth of Malachi—testifying that he [Elijah] should be sent . . . to turn the hearts" (D&C 110:14–15). Then the priesthood was revealed by the hand of Elijah (see Joseph Smith—History 1:38) since the sealing keys of Elijah are necessary, as Joseph Smith said, to administer all the ordinances of the priesthood in righteousness.[2] Then the gaping hole from the loss of true temple worship finally had a foundation and authority upon which to fill it with righteousness acceptable to God for our honor and glory (see D&C 124:34).

The Scriptural Temple

Even the great temple work of the millennial dispensation was foreshadowed with the prophecy about Elijah and the turning of hearts when the Lord said in reference to the grand council of Adam-ondi-Ahman before His Second Coming:

> I will drink of the fruit of the vine with you on the earth. . . .
>
> And also Elijah, unto whom I have committed the keys of the power of turning the hearts of the fathers to the children, and the hearts of the children to the fathers, that the whole earth may not be smitten with a curse. . . .
>
> Unto whom I have committed the keys of my kingdom . . . for the fulness of times, in the which I will gather together in one all things, both which are in heaven, and which are on earth. (D&C 27:5, 9, 13)

Thus we see that an important scriptural temple pattern is that the prophecies concerning Elijah and the turning of hearts always foreshadow the introduction and instruction of temple work. The importance of the spirit and power of Elijah cannot be overemphasized because if we perform temple ordinances and keep temple covenants, "the power of Elijah," as Joseph Smith said, "is sufficient to make our calling and election sure."[3] One interesting, implied blessing for turning hearts is "[renouncing] war and [proclaiming] peace" (D&C 98:16) as a foreshadowing of millennial peace.

The turning of the heart to God the Father starts at a very young age. Shortly after birth, we receive a name and a blessing as the hearts of our heavenly and earthly fathers turn toward us as newborn in mortality. Often we are given a family or scriptural name so "that when [we] remember [our] names [we] may remember them" (Helaman 5:6). In Primary our hearts begin to turn toward our Heavenly Father as we learn that we are His children. At baptism, we take upon us a new name. It is the name of Christ, the Father of our spiritual rebirth. As we emulate His name, Christ will spiritually beget us with a mighty change of heart. Our changed hearts will then turn to our Father in Heaven, because with this new heart we can again become His sons and daughters (see Mosiah 5:7; 27:25).

Later, the blessing at the hand of a patriarch is an extension of the blessing and promises of the patriarch fathers who received the promises by covenant from God. In this patriarchal blessing, we learn of our royal lineage and our obligation to become the seed of Abraham and to do the works of Abraham by proselyting the gospel. In this special blessing the promises given to the patriarch fathers are planted in our hearts.

When a young man receives the priesthood, he obtains the oath and covenant of the Father. He is given the obligation to carry the keys of salvation to his fellow men and his fathers by becoming a true messenger of the Father. Promising all that He has, the Father turns his heart towards all those who receive the oath and covenant of the priesthood to become kings and queens of righteousness.

When young men and women receive their temple endowment, they make covenants to be the salt and light of the world in bringing salvation for the living and the dead, and building up the kingdom of God. With these covenants written in their hearts, they turn to their fathers and fellow men as kings and queens of righteousness.

When a man and a woman enter the Holy Order of Matrimony, they promise to turn their hearts first to each other, then to their children, planting in the hearts of these children the promises that they have received. Thus "great things" are required at the hand of their mothers and fathers (see D&C 29:48). Because of these prom-ises and their parents' love, these children will turn their hearts to their earthly parents and then to their Heavenly Parents. The cycle of turning the hearts is renewed.

By teaching the importance of the temple and the obligation of the everlasting covenant to our children, the works of Abraham and the gospel of Abraham will continue, fulfilling the promise pro-nounced by Elias in the Kirtland temple:

> After this, Elias appeared, and committed the dispensation of the gospel of Abraham, saying that in us and our seed all generations after us should be blessed. (D&C 110:12)

The fathers turn their hearts to us with their recorded voices from the dust.

With the spirit of Elias and Elijah, the promises of the Father from the fathers are planted in our hearts until they turn to a mighty change of heart. It is interesting that hard hearts, broken hearts, and pure hearts were all present in the temple when Jacob gave his sermon (see Jacob 2:10–11). He blessed pure hearts to "receive the pleasing word of God, and feast upon his love" (Jacob 3:2). This event demonstrated the mighty change of heart that can occur in the temple. It showed a personal meaning of "turning the hearts." This change of heart will turn our hearts to our fathers ("their fathers") who await the promises in spirit prison and to our fellow men who are still in the prison house of mortality (see D&C 123:12).

The hearts of the fathers and the prophets (see D&C 98:16–17) are turning towards the house of Israel, literal and adopted, since those of this house "must come to a knowledge of [their] fathers" (Mormon 7:5). After explaining to his "brethren" the allegory of the olive tree taught by Lehi, Nephi reminded them of the obligation of the "seed" of Abraham: "Wherefore, our father hath not spoken of our seed alone, but also of all the houses of Israel, pointing to the covenant which should be fulfilled in the latter days; which covenant the Lord made to our father Abraham, saying: In thy seed shall all the kindreds of the earth be blessed" (1 Nephi 15:18).

Nephi had already explained to his brethren that in the latter days the fulness of the gospel of the Messiah would come to the Gentiles and from the Gentiles to the remnant of the seed of Lehi. This turning of hearts is the often prophesied covenant of the Father that He will keep with the house of Israel for the redemption of Zion (see D&C 49:24–25). At the time of "the fulness of the Gentiles" (Romans 11:25; see also Luke 21:24; D&C 45:30), "all Israel shall be saved" (Romans 11:26) by a final welding or grafting together (see Jacob 5:52–60, 67–68; compare Romans 11:16–27) because "God is able to graft them in again" (Romans 11:23). Then "the saints shall come forth from the four quarters of the earth" (D&C 45:46) because their hearts are turned to their Father in Heaven and to each other. "For this is my covenant unto them" (Romans 11:27).

When we perform temple ordinances and keep temple covenants, our hearts will not only turn to our Father in Heaven but eventually it will be sealed to Him. To advance this great sealing of hearts, this welding link, the hearts of fathers will be turned and welded to their gospel seed (see Malachi 4:6) if this seed keeps the light of the fulness of the gospel (see D&C 45:28) burning. This light is in the everlasting covenant of the Father (see D&C 66:2) that shines as a light to the world and a standard for His people (see D&C 45:9). We who worship in the temple are the gospel seed, the seed of Abraham, because we have accepted the welding obligation of the everlasting covenant in the dispensation of the fulness of times.

A new line on a pedigree chart is produced by the welding of DNA but this new line is only welded to the eternal chain by the turning of hearts in temples. Ancestral links are not welded just by remembering our ancestors and doing genealogical research. They are welded or sealed by the power of the priesthood in temples.

> The priesthood hath continued through the lineage of your fathers—
>> For ye are lawful heirs, according to the flesh, and have been hid from the world with Christ in God—
>> Therefore your life and the priesthood have remained, and must needs remain through you and your lineage until the restoration of all things. (D&C 86:8–10)

Priesthood power has been available from the beginning and will be to the end of time. Worthy heirs of this priesthood power must remain for lineages to be linked.

"If it so be that ye are righteous, [by the power of the priesthood] then are ye blessed [in the resurrection] with your fathers who have gone before you" (Mormon 6:21). Thus "pro-sel-lighting" to turn and seal hearts in temples is our obligation in the Abrahamic covenant, both in this world and in the world of spirits, in order to bless all the nations, kindreds, and families of the earth:

> And thou shalt be a blessing unto thy seed after thee, that in their hands they shall bear this ministry and Priesthood unto all nations;
>> And I will bless them through thy name; for as many as receive this Gospel shall be called after thy name, and shall be accounted to thy seed. . . .
>> For I give unto thee a promise that this right shall continue in thee, and in thy seed after thee . . . shall all the families of the earth be blessed, even with the blessings of the Gospel, which are the blessings of salvation, even of life eternal. (Abraham 2:9–11)

The charge to "pro-sel-light" was committed by the Lord "into [the] hands" (see D&C 110:16) of the elders of the Church in this dispensation, fulfilling the declaration to Abraham that "in their hands" (Abraham 2:9) the ministry and priesthood would go forth. The Lord is still telling the "elders of [His] church" today that the keys of salvation for our waiting fathers and fellow men are in our hands if the promises are planted in our hearts by the power of the Holy Spirit:

> Again I say, hearken ye elders of my church, whom I have appointed: Ye are not sent forth to be taught, but to teach the children of men the things which I have put into your hands by the power of my spirit. (D&C 43:15)

"By the wisdom of God, [these things] remained safe in [our] hands, until [we accomplish] by them what is required at [our] hand" (Joseph Smith—History 1:60). When we put the fulness of the gospel into the hands of our neighbors, we can both enjoy the "great blessings the Father hath in his own hands" (D&C 78:17).

As the gospel seed of Abraham, our obligation in the everlasting Abrahamic covenant is to bear the Lord's name with the fulness of His gospel and priesthood "throughout all the earth" (Exodus 9:16; see also Abraham 2:6). We are to bless all the families and kindreds from the beginning to the end of the earth with the blessings of salvation, even eternal life. Those who embrace the fulness of the gospel will bless all the kindreds and families of the earth, dead or alive, with the blessings of eternal life through missionary work, both on earth and in the world of spirits. The purpose of this missionary work is to "push the people together from the ends of the earth" (D&C 58:45) in order to "push many people to Zion" (D&C 66:11). The push is to bring souls to base camp and prepare them to do temple work in order to climb "the mountain of [their] inheritance . . . the Sanctuary" (see Exodus 15:17). Through temple ordinances and covenants, all the families (sealed families) and kindreds (sealed relatives) of the earth shall be blessed with the fulness of the gospel.

We who embrace the everlasting covenant in the last days have the obligation of performing this temple work to bless all the kindreds and families who cannot do this work for themselves. If we do not do this work then "their names shall not be found, neither the names of the fathers, nor the names of the children written in the book of the law of God" (D&C 85:5). "And all they who are not found written in the book of remembrance shall find none inheritance in that day, but they shall be cut asunder" (see D&C 85:9–12) and "wasted away, both root and branch" (D&C 109:52). On the threshold of the Great Apostasy, the Apostle John, seeking hope for the meridian Saints, saw the great salvation of a great multitude dressed in temple clothing through the great temple work of the dispensation of the fulness of times:

> And this I beheld, and, lo, a great multitude, which no man could number, of all nations, and kindreds, and people, and tongues, stood before the throne, and before the Lamb, clothed with white robes, and palms in their hands. (Revelation 7:9)

Climbing Mount Zion with our kindred, alive and dead, by turning hearts in temples is our imperative obligation and privilege because the dispensation of the fulness of times is "the dispensation of the fulness of the priesthood"[4] in temples. Thus the covenant with Abraham will be fulfilled in the latter days.

Grown Up in the Lord: Receiving a Fulness of the Abrahamic Covenant

The Abrahamic covenant is a covenant of salt because it preserves in purity the knowledge and keys of salvation in the power of the priesthood of God. This knowledge and these keys are in the ordinances and covenants that we make in the temple. This includes the crowning covenant, the everlasting covenant of marriage. These keys are the "key to the knowledge of God" (D&C 84:19), which unlock the power to become as God, with eternal lives.

To become as God we must develop a divine nature. We develop this divine nature by growing up in the temple. There we acquire, through the power of Christ, all of the graces and truths of His divine nature. Symbolically in the endowment we put on a divine nature as we are clothed with the robes of righteousness. We are fully clothed when we have the divine nature of charity, which is fully practiced in the celestial law of consecration with the virtue and holiness of one-ness (see D&C 38:24–27; 46:7).

It is interesting that with the verses of scripture most often quoted as a calling to those who wish to become true messengers with salt and light to the world, the graces of a divine nature are again mentioned: "Remember faith, virtue, knowledge, temperance, patience, brotherly kindness, godliness, charity, humility, diligence" (D&C 4:6).

The endowment teaches us that as we become more righteous (symbolically more completely clothed in the robes of righteousness), we receive more priesthood power until we receive a fulness of the priesthood. We become "clothed with power and authority" (D&C 138:30). When we receive and keep the fulness of the Melchizedek Priesthood in the temple, we become kings and queens of righteous-ness (*Melchiah* means Jehovah is king, *Zadok* means righteous[5]), truly emulating the Savior. The Savior taught the Nephites at the temple of the land Bountiful their obligation to "pro-sel-light" by emulating Him: "Verily, verily, I say unto you, this is my gospel; and ye know the things that ye must do in my church; for the works which ye have seen me do that shall ye also do" (3 Nephi 27:21).

The works of the Savior are described as "miracles and wonders and signs" (Acts 2:22). *Semeion*, a Greek word often associated with Christ's miracles, means a *sign* that reveals the character of the person who performs the miracle. Christ revealed His character through his works in that He always used his power in compliance with the will of His Father and applied it with great compassion on those who received it. The power for His works comes through the doctrine of the priesthood (see D&C 121:41–45) when we are clothed with the robes of righteousness.

> Yea, and if it had not been for his matchless power, and his mercy, and his long-suffering towards us, we should unavoidably have been cut off from the face of the earth. (Alma 9:11)

This is the work "that shall ye also do" (3 Nephi 27:21).

When we receive the fulness of the priesthood, we receive the fulness of the Abrahamic covenant—the "oath and covenant" of the Father (see D&C 84:40), for "all that [the] Father hath shall be given unto him" (see D&C 84:38). With this priesthood we have access to great power for "a man may have great power given him from God" (Mosiah 8:16; see also Alma 8:31), in the form of "power and authority from God" (Alma 5:3).

> God having sworn . . . with an oath . . . that every one being ordained after this order and calling should have power, by faith, to break mountains, to divide the seas, to dry up waters, to turn them out of their course;
>
> To put at defiance the armies of nations, to divide the earth, to break every band, to stand in the presence of God; to do all things according to his will, according to his command, subdue principalities and powers, and this by the will of the Son of God. (Joseph Smith Translation, Genesis 14:30–31)

However, we are expected to practice what we learn in the temple, and exercise the power of the priesthood in everyday life, with "kindness and pure knowledge" (see D&C 121:41–42) to "succor the weak" (see D&C 81:5). We are to use priesthood power only in accordance with the will and counsel of God or we "shall have no power" (see D&C 3:4; 136:19).

Nephi, the son of Helaman, is a great example of one who sought the will of the Lord to keep his commandments "with such unwearyingness" (Helaman 10:5) that he received total confidence from the Lord in His sealing power:

> I will bless thee forever; and I will make thee mighty in word and in deed, in faith and in works; yea, even that all things shall be done unto thee according to thy word, for thou shalt not ask that which is contrary to my will.
>
> Behold, I give unto you power, that whatsoever ye shall seal on earth shall be sealed in heaven; and whatsoever ye shall loose on earth shall be loosed in heaven; and thus shall ye have power among this people. (Helaman 10:5, 7)

As a benefit for our fellow men and the glory of God, seeking signs and wonders through the power of the priesthood comes only by faith in God. What a contrast this truth is with the practice of priestcraft in the world today: "Wherefore, I, the Lord, am not pleased with those among you who have sought after signs and wonders for faith, and not for the good of men unto my glory" (D&C 63:12).

By following the counsel of the Lord for his glory we will grow up in the temple and there receive the fulness of the Abrahamic Covenant. And thus, by "growing up" in the Lord in His temple, we become the salt and light of the earth, blessed with the powers of heaven. By turning our hearts to the Lord and growing up in Him with His power, we have the power to grow a tree of life within us. As the seed of Abraham we are the seed of this tree of life. When we turn our hearts to each other by grafting and sealing families and kindreds in temples, our tree of life grows new branches. The people in our lives that we have edified by the power of the priesthood become fruit of this tree of life and produce seed for a new tree of life. All of these trees of life are grafted to God's tree of life.

Views from the Summit of Mount Zion

If a writer's aim be logical conviction, he must spare no logical pains, not merely to be understood, but to escape being misunderstood; where his object is to move by suggestion, to cause to imagine, then let him assail the soul of his reader as the wind assails an aeolian harp. If there be music in my reader, I would gladly wake it.[1]

So that the temple becomes the most powerful spiritual motivation in our lives, I hope the music of Moroni's "moonlight sonata" in the music of the *scriptural temple* has awakened the music within our souls. Being "filled with the Holy Ghost," I hope that we like Joseph and Oliver can say, "our minds being now enlightened, we began to have the scriptures laid open to our understandings, and the true meaning and intentions of their more mysterious passages revealed unto us in a manner which we never could attain to previously, nor ever before had thought of" (Joseph Smith—History 1:74). I hope the heralding and mellifluous message from the trumpet of Moroni, which declares "come unto Christ" and turn your heart to your fathers and the Father, will draw us to the temple as the power of Christ draws us to Him (see D&C 88:63). There we will enjoy the complete composition.

The Message of Mount Zion

As we have journeyed through the *scriptural temple* in climbing the mountain of the Lord's house, we have seen consistent temple messages through time and on both hemispheres. These messages are in the stick of Judah and the stick of Joseph. They are in the scriptures of the dispensation of the fulness of times. Now, they are all one in our hands (see Ezekiel 37:16–17). To read, ponder, and pray is only the beginning of searching the scriptures (see Joshua 1:8; John 5:39). Temple worship continues this search for eternal life as we come to see the great view of this ever-expanding *scriptural temple* through the spirit of prophecy and revelation.

A clear temple message woven through the scriptures explains how we make the mighty change in preparation to meet God. Since the law of Moses, a law of sanctification through sacrifice and Atonement, was centered in the temple, even more should the fulness of the gospel in the dispensation of the fulness of times be centered in the temple. This is where we prepare to meet God by learning to worship the Lord in "the beauty of holiness" (Psalm 29:2) until we are "sanctified in holiness" (D&C 133:35), "without which no man shall see the Lord" (Hebrews 12:14). We are not only to remember the Lord but like Jonah, "[His] house also, to keep and preserve it holy" (D&C 117:16). We are to remember its "holy grounds . . . holy ordinances . . . and holy words" (D&C 124:46) so that one day we shall be prepared to receive its great and last promise. "It shall be holy, or the Lord your God will not dwell therein" (D&C 124:24).

Moses learned about the sacred nature of holiness when he ascended higher on Mount Sinai and was told to remove his shoes because "the place whereon thou standest is holy ground" (Exodus 3:5). Symbolically, nature also teaches us about holiness. The higher the mountain peak, the more it remains covered with white snow, the color of holiness. Josephus described the temple at Jerusalem as appearing "to strangers, when they were at a distance, like a mountain of snow; for as to those parts of it that were not gilt, they appeared exceeding white."[2] *The message is that the higher we climb the mountain of the Lord's house the more holiness we find.*

The quintessential quality of holiness in which we should find beauty and joy was revealed to the children of Israel in the Sinai. When

Moses brought them before the temple mount, "the Lord descended upon it in fire" (Exodus 19:18). The Semitic root for the word *love* is *hav*. It means to warm, to kindle, or set on fire.[3] If God is love (1 John 4:8) and he dwells in a consuming fire (Hebrews 12:29) of everlasting burnings (Isaiah 33:14), then the depth, breadth, and longevity of His love is expressed in His burnings. From the small burning bush that would not be consumed to the whole temple mount, flaming and smoking with fire, *pure love that consumes all pride but never extinguishes its light and warmth for humility is the holiness of God* (see Exodus 15:11; 18:11; Isaiah 9:12, 17, 21; 10:4). The fire of pure love "shall try every man's work of what sort it is" (1 Corinthians 3:13). Elijah the Prophet precisely declared this symbolic truth when he said, "the God that answereth by fire, let him be God" (1 Kings 18:24), for "after the [consuming] fire [comes] a still small voice" (1 Kings 19:12) of love.

The Apostle Paul connected pure love and holiness when he wrote to the Thessalonian Saints,

> And the Lord make you to increase and abound in *love* one toward another, and toward all men. . . .
>
> To the end he may establish your hearts unblameable in *holiness* before God. (1 Thessalonians 3:12–13; emphasis added)

The baptism of fire is symbolic of the essence of holiness because it is the baptism of pure love. Baptism by the Holy Spirit is baptism by "the spirit of burning" (Isaiah 4:4) where the field is "white already to be burned" (D&C 31:4). "And behold, the Holy Spirit of God did come down from heaven, and did enter into their hearts, and they were filled as if with fire" (Helaman 5:45).

Nephi expressed his baptism of fire as the baptism of pure love when he said, "He hath filled me with his love, even unto the consuming of my flesh" (2 Nephi 4:21). *If we are to find beauty and joy in holiness then we must acquire the beauty and joy of pure love.* The Lord commanded us to "practice virtue and holiness" by keeping the first two great commandments of love (see D&C 38:24). It is only in the temple, where the power of godliness is manifest through its ordinances, that we will receive the beauty and joy of pure love as a gift from God.

The Scriptural Temple

When the children of Israel crossed the Jordan into the land of Canaan, the Lord again taught them the importance of coming to the temple (see Joshua 8:30–35). All the tribes of Israel gathered in a valley between Mount Ebal and Mount Gerizim, representing an important choice in their lives. From mount Ebal the cursings for disobedience were pronounced. From Mount Gerizim the blessings of obedience were pronounced (see Deuteronomy 27:12–13). The children of Israel surrounded the Ark of the Covenant in the valley between these two mounts. They were to decide if obedience to the covenant of the Lord contained in the ark would be the center of their lives. Obedience to the Lord would give them the power and blessings of the temple sanctuary at Shiloh that they "dwelled safe" (1 Samuel 12:11) in the mountains of Ephraim. "For this [the law and revelations of God] is your wisdom and your understanding in the sight of the nations" (Deuteronomy 4:6) to be "a holy people unto himself," "high above all nations" (Deuteronomy 28:1, 9). Likewise, the Lord declares to His Saints today, "Arise and shine forth, that thy light may be a standard for the nations; and that the gathering together upon the land Zion, . . . may be for a defense, and for a refuge" (D&C 115:5–6).

Latter-day Saints often hear the phrase *in the world but not of the world*. Yet in light of 1 John 2:16, "For all that is in the world, . . . is not of the Father, but is of the world," we cannot be in the world and not be part of the world. In His Intercessory Prayer, the Savior prayed, "not that thou shouldest take them out of the world, but that thou shouldest keep them from the evil" (John 17:15). As the salt and light the Abrahamic covenant, we who worship in the temple are protected from and overcome the evil of the world. While we must pass through Babylon as we seek Zion, only strict obedience to the Lord will bring us to Zion. Through the *scriptural temple*, Mount Zion's message for us today is the same as that pronounced on Mounts Gerizim and Ebal. The Lord is continually trying to separate us from Babylon and bring us to Zion. He does this by placing temple mounts in our midst then warning us with cursings for disobedience in climbing worldly mountains and pronouncing blessings for obedience in climbing Mount Zion.

As Mount Gerizim was in contrast to Mount Ebal and the Tower of Babel was in contrast to the staircase tower of Jacob's vision, Mount Babylon is today in contrast with Mount Zion. One is formed by the hand of man for the purpose of selfish idolatry. The other is formed by the hand of God for the exaltation of man. We must choose which mount we will climb. We cannot stand on both (see Amos 6:1; 2 Corinthians 6:14–18).

The scriptures tell us of the fate of both Mount Babylon and Mount Zion in the last days:

- Mount Babylon:

Behold, I am against thee [Babylon], O destroying [corrupting] mountain, saith the Lord, which destroyest all the earth: and I will stretch out mine hand upon thee, and roll thee down from the rocks, and will make thee a *burnt mountain*.

And they shall not take of thee a stone for a corner, nor a stone for foundations; but thou shalt be desolate for ever, saith the Lord. (Jeremiah 51:25–26; compare Isaiah 28:16)

And I [the Lord] will not spare any that remain in Babylon (D&C 64:24)

- Mount Zion:

Thou sawest till that a stone was cut out without hands, which smote the image upon his feet that were of iron and clay [Mount Babylon], and brake them to pieces. . . .

And the stone that smote the image became a great mountain, and filled the whole earth. (Daniel 2:34–35; see D&C 103:7; 109:72)

Truly, "the joy of the whole earth, is Mount Zion" (Psalm 48:2).

If we cannot stand on both Mount Babylon and Mount Zion or serve both God and mammon, then the song in our hearts should be the song of the elders of Israel, "O Babylon, O Babylon, we bid thee farewell; We're going to the mountains of Ephraim to dwell"[4] as we "flee unto Zion and . . . flee unto Jerusalem, unto the mountains of the Lord's house" (D&C 133:12–13).

The Great View of a Better World

As the stone cut without hands rolls forth to become the great Mount Zion that fills the whole earth, I hope we feel the urgency and responsibility for the preparation of the redemption of Zion and the gathering together in one all things in Christ. This preparation and gathering must pass up the spiritual Mount Zion, the mountain of the House of the Lord. It is this spiritual mount that each of us must climb, to see and be part of the great "gathering in one" of the Lord, that we will be prepared for the redemption of Zion. We can only climb Mount Zion with the Savior's rope with a "perfect brightness" and "full assurance" of hope in the Atonement of our guide Jesus Christ. By the power of Christ's Atonement, we can only reach the summit of Mount Zion if our bowels are filled with the spirit of prophecy and revelation and we are baptized with fire and the Holy Ghost. The Prophet Ether exhorted the people of Coriantumr to have faith and hope in Christ for the great view of a "better world." Then, like the Apostle Paul (see Hebrews 6:18–19), Ether gave the image of the climb of Mount Zion to obtain the summit and see the great view:

> Wherefore, whoso believeth in God might with surety hope for a better world, yea, even a place at the right hand of God, which hope cometh of faith, maketh an anchor to the souls of men, which would make them sure and steadfast, always abounding in good works, being led to glorify God. (Ether 12:4)

In Moroni's commentary on faith, hope, and charity, he alludes to the temple when he remembers that Christ "hast prepared a house for man, yea, even among the mansions of thy Father, in which man might have a more excellent hope" (see Ether 12:32). Once we have seen even glimpses of the great view of this "better world" in the temple, we will desire to "lay aside the things of this world, and seek for the things of a better" (D&C 25:10). With this more excellent hope, we can obtain a pure heart with pure love to do "good continually" (see Moroni 7:13). Pure love is possible "because of the spirit of the Lord Omnipotent, which has wrought a mighty change in us, or in our hearts, that we have *no more disposition to do evil*, but to do good continually. And we, ourselves, also, through the infinite goodness of God, and the manifestations of his Spirit, have *great views*" (Mosiah 5:2–3; emphasis added).

The Prophet Joseph Smith taught about achieving this great view when he said:

The nearer man approaches perfection (by heed and diligence given to the light communicated from heaven to his intellect), *the clearer are his views*, and the greater his enjoyment, till he has overcome the evils of his life and lost every desire for sin.[5]

To Reach the Summit: Come unto Christ

When we glimpse the great view, we will hear Moroni and the Holy Spirit calling us to come unto Christ. When we come unto Him, we will better understand His greatness and His Atonement. Because of His Atonement the covering He provides for the nakedness of our fall is the garment of salvation. As we climb back to the presence of our Father in Heaven, the Savior clothes us with the robes of righteousness. As the Savior said: "Solomon, in all his glory, was not arrayed like one of these [lilies of the field]. Even so will [I] clothe you" (3 Nephi 13:29–30). We should seek this holy covering of our Savior, eschewing "the garments spotted with the flesh" (D&C 36:6; see also Jude 1:23).

We are clothed in Christ's holy covering when we learn to take His name upon us and become His spiritually begotten children. Taking His name upon us and becoming His children is the key that will unlock the mysteries of God for our honor and glory. This spiritual birth to a mighty change of heart only occurs through true temple worship where the fulness of the Melchizedek Priesthood is found (see D&C 84:19). For "therein are the keys of the holy priesthood ordained, that you may receive honor and glory" (see D&C 124:34). Without Christ's covering we could not climb Mount Zion to obtain the keys and make the mighty change to return to our Father in Heaven.

In climbing Mount Zion we will be endowed or filled with charity, the pure love of Christ (see Psalm 24:34). With this crowning quality through the power of the Atonement we will become "new creatures" with a mighty change of heart. *This is the great paradigm shift of the gospel and it only occurs within the temple paradigm.* By the matchless power of an infinite Atonement, in the temple our hearts and bodies are renewed and sanctified as we perform the ordinances and keep the covenants of His Holy Order.

In verses laden with temple meaning, the Apostle Paul understood the importance of being drawn to Christ with "true hearts" (real intent, broken hearts), that our hearts and bodies be purified by Him in the "house of God":

> And having an high priest over the house of God ;
> Let us draw near with a true heart in full assurance of faith, having our hearts sprinkled [purified] from an evil conscience, and our bodies washed with pure water [the pure blood of Christ from the well of salvation]. (Hebrews 10:21–22)

To be drawn to Christ with a true heart and receive His gift of perfect love, we must repent by obedience and sacrifice to His covenants:

> For, behold, the Lord your Redeemer suffered death in the flesh; wherefore he suffered the pain of all men, that all men might repent and come unto him.
> And he hath risen again from the dead, that he might bring all men unto him, on conditions of repentance.
> And how great is his joy in the soul that repenteth! (D&C 18:11–13)

I hope we are men and women to match His mountain and His message through repentance. Just like the dead, we "who repent will be redeemed, through obedience to the ordinances of the house of the God" (D&C 138:58). As a gift for repentance and obedience to the ordinances of house of God, we will be given the fulness of the Holy Spirit: His gift of sanctification and the gift of the spirit of prophecy and revelation, even the more sure word of prophecy. Because of the Atonement and by this gift of the Holy Ghost, we will be lifted up to not only see the great view but to become part of it.

The Savior eloquently explained how those who are drawn or brought to him will be "lifted up" to the summit of Mount Zion. First, He was lifted up in the crucifixion to draw men to Him (see 3 Nephi 27:14). Then, because of Christ's Atonement, the Father will provide the power to resurrect all men to be lifted up and stand before Christ to be judged (see 3 Nephi 27:14–15). Those who have obeyed Christ's gospel by doing His works will be "lifted up at the last day" (3 Nephi 27:22) and exalted on the summit of Mount Zion. Again, there is deep significance in Mormon's statement, "may Christ lift thee up" (Moroni 9:25).

As Joseph Smith implied, for this great lift in the gift of exaltation let us climb with our Savior to the summit, to that within the veil, and obtain eternal lives:

> It is one thing to be on the mount and hear the excellent voice. &c., &c., and another to hear the voice declare to you, You have a part and lot in that kingdom.[6]

The Bond of the Great Covenant

Through the *scriptural temple*, we begin to understand the importance of making and keeping covenants with the Lord. The Lord requires that we make covenants with each other and with Him, that we may be "knit together as one man" (Judges 20:11) and committed by the power of love:

> And I will bring you out from the people, and will gather you out of the countries wherein ye are scattered, with a mighty hand, and with a stretched out arm, and with fury poured out.
>
> And I will bring you into the wilderness of the people, and there will I plead with you face to face.
>
> Like as I pleaded with your fathers in the wilderness of the land of Egypt, so will I plead with you, saith the Lord God.
>
> And I will cause you to pass under the rod [be straightened by His will or commandments], and I will bring you into the bond of the covenant. (Ezekiel 20:34–37)

Again, our Guide and Savior led the way. He passed under the rod (the will) of His Father, that He would be brought into the bond of love through the covenant with His Father.

The greatest covenant of all was completed on the northern end of Mount Moriah, a natural and most sacred altar. This covenant was between the Father and the Son:

> But, behold, my Beloved son, which was my Beloved and Chosen from the beginning, said unto me—Father, thy will be done, and the glory be thine forever. (Moses 4:2; see also 3 Nephi 27:13–14)

> And this is the will of Him that sent me, that every one which seeth the Son, and believeth on Him, may have everlasting life: and I will raise him up at the last day. (John 6:40)

This is the oath and covenant of the priesthood.

On the sacred Mount of Olives and Mount Moriah, Jesus Christ culminated this covenant with His Father. Because of the bond of perfect love for us and His Father, He suffered and sacrificed His life that we might be lifted up to live eternal lives.

> Which suffering caused myself, even God, the greatest of all, to tremble because of pain, and to bleed at every pore; and to suffer both body and spirit, and would that I might not drink the bitter cup and shrink—
>
> Nevertheless, glory be to the Father and I partook and finished my preparations unto the children of men. (D&C 19:18–19)

> I have glorified thee on the earth: I have finished the work which thou gavest me to do.
>
> And now, O Father, glorify thou me with thine own self with the glory which I had with thee before the world was. (John 17:4–5; see also Matthew 26:39)

> When Jesus therefore had received the vinegar, he said, It is finished: and he bowed his head, and gave up the ghost. (John 19:30)

As the great example of one who keeps his covenants, Christ "suffered the will of the Father in all things from the beginning" (3 Nephi 11:11).

Nephi recognized the covenant relationship between the Father and the Son, and the importance of the same relationship between us and the Son when he said,

> For the Lord covenanteth with none save it be with them that repent and believe in his Son, who is the Holy One of Israel. (2 Nephi 30:2)

By keeping the fulness of our covenants with the Son, we keep the covenants that He kept with His Father. We do the will of the Father by entering, in the name of the Son, the narrow gate and following the strait path to eternal life. All covenants we make with

God pass through pieces of our flesh (see Genesis 15:10, 17–18; Jeremiah 34:18) in the trials and blessings of mortal life. Covenants which have passed through the rent veil of the flesh of His Son (see Hebrews 10:20) are valid between us and the Father when we pass through ordinances of the flesh to write these covenants in our hearts.

The fulness of the bond of the covenants, in pressing forward with a steadfastness in Christ, feasting upon His words, and becoming spiritually begotten by Him, occurs in the temple. *The effect of steadfastness in temple worship is to learn how to love God and all men* (see Mosiah 2:4). This is the "bond of the covenant." This quality of love from the heart helps us endure to the end and seals us for eternal life:

> Know ye not that He was holy? But notwithstanding he being holy, he showeth unto the children of men that, according to the flesh he humbleth himself before the Father, and witnesseth unto the Father that he would be obedient unto him in keeping his commandments.
>
> And again, it showeth unto the children of men the straitness of the path, and the narrowness of the gate, by which they should enter, he having set the example before them.
>
> And he said unto the children of men: Follow thou me. Wherefore, my beloved brethren, can we follow Jesus save we shall be willing to keep the commandments of the Father?
>
> And I heard a voice from the Father, saying: Yea, the words of my Beloved are true and faithful. He that endureth to the end, the same shall be saved.
>
> And now, my beloved brethren, I know by this that unless a man shall endure to the end, in following the example of the Son of the living God, he cannot be saved.
>
> And now, my beloved brethren, after ye have gotten into the strait and narrow path, I would ask if all is done? Behold I say unto you, Nay. . . .
>
> Wherefore, ye must press forward with a steadfastness in Christ, having a perfect brightness of hope, and a love of God and all men. Wherefore, if ye shall press forward, feasting upon the word of Christ, and endure to the end, behold, thus saith the Father: Ye shall have eternal life. (2 Nephi 31:7, 9–10, 15–16, 19–20)

The secret of enduring faithful to the end of mortality and enduring everlastingly is to follow Christ in filling our hearts with pure love "which love endureth by diligence unto prayer" (Moroni 8:26). We must connect with the powers of heaven because pure love is connected with the powers of heaven (see D&C 121:41, 45). Saul was "turned into another man" (1 Samuel 10:6) by the Spirit of the Lord because "God gave him another heart" (1 Samuel 10:9). But Saul did not endure by diligence unto prayer "in obeying the voice of the Lord" (see 1 Samuel 15:22). Therefore, "the Lord . . . sought him a man after his own heart" (1 Samuel 13:14), a pure heart filled with charity. "Charity never faileth" (Moroni 7:46) because it is "everlasting love" (Moroni 8:17) and "endureth all things" (Moroni 7:45).

Steadfastly Seeking the Summit: Being Drawn to Mount Zion

There is no written guideline for temple activity. An unwritten tradition is temple attendance once a month. However, as my understanding of the importance of the temple has grown, my desire to be in it has greatly increased. I now understand Luke's declaration of Christ in the temple when he said:

> And he taught daily in the temple. . . . For all the people were very attentive to hear him. (Luke 19:47–48)

If we knew that Christ was teaching daily in the temple, would we not eagerly and attentively go to hear Him? Would we not "labor exceedingly all that night, that [we] might be on the marrow in the place where Jesus should show himself" (3 Nephi 19:3)? Yet, is He not still teaching daily in the temple? Is He not, through the power of the Holy Spirit in the temple, expounding all the scriptures, both great and small, into one (see 3 Nephi 23:6, 14; 26:1) *scriptural temple* by expounding the things concerning Himself (see Luke 24:27)? If we who go to the temple still ask, "What think ye of Jesus, will he not come to the feast?" (see Joseph Smith Translation, John 11:56), then we are not being taught of Jesus Christ by the Spirit in the temple and will sadly one day hear Christ say, "I sat daily with you teaching in the temple, and ye laid no hold on me" (Matthew 26:55).

I wish I could go daily, but I would feel spiritually hungry if I did not attend the temple as much as I attend church on the Sabbath.

Yet my goal is to be like the Prophetess Anna, whether in or out of the temple, who "departed not from the temple, but served God with fastings and prayers night and day" (Luke 2:37). Therefore, like Simeon, she received the great and last promise of the temple.

If, for reasons of inaccessibility or worthiness, we cannot visit the house of the Lord, we should strive to make ourselves, our homes, and our assemblies as temples (see Exodus 33:10) until the day that "every one which [seeks] the Lord [goes] out unto the tabernacle" (Exodus 33:7). Ascending to holiness in His house and our homes is proof to the Lord of our desires to draw near to Him. Then the Lord, through His Holy Spirit, will draw near to us. We need to be drawn to the temple like King David:

> One thing I have desired of the Lord, that will I seek after; that I may dwell in the house of the Lord all the days of my life, to behold the beauty of the Lord, and to inquire in his temple. (Psalm 27:4)

Surely goodness and mercy will follow us all the days of our lives because we seek to dwell in the house of the Lord forever (see Psalm 23:6).

The more we inquire in the temple and behold the beauty of the Lord, the more we are drawn out of Babylon into Zion. The more we acquire the quality of charity, the more we desire to renounce the laws of competition and profits for the oneness of the law of consecration "continuing daily with one accord in the temple" (see Acts 2:44–46).

It is a glimpse of the reality of the great view, and the great and last promise of the temple, that draws me to this sacred place. It is to the words of Christ taught by the Holy Spirit that I want to be very attentive while in the temple. There, I want to offer up my "most holy desires" (D&C 95:16) that I might hear the "words of eternal life" and "peaceable things of immortal glory" (Moses 6:59, 61), receiving "revelation upon revelation, knowledge upon knowledge" of the mysteries of God and "that which bringeth life eternal" (see D&C 42:61).

I want to be able to say as Abraham: "Thy servant hath sought Thee earnestly; now I have found thee" (Abraham 2:12). I want to be a true messenger and be called as Abraham "the Friend of God" (James 2:23). It is the friend of God that becomes the seed of Abraham (see

Isaiah 41:8) and receives the great and last promise of the temple (see D&C 88:3). To this end, I want to climb Mount Zion and reach the summit, for I am beginning to see that "eye hath not seen, nor ear heard, neither have entered into the heart of man, the things which God hath prepared for them that love him" (1 Corinthians 2:9).

Certainly, the great view, even a glimpse of the summit of Mount Zion, is worth the climb for as Joseph Smith said:

> Could you gaze into heaven five minutes, you would know more than you would by reading all that ever was written on the subject.[7]

Let Us Go Up to the Summit of Mount Zion

May we find through the temple the path of salvation and exaltation to "the things which God hath prepared for them that love Him" (1 Corinthians 2:9). For this great view, we need to heed the words of true messengers and prophets of this dispensation as foretold by the prophet of a former dispensation:

> And many people shall go and say, Come ye, and let us go up to the mountain of the Lord, to the house of the God of Jacob; and he will teach us of his ways, and we will walk in his paths. (Isaiah 2:3)

While leaving the Salt Lake Temple one day, I started up the exit stairs and looked at a portrait of a prophet of this dispensation. My eyes caught the penetrating words on a directional sign below the portrait of Lorenzo Snow, the first president of the Salt Lake temple. The sign read "Up Only." This is the temple message that Lorenzo Snow, a man who personally received the great and last promise of the temple, would leave for us today. As the Prophet Isaiah said "let us go up [only] to the mountain of the Lord" (Isaiah 2:3), so the Prophet Lorenzo Snow would have us oppose gravity and go up only to and in the temple.

Once we enter the gate, the path up Mount Zion is "up only." This does not mean that as we follow the Savior up Mount Zion, all in our lives will go up and go well. For even the Savior had to descend below all things to be the light of truth (see D&C 88:6). In our climb up Mount Zion there will be tribulations and trials, but as we follow our Savior with a perfect brightness of hope, even the "downs" will transcend to up only. With the faith of Nephi in the power of the Lord's deliverance, "let us go up" (see 1 Nephi 4:1–3) to the summit of Mount Zion.

Enticed more and more by the fruit of the tree of life (the view of the love of God at the summit of Mount Zion), and less and less by the forbidden fruit (the views of the world), we will hear the call of the Prophet Joseph Smith encouraging us to the summit of Mount Zion:

> Brethren, shall we not go on in so great a cause? Go forward and not backward. Courage, brethren; and on, on to the victory! Let your hearts rejoice, and be exceedingly glad . . . for the prisoners shall go free.
>
> Let the mountains [temples] shout for joy. . . . Let all the sons of God shout for joy! And let the eternal creations declare his name forever and ever! . . . How glorious is the voice we hear from heaven, proclaiming in our ears glory, and salvation, and honor, and immortality, and eternal life; kingdoms, principalities, and powers! (D&C 128:22–23)

Inviting those desiring perfection to likewise focus, let us climb Mount Zion like the Apostle Paul who focused his climb on the mark of its summit.

> I press toward the mark for the prize of the high calling of God in Christ Jesus.
>
> Let us therefore, as many as be perfect, be thus minded. (Philippians 3:14–15)

The Great View at the Summit: The Fulness of the Lord's Work

As we steadfastly press forward to climb Mount Zion, the glorious view (see 2 Nephi 1:24) at the summit will become more and more real to us. It is upon the summit of Mount Zion that we will see the fulness of the Lord's work, "When the Lord hath performed his whole work upon Mount Zion" (2 Nephi 20:12).

To those who climb Mount Zion in the dispensation of the fulness of times is given the responsibility to be the savor and saviors of our fellow men. We carry out the "whole work" of the Lord when

The Scriptural Temple

"our whole labor shall be in Zion" (D&C 30:11) in gathering together all dispensations in one through temple work:

> For unto you, [the First Presidency, the Twelve, and all those appointed with them] is the power of this priesthood given, for the last days and for the last time, in the which is the dispensation of the fulness of times.
> Which power you hold, in connection with all those who have received a dispensation at any time from the beginning of creation. (D&C 112:30–31)

> For it [temple work] is necessary in the ushering in of the dispensation of the fulness of times, which dispensation is now beginning to usher in, that a whole and complete and perfect union, and welding together of dispensations, and keys, and powers, and glories should take place, and be revealed from the days of Adam even to the present time. (D&C 128:18)

Once "the whole work upon Mount Zion" is completed and all things become one in Christ, the earth will be celestialized and temple work as we know it will no longer be needed (see D&C 130:7–11). Then, the great and last promise of the temple—or dwelling in the eternal presence of God and His Son—will be our temple:

> And I saw no temple therein: for the Lord God Almighty and the Lamb are the temple of it. (Revelation 21:22)

When we see this great view, we will "sing the song of the Lamb, day and night forever and ever" (D&C 133:56), for He is the perfect reflection of the great view. Reaching the summit of Mount Zion and entering the "heavenly place," we will receive the fulness of the Lord:

> They are they who are priests and kings, who have received of his fulness, and of his glory;
> These are they who are come unto Mount Zion, and unto the city of the living God, the heavenly place, the holiest of all. (D&C 76:56, 66)

The celestial city of God, a heavenly and holy place, is the great and glorious view before our eyes at the summit of Mount Zion. It is worth every obedient act, and every personal sacrifice to climb the mountain of the house of the Lord. It is worth holding fast to the rod of iron for it leads to the tree of life and fountain of living waters. These represent a fulness of the love of God found at the summit of Mount Zion (see 1 Nephi 25:11).

As we hold fast and climb, partaking of the fruit and drinking the water, we become holy. We become new creatures with a mighty change of heart. When we taste the exquisite sweetness of the fruit of the tree of life, our desire for righteousness will not be satisfied until we experience a fulness of joy that can only continue in the city of the living God with the full power of His love.

Even in this life, we can experience a measure of full joy in the temple. King Benjamin and his people truly found joy in the temple. The scriptural account in Mosiah explains how they arrived at this joy. Those who heard King Benjamin's address at the temple of Zarahemla were asked to open their ears, hearts, and minds so that the mysteries of God could be unfolded to their view (see Mosiah 2:9). With the manifestation of God's spirit, they were able to witness great views of that which is to come (see Mosiah 5:3), even to an understanding of the mysteries of God. Then they saw the awful view of their carnal state (see Mosiah 4:2). This contrast caused them to all cry with one voice to have the fulness of the atoning blood of Christ applied to them so that not only their sins would be forgiven but that their hearts would be purified (see Mosiah 4:2). Then because of their great faith, the atoning power of Christ and the sanctifying power of the Spirit came upon them and they were filled with joy and peace (see Mosiah 4:3). With this mighty change wrought in their hearts, filling them with the joy and peace of pure love, they had no more disposition to do evil but to do good continually (see Mosiah 5:2).

Thank God for the fulness of joy found in the everlasting covenant of the temple. Thank God for the dispensation of the fulness of times, the dispensation of the fulness of temples.

> And for this cause, that men might be made partakers of the glories which were to be revealed, the Lord sent forth the fulness of his gospel, his everlasting covenant, reasoning in plainness and simplicity—
> And unto him that repenteth and sanctifieth himself before the Lord shall be given eternal life. (D&C 133:57, 62)

The Summit: Being Sealed to
the Father with Eternal Life

Eternal life, the greatest gift of God, is the summit of Mount Zion. There we will come to know our Eternal Father and then, as Joseph Smith said, we will come to know ourselves. We will see things as we really are (see D&C 76:94).[8] Eternal life is the great and last promise of the temple:

> Wherefore, I now send upon you another Comforter, even upon you my friends, that it may abide in your hearts, even the Holy Spirit of promise; which other Comforter is the same that I promised unto my disciples, as is recorded in the testimony of John.
>
> This Comforter is the promise which I give unto you of eternal life, even the glory of the celestial kingdom. (D&C 88:3–4)

For this greatest of gifts, I hope we are beginning to glimpse, as President McKay said, the importance of the temple. At age 91, while addressing General Authorities in the temple about the endowment, President McKay said: "Brethren, I think I am finally beginning to understand."[9]

Progressing from a glimpse to understanding can be a lifelong pursuit, but "in due time" if we continue to climb Mount Zion, we will be exalted (see 1 Peter 5:6). Joseph Smith said the climb of Mount Zion will continue beyond this life:

> When you climb up a ladder, you must begin at the bottom, and ascend up step by step, until you arrive at the top; and so it is with the principles of the Gospel—you must begin with the first, and go on until you learn all the principles of exaltation. But it will be a great while after you have passed through the veil before you will have learned them. It is not all to be comprehended in this world; it will be a great work to learn our salvation and exaltation even beyond the grave.[10]

A preparation for the great and last promise of the temple is to receive spiritual gifts through the gift of the Holy Spirit. As we grow up in the temple, we are endowed with these gifts as graces or virtues, the greatest of which is charity. Therefore the Apostle Paul said:

"Follow after charity, and desire spiritual gifts" (1 Corinthians 14:1).

An important key to finding the Father of our spirits again, and becoming like Him, is to have the Holy Ghost as our constant companion. He is the one who gives us the knowledge of Jesus Christ, the grand key who unlocks the veil to the Father and His Kingdom of Heaven. This constant companionship occurs when our thoughts are garnished unceasingly with virtue and our bowels are filled with charity towards all men (see D&C 121:45–46) or in other words, when we have a fulness of the gifts of the Spirit.

Therefore, an important part of the great and last promise of the temple is to receive a fulness (see D&C 109:15) or constant companionship of the Holy Ghost. With this gift, we will be prepared, our lamps full with all the spiritual gifts, because with the constant companionship of the Holy Spirit, we will practice virtue and holiness before the Lord continually (see D&C 46:33). Only then will our dominion be an everlasting dominion. Truth and righteousness will flow unto us forever and ever as the Holy Spirit leads us to the companionship of Christ, the Second Comforter. *These Comforters, Christ and the Holy Spirit, will plead our cause and seal us to the Father with eternal life.*

Joseph Smith taught that this sealing will be accomplished through the great and last promise of the temple when our knowledge of Christ parts the temple veil to the glories of the Kingdom of Heaven.

> For the day must come when no man need say to his neighbor, Know ye the Lord; for all shall know Him [all who have reached the summit of Mount Zion] . . . from the least to the greatest [Jeremiah 31:34; Hebrews 8:11; D&C 84:98]. How is this to be done? It is to be done by this sealing power, and the other comforter spoken of, which will be manifest by revelation.[11]

> Knowledge through our Lord and Savior Jesus Christ is the grand key that unlocks [parts the veil to] the glories and mysteries of the Kingdom of Heaven.[12]

While we make this climb of Mount Zion, the Holy Spirit will open our minds and hearts in the temple, teaching us the way of salvation. He will lead us to Christ, who will take us to the summit of

The Scriptural Temple

Mount Zion. At the summit, no longer spiritual orphans but rather spiritually begotten children of Christ with a mighty change of heart, we will "sing at the height of Zion" (Jeremiah 31:12):

> High on the mountain top a banner is unfurled.
>> Ye nations, now look up; It waves to all the world. . . .
>> For God remembers still His promise made of old
>> That He on Zion's hill truths standard would unfold![13]

When we finally "stand upon Mount Zion, which shall be the city of New Jerusalem" (D&C 84:2), we shall "dwell in the house of the Lord for ever" (Psalm 23:6). At the summit of Mount Zion, "a glorious high throne from the beginning is the place of our sanctuary" (Jeremiah 17:12). We will have come again to our Father in Heaven.

As this great and glorious view of the summit of Mount Zion becomes real in our minds and hearts, we will want to develop the intimate, marriage covenant relationship with Christ that He desires. We will want to expose our hearts to Him and let Him have "full sway" (Alma 42:30) in them. Then the temple will become the most powerful spiritual motivation in our lives because pure love through a mighty change of heart has become the most powerful spiritual motivation in our lives. Through the teaching and sanctifying power of the Holy Spirit, the sayings and teachings of Christ in the *scriptural temple* will draw us to His temple with powerful spiritual motivation to receive grace for grace as He did. Then we can come unto the Father in His name and receive of His fulness:

> And every one that hearkeneth to the voice of the Spirit cometh unto God, even the Father. (D&C 84:47)

> I give unto you these sayings that you may understand and know how to worship, and know what you worship, that you may come unto the Father in my name, and in due time receive of his fulness.
>> For if you keep my commandments you shall receive of his fulness, and be glorified in me as I am in the Father; therefore, I say unto you, you shall receive grace for grace. (D&C 93:19–20)

The fulfillment of this promise is the great and last promise of the temple for those who overcome the world to serve God. To overcome is to come over completely to the power of God's pure love through our repentance and the gifts of Christ's Atonement. The great promises, including the great and last promise of the *scriptural temple*, are granted to those who overcome (see Revelation 2:7, 11, 27–28; 3:4–5, 11, 12, 20–21).

When we "overcome all things" (D&C 76:60) we will be glorified in the Son as He is in the Father. Then we will "[comprehend] all things" (D&C 88:41) and "inherit all things" (Revelation 21:7). We will have reached the summit of Mount Zion which is "above all things" (D&C 88:41). There we will know "the fulness of him that filleth all in all" (Ephesians 1:23). There "all things are subject unto [us]" (D&C 132:20) because "above all these things [we have] put on charity" (Colossians 3:14). "Yea, [charity] is the love of God, . . . wherefore, it is the most desirable above all things. . . . Yea, and the most joyous to the soul" (1 Nephi 11:22–23).

Endnotes

The Temple Paradigm

1. Truman G. Madsen, *The Highest in Us* (Salt Lake City: Bookcraft, 1978), 102–3.
2. Ezra Taft Benson, "What I Hope You Will Teach Your Children About the Temple," *Ensign*, August 1985, 6–10.
3. Joseph Smith, *Teachings of the Prophet Joseph Smith*, compiled by Joseph Fielding Smith (Salt Lake City: Deseret Book, 1976), 193.
4. Sidney B. Sperry, *Paul's Life and Letters* (Salt Lake City: Bookcraft, 1973), 176.
5. Joseph Smith, *Lectures on Faith* (Salt Lake City: Deseret Book, 1985), 6:7.
6. William Shakespeare, "As You Like It," 2.7., 139–66.
7. Hugh W. Nibley, "Abraham's Temple Drama" in *The Temple in Time and Eternity* (Provo, Utah: Foundation for Ancient Research and Mormon Studies, 1999), 36.
8. C. S. Lewis, *The Great Divorce* (New York: Touchstone, 1996), 72.
9. Dietrich Bonhoeffer, *The Cost of Discipleship* (New York: Touchstone, Simon & Schuster, 1995), 19–20.
10. Joseph Smith, *Teachings of the Prophet Joseph Smith*, 162.
11. Truman G. Madsen, "The Temple and the Atonement" in *Temples of the*

Ancient World (Salt Lake City: Deseret Book, 1994), 72.

12. John A. Widtsoe, "Temple Worship," *The Utah Genealogical and Historical Magazine*, Vol. 12, April 1921, 50–51.

13. Gordon B. Hinckley, "Some Thoughts on Temple, Retention of Converts, and Missionary Service," Ensign, November 1997, 49.

14. "My Country, 'Tis of Thee," *Hymns*, no. 339.

15. Elmer W. Lammi, "Moroni Statue Tops DC Spire," *Church News*, May 19, 1973, 3.

Seeking the Source of Temple Worship in the Holy Land

1. David B. Galbraith, D. Kelly Ogden, and Andrew C. Skinner, *Jerusalem: the Eternal City* (Salt Lake City: Deseret Book, 1996), 260.

2. Howard W. Hunter, "Exceeding Great and Previous Promises," *Ensign*, November 1994, 8.

3. Gordon B. Hinckley, "The Symbol of Our Faith" *Ensign*, April 2005, 3.

4. Ezra T. Benson, "What I Hope You Will Teach Your Children about the Temple," *Ensign*, August 1985, 9.

5. Joseph Smith, *Teachings of the Prophet Joseph Smith*, 151.

6. John M. Lundquist, "What Is a Temple? A Preliminary Typology," in *Temples of the Ancient World*, 84.

7. John M. Lundquist, "Temple, Covenant, and Law in the Ancient Near East and in the Old Testament," in *Temples of the Ancient World*, 272–94.

8. Richard L. Bushman, *Believing History* (New York: Columbia University Press, 2004), 186.

9. Joseph Smith, *Teachings of the Prophet Joseph Smith*, 57–58.

The Mountain of Holiness

1. M. Catherine Thomas, "The Brother of Jared at the Veil," in *Temples of the Ancient World*, 389.

2. Donald W. Parry, "Garden of Eden: Prototype Sanctuary," in *Temples of the Ancient World*, 133.

3. Paul Thomas Smith and Matthew B. Brown. *Symbols in Stone* (American Fork, Utah: Covenant Communications, 1997), 15.

4. Joseph Smith, *Teachings of the Prophet Joseph Smith*, 158–59.

5. Orson F. Whitney, *The Life of Heber C. Kimball* (Salt Lake City: Bookcraft, 1992), 209.

6. Leland H. Gentry, "Adam-Ondi-Ahman, A Brief Historic Survey," *Brigham Young University Studies*, Vol. 13, No. 4, 561.

7. Brigham Young, *Journal of Discourses*, 26 vols. (Liverpool: R. D. and S. W. Richards, 1854–56), 336–37.

Endnotes

8. Irving Stone, *Men to Match My Mountains* (Garden City, New York: Doubleday & Company, 1956).

9. Andrew F. Ehat and Lyndon W. Cook, *The Words of Joseph Smith* (Orem, Utah: Grandin Book, 1993), 119–20.

10. Joseph Smith, *Lectures on Faith*, 2:55.

11. David B. Galbraith, D. Kelly Ogden, and Andrew C. Skinner, *Jerusalem: the Eternal City*, 248.

12. John M. Lindquist, "The Legitimizing Role of the Temple in the Origin of the State," in *Temples of the Ancient World*, 184–85.

13. Joseph Smith, *Teachings of the Prophet Joseph Smith*, 323.

Ascending the Mountain of Holiness

1. David B. Galbraith, D. Kelly Ogden, and Andrew C. Skinner, *Jerusalem: the Eternal City*, 192.

2. Ibid., 241–42.

3. Ibid., 245–46.

4. "The Old Testament and New Testament Faith," *Heart and Mind*. (Grand Rapids, Michigan: Institute of Religious Research, 1997), 5.

5. William J. Hamblin, "Temple Motifs in Jewish Mysticism," in *Temples of the Ancient World*, 444.

6. Ibid., 461.

7. Lamar C. Berrett and D. Kelly Ogden, *Discovering the World of the Bible* (Provo, Utah: Grandin Book, 1996), 134.

8. Ioan Petru Colianu, "Ascension," *Encyclopedia of Religion*, Mircea Eliade Edition (New York: Macmillan, 1987), 1:435–41.

9. William J. Hamblin, "Temple Motifs in Jewish Mysticism," in *Temples of the Ancient World*, 442, 447.

10. M. Catherine Thomas, "The Brother of Jared at the Veil," in *Temples of the Ancient World*, 389.

11. Avraham Gileadi, *Isaiah Decoded* (Escondido, California: Hebraeus Press, 2002).

12. M. Catherine Thomas, "Hebrews: To Ascend the Holy Mount," in *Temples of the Ancient World*, 480.

The Camp of Israel: Base Camp of Mount Zion

1. Richard Neitzel Holzapfel, *The Exodus Story* (Salt Lake City: Bookcraft, 1997), 67.

2. Brent L. Top, A Peculiar Treasure (Salt Lake City: Bookcraft, 1997), 2.

3. *Old Testament Student Manual Genesis–2 Samuel* (Salt Lake City: The Church of Jesus Christ of Latter-day Saints, 1980), 152.

4. Joseph Smith, *History of the Church*, edited by B. H. Roberts (Salt Lake

City: Deseret Book, 1980), 5:423–24.

Equipped for the First Ascent: Initiation to Mount Zion

1. Joseph Smith, *History of the Church*, 6:184–85.

2. John D. Charles *Endowed from on High* (Bountiful, Utah: Horizon Publishers, 1997), 42, 52–54.

3. Joseph Smith, *Teachings of the Prophet Joseph Smith*, 51.

4. John A. Widtsoe, "The House of the Lord," *Improvement Era*, April 1936, 228.

5. Joseph Smith, *Teachings of the Prophet Joseph Smith*, 328.

6. Ibid., 137.

7. Joseph F. Smith, *Gospel Doctrine* (Salt Lake City: Deseret Book), 15.

8. C. S. Lewis, *Mere Christianity* (New York: Touchstone, 1980), 111.

9. Joseph Smith, *Teachings of the Prophet Joseph Smith*, 151.

10. Brigham Young, *Journal of Discourses*, 19:153–54.

11. William G. Hartley, "How Shall I Gather?" *Ensign*, October 1997, 9.

12. Byron R. Merrill, *Elijah: Yesterday, Today, and Tomorrow* (Salt Lake City: Bookcraft, 1997), 56.

13. Johan B. MacDonald, *The Holiness of Everyday Life* (Salt Lake City: Deseret Book, 1995), 4, 8.

14. Orson F. Whitney, "Latter-day Saint Ideals and Institutions," *Improvement Era*, August 1927, 851.

15. Jay A. Parry and Donald W. Parry, *Understanding the Book of Revelation* (Salt Lake City: Deseret Book, 1998), 299.

16. John A. Widtsoe, "Temple Worship," 62.

17. John D. Charles *Endowed from on High*, 38.

18. Marvin Wilson, *Our Father Abraham* (Grand Rapids, Colorado: Eerdmans Publishing, 1989), 205.

19. Joseph Smith, *Lectures on Faith*, 1:9, 13, 16; 3:2–5; 6:7.

20. Bruce R. McConkie, *Doctrinal New Testament Commentary* (Salt Lake City: Bookcraft, 1965), 3:485.

21. Joseph Smith, *Teachings of the Prophet Joseph Smith*, 298.

22. Ibid., 322.

23. Ibid., 349.

24. John D. Charles *Endowed from on High*, 35.

25. Henry B. Eyring, "Witnesses for God," *Ensign*, November 1996, 32.

26. Joseph F. Smith, *Doctrines of Salvation* (Salt Lake City: Bookcraft, 1995), 1:156.

27. Brigham Young, *Journal of Discourses*, 21:194.

Endnotes

The Great Endowment: The Purifying Power of Mount Zion

1. John W. Welch, *Illuminating the Sermon at the Temple and Sermon on the Mount* (Provo, Utah: Foundation of Ancient Research and Mormon Studies Provo, 1999), 85.

2. Donna B. Nielson, *Beloved Bridegroom* (Onyx Press, 1999), 99.

3. Brigham Young, *Journal of Discourses*, 2:31.

4. Joseph Smith, *Teachings of the Prophet Joseph Smith*, 237.

5. H. Burke Peterson, "The Temple and Its Influence in Perfecting the Members of the Church," First Quorum of Seventy meeting, February 20, 1986.

6. Boyd K. Packer, *The Holy Temple* (Salt Lake City: Bookcraft, 1980), 42.

7. Carlos E. Asay, "Temple blessings and Applications," 5.

8. Donna B. Nielsen, *Beloved Bridegroom*, 99.

9. Virginia H. Pearce, *A Heart like His* (Salt Lake City: Deseret Book, 2006), 90.

10. Laura M. Brotherson, *And They Were Not Ashamed* (Boise: Inspire Book, 2004), 211.

11. John W. Welch, "Benjamin's Covenant: A Precursor of the Sacrament Prayers" in *King Benjamin's Speech* (Provo, Utah: Foundation for Ancient Research and Mormon Studies, 1998), 208.

12. Joseph Smith, *Teachings of the Prophet Joseph Smith*, 355.

13. C. S. Lewis, *Mere Christianity*, 88.

14. Joseph Smith, *History of the Church*, 6:428.

15. Robert L. Millet, *Another Testament of Jesus Christ in First Nephi: The Doctrinal Foundation* (Salt Lake City: Bookcraft, 1988), 165–66.

16. Matthew B. Brown, *The Gate of Heaven* (American Fork, Utah: Covenant Communications, 1999), 112.

17. Joseph Smith, *History of the Church*, 5:215–16.

18. M. Catherine Thomas, "Hebrews: To Ascend the Holy Mount," in *Temples of the Ancient World*, 485.

19. Interpretive adaptation of lecture given by Wayne Brickey, *Tel Aviv*, December 29, 1996.

A Full View of Mount Zion

1. Joseph Smith, *Teachings of the Prophet Joseph Smith*, 343.

2. Ibid., 308.

3. Joseph Smith, *History of the Church*, 5:527.

4. F. Andrew Ehat and Lyndon W. Cook, *The Words of Joseph Smith* (Provo, Utah: Grandin Book Company, 1993), 286. (Heber C. Kimball journal kept by William Clayton, December 26, 1845; Church Archives).

5. Orson Pratt, *The Seer*, Vol. 1, No. 10 (1853).

6. Joseph Smith, *Lectures on Faith*, 5:60.

7. Joseph Fielding Smith, *Elijah the Prophet and His Mission* (Salt Lake City: Deseret Book, 1957), 46.

8. Bruce K. Satterfield, *The Family Under Siege: The Role of Man and Woman* (BYU–Idaho Education Week address, June 7, 2001).

9. Avraham Gileadi, *Studies in the Book of Mormon* (Escondido, California: Hebraeus Press, 2005), 125.

10. Orson F. Whitney, in Conference Report, April 1929, 110.

11. Joseph Smith, *Teachings of the Prophet Joseph Smith*, 321.

12. Joseph Smith, *History of the Church*, 6:254.

13. F. Andrew Ehat and Lyndon W. Cook, *The Words of Joseph Smith*, 329.

The Great and Last Promise: Reaching the Summit of Mount Zion with a Great and Last Sacrifice

1. Joseph Smith, *Teachings of the Prophet Joseph Smith*, 150–51.

2. Ezra T. Benson, "What I Hope You Will Teach Your Children about the Temple," 495.

3. John A. Widtsoe, "Temple Worship."

4. Bruce R. McConkie, *A New Witness for the Articles of Faith* (Salt Lake City: Deseret Book, 1985), 495.

5. Joseph Smith, *Lectures on Faith*, 2:55.

6. Joseph Smith, *History of the Church*, 5:389.

7. Bruce R. McConkie, Bruce R. *The Promised Messiah* (Salt Lake City: Deseret Book, 1978), 584.

8. Joseph Smith, *Lectures on Faith*, 6:12.

9. Joseph Smith, *Teachings of the Prophet Joseph Smith*, 162.

10. Lawrence Wright, "Forcing the End" *The New Yorker*, July 20, 1998, 42–53.

11. "God of Our Fathers, Known of Old," *Hymns*, no. 80.

12. Avraham Gileadi, *The Literary Message of Isaiah* (Escondido, California: Hebraeus Press, 1994), 68.

13. Donna B. Nielsen, *Beloved Bridegroom*, iii.

14. Laura M. Brotherson, *And They Were Not Ashamed*, 149.

15. Adaptive interpretation of lecture by Wayne Brickey on the roof of Simon the Tanner's dwelling, December 30, 1996.

16. C. S. Lewis, *Mere Christianity*, 112.

17. Donna B. Nielsen, *Beloved Bridegroom*, 39.

18. John W. Weltch, *Illuminating the Sermon at the Temple and Sermon on the Mount*, 63.

Endnotes

19. Adaptive interpretation of a lecture by Wayne Brickey at the Sermon on the Mount memorial, December 28, 1996.

20. John M. Pontius, *Following the Light of Christ into His Presence* (Springville, Utah: Cedar Fort, 1997), 70.

21. Howard W. Howard, "A More Excellent Way," *Ensign*, May 1992, 61–63.

22. Michael Wilcox, Education Week lecture, Brigham Young University, 1997.

23. Gordon B. Hinckley address at the dedication of Taipei Taiwan Temple, 1984.

24. Richard L. Evans, "An Open Door," *Selections from Thoughts for 100 Days and the Spoken Word*, Vol. 2 (Publishers Press, 1966).

25. Viktor E. Frankl, *Man's Search for Meaning* (New York: Washington Square Press, 1985), 56–57.

26. O Love That Glorifies the Son," *Hymns*, no. 295.

Climbing Up to the Summit of Mount Zion: Lord, How Is It Done?

1. Joseph Smith, *Lectures on Faith*, 5:2.

2. George Q. Cannon, *Millennial Star*, April 23, 1894, 260–61.

3. Henry B. Eyring, CES fireside, September 8, 1996.

4. Royden G. Derrick, *Temples of the Last Days* (Salt Lake City: Bookcraft, 1987), 53.

5. John W. Welch, *Illuminating the Sermon at the Temple and Sermon on the Mount*, 172.

6. Bruce C. Hafen and Marie K. Hafen, "Bridle All Your Passions," *Ensign*, February 1994, 14–18.

7. Parley P. Pratt, *Key to the Science of Theology*, Classics in Mormon Literature Series (Salt Lake City: Deseret Book, 1978), 61.

8. Parley P. Pratt, *Autobiography of Parley P. Pratt* (Salt Lake: Deseret Book, 1979), 260.

9. Brigham Young, *Journal of Discourses*, 9:3.

10. Susan Savage, "Temple Snow," Ensign, January 1986.

11. Spencer W. Kimball, "Becoming the Pure in Heart," *Ensign*, March 1985.

12. Joseph Smith, Kirtland High Council minutes, August 8, 1834 (*History of the Church*, 2:239).

13. Lorenzo Snow, Millennial Star, Vol. 50, No. 25, 392.

14. Bruce R. McConkie, A New Witness for the Articles of Faith (Salt Lake City: Deseret Book, 1985), 602.

15. Joseph Smith, *History of the Church*, 2:268.

16. Joseph Smith, *Teachings of the Prophet Joseph Smith*, 66.

The Bond of Perfectness: The Only Way to the Summit of Mount Zion

1. Joseph Smith, *Teachings of the Prophet Joseph Smith*, 330.
2. Donna B. Nielsen, *Beloved Bridegroom*, 31–32.
3. M. Catherine Thomas, "The Brother of Jared at the Veil," in *Temples of the Ancient World*, 388.
4. "O Ye Mountains High," *Hymns*, no. 34.
5. Robert Robinson, "Come, Thou Fount of Every Blessing" arranged by Mack Wilberg, *Wyeths' Repository of Sacred Music*.
6. C. S. Lewis, *Weight of Glory and Other Addresses* (New York: Colliers Book, Macmillan, 1980), 92.
7. Joseph Smith, *History of the Church*, 6:230.
8. Truman Madsen, "The Temple and the Atonement," in *Temples of the Ancient World*, 66–67.
9. Francis Bacon, quotation from "Of Revenge," *The Oxford Dictionary of Quotations* (Oxford: Oxford University Press, 1980), 27.
10. "Father in Heaven, We Do Believe," *Hymns*, no. 180.
11. Joan B. MacDonald, *The Holiness of Everyday Life* (Salt Lake City: Deseret Book, 1995), 47.
12. "How Firm a Foundation," *Hymns*, no. 85.
13. M. Catherine Thomas, "The Brother of Jared at the Veil," in *Temples of the Ancient World*, 388–89.
14. Joseph Smith, *Lectures on Faith*, 4:14–15.
15. "I Stand All Amazed," *Hymns*, no. 193.
16. Orson F. Whitney, *Through Memory's Halls* (Zion's Printing and Publishing, 1930), 83.
17. Melvin J. Ballard, *Crusade for Righteousness* (Salt Lake City: Bookcraft. 1966), 138–39.
18. Tad R. Callister, *The Infinite Atonement* (Salt Lake City: Deseret Book, 2000), 27.
19. Michael Wilcox, Education Week lecture, Brigham Young University, 1997.
20. Joseph Smith, *Teachings of the Prophet Joseph Smith*, 193.

The Wells of Salvation: Sustaining the Ascent of Mount Zion

1. David B. Galbraith, D. Kelly Ogden, and Andrew C. Skinner, *Jerusalem: the Eternal City*, 24.
2. Ibid., 17–18.
3. Alfred Lord Tennyson, "In Memory of A. H. H. (1850)," *The Oxford*

Endnotes

Dictionary of Quotations (Oxford: Oxford University Press, 1980), 535.

4. Dietrich Bonhoeffer, *The Cost of Discipleship* (New York: Touchstone, 1995), 149–50.

5. W. D. Longstaff, "Take Time to Be Holy," arranged by John Longhurst (Orem, Utah: Sonos, 1991).

6. Joseph Smith, *Teachings of the Prophet Joseph Smith*, 286.

7. S. Michael Wilcox, *House of Glory* (Salt Lake City: Deseret Book, 1995), 41.

8. Joseph Smith, *History of the Church*, 9:317.

9. Joseph F. Smith "Salvation for the Living and the Dead," *Relief Society Magazine*, 5:678.

10. Spencer W. Kimball, proceedings of the Priesthood Genealogy Research Seminar, Brigham Young University, August 4, 1977, 4.

11. S. Michael Wilcox, *House of Glory*, 41.

Stand in Holy Places: Safety in Climbing Mount Zion

1. S. Michael Wilcox, *House of Glory* (Salt Lake City: Deseret Book, 1995), 64.

2. Joseph Smith, The Personal Writings of Joseph Smith, compiled and edited Dean C. Jessee (Salt Lake City: Deseret Book, 1984), 288.

3. Vaughn J. Featherstone, "A Haven in a World of Turmoil," special meeting of the Seventy at the St. George and Manti Utah Temples; see also The Incomparable Christ (1995), 3–6.

4. "Guide Us, Oh Thou Great Jehovah," *Hymns*, no. 83.

5. John A. Widtsoe, "Temple Worship," 51.

6. William J. Hamblin, Temple Motifs in John 17 (Provo, Utah: Foundation for Ancient Research and Mormon Studies, 1995).

The Salt and Light of the Covenant:
Preserving the Endowment of Mount Zion

1. John A. Widtsoe, "The House of the Lord," 228.

2. Joseph Smith, *Teachings of the Prophet Joseph Smith*, 172.

3. Ibid., 338.

4. Ibid., 258.

5. Gib Kocherhans, "The Name 'Melchizedek': Some Thoughts on Its Meaning and the Priesthood It Represents," *Ensign*, September 1980, 16.

Views from the Summit of Mount Zion

1. George MacDonald, *The Gifts of the Child Christ and Other Tales* (Grand Rapids, Colorado: Eerdmans Publishing, 1996), 1:28.

2. William Whiston (translator), *The Complete Works of Josephus* (Massachusetts: Henrickson Peabody, 1987), 708.

3. Donna B. Nielsen, *Beloved Bridegroom*, 13.

4. "Ye Elders of Israel," *Hymns*, no. 319.

5. Joseph Smith, *Teachings of the Prophet Joseph Smith*, 51.

6. Joseph Smith, *History of the Church*, 5:403.

7. Joseph Smith, *History of the Church*, 6:50.

8. Robert L. Millet, *Alive in Christ: The Miracle of Spiritual Rebirth* (Salt Lake City: Desert Book, 1997), 28.

9. Boyd K. Packer, *The Holy Temple*, 263.

10. Joseph Smith, *Teachings of the Prophet Joseph Smith*, 348.

11. Joseph Smith, *History of the Church*, 3:380.

12. Joseph Smith, *Teachings of the Prophet Joseph Smith*, 298.

13. "High on the Mountain Top," *Hymns*, no. 5.

About the Author

In 1963, Mark H. Greene III was climbing mountains in Colorado for a better view—especially of himself. Little did he know, then, that thirty-three years later, he would be facing the most challenging mountain of his life. It is Mount Zion, the mountain of the Lord's house. Now he knows that if he can reach the summit of this mountain, he will see the "great view."

Mark has been an orthopedic surgeon, specializing in hand and upper lib surgery in Salt Lake City and Illinois for the past thirty-three years. He has served in a variety of Church callings, including a full-time mission to Belgium and France.

After his mission, Mark married the beautiful Jill Stephenson. They have six children: Brian, Lara, Lys-An, Linsey, Leslee, and Stephen. All them are uniquely special and have brought Mark and Jill great joy.

Some of Doctor Greene's patients call him triplesticks because of the Roman numeral *III* ending his name, which represents three generations of Mark Greenes. He appreciates this sobriquet because it reminds him of the name he bears and the ancestry it represents. His father was also an orthopedic hand surgeon, and his grandfather was

About the Author

a professor of finance at the University of Utah. He still, on occasion, sees patients who remember these wonderful men.

Mount Zion requires climbing it with others, especially family and ancestors. Then lasting relationships will develop.